Rumiko Takahashi

The spotlight on Rumiko Takahashi's career began in 1978 when she won an honorable mention in Shogakukan's annual New Comic Artist Contest for *Those Selfish Aliens*. Later that same year, her boy-meets-alien comedy series, *Urusei Yatsura*, was serialized in *Weekly Shonen Sunday*. This phenomenally successful manga series was adapted into anime format and spawned a TV series and half a dozen theatrical-release movies, all incredibly popular in their own right. Takahashi followed up the success of her debut series with one blockbuster hit after another—*Maison Ikkoku* ran from 1980 to 1987, *Ranma ½* from 1987 to 1996, and *Inuyasha* from 1996 to 2008. Other notable works include *Mermaid Saga*, *Rumic Theater*, and *One-Pound Gospel*.

Takahashi won the prestigious Shogakukan Manga Award twice in her career, once for *Urusei Yatsura* in 1981 and the second time for *Inuyasha* in 2002. A majority of the Takahashi canon has been adapted into other media such as anime, live-action TV series, and film. Takahashi's manga, as well as the other formats her work has been adapted into, have continued to delight generations of fans around the world. Distinguished by her wonderfully endearing characters, Takahashi's work adeptly incorporates a wide variety of elements such as comedy, romance, fantasy, and martial arts. While her series are difficult to pin down into one simple genre, the signature style she has created has come to be known as the "Rumic World." Rumiko Takahashi is an artist who truly represents the very best from the world of manga.

KU-477-537

RIN-NE
VOLUME 5
Shonen Sunday Edition

STORY AND ART BY
RUMIKO TAKAHASHI

© 2009 Rumiko TAKAHASHI/Shogakukan
All rights reserved.
Original Japanese edition "KYOUKAI NO RINNE"
published by SHOGAKUKAN Inc.

Translation/Christine Dashiell
Touch-up Art & Lettering/Evan Waldinger
Design/Yukiko Whitley
Editor/Mike Montesa

The rights of the author(s) of the work(s) in this
publication to be so identified have been asserted in
accordance with the Copyright, Designs and Patents Act
1988. A CIP catalogue record for this book is available
from the British Library.

The stories, characters and incidents mentioned in
this publication are entirely fictional.

No portion of this book may be reproduced or
transmitted in any form or by any means without
written permission from the copyright holders.

Printed in the U.S.A.

Published by VIZ Media, LLC
P.O. Box 77010
San Francisco, CA 94107

10 9 8 7 6 5 4 3 2 1
First printing, March 2011

www.viz.com   WWW.SHONENSUNDAY.COM

PARENTAL ADVISORY
RIN-NE is rated T+ for Older Teen and is
recommended for ages 16 and up.
ratings.viz.com

Story and Art by
Rumiko Takahashi

RIN-NE

りんね

Characters

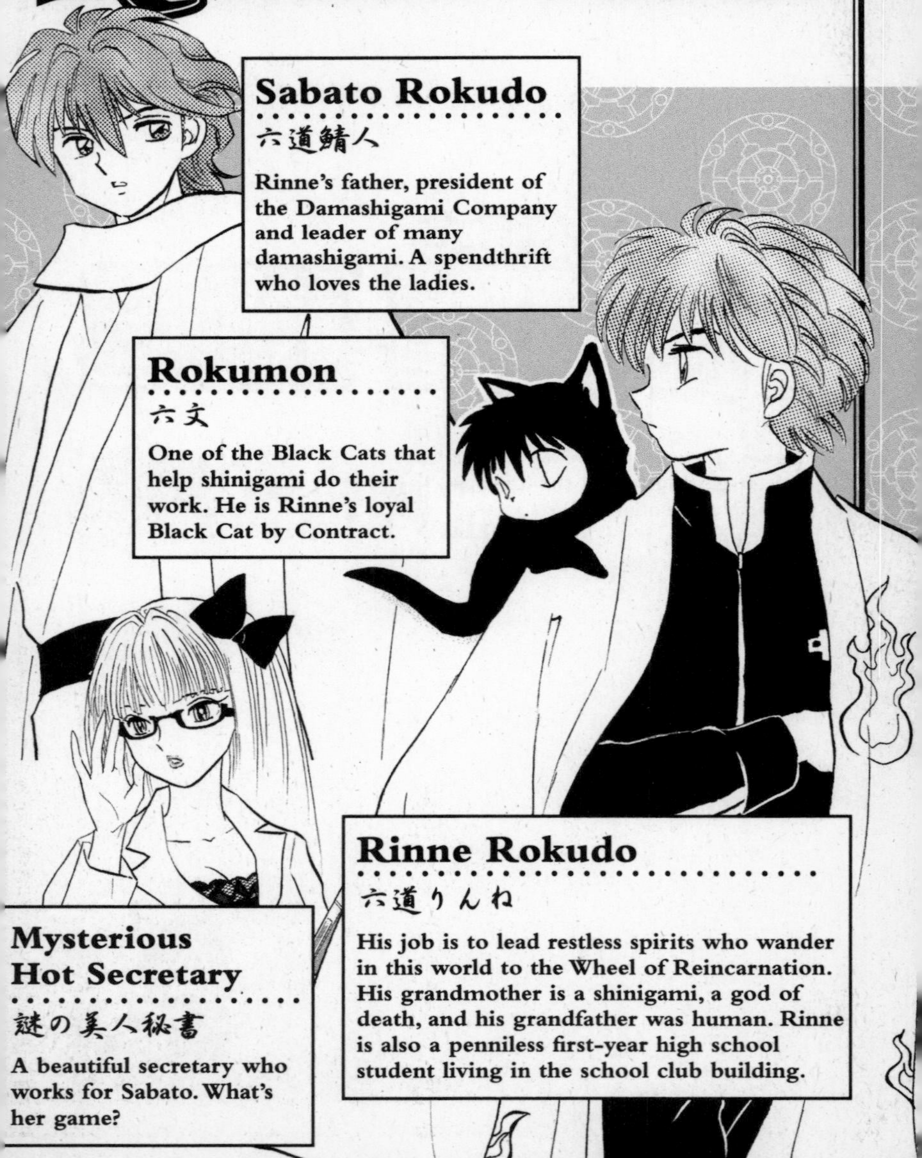

Sabato Rokudo

六道鯖人

Rinne's father, president of the Damashigami Company and leader of many damashigami. A spendthrift who loves the ladies.

Rokumon

六文

One of the Black Cats that help shinigami do their work. He is Rinne's loyal Black Cat by Contract.

Rinne Rokudo

六道りんね

His job is to lead restless spirits who wander in this world to the Wheel of Reincarnation. His grandmother is a shinigami, a god of death, and his grandfather was human. Rinne is also a penniless first-year high school student living in the school club building.

Mysterious Hot Secretary

謎の美人秘書

A beautiful secretary who works for Sabato. What's her game?

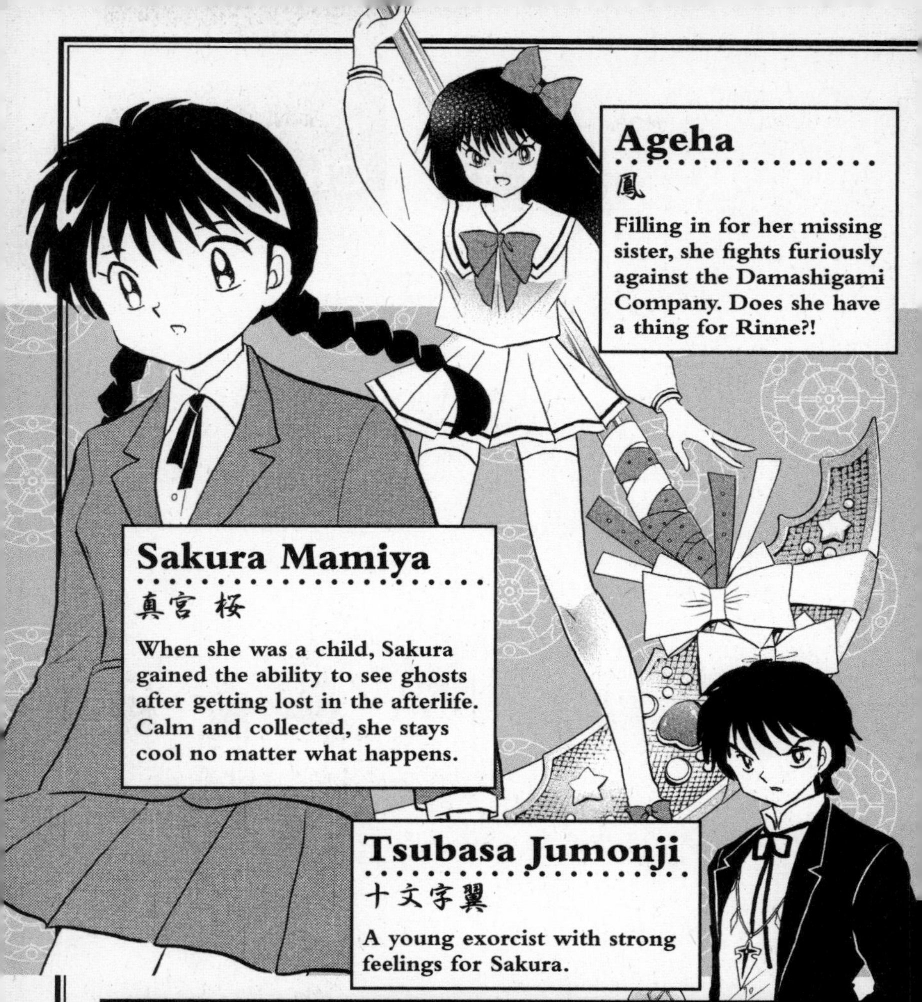

Ageha

鳳

Filling in for her missing sister, she fights furiously against the Damashigami Company. Does she have a thing for Rinne?!

Sakura Mamiya

真宮 桜

When she was a child, Sakura gained the ability to see ghosts after getting lost in the afterlife. Calm and collected, she stays cool no matter what happens.

Tsubasa Jumonji

十文字翼

A young exorcist with strong feelings for Sakura.

The Story So Far

Together, Sakura, the girl who can see ghosts, and Rinne the shinigami (sort of) spend their days helping spirits that can't pass on reach the afterlife, and deal with all kinds of strange phenomena at their school.

One day, while handling a case, Rinne is interrupted by a spirited young shinigami girl named Ageha. She thinks Rinne is a damashigami, a shinigami gone bad, who leads humans who aren't meant to die yet to the afterlife, to pad their quotas. Ageha is filling in for her missing sister and is dedicated to crushing the Damashigami Company. Little does she know, Rinne is the son of the Damashigami Company president!

Contents

Chapter 39: The Hot Secretary's True Identity......7

Chapter 40: Rich Girl......25

Chapter 41: Just a Simple Thanks......43

Chapter 42: Soul Eater King......61

Chapter 43: The Unopenable Bookshelves......79

Chapter 44: Roses and Soy Sauce......97

Chapter 45: The Cursed Track Star......115

Chapter 46: I Don't Want Him to Know......134

Chapter 47: The Haunted Cedar......153

Chapter 48: Yo-Yo Memories......171

CHAPTER 39: THE HOT SECRETARY'S TRUE IDENTITY

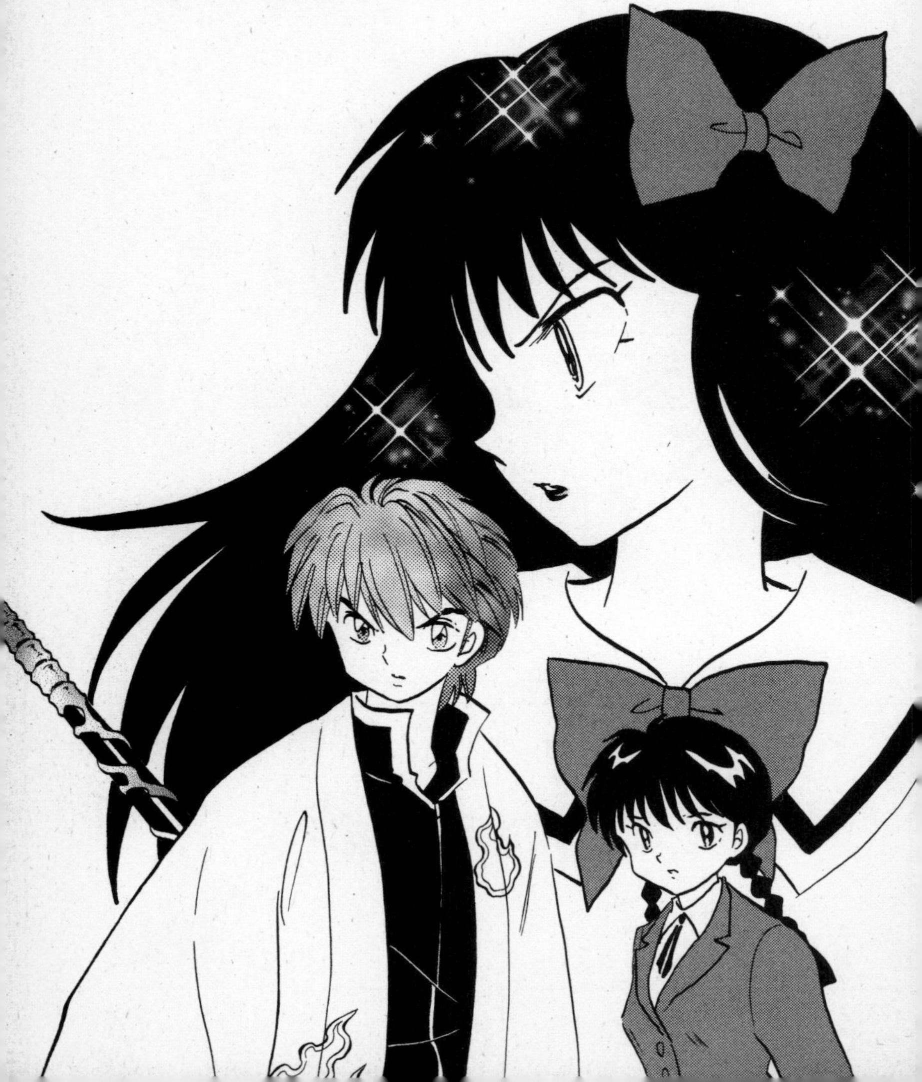

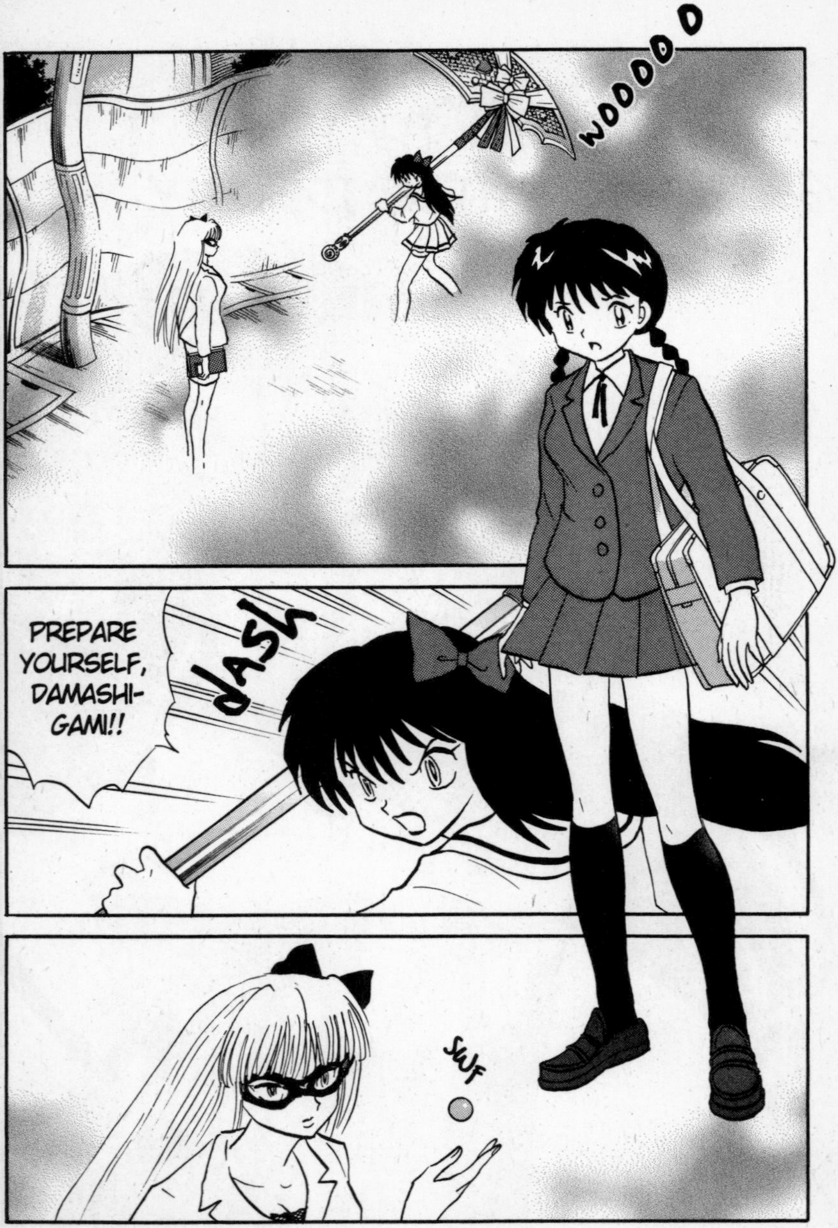
WOOOOD
DASH
PREPARE YOURSELF, DAMASHI-GAMI!!
SWF

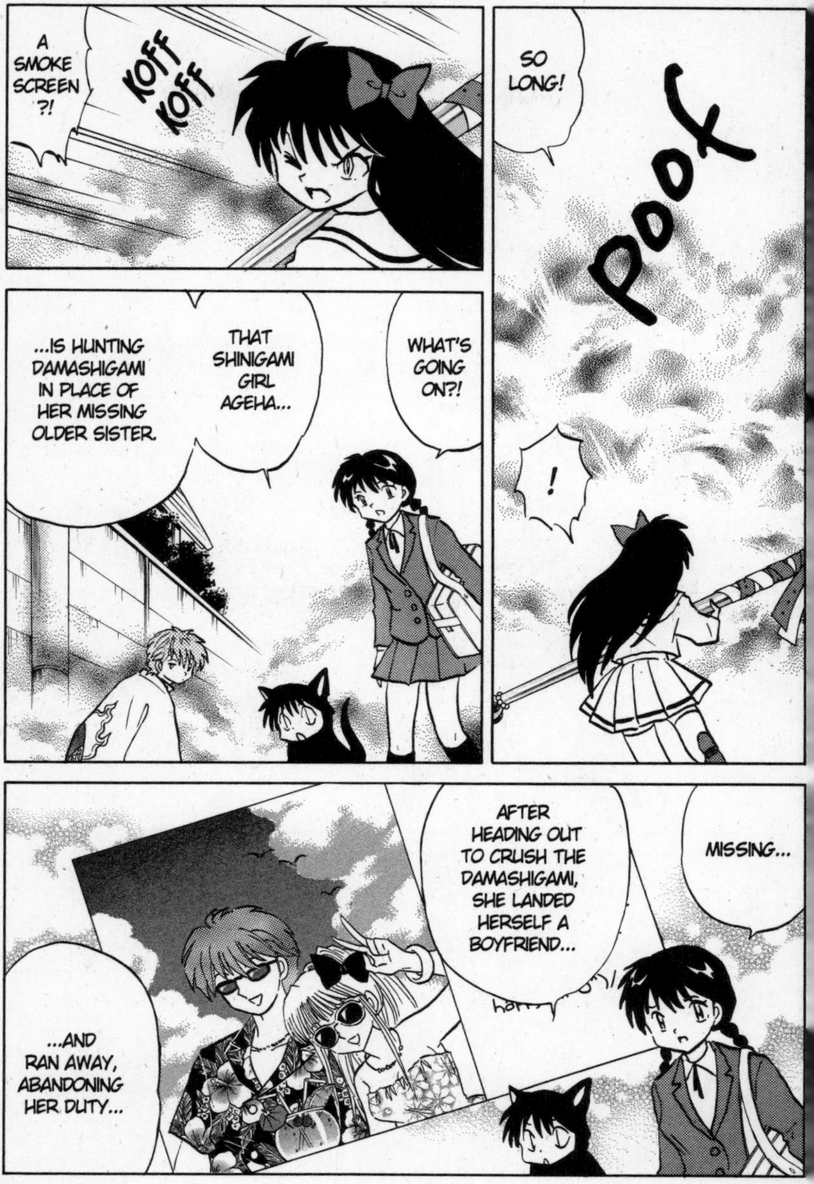
SO LONG!
POOF
!
A SMOKE SCREEN ?!
KOFF KOFF
WHAT'S GOING ON?!
THAT SHINIGAMI GIRL AGEHA...
...IS HUNTING DAMASHIGAMI IN PLACE OF HER MISSING OLDER SISTER.
MISSING...
AFTER HEADING OUT TO CRUSH THE DAMASHIGAMI, SHE LANDED HERSELF A BOYFRIEND...
...AND RAN AWAY, ABANDONING HER DUTY...

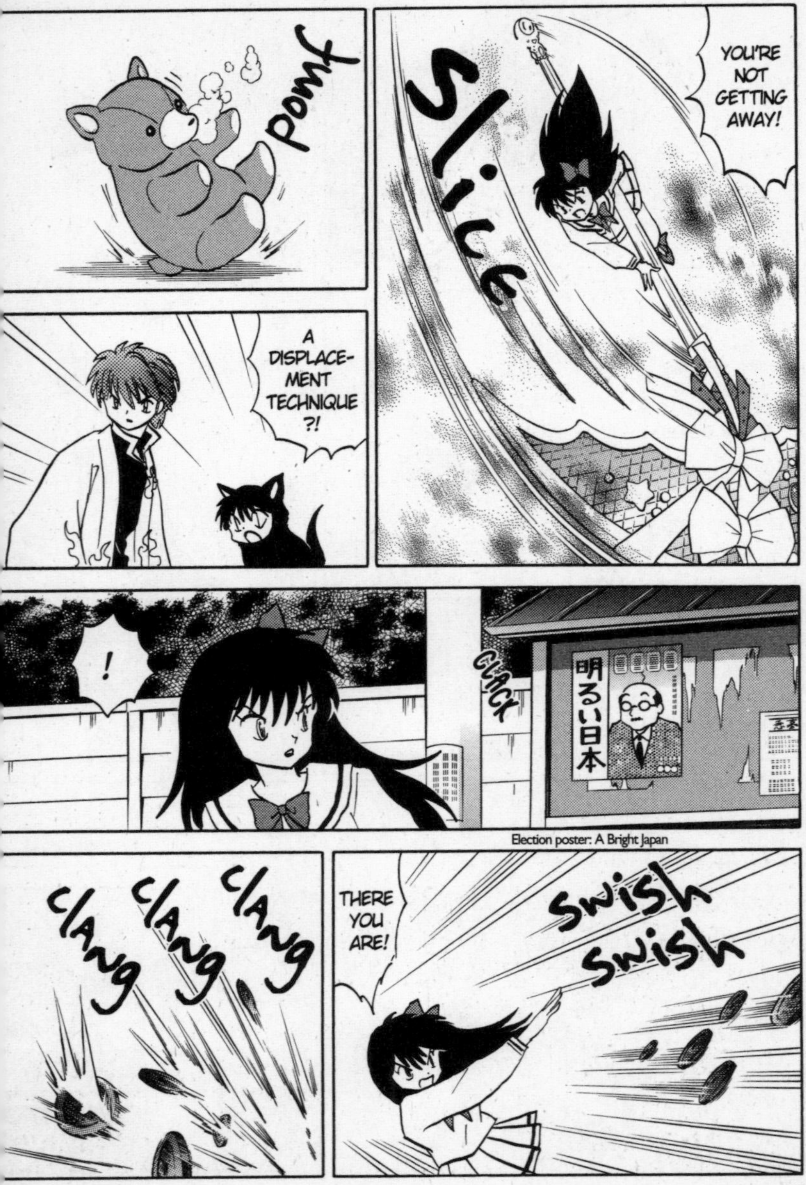

YOU'RE NOT GETTING AWAY!
slice
pomf
A DISPLACEMENT TECHNIQUE ?!
明るい日本
CLACK
!
Election poster: A Bright Japan
THERE YOU ARE!
swish swish
clang clang clang

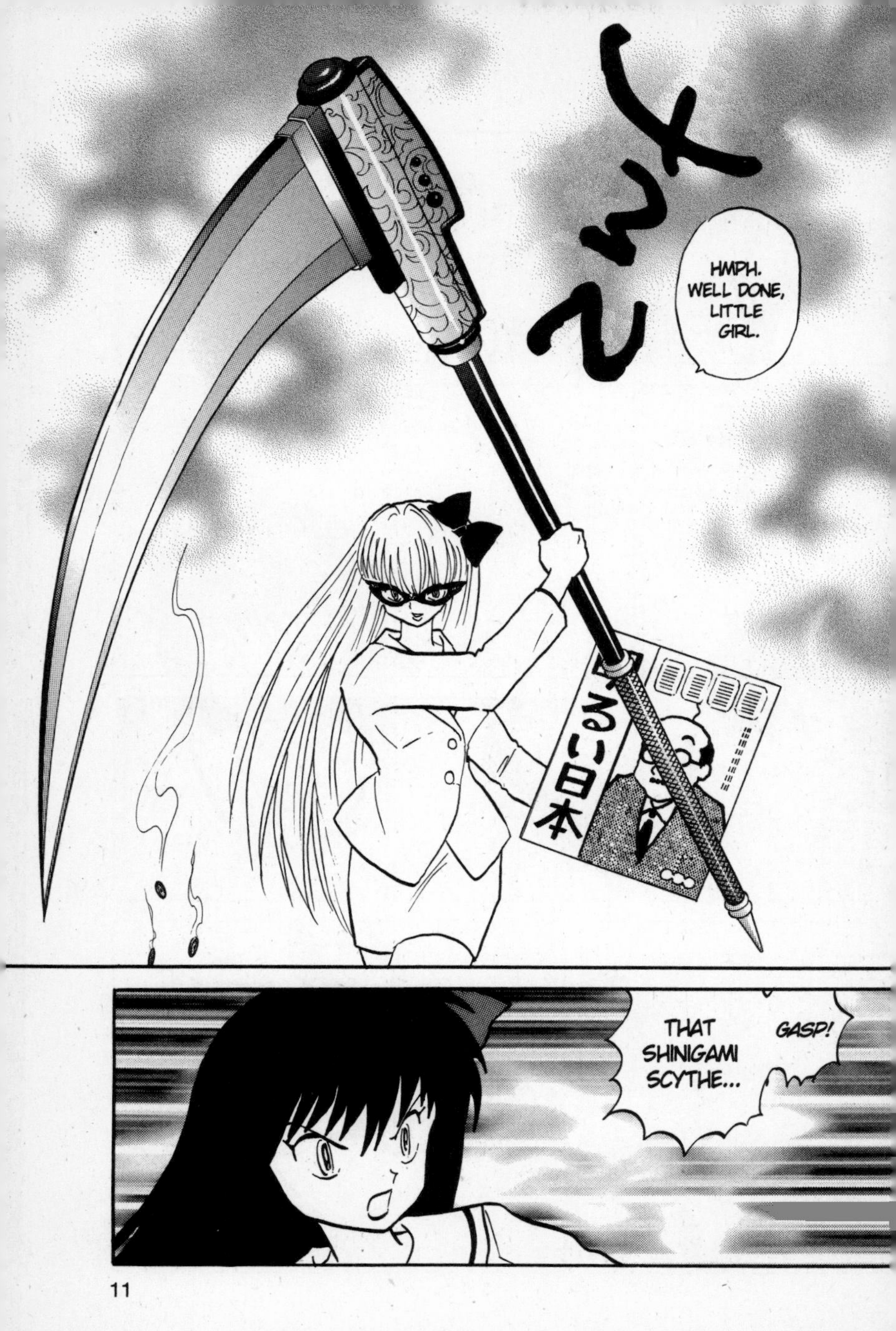
HMPH. WELL DONE, LITTLE GIRL.
GASP!
THAT SHINIGAMI SCYTHE...

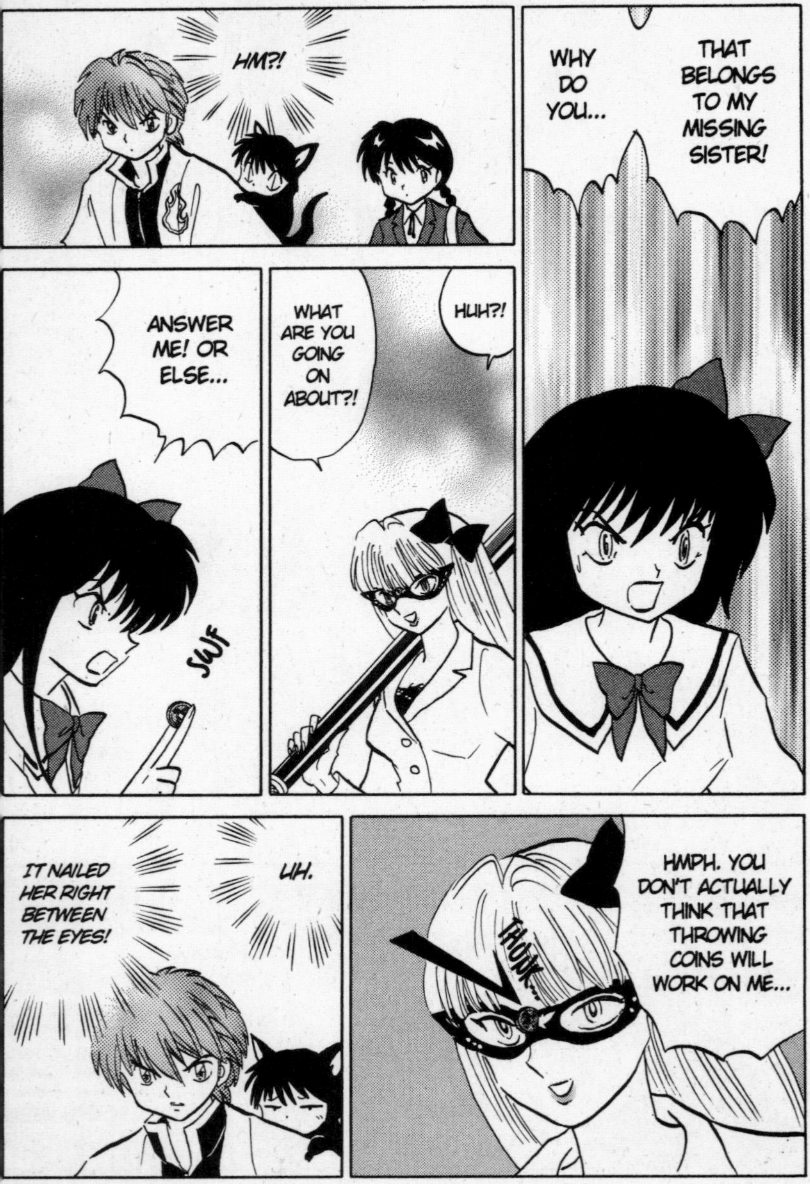
THAT BELONGS TO MY MISSING SISTER!
WHY DO YOU...
HM?!
HUH?!
WHAT ARE YOU GOING ON ABOUT?!
ANSWER ME! OR ELSE...
SWF
HMPH. YOU DON'T ACTUALLY THINK THAT THROWING COINS WILL WORK ON ME...
THUNK...
UH.
IT NAILED HER RIGHT BETWEEN THE EYES!

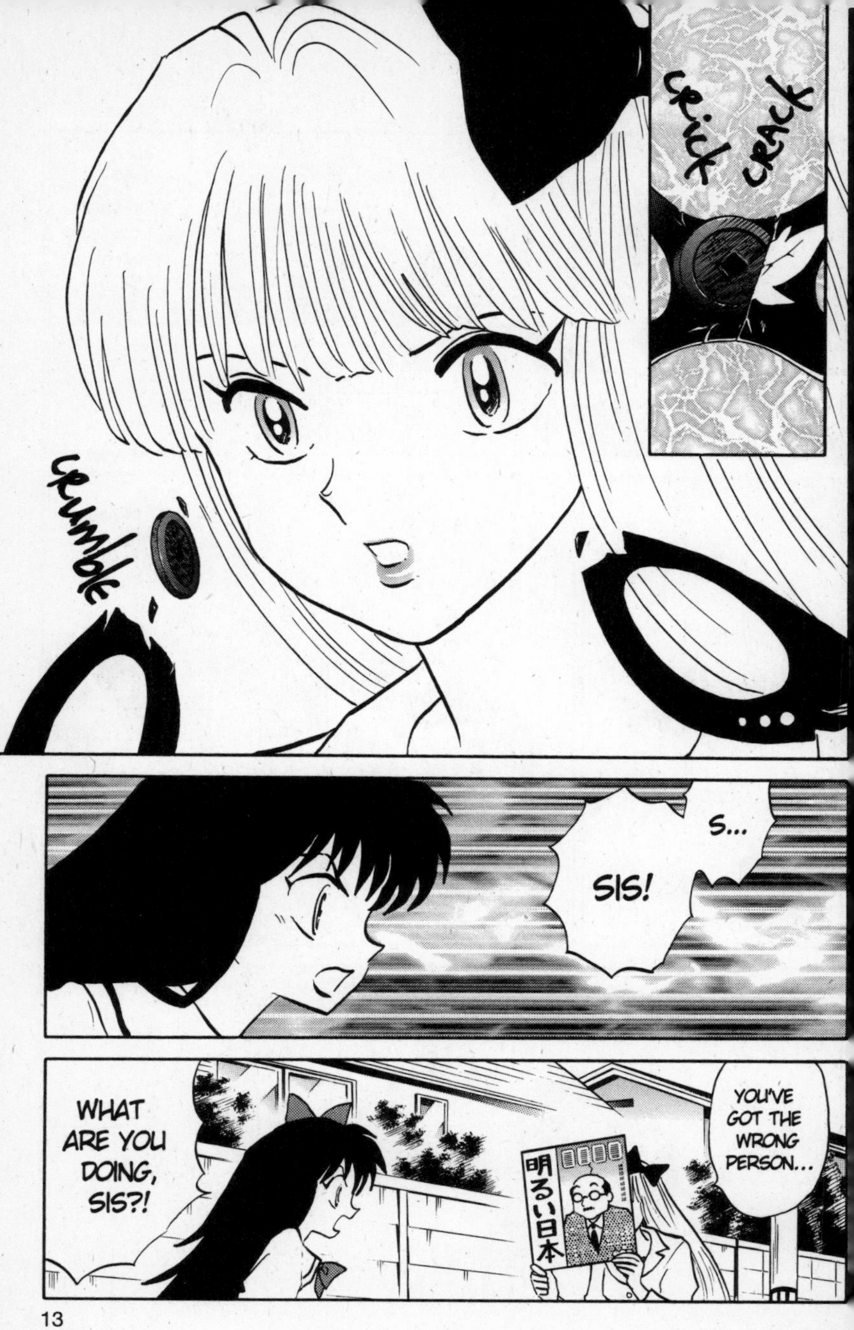
CRACK
crick
crumble
S...
SIS!
YOU'VE GOT THE WRONG PERSON...
明るい日本
WHAT ARE YOU DOING, SIS?!

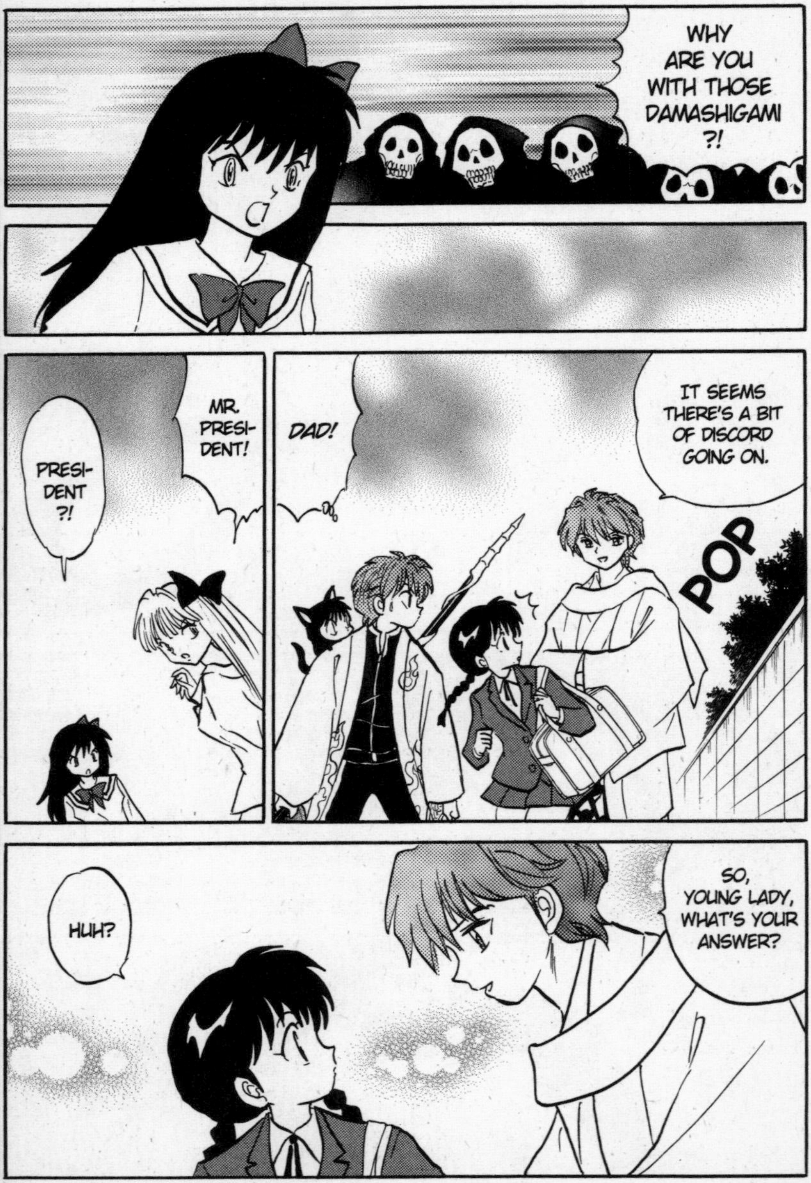
WHY ARE YOU WITH THOSE DAMASHIGAMI ?!
IT SEEMS THERE'S A BIT OF DISCORD GOING ON.
POP
DAD!
MR. PRESI- DENT!
PRESI- DENT ?!
SO, YOUNG LADY, WHAT'S YOUR ANSWER?
HUH?

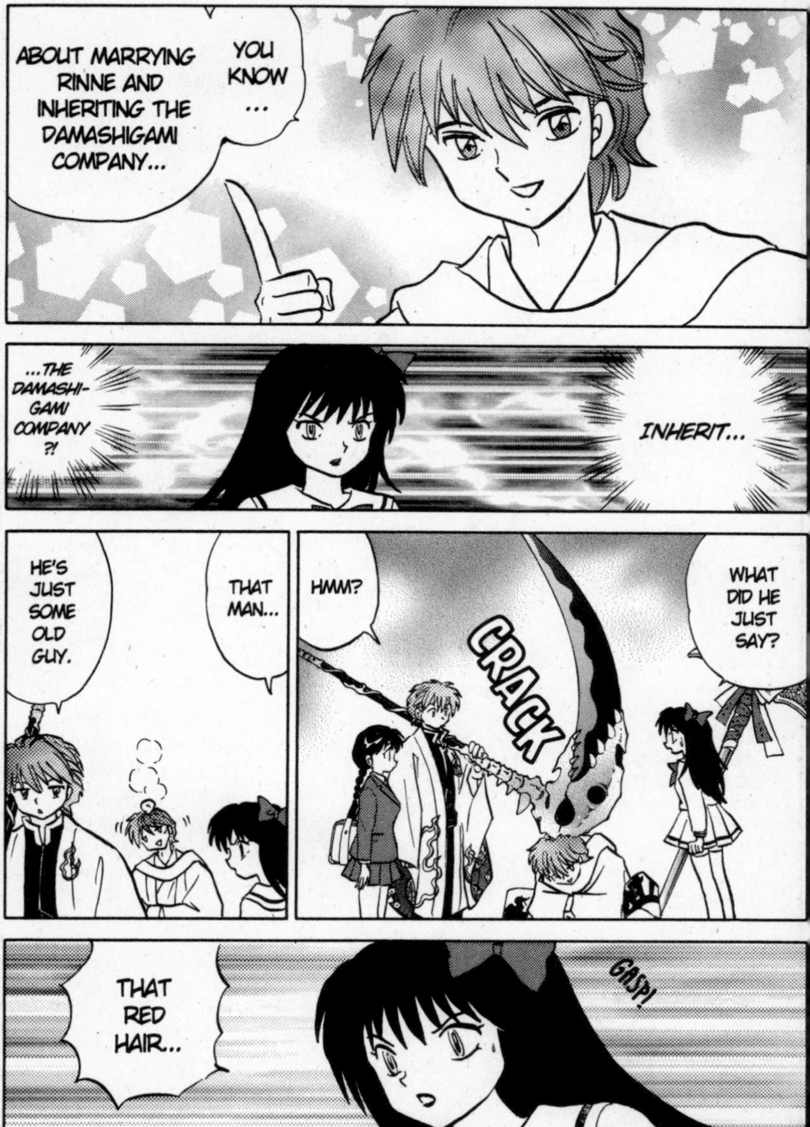
YOU KNOW ...
ABOUT MARRYING RINNE AND INHERITING THE DAMASHIGAMI COMPANY...
INHERIT...
...THE DAMASHI-GAMI COMPANY ?!
WHAT DID HE JUST SAY?
HMM?
CRACK
THAT MAN...
HE'S JUST SOME OLD GUY.
GASP!
THAT RED HAIR...

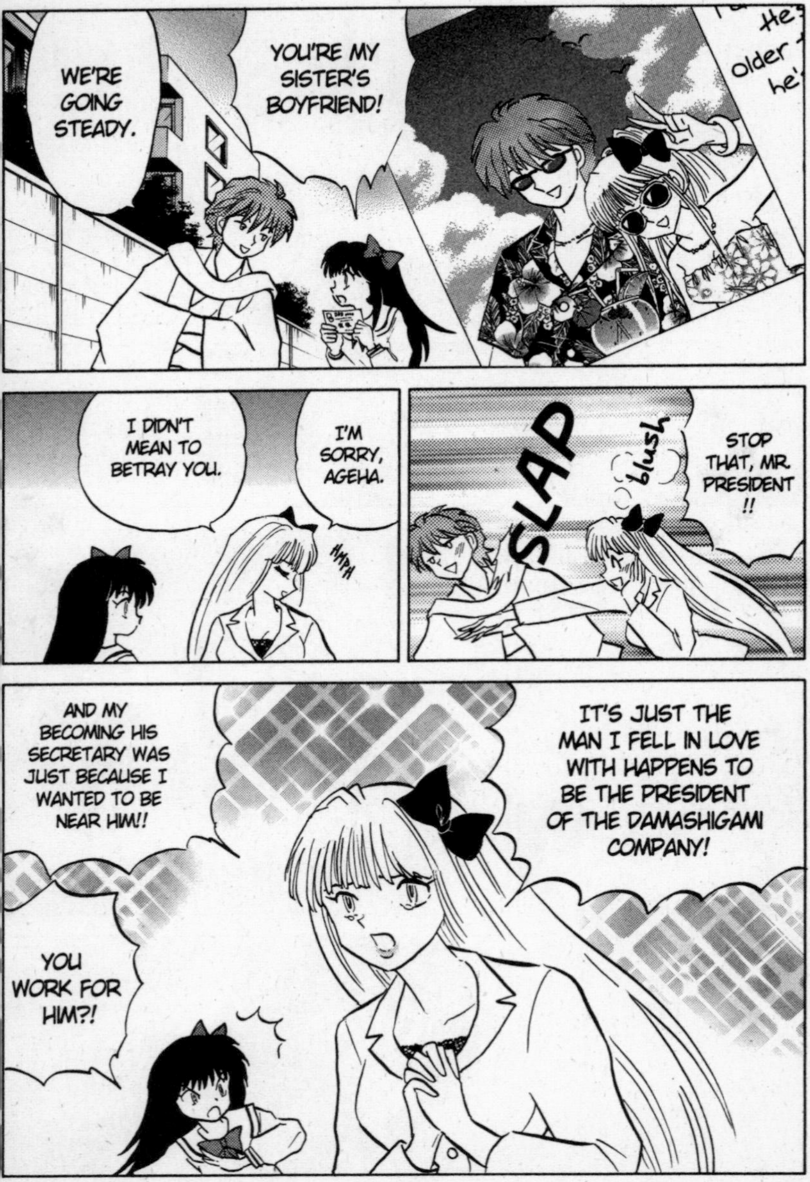
YOU'RE MY SISTER'S BOYFRIEND!
WE'RE GOING STEADY.
STOP THAT, MR. PRESIDENT !!
blush
SLAP
I'M SORRY, AGEHA.
HMPH
I DIDN'T MEAN TO BETRAY YOU.
IT'S JUST THE MAN I FELL IN LOVE WITH HAPPENS TO BE THE PRESIDENT OF THE DAMASHIGAMI COMPANY!
AND MY BECOMING HIS SECRETARY WAS JUST BECAUSE I WANTED TO BE NEAR HIM!!
YOU WORK FOR HIM?!

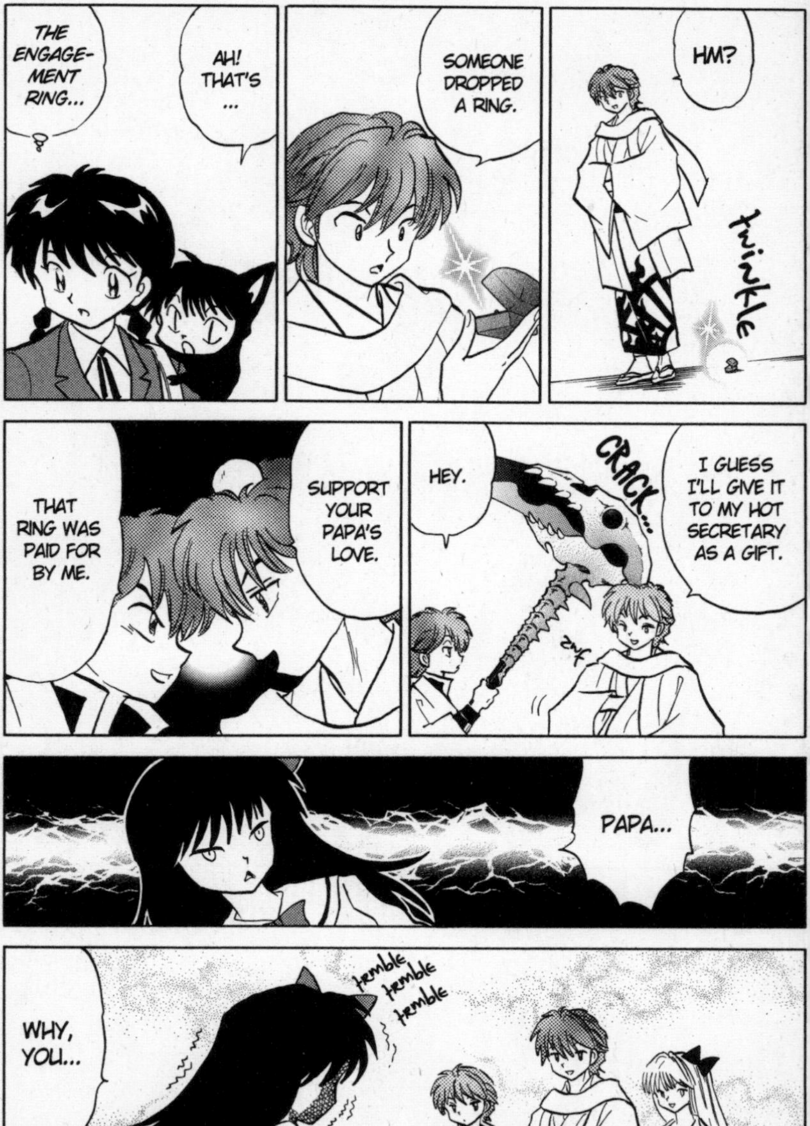
HM?
twinkle
SOMEONE DROPPED A RING.
AH! THAT'S ...
THE ENGAGEMENT-MENT RING...
I GUESS I'LL GIVE IT TO MY HOT SECRETARY AS A GIFT.
CRACK...
HEY.
SUPPORT YOUR PAPA'S LOVE.
THAT RING WAS PAID FOR BY ME.
PAPA...
tremble tremble tremble
WHY, YOU...

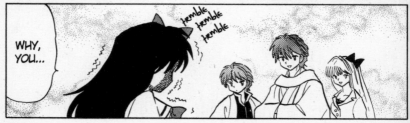

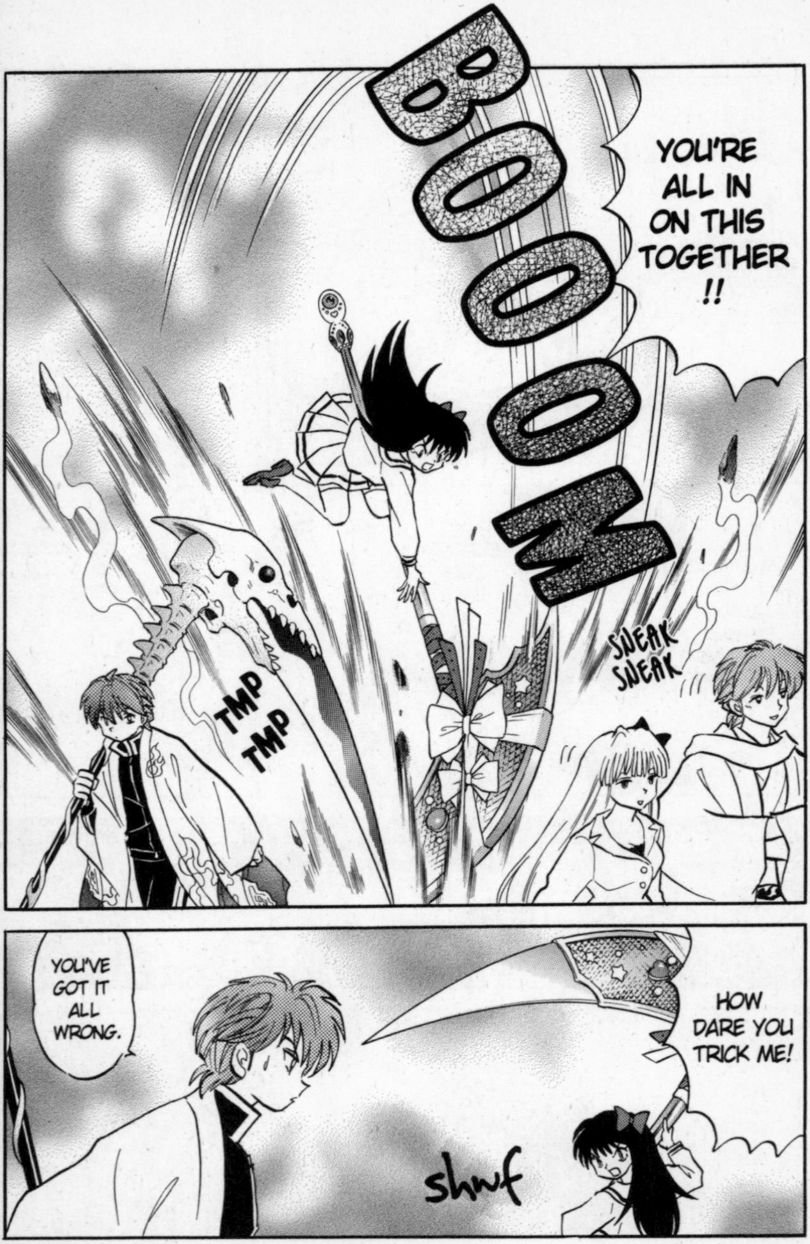
BOOOOM
YOU'RE ALL IN ON THIS TOGETHER!!
SNEAK SNEAK
TMP TMP
HOW DARE YOU TRICK ME!
shwf
YOU'VE GOT IT ALL WRONG.

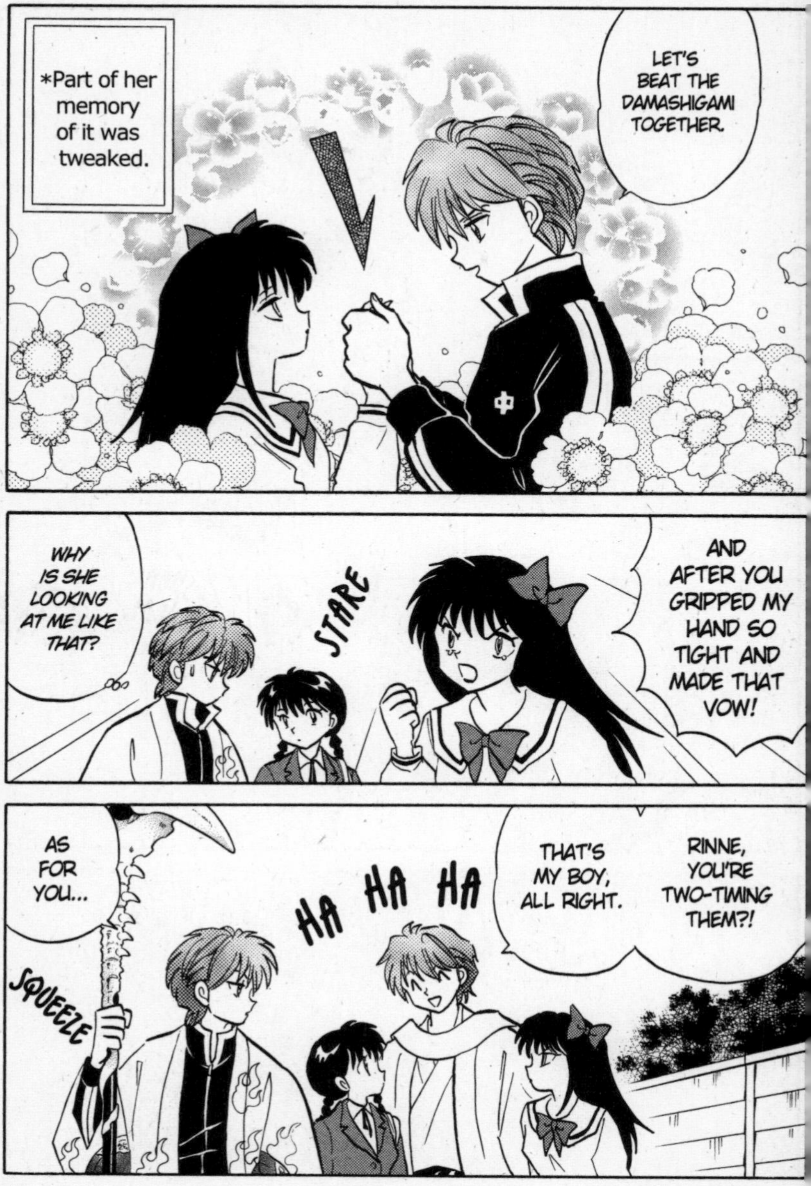
LET'S BEAT THE DAMASHIGAMI TOGETHER.
*Part of her memory of it was tweaked.
AND AFTER YOU GRIPPED MY HAND SO TIGHT AND MADE THAT VOW!
STARE
WHY IS SHE LOOKING AT ME LIKE THAT?
RINNE, YOU'RE TWO-TIMING THEM?!
THAT'S MY BOY, ALL RIGHT.
HA HA HA
AS FOR YOU...
SQUEEZE

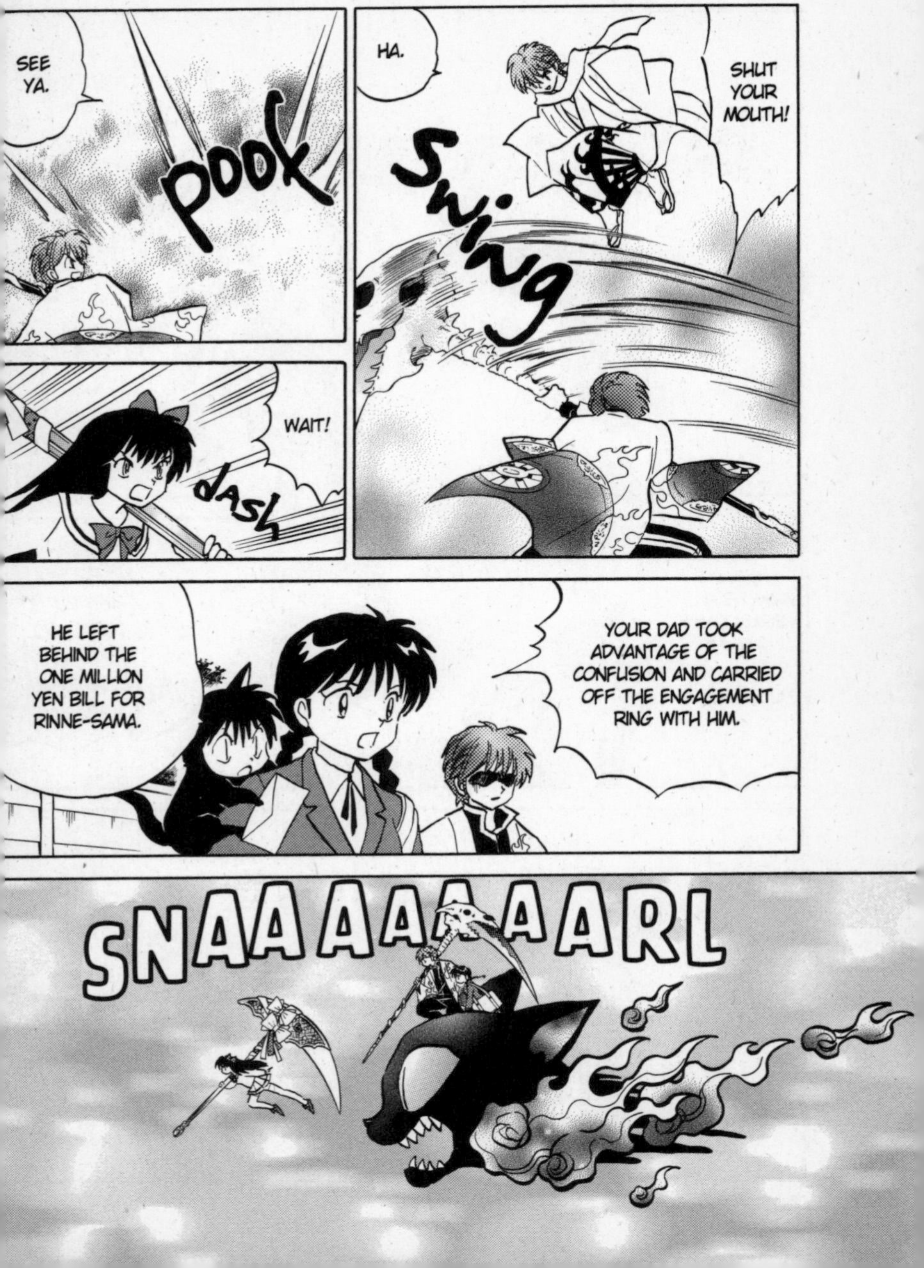
HA.
SHUT YOUR MOUTH!
SWING
SEE YA.
POOK
WAIT!
DASH
YOUR DAD TOOK ADVANTAGE OF THE CONFUSION AND CARRIED OFF THE ENGAGEMENT RING WITH HIM.
HE LEFT BEHIND THE ONE MILLION YEN BILL FOR RINNE-SAMA.
SNAAAAAARL

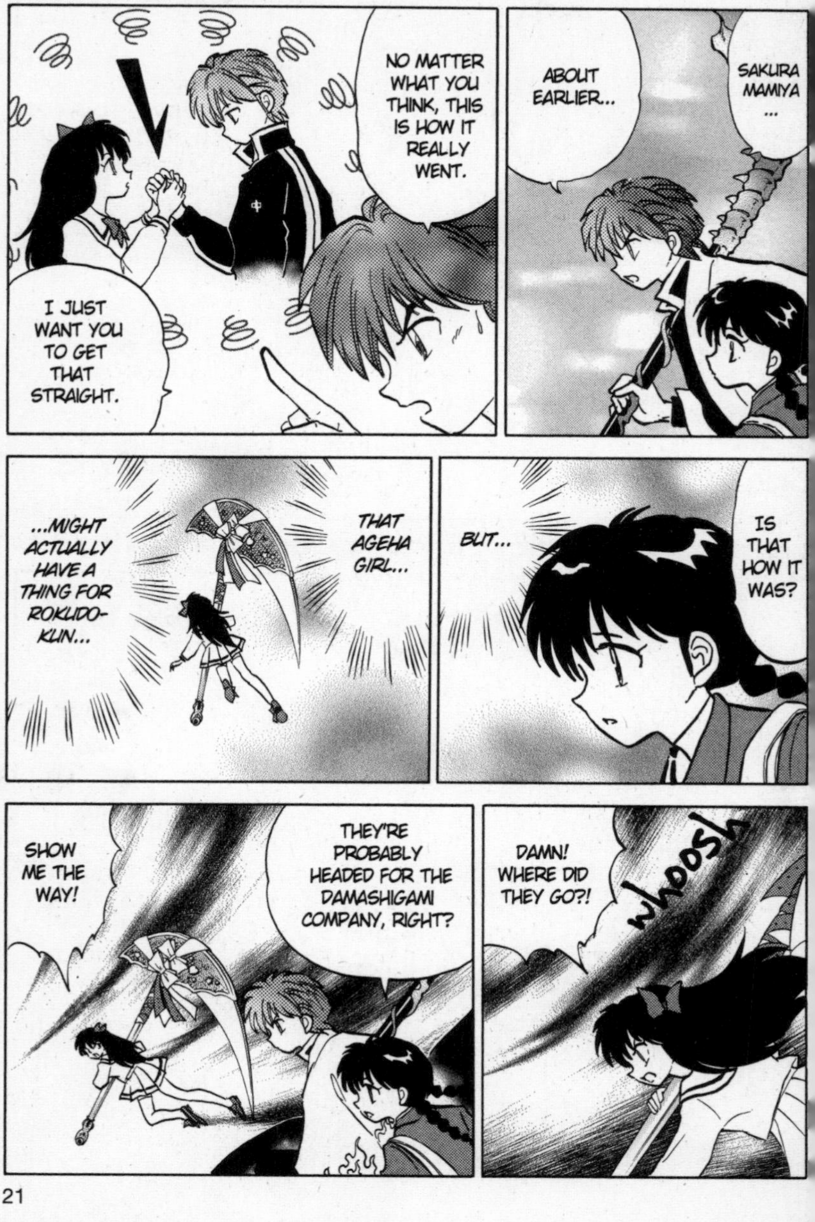
SAKURA MAMIYA ...
ABOUT EARLIER...
NO MATTER WHAT YOU THINK, THIS IS HOW IT REALLY WENT.
I JUST WANT YOU TO GET THAT STRAIGHT.
IS THAT HOW IT WAS?
BUT...
THAT AGEHA GIRL...
...MIGHT ACTUALLY HAVE A THING FOR ROKUDO-KUN...
whoosh
DAMN! WHERE DID THEY GO?!
THEY'RE PROBABLY HEADED FOR THE DAMASHIGAMI COMPANY, RIGHT?
SHOW ME THE WAY!

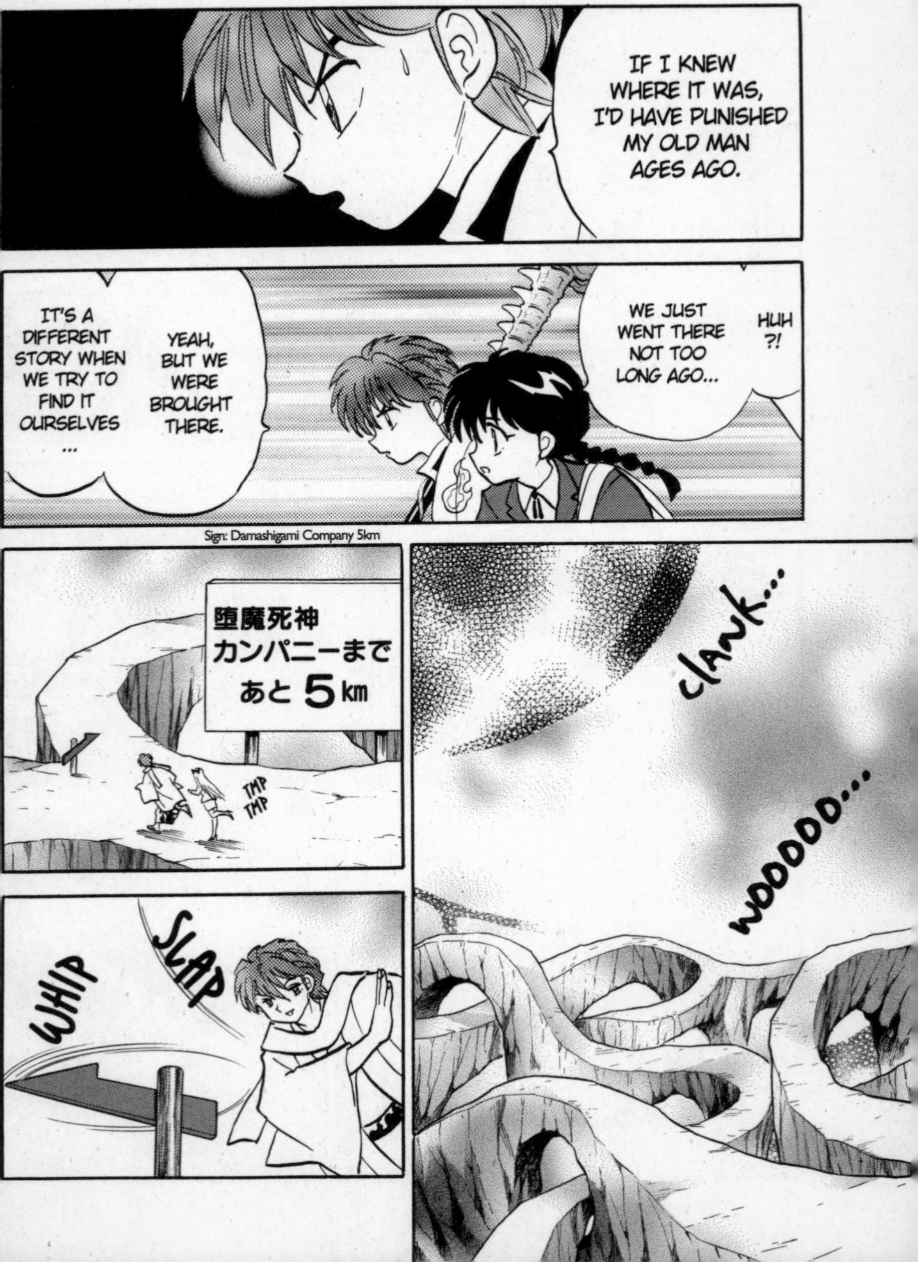
IF I KNEW WHERE IT WAS, I'D HAVE PUNISHED MY OLD MAN AGES AGO.
HUH ?!
WE JUST WENT THERE NOT TOO LONG AGO...
YEAH, BUT WE WERE BROUGHT THERE.
IT'S A DIFFERENT STORY WHEN WE TRY TO FIND IT OURSELVES ...
clank...
WOOOOOD...
Sign: Damashigami Company 5km
堕魔死神
カンパニーまで
あと 5 km
TMP TMP
SLAP
WHIP

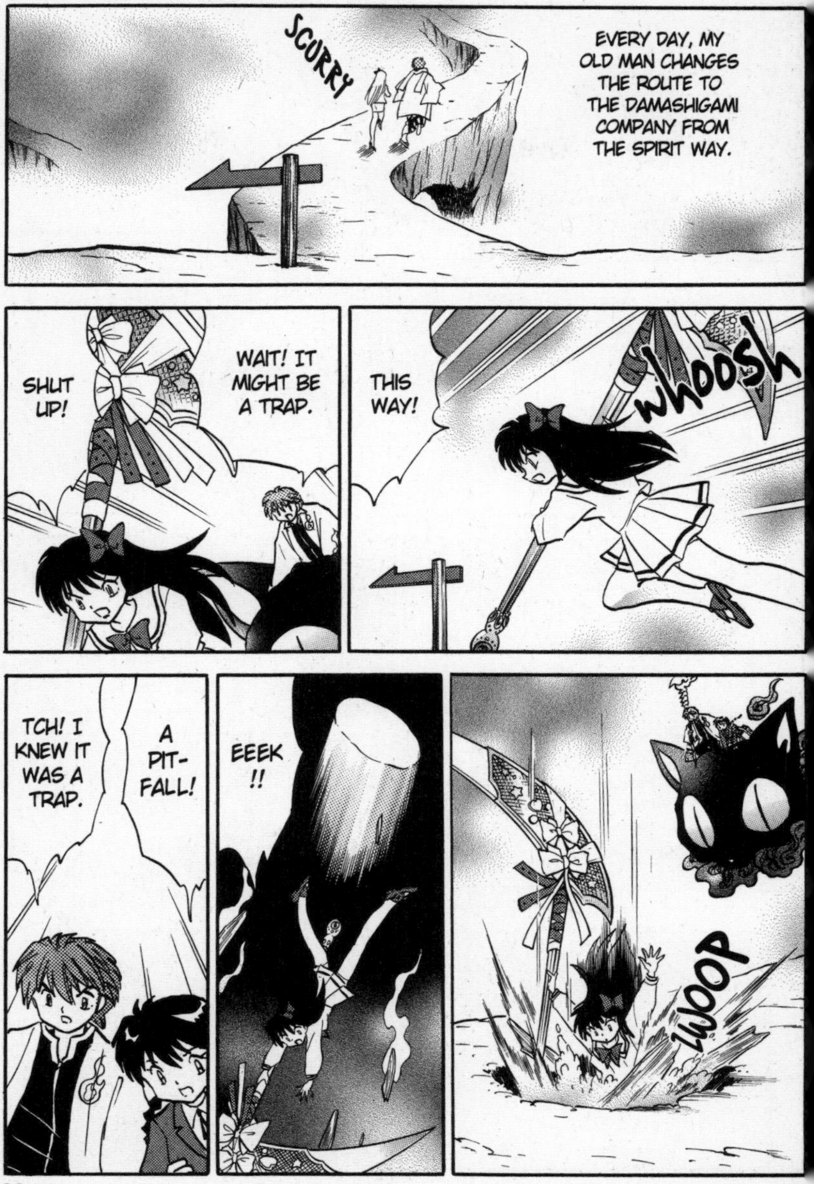
EVERY DAY, MY OLD MAN CHANGES THE ROUTE TO THE DAMASHIGAMI COMPANY FROM THE SPIRIT WAY.
SCURRY
THIS WAY!
WHOOSH
WAIT! IT MIGHT BE A TRAP.
SHUT UP!
WOOP
EEEK !!
A PIT-FALL!
TCH! I KNEW IT WAS A TRAP.

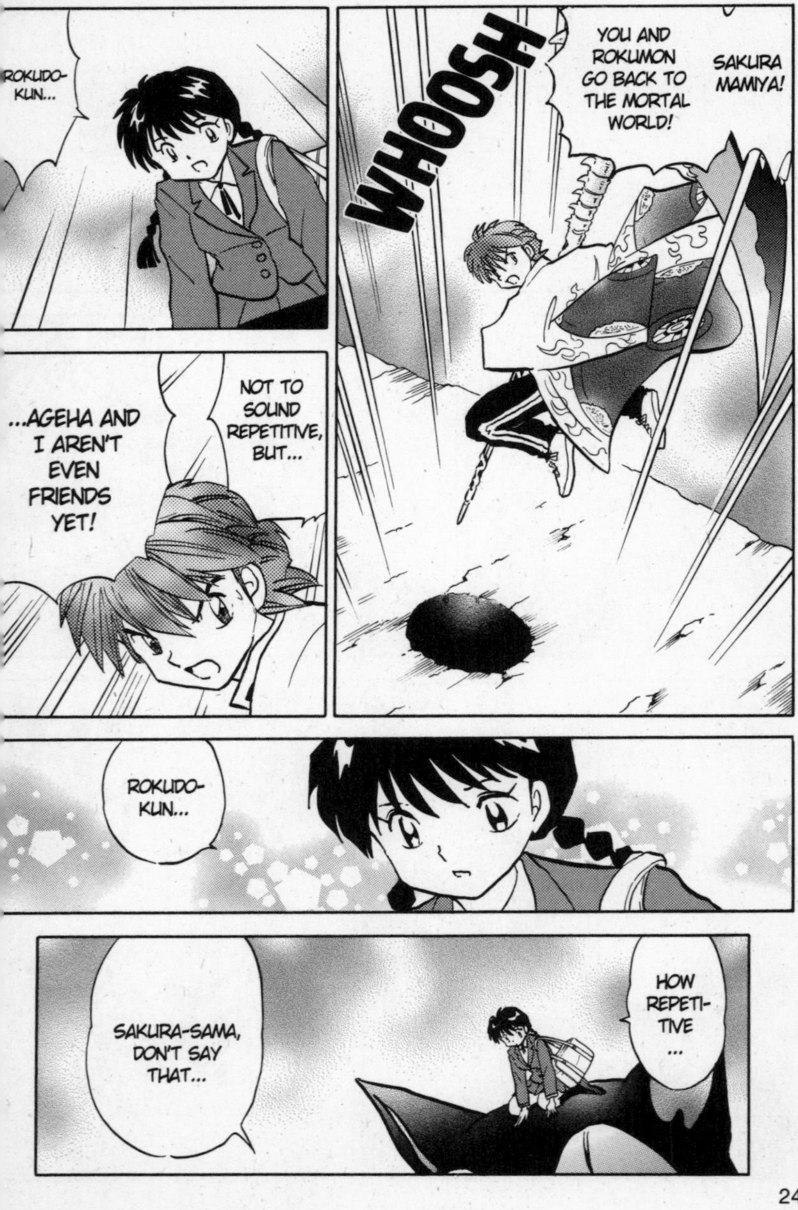
SAKURA MAMIYA!
YOU AND ROKUMON GO BACK TO THE MORTAL WORLD!
WHOOSH
ROKUDO-KUN...
NOT TO SOUND REPETITIVE, BUT...
...AGEHA AND I AREN'T EVEN FRIENDS YET!
ROKUDO-KUN...
HOW REPETI-TIVE ...
SAKURA-SAMA, DON'T SAY THAT...

CHAPTER 40: RICH GIRL

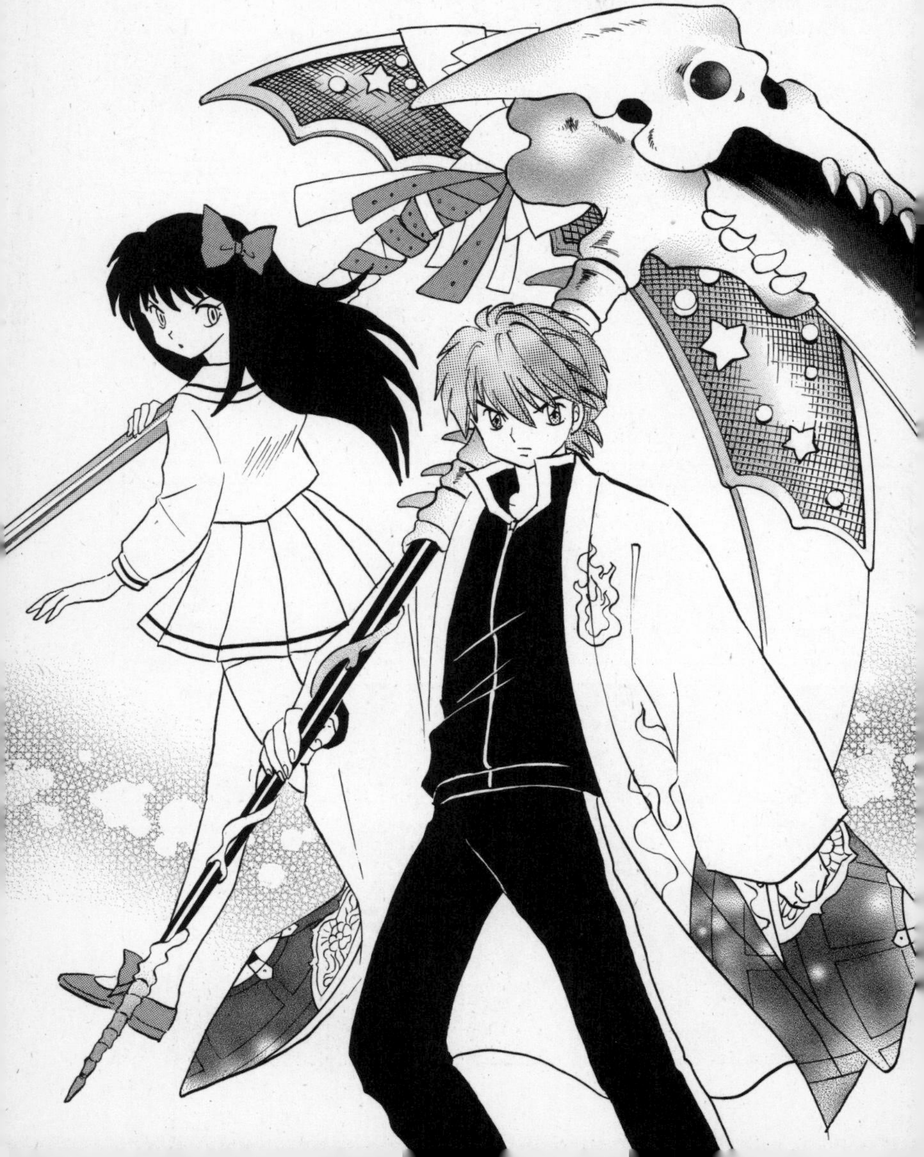

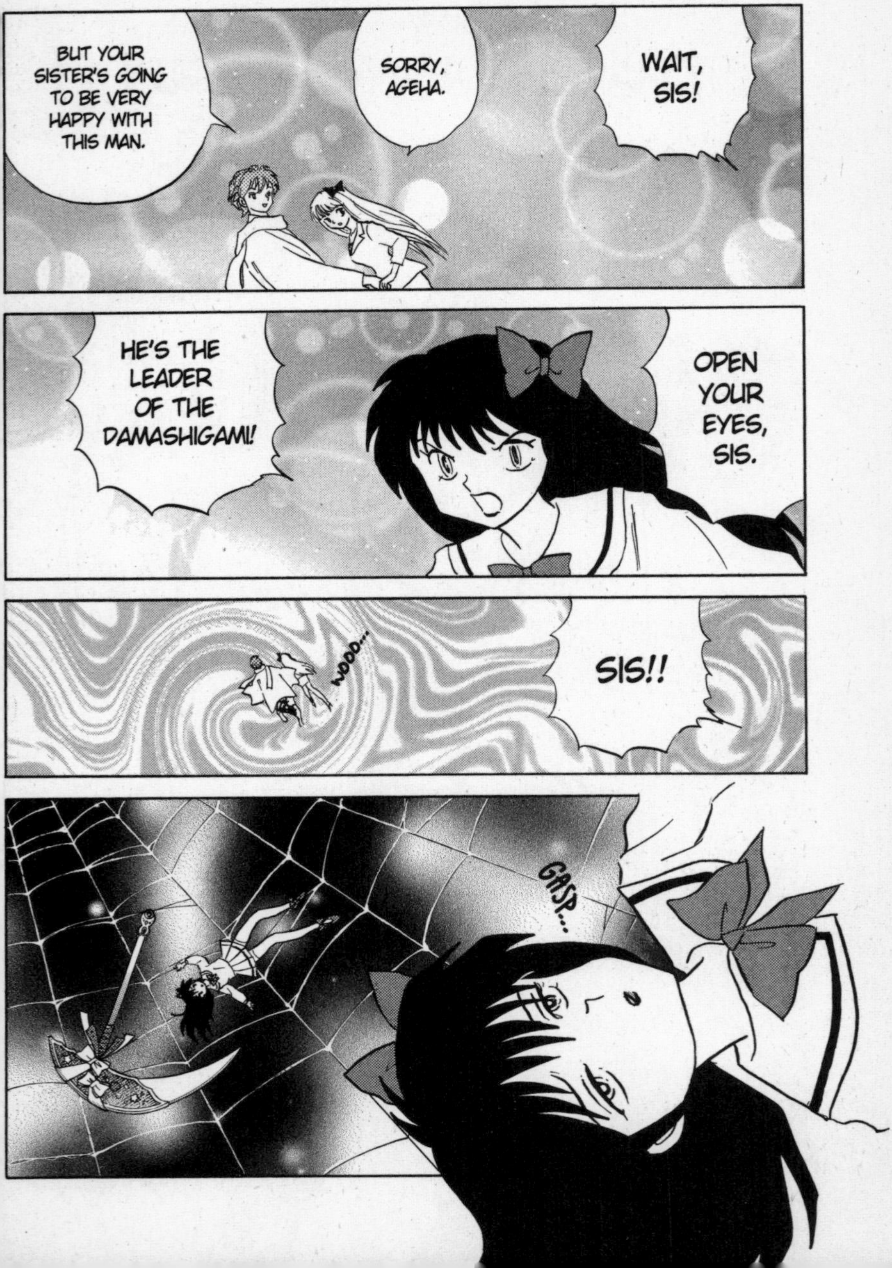
WAIT, SIS!
SORRY, AGEHA.
BUT YOUR SISTER'S GOING TO BE VERY HAPPY WITH THIS MAN.
OPEN YOUR EYES, SIS.
HE'S THE LEADER OF THE DAMASHIGAMI!
SIS!!
WOOO...
GASP...

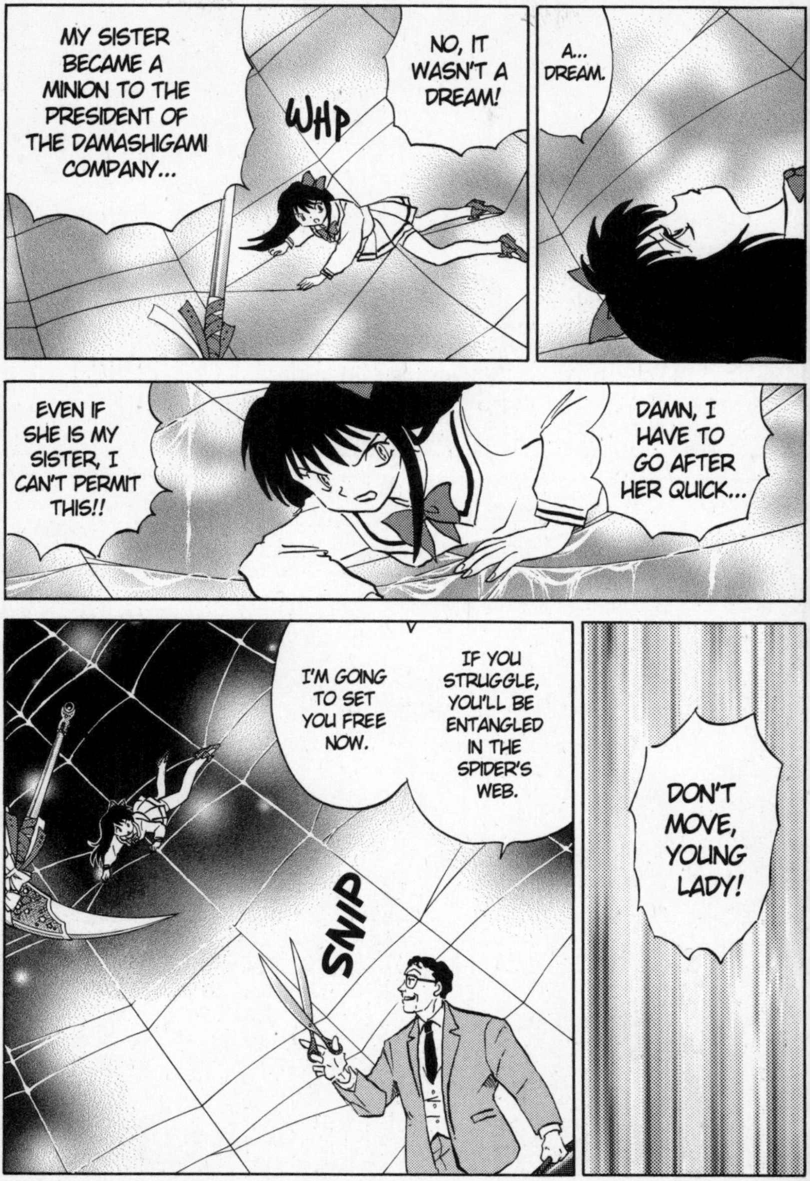
A... DREAM.
NO, IT WASN'T A DREAM!
WHP
MY SISTER BECAME A MINION TO THE PRESIDENT OF THE DAMASHIGAMI COMPANY...
DAMN, I HAVE TO GO AFTER HER QUICK...
EVEN IF SHE IS MY SISTER, I CAN'T PERMIT THIS!!
DON'T MOVE, YOUNG LADY!
IF YOU STRUGGLE, YOU'LL BE ENTANGLED IN THE SPIDER'S WEB.
I'M GOING TO SET YOU FREE NOW.
SNIP

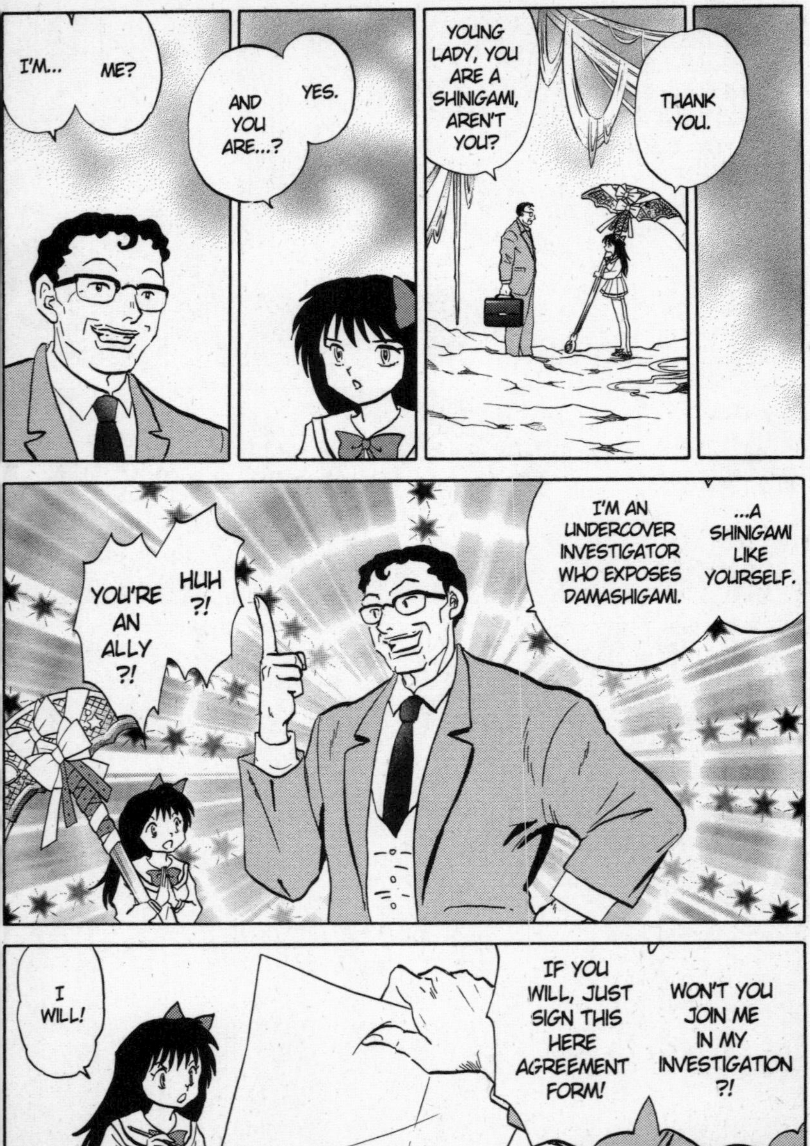
THANK YOU.
YOUNG LADY, YOU ARE A SHINIGAMI, AREN'T YOU?
YES.
AND YOU ARE...?
ME?
I'M...
I'M AN UNDERCOVER INVESTIGATOR WHO EXPOSES DAMASHIGAMI.
...A SHINIGAMI LIKE YOURSELF.
HUH ?!
YOU'RE AN ALLY ?!
WON'T YOU JOIN ME IN MY INVESTIGATION ?!
IF YOU WILL, JUST SIGN THIS HERE AGREEMENT FORM!
I WILL!

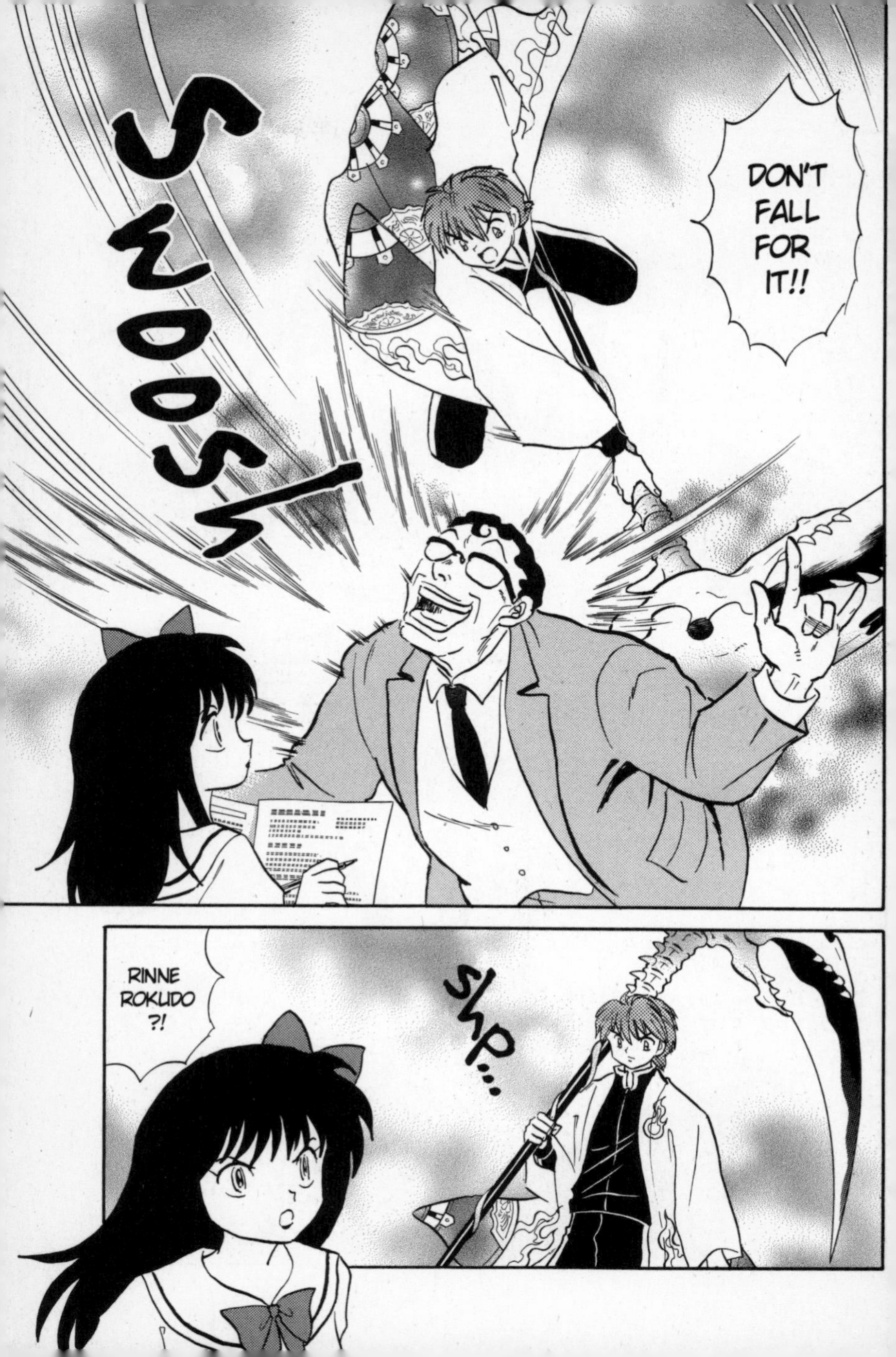
DON'T FALL FOR IT!!
SWOOSH
SHP...
RINNE ROKUDO ?!

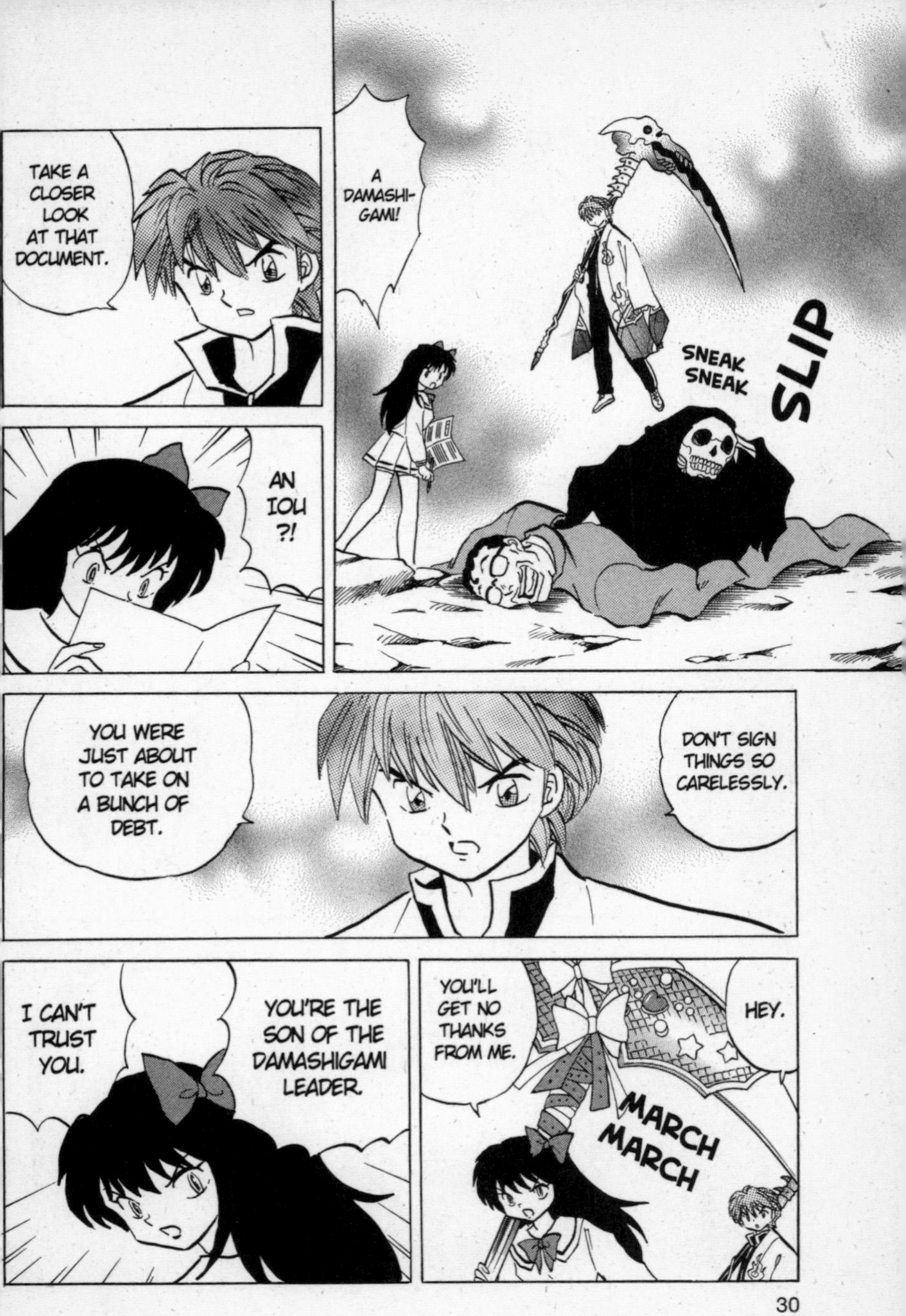
A DAMASHIGAMI!
SNEAK SNEAK
SLIP
TAKE A CLOSER LOOK AT THAT DOCUMENT.
AN IOU ?!
DON'T SIGN THINGS SO CARELESSLY.
YOU WERE JUST ABOUT TO TAKE ON A BUNCH OF DEBT.
HEY.
YOU'LL GET NO THANKS FROM ME.
MARCH MARCH
YOU'RE THE SON OF THE DAMASHIGAMI LEADER.
I CAN'T TRUST YOU.

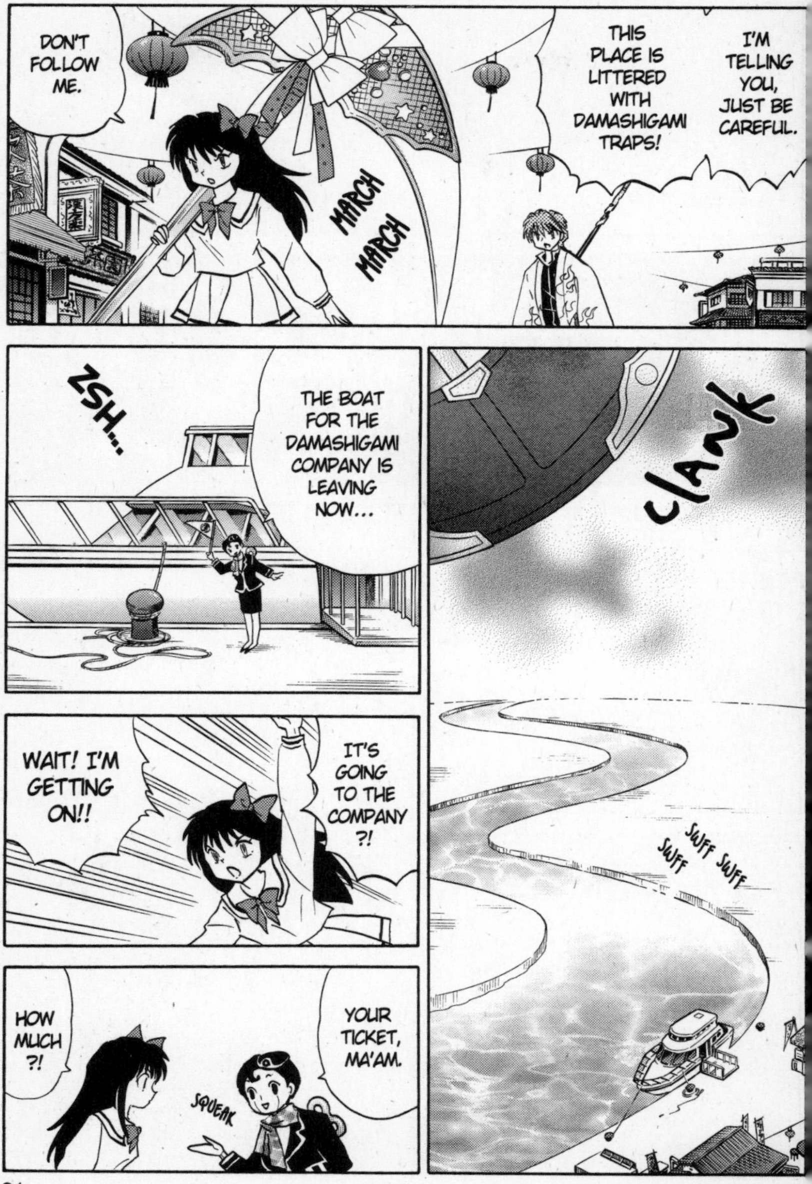
I'M TELLING YOU, JUST BE CAREFUL.
THIS PLACE IS LITTERED WITH DAMASHIGAMI TRAPS!
DON'T FOLLOW ME.
MARCH
MARCH
CLANK
SWFF SWFF
SWFF
THE BOAT FOR THE DAMASHIGAMI COMPANY IS LEAVING NOW...
ZSH...
IT'S GOING TO THE COMPANY?!
WAIT! I'M GETTING ON!!
YOUR TICKET, MA'AM.
SQUEAK
HOW MUCH?!

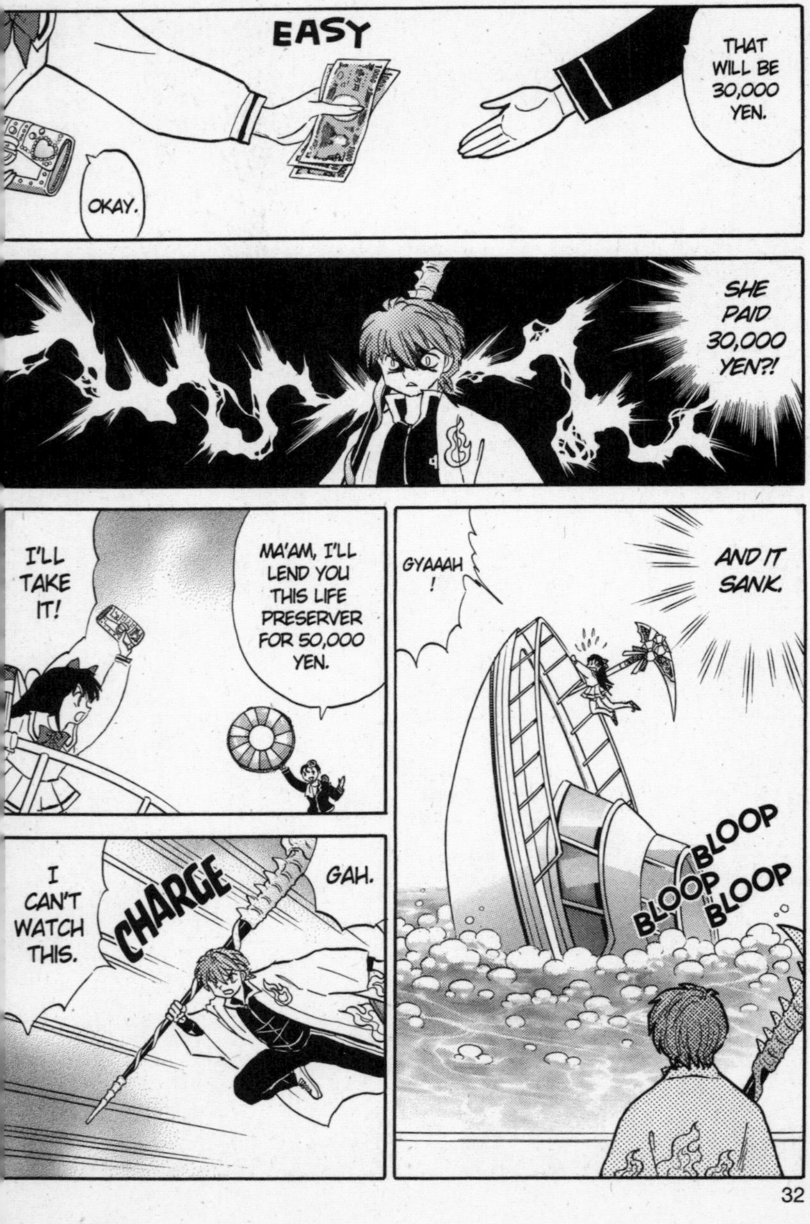
THAT WILL BE 30,000 YEN.
EASY
OKAY.
SHE PAID 30,000 YEN?!
AND IT SANK.
GYAAAH!
BLOOP BLOOP BLOOP BLOOP
MA'AM, I'LL LEND YOU THIS LIFE PRESERVER FOR 50,000 YEN.
I'LL TAKE IT!
GAH.
CHARGE
I CAN'T WATCH THIS.

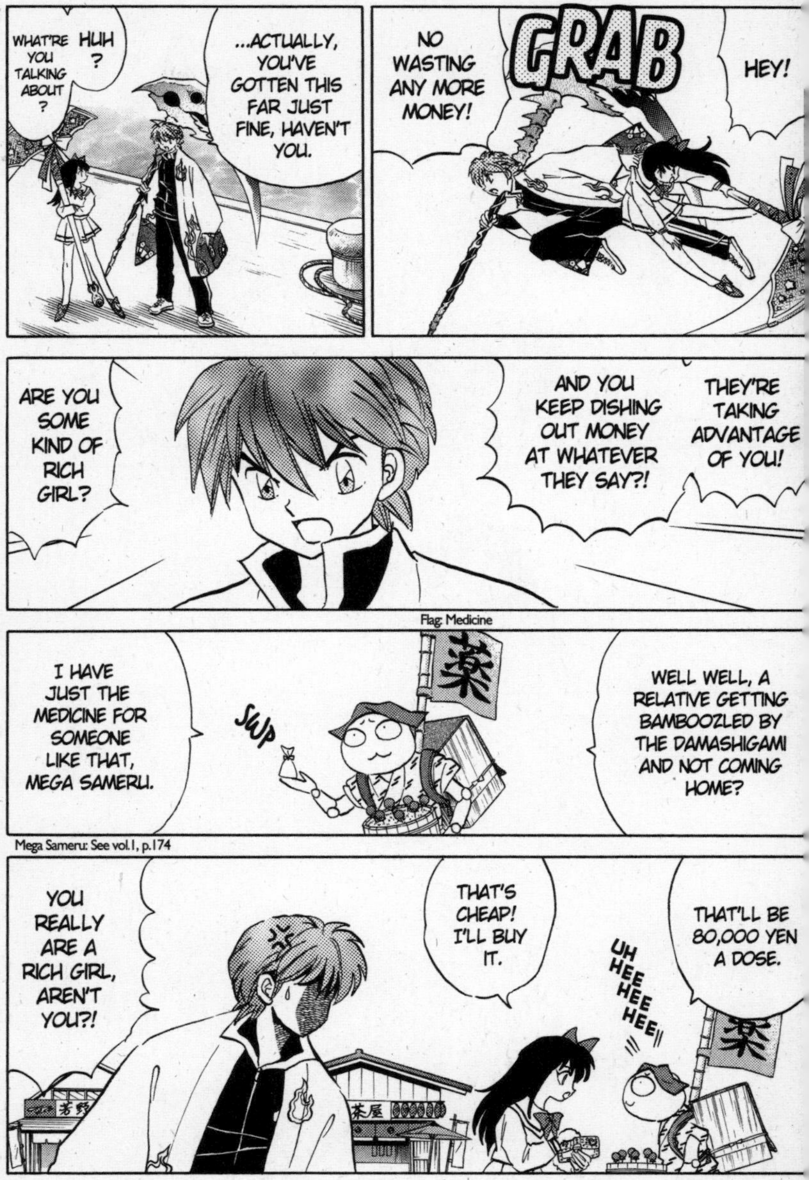
HEY!
GRAB
NO WASTING ANY MORE MONEY!
...ACTUALLY, YOU'VE GOTTEN THIS FAR JUST FINE, HAVEN'T YOU.
HUH?
WHAT'RE YOU TALKING ABOUT?
THEY'RE TAKING ADVANTAGE OF YOU!
AND YOU KEEP DISHING OUT MONEY AT WHATEVER THEY SAY?!
ARE YOU SOME KIND OF RICH GIRL?
薬
WELL WELL, A RELATIVE GETTING BAMBOOZLED BY THE DAMASHIGAMI AND NOT COMING HOME?
SWP
I HAVE JUST THE MEDICINE FOR SOMEONE LIKE THAT, MEGA SAMERU.
THAT'LL BE 80,000 YEN A DOSE.
UH HEE HEE HEE
THAT'S CHEAP! I'LL BUY IT.
YOU REALLY ARE A RICH GIRL, AREN'T YOU?!

Flag: Medicine

Mega Sameru: See vol.1, p.174

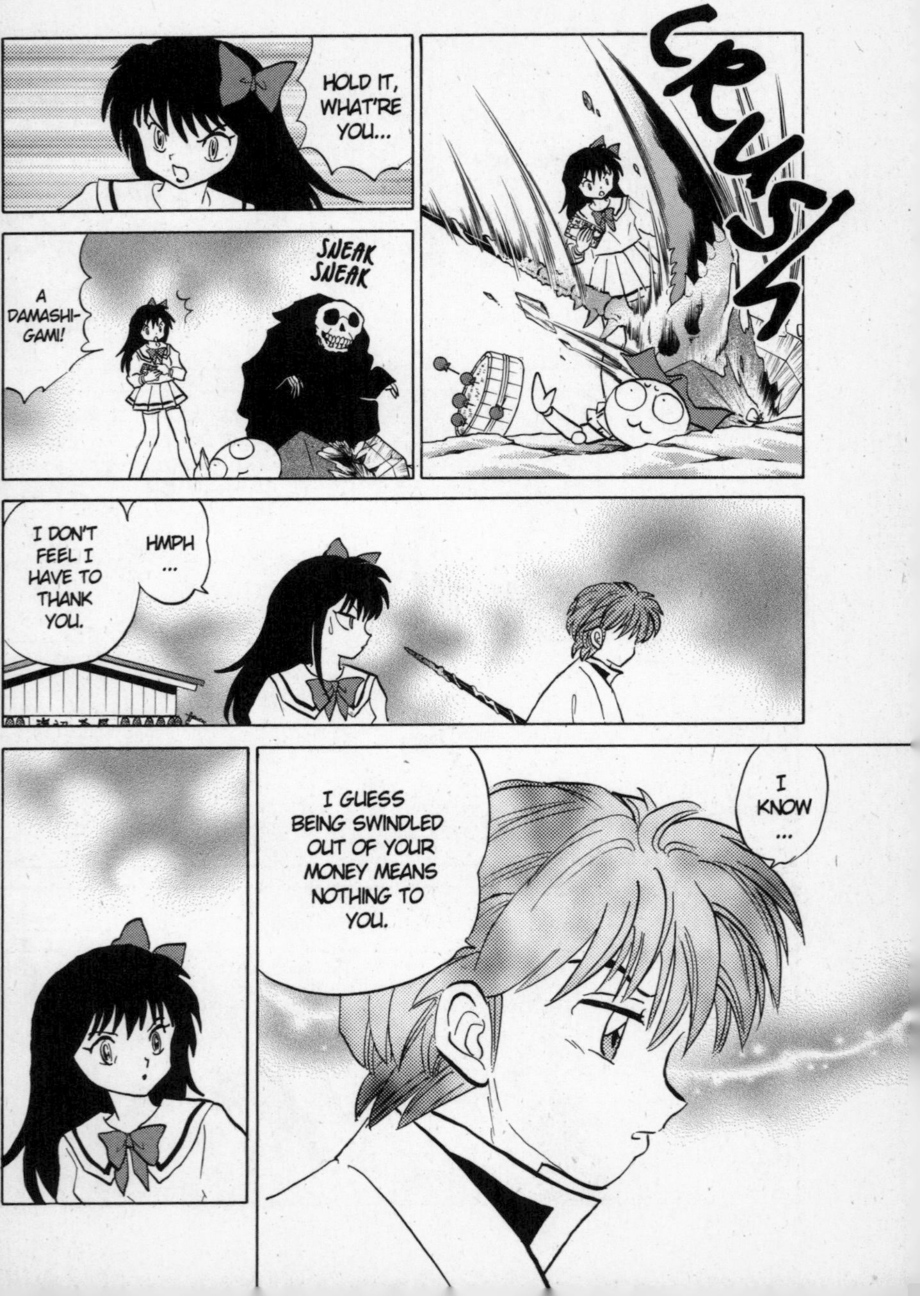
CRUSH
HOLD IT, WHAT'RE YOU...
SNEAK SNEAK
A DAMASHI-GAMI!
HMPH ...
I DON'T FEEL I HAVE TO THANK YOU.
I KNOW ...
I GUESS BEING SWINDLED OUT OF YOUR MONEY MEANS NOTHING TO YOU.

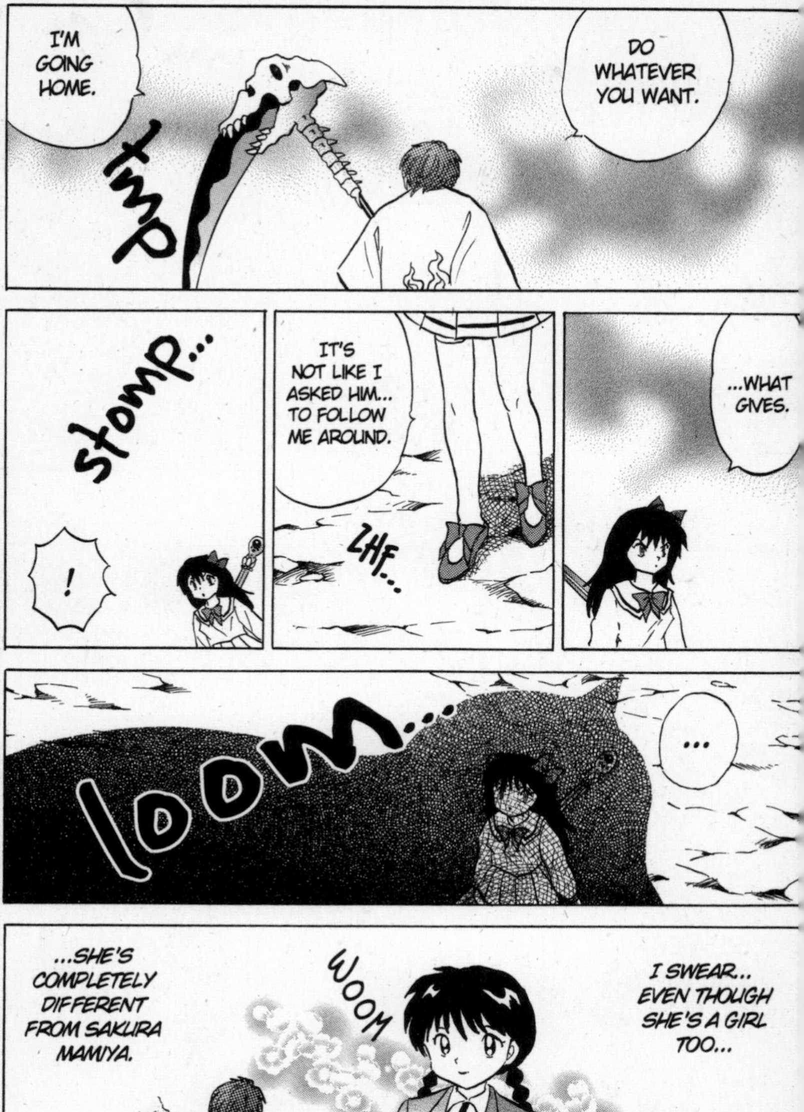
DO WHATEVER YOU WANT.
I'M GOING HOME.
tmp
...WHAT GIVES.
IT'S NOT LIKE I ASKED HIM... TO FOLLOW ME AROUND.
ZHF...
stomp...
!
...
loom...
I SWEAR... EVEN THOUGH SHE'S A GIRL TOO...
WOOM
...SHE'S COMPLETELY DIFFERENT FROM SAKURA MAMIYA.

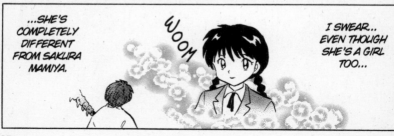

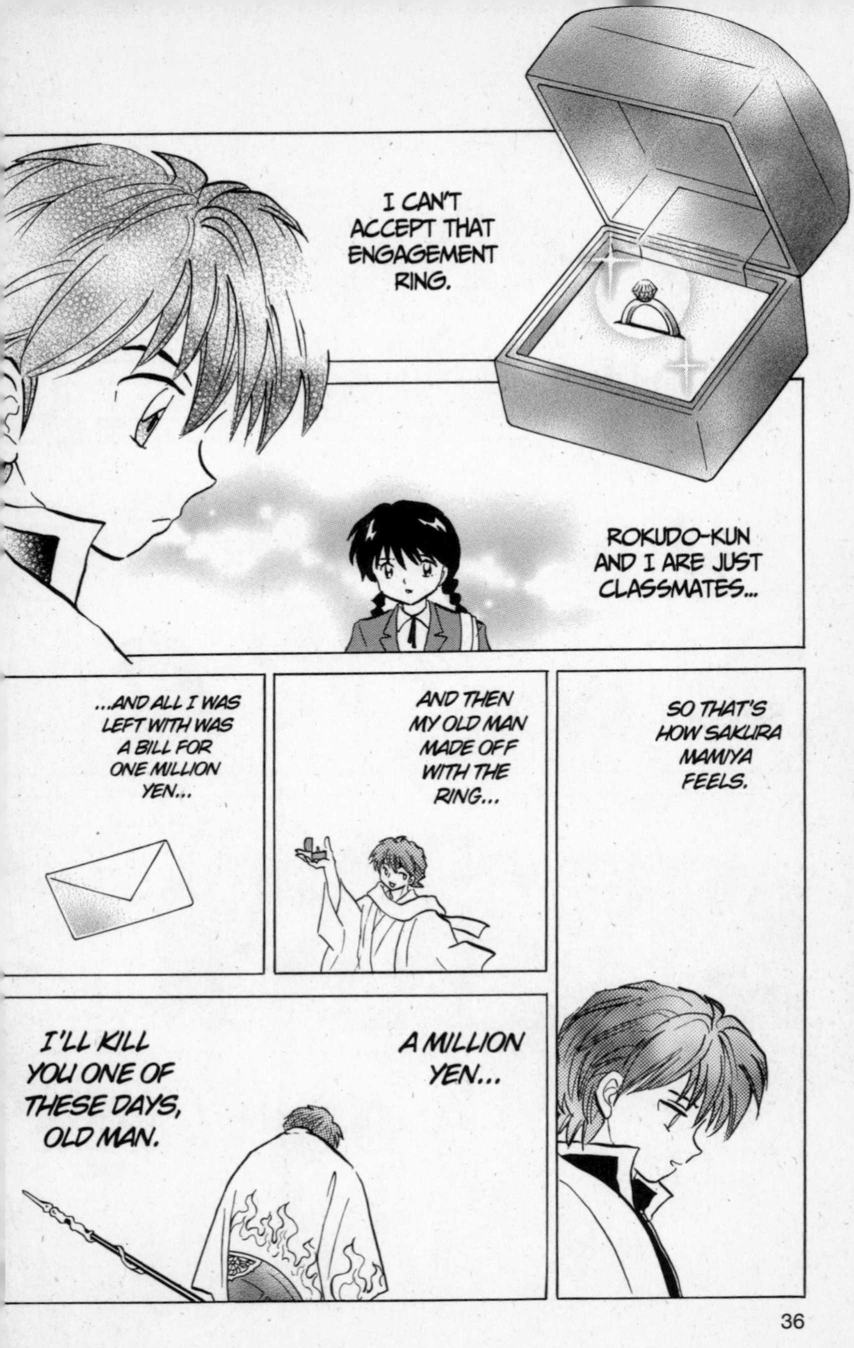

I CAN'T ACCEPT THAT ENGAGEMENT RING.
ROKUDO-KUN AND I ARE JUST CLASSMATES...
SO THAT'S HOW SAKURA MAMIYA FEELS.
AND THEN MY OLD MAN MADE OFF WITH THE RING...
...AND ALL I WAS LEFT WITH WAS A BILL FOR ONE MILLION YEN...
A MILLION YEN...
I'LL KILL YOU ONE OF THESE DAYS, OLD MAN.

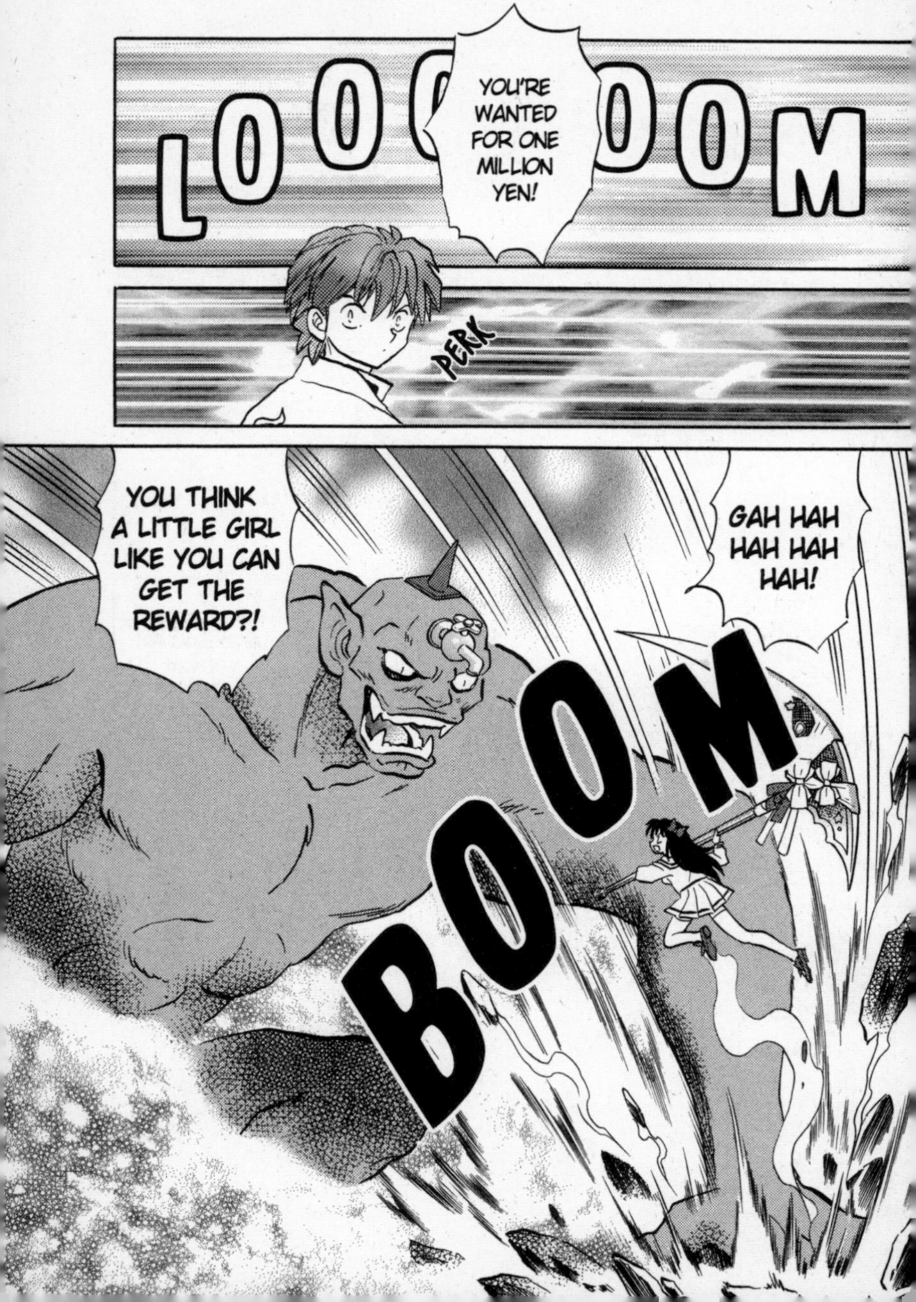
LOOO OOM
YOU'RE WANTED FOR ONE MILLION YEN!
PERK
GAH HAH HAH HAH HAH!
YOU THINK A LITTLE GIRL LIKE YOU CAN GET THE REWARD?!
BOOM

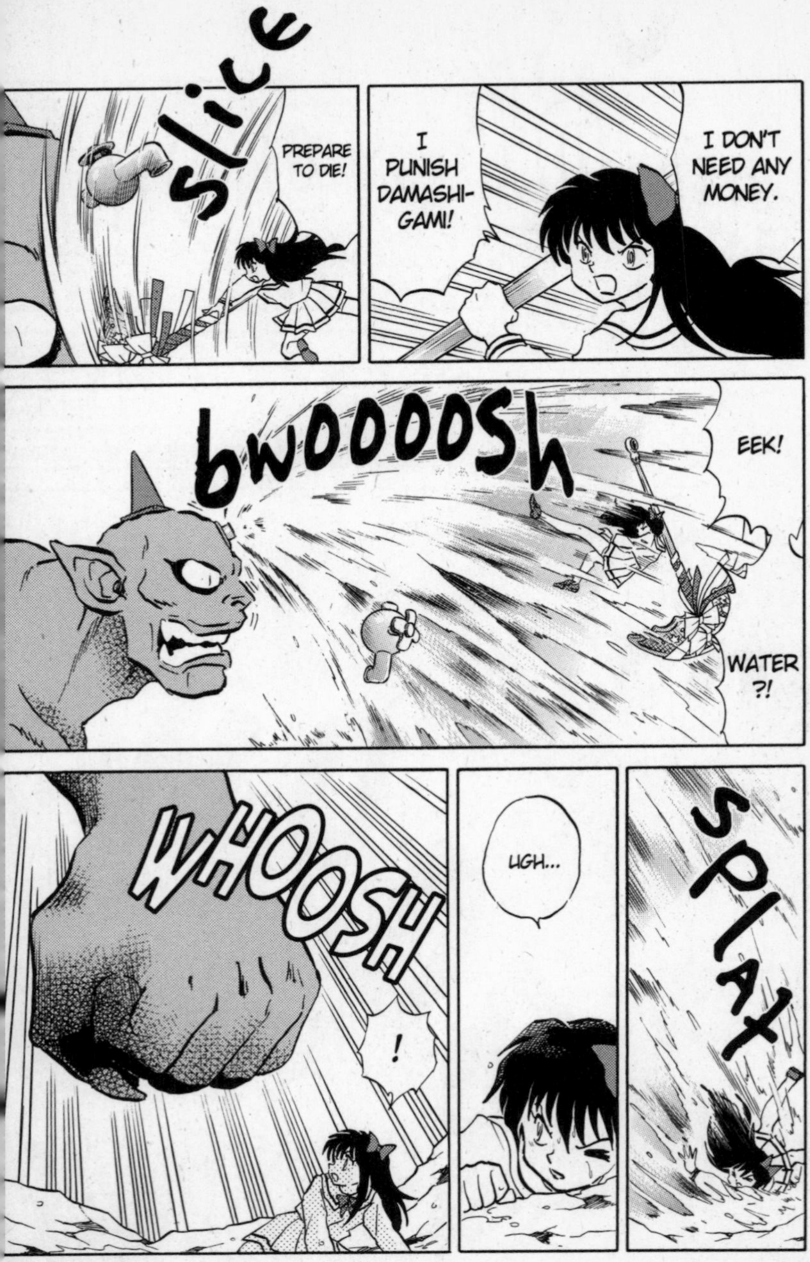
I DON'T NEED ANY MONEY.
I PUNISH DAMASHI-GAMI!
slice
PREPARE TO DIE!
EEK!
bwoooosh
WATER ?!
splat
UGH...
WHOOSH
!

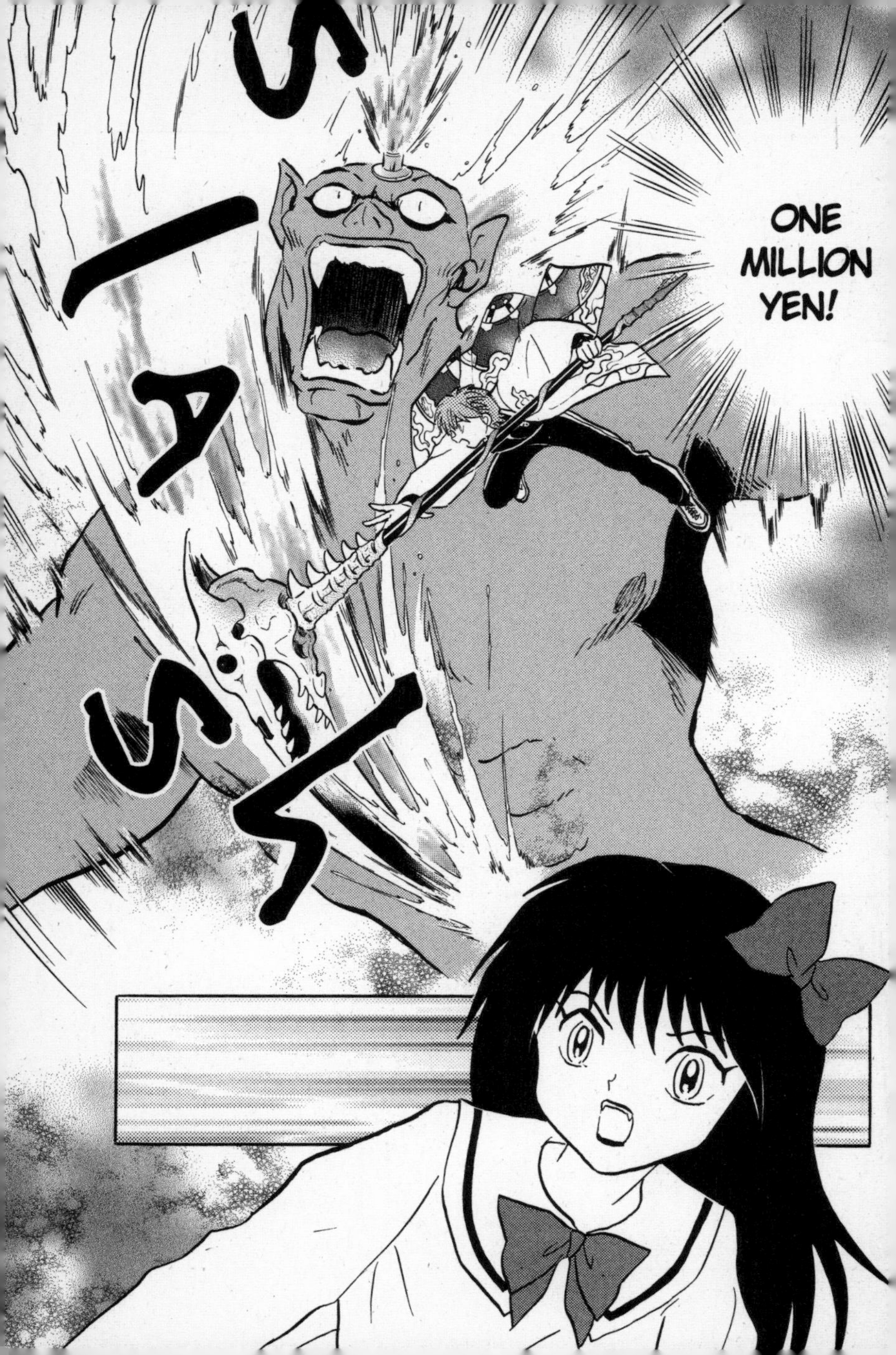
ONE MILLION YEN!
SLASH

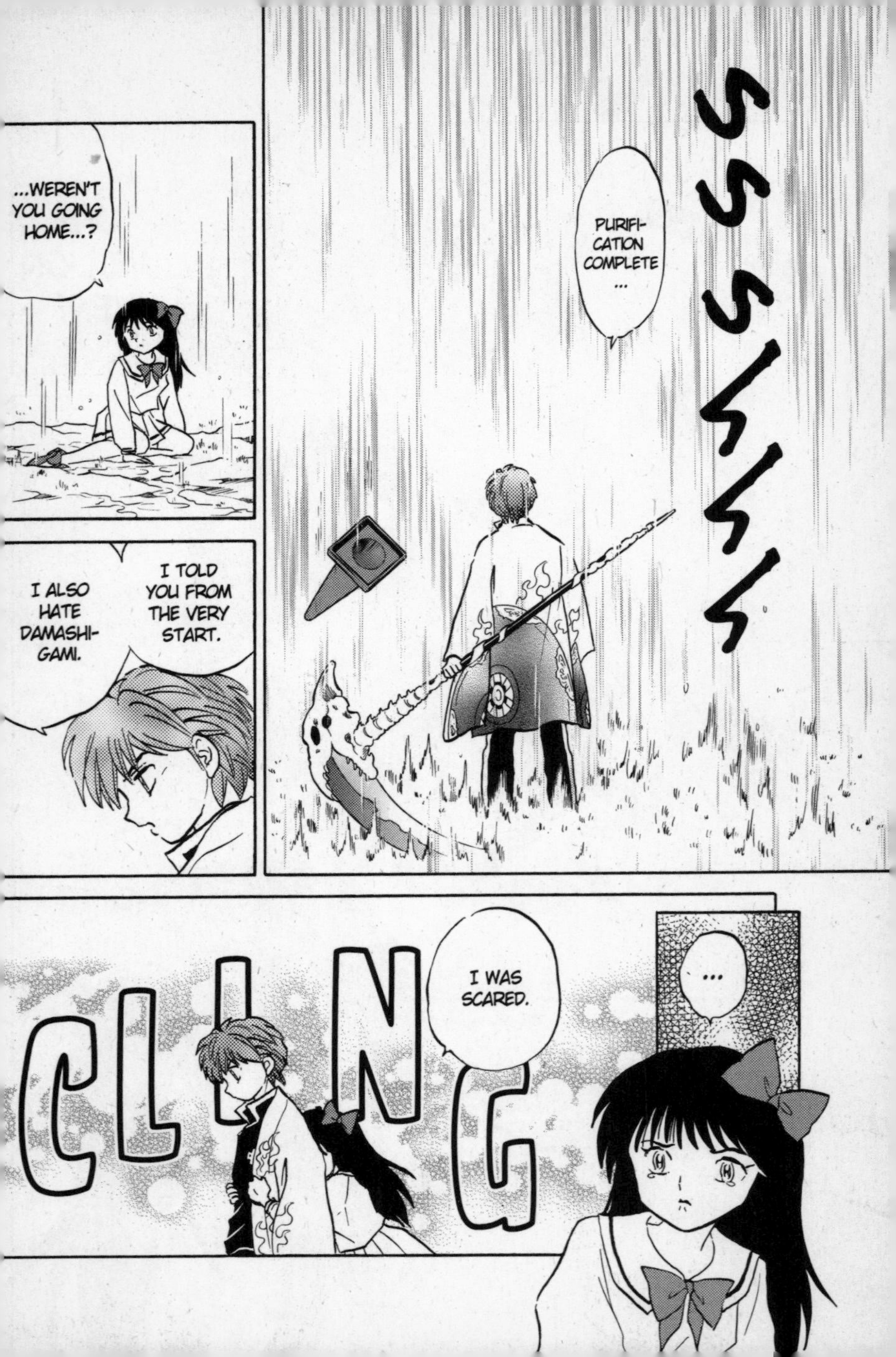
SSSSSSSS
PURIFICATION COMPLETE...
...WEREN'T YOU GOING HOME...?
I TOLD YOU FROM THE VERY START.
I ALSO HATE DAMASHIGAMI.
...
I WAS SCARED.
CLING

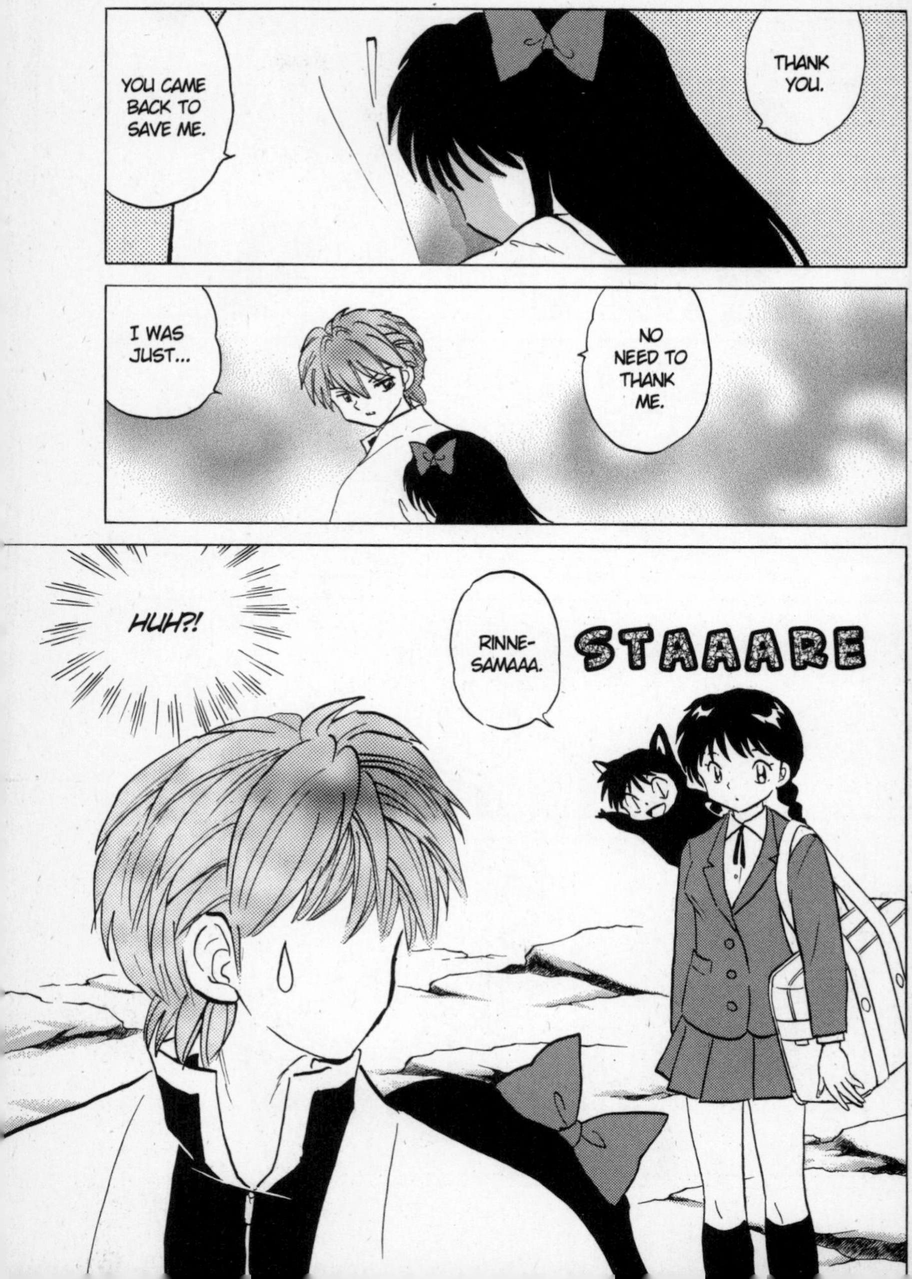
THANK YOU.
YOU CAME BACK TO SAVE ME.
NO NEED TO THANK ME.
I WAS JUST...
STAAARE
RINNE-SAMAAA.
HUH?!

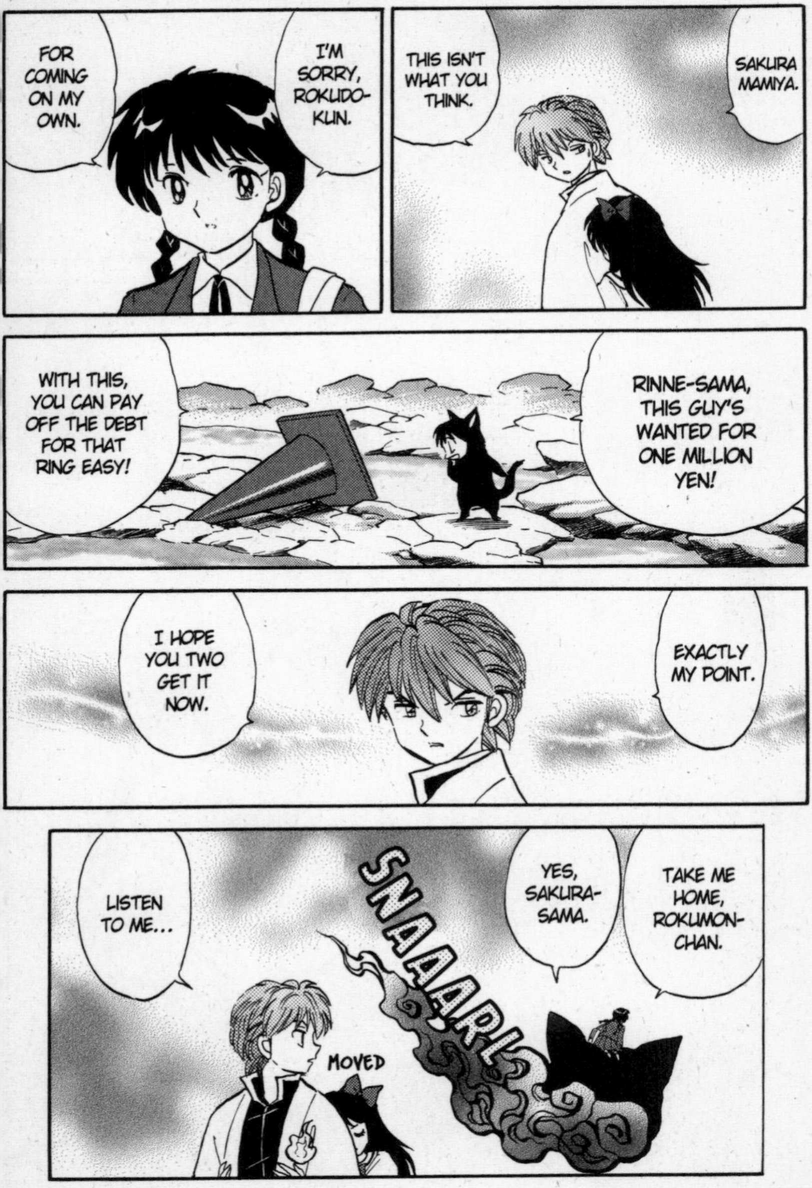
SAKURA MAMIYA.
THIS ISN'T WHAT YOU THINK.
I'M SORRY, ROKUDO-KUN.
FOR COMING ON MY OWN.
RINNE-SAMA, THIS GUY'S WANTED FOR ONE MILLION YEN!
WITH THIS, YOU CAN PAY OFF THE DEBT FOR THAT RING EASY!
EXACTLY MY POINT.
I HOPE YOU TWO GET IT NOW.
TAKE ME HOME, ROKUMON-CHAN.
YES, SAKURA-SAMA.
SNAAARL
LISTEN TO ME...
MOVED

CHAPTER 41: JUST A SIMPLE THANKS

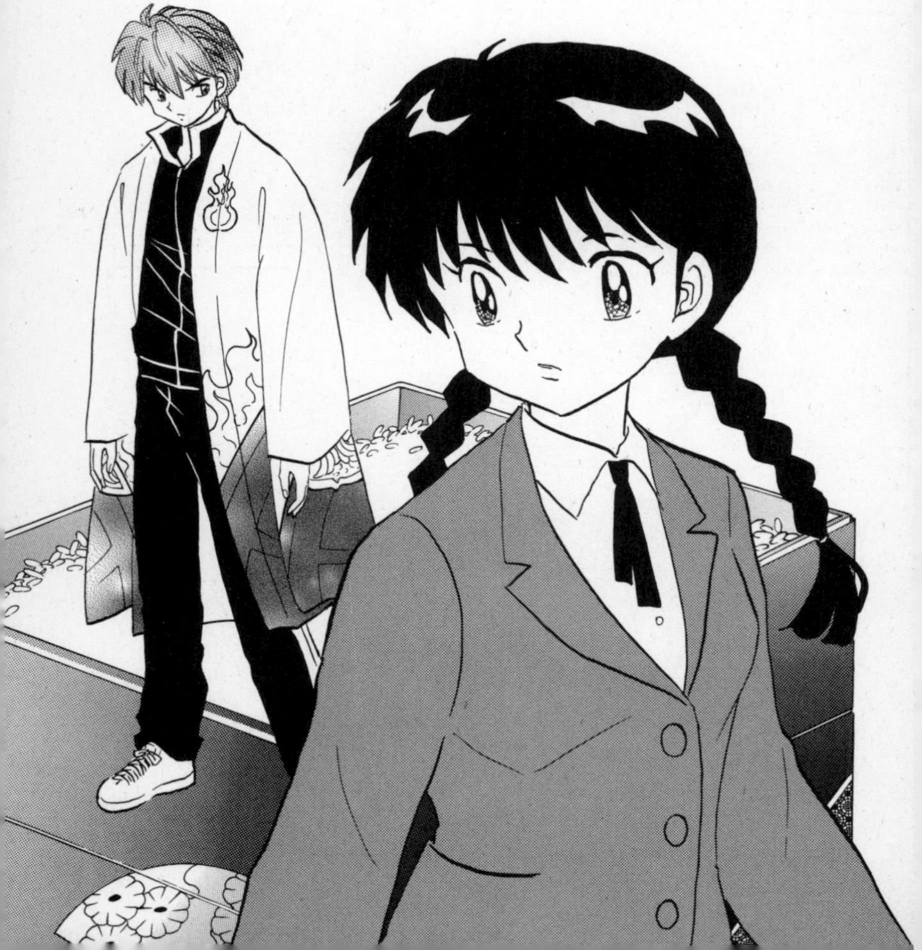

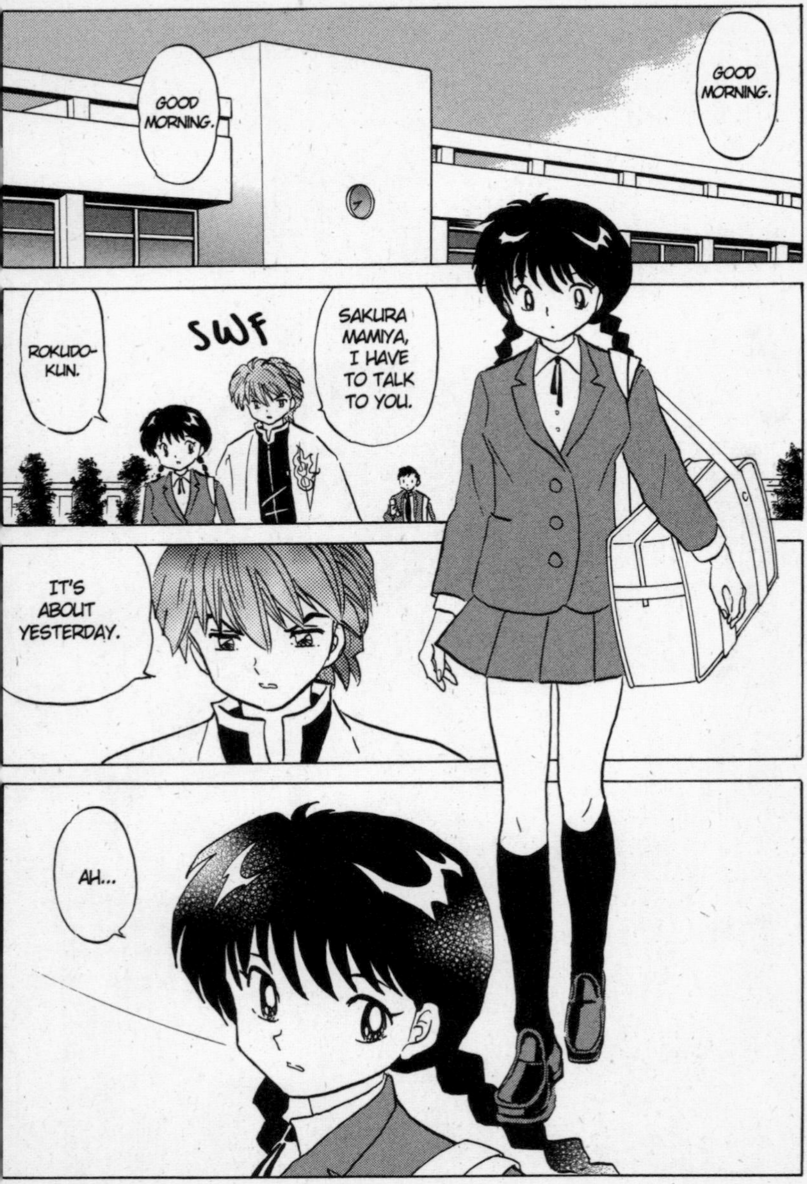
GOOD MORNING.
GOOD MORNING.
SAKURA MAMIYA, I HAVE TO TALK TO YOU.
SWF
ROKUDO-KUN.
IT'S ABOUT YESTERDAY.
AH...

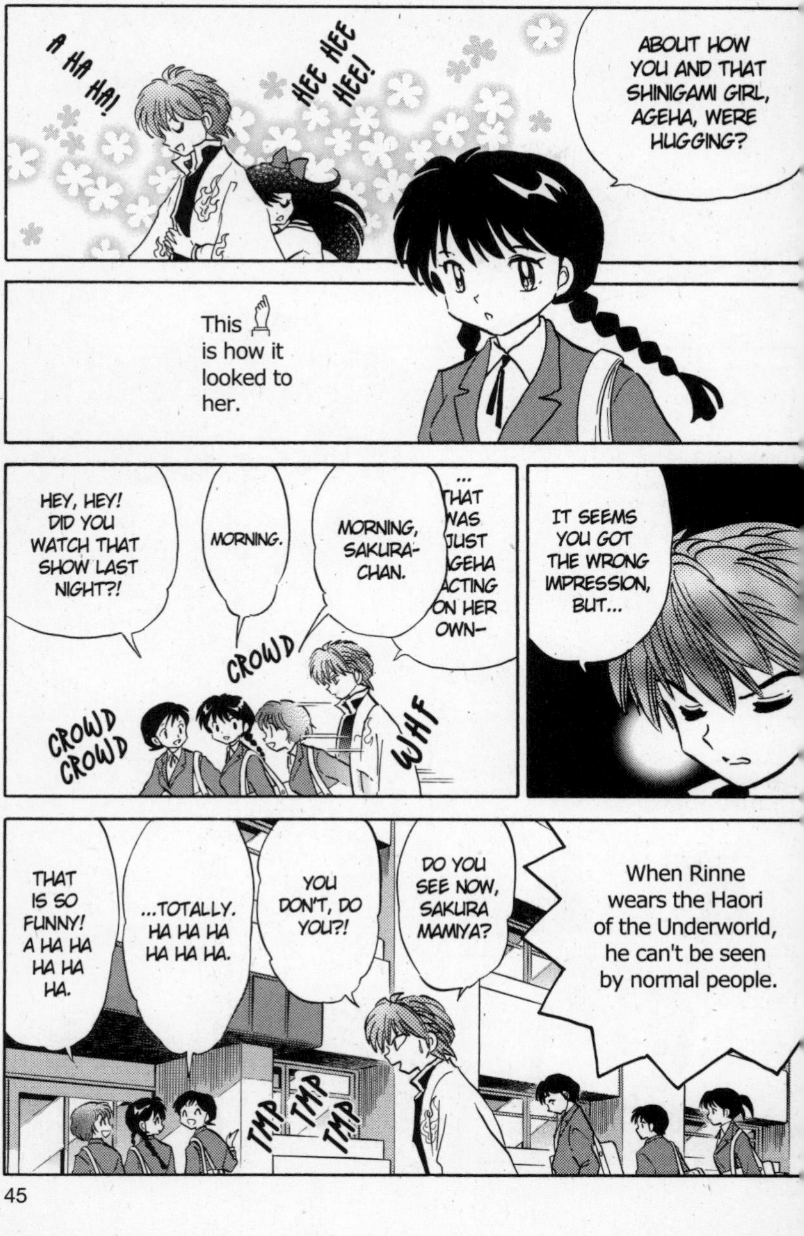
ABOUT HOW YOU AND THAT SHINIGAMI GIRL, AGEHA, WERE HUGGING?
HEE HEE HEE!
A HA HA!
This is how it looked to her.
IT SEEMS YOU GOT THE WRONG IMPRESSION, BUT...
...THAT WAS JUST AGEHA ACTING ON HER OWN–
MORNING, SAKURA-CHAN.
MORNING.
HEY, HEY! DID YOU WATCH THAT SHOW LAST NIGHT?!
WHF
CROWD
CROWD CROWD
When Rinne wears the Haori of the Underworld, he can't be seen by normal people.
DO YOU SEE NOW, SAKURA MAMIYA?
YOU DON'T, DO YOU?!
...TOTALLY. HA HA HA HA HA HA.
THAT IS SO FUNNY! A HA HA HA HA HA.
TMP TMP TMP

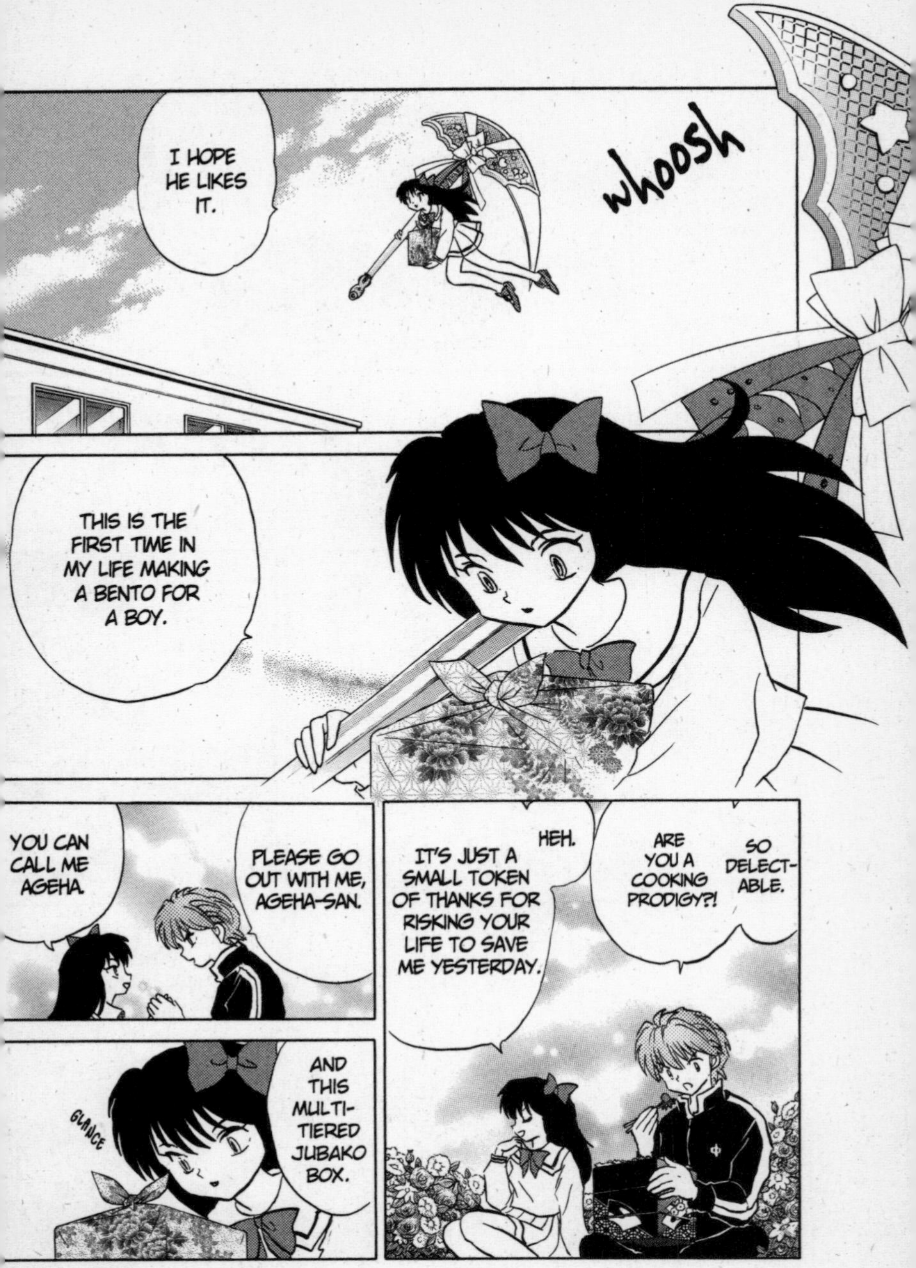
whoosh
I HOPE HE LIKES IT.
THIS IS THE FIRST TIME IN MY LIFE MAKING A BENTO FOR A BOY.
SO DELECTABLE.
ARE YOU A COOKING PRODIGY?!
HEH.
IT'S JUST A SMALL TOKEN OF THANKS FOR RISKING YOUR LIFE TO SAVE ME YESTERDAY.
PLEASE GO OUT WITH ME, AGEHA-SAN.
YOU CAN CALL ME AGEHA.
AND THIS MULTI-TIERED JUBAKO BOX.
GLANCE

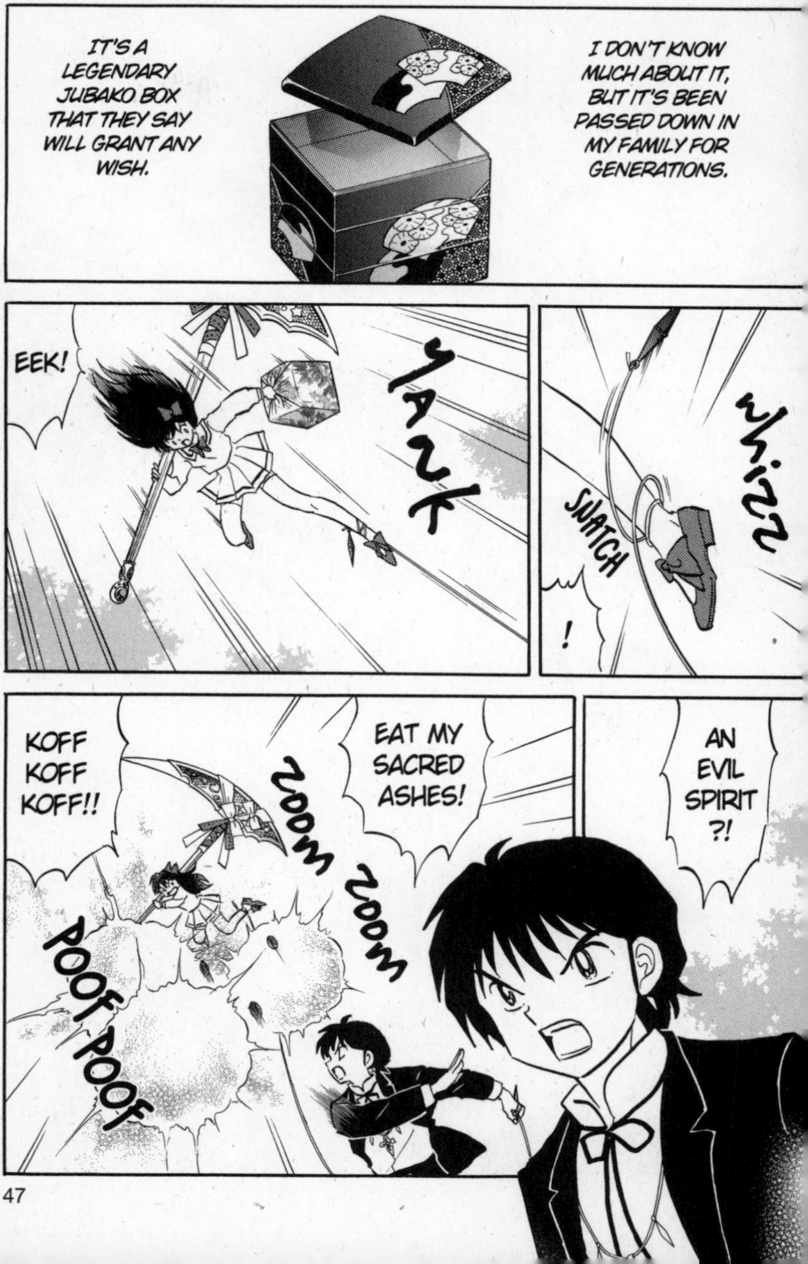
I DON'T KNOW MUCH ABOUT IT, BUT IT'S BEEN PASSED DOWN IN MY FAMILY FOR GENERATIONS.
IT'S A LEGENDARY JUBAKO BOX THAT THEY SAY WILL GRANT ANY WISH.
WHIZZ
SWATCH
!
YANK
EEK!
AN EVIL SPIRIT ?!
EAT MY SACRED ASHES!
ZOOM
ZOOM
KOFF KOFF KOFF!!
POOF POOF POOF

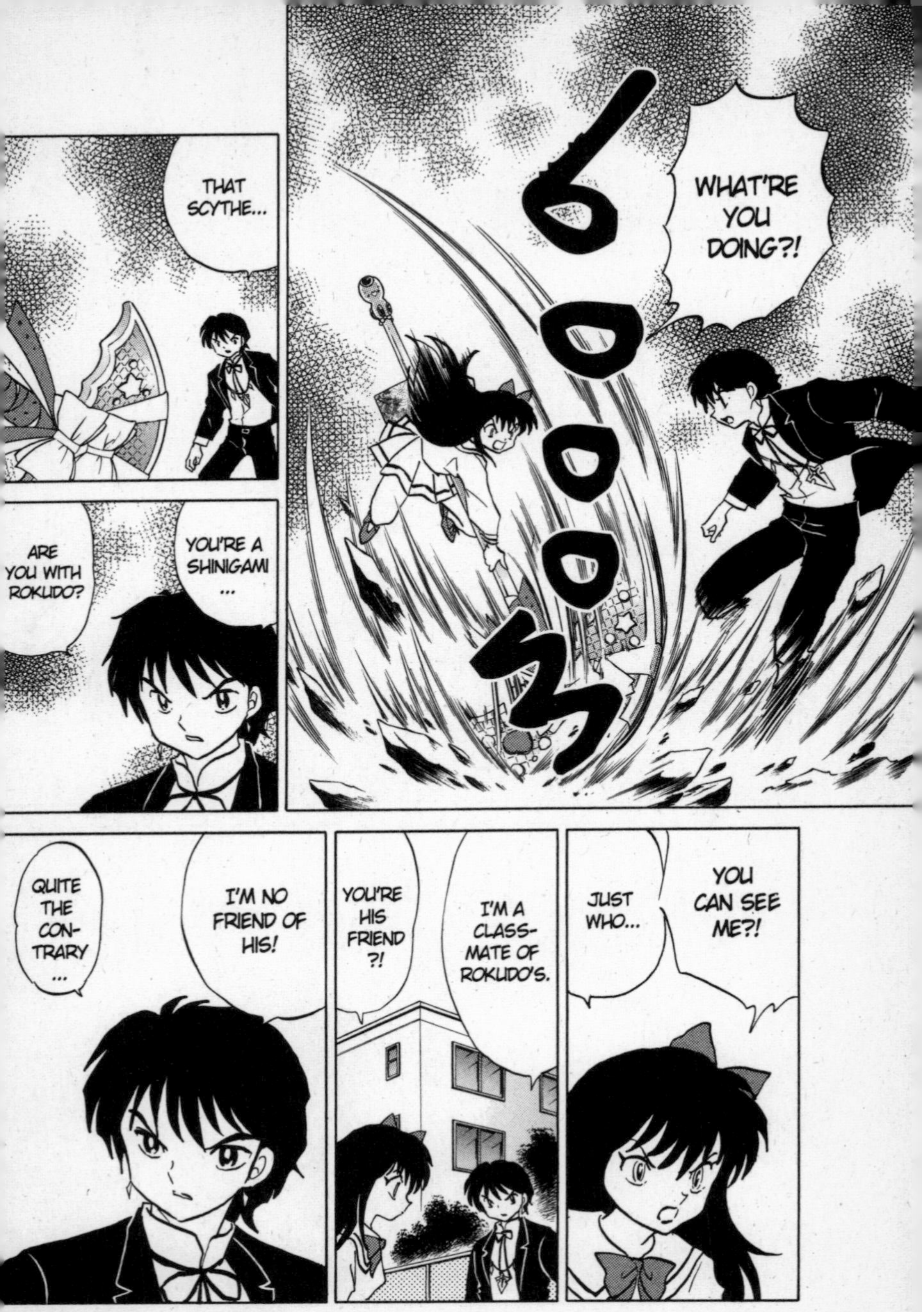
WHAT'RE YOU DOING?!
DOOOM
THAT SCYTHE...
YOU'RE A SHINIGAMI ...
ARE YOU WITH ROKUDO?
YOU CAN SEE ME?!
JUST WHO...
I'M A CLASS-MATE OF ROKUDO'S.
YOU'RE HIS FRIEND ?!
I'M NO FRIEND OF HIS!
QUITE THE CON-TRARY ...

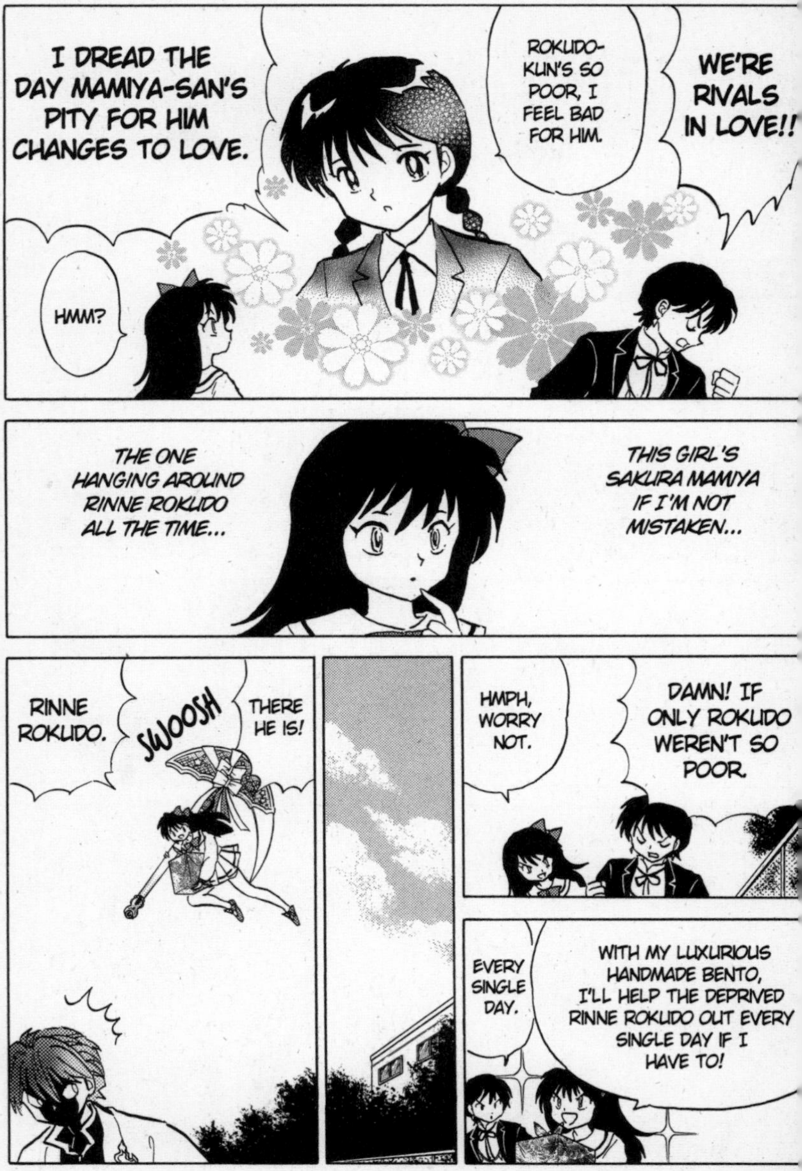
WE'RE RIVALS IN LOVE!!
ROKUDO-KUN'S SO POOR, I FEEL BAD FOR HIM.
I DREAD THE DAY MAMIYA-SAN'S PITY FOR HIM CHANGES TO LOVE.
HMM?
THIS GIRL'S SAKURA MAMIYA IF I'M NOT MISTAKEN...
THE ONE HANGING AROUND RINNE ROKUDO ALL THE TIME...
DAMN! IF ONLY ROKUDO WEREN'T SO POOR.
HMPH, WORRY NOT.
WITH MY LUXURIOUS HANDMADE BENTO, I'LL HELP THE DEPRIVED RINNE ROKUDO OUT EVERY SINGLE DAY IF I HAVE TO!
EVERY SINGLE DAY.
THERE HE IS!
SWOOSH
RINNE ROKUDO.

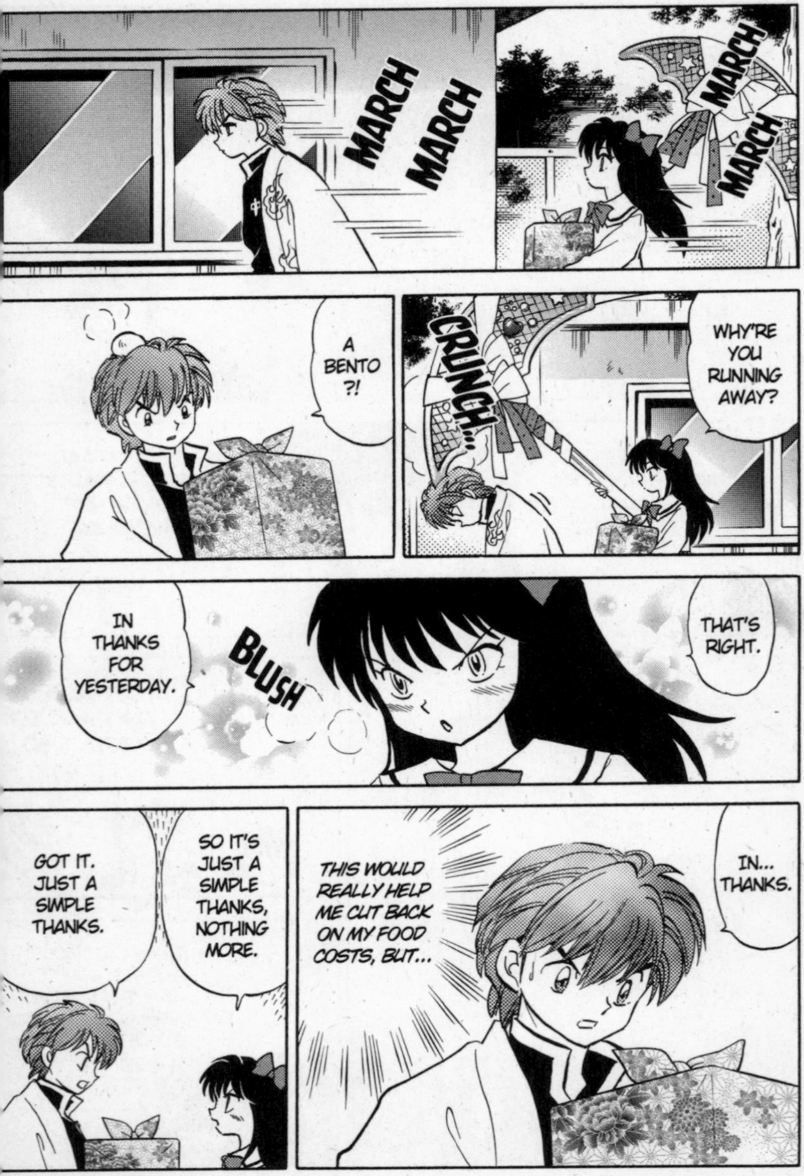
MARCH
MARCH
MARCH
MARCH
WHY'RE YOU RUNNING AWAY?
CRUNCH...
A BENTO ?!
THAT'S RIGHT.
BLUSH
IN THANKS FOR YESTERDAY.
IN... THANKS.
THIS WOULD REALLY HELP ME CUT BACK ON MY FOOD COSTS, BUT...
SO IT'S JUST A SIMPLE THANKS, NOTHING MORE.
GOT IT. JUST A SIMPLE THANKS.

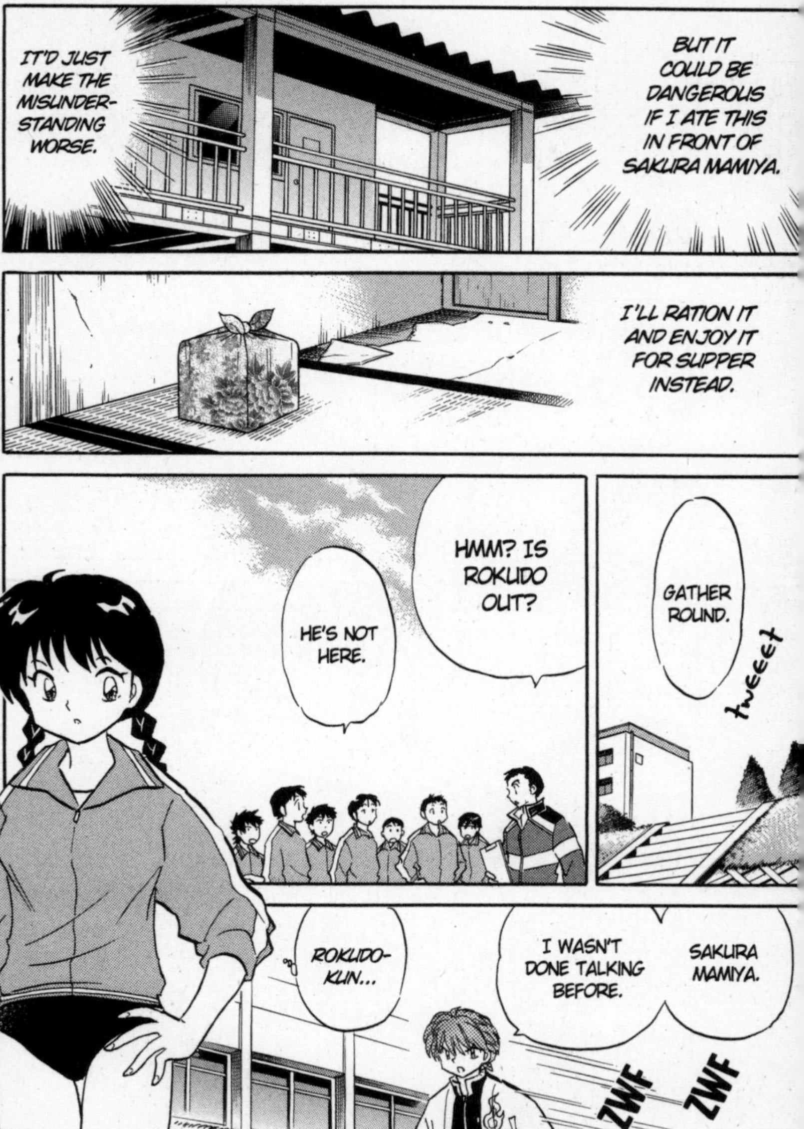
BUT IT COULD BE DANGEROUS IF I ATE THIS IN FRONT OF SAKURA MAMIYA.
IT'D JUST MAKE THE MISUNDER-STANDING WORSE.
I'LL RATION IT AND ENJOY IT FOR SUPPER INSTEAD.
GATHER ROUND.
tweeet
HMM? IS ROKUDO OUT?
HE'S NOT HERE.
SAKURA MAMIYA.
I WASN'T DONE TALKING BEFORE.
ZWF
ZWF
ROKUDO-KUN...

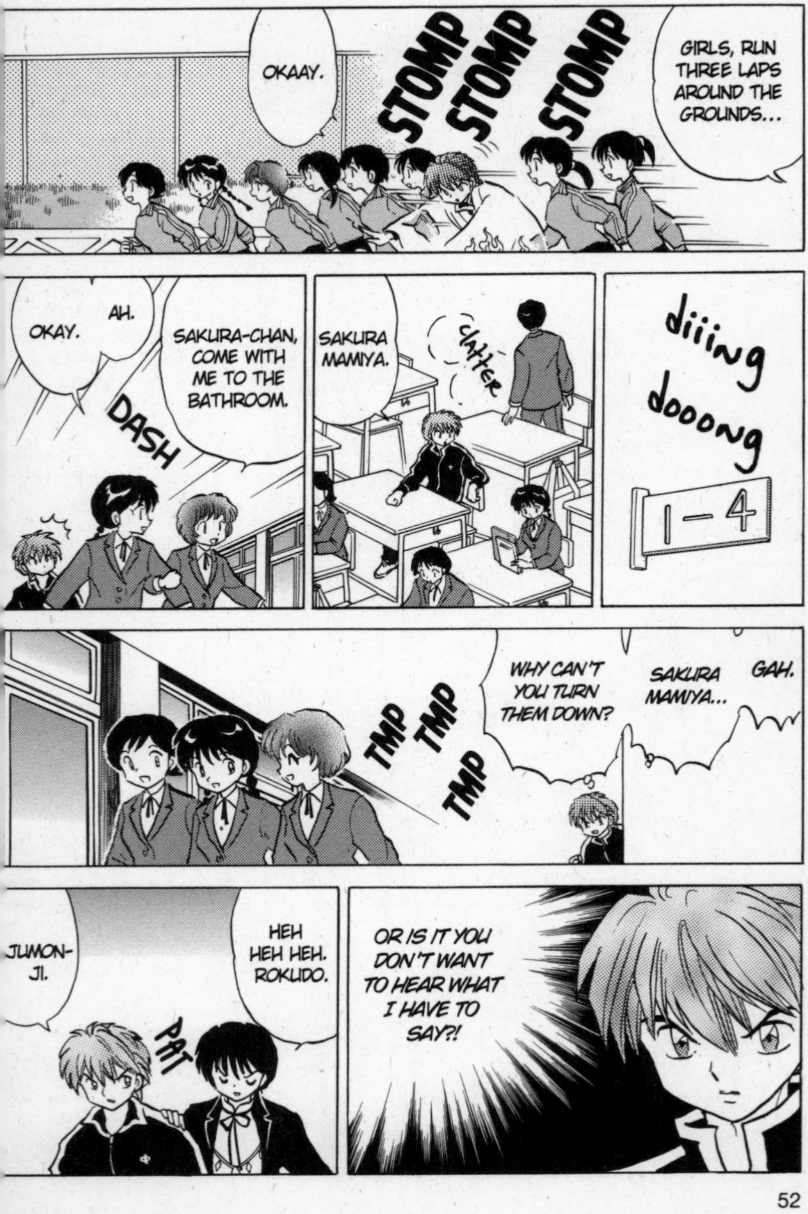
GIRLS, RUN THREE LAPS AROUND THE GROUNDS...
STOMP
STOMP
STOMP
OKAAY.
diiing dooong
1-4
clatter
SAKURA MAMIYA.
SAKURA-CHAN, COME WITH ME TO THE BATHROOM.
DASH
AH.
OKAY.
GAH.
SAKURA MAMIYA...
WHY CAN'T YOU TURN THEM DOWN?
TMP
TMP
TMP
OR IS IT YOU DON'T WANT TO HEAR WHAT I HAVE TO SAY?!
HEH HEH HEH. ROKUDO.
PAT
JUMON-JI.

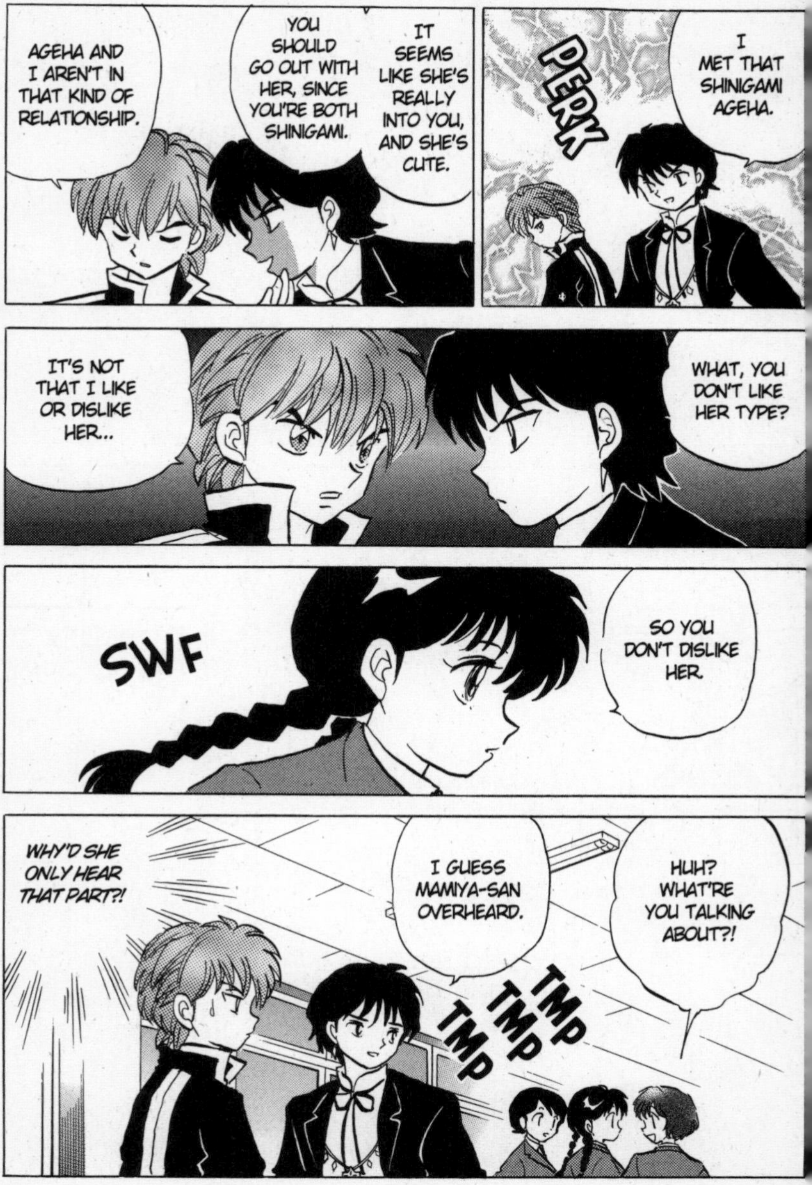
PERK
I MET THAT SHINIGAMI AGEHA.
IT SEEMS LIKE SHE'S REALLY INTO YOU, AND SHE'S CUTE.
YOU SHOULD GO OUT WITH HER, SINCE YOU'RE BOTH SHINIGAMI.
AGEHA AND I AREN'T IN THAT KIND OF RELATIONSHIP.
WHAT, YOU DON'T LIKE HER TYPE?
IT'S NOT THAT I LIKE OR DISLIKE HER...
SO YOU DON'T DISLIKE HER.
SWF
HUH? WHAT'RE YOU TALKING ABOUT?!
TMP TMP TMP
I GUESS MAMIYA-SAN OVERHEARD.
WHY'D SHE ONLY HEAR THAT PART?!

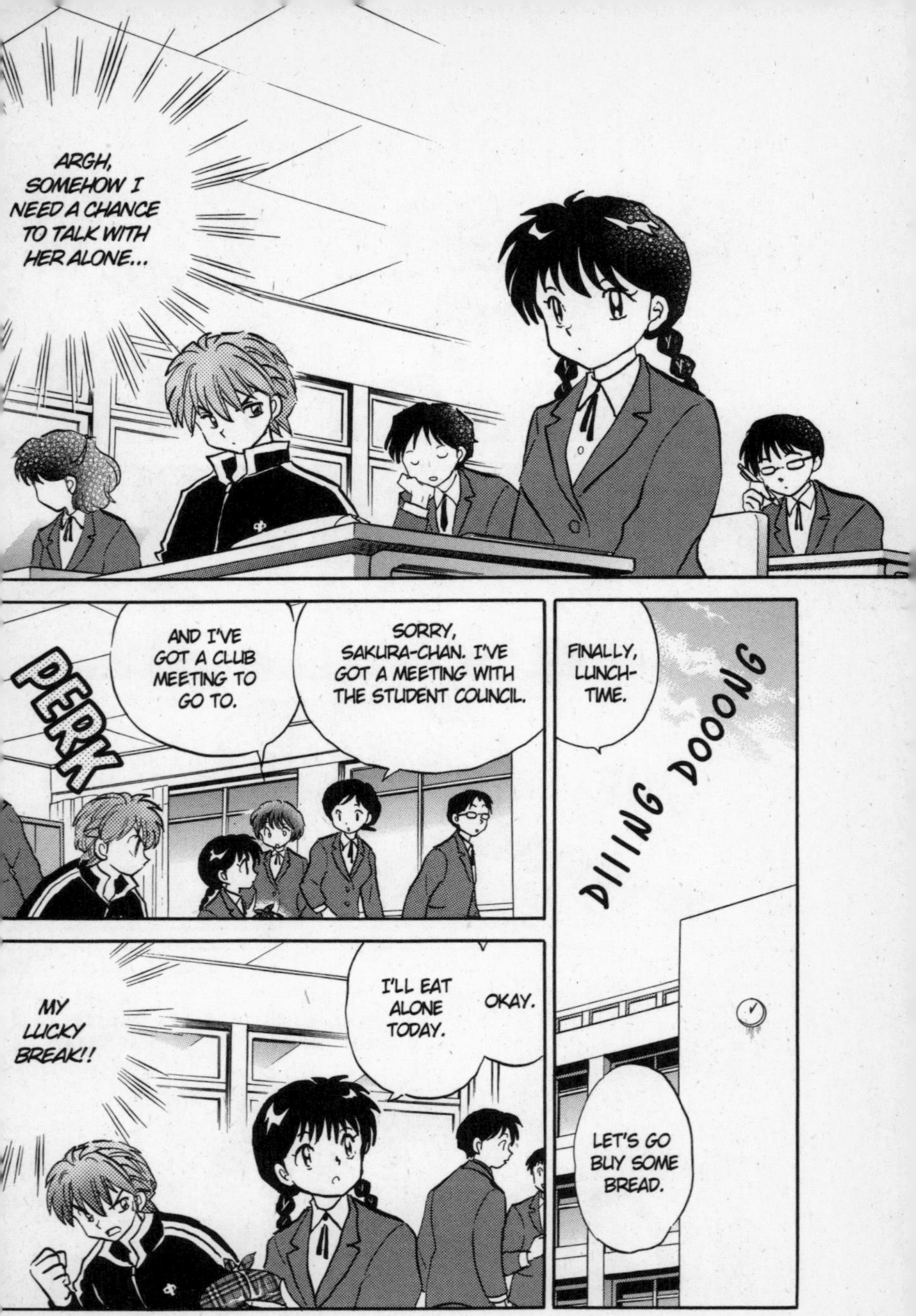
ARGH, SOMEHOW I NEED A CHANCE TO TALK WITH HER ALONE...
FINALLY, LUNCH-TIME.
DIIING DOOONG
LET'S GO BUY SOME BREAD.
SORRY, SAKURA-CHAN. I'VE GOT A MEETING WITH THE STUDENT COUNCIL.
AND I'VE GOT A CLUB MEETING TO GO TO.
PERK
OKAY.
I'LL EAT ALONE TODAY.
MY LUCKY BREAK!!

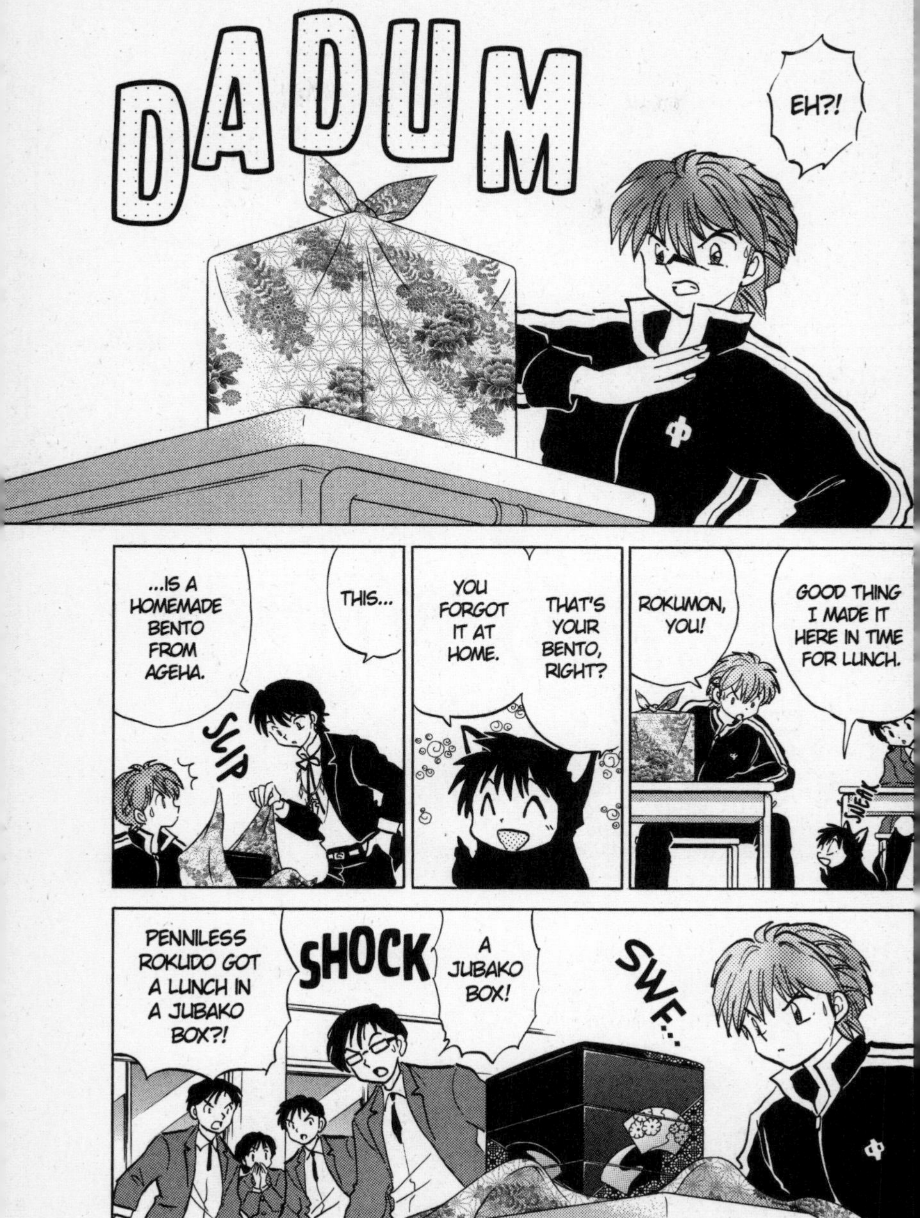
DADUM
EH?!
GOOD THING I MADE IT HERE IN TIME FOR LUNCH.
ROKUMON, YOU!
SQUEAK
THAT'S YOUR BENTO, RIGHT?
YOU FORGOT IT AT HOME.
THIS...
...IS A HOMEMADE BENTO FROM AGEHA.
SLIP
SWF...
A JUBAKO BOX!
SHOCK
PENNILESS ROKUDO GOT A LUNCH IN A JUBAKO BOX?!

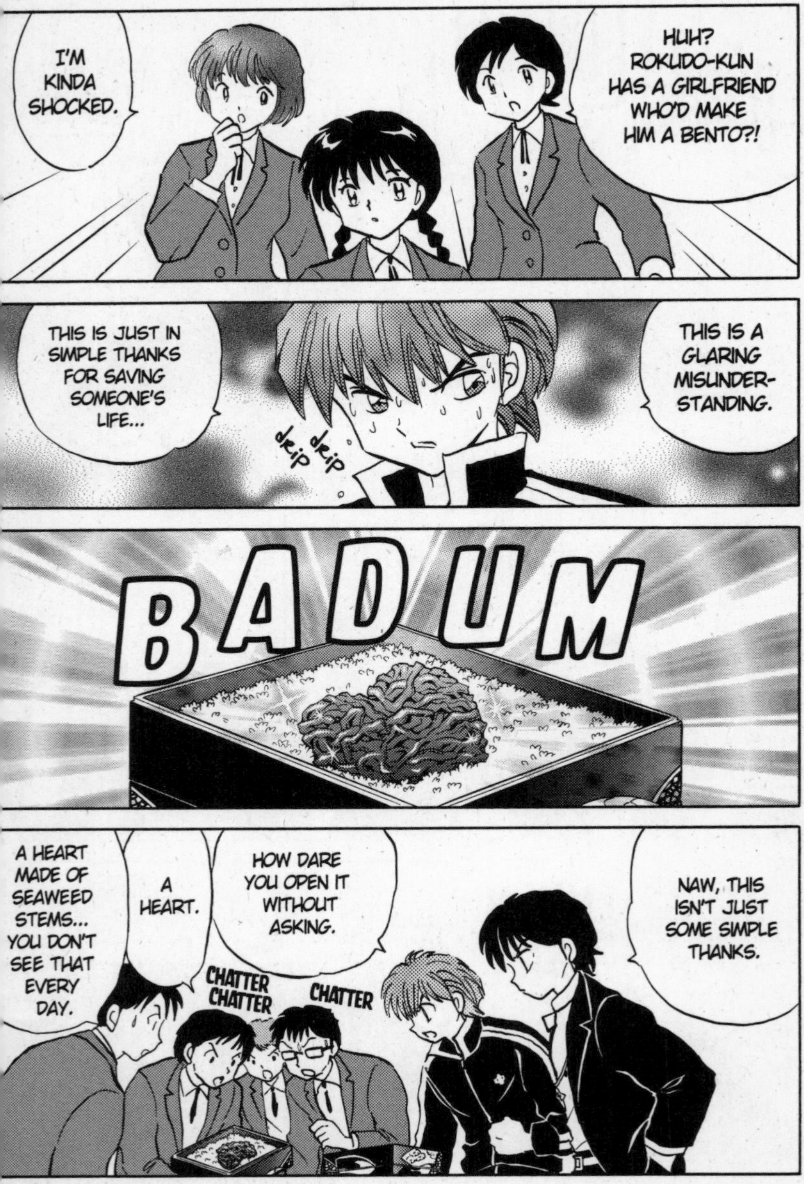
HUH? ROKUDO-KUN HAS A GIRLFRIEND WHO'D MAKE HIM A BENTO?!
I'M KINDA SHOCKED.
THIS IS A GLARING MISUNDER-STANDING.
THIS IS JUST IN SIMPLE THANKS FOR SAVING SOMEONE'S LIFE...
drip drip
BADUM
NAW, THIS ISN'T JUST SOME SIMPLE THANKS.
CHATTER
HOW DARE YOU OPEN IT WITHOUT ASKING.
CHATTER CHATTER
A HEART.
A HEART MADE OF SEAWEED STEMS... YOU DON'T SEE THAT EVERY DAY.

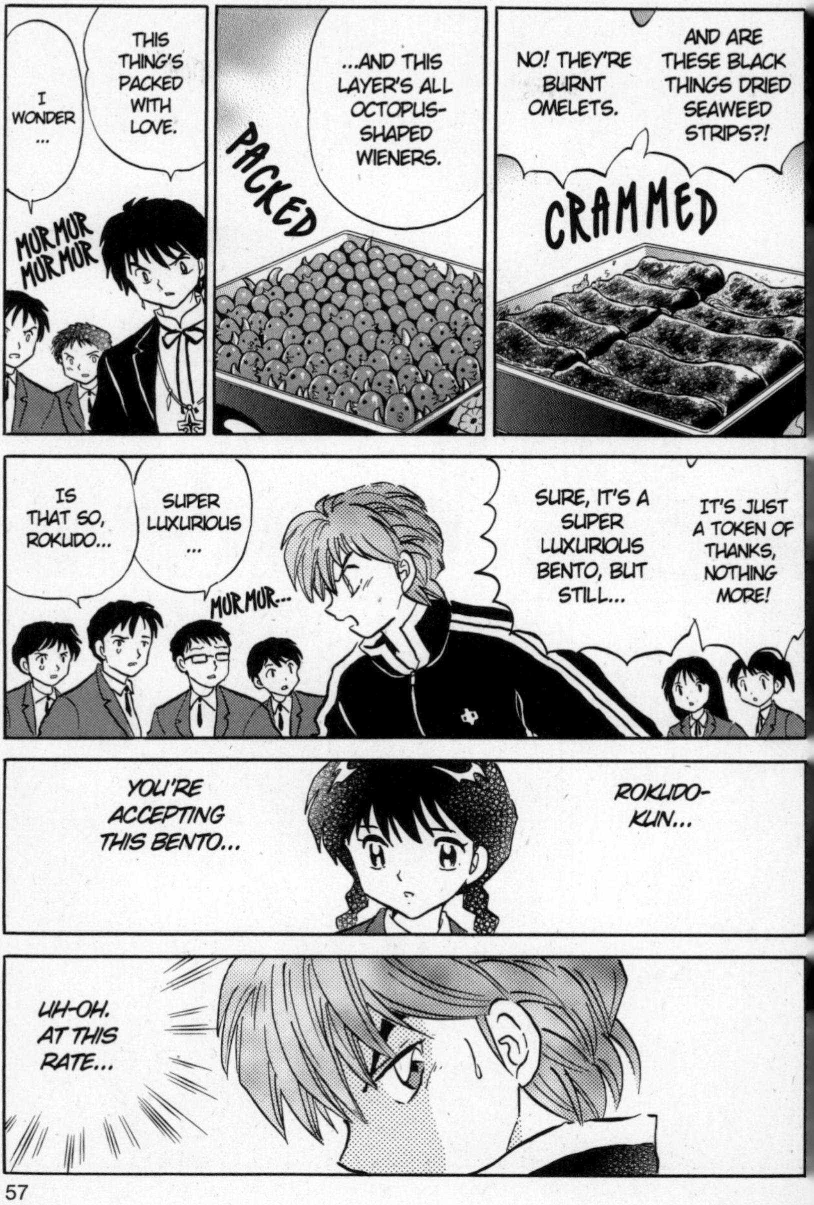

AND ARE THESE BLACK THINGS DRIED SEAWEED STRIPS?!
NO! THEY'RE BURNT OMELETS.
CRAMMED
...AND THIS LAYER'S ALL OCTOPUS-SHAPED WIENERS.
PACKED
THIS THING'S PACKED WITH LOVE.
I WONDER...
MUR MUR MUR MUR
IT'S JUST A TOKEN OF THANKS, NOTHING MORE!
SURE, IT'S A SUPER LUXURIOUS BENTO, BUT STILL...
SUPER LUXURIOUS...
IS THAT SO, ROKUDO...
MUR MUR...
ROKUDO-KUN...
YOU'RE ACCEPTING THIS BENTO...
UH-OH. AT THIS RATE...

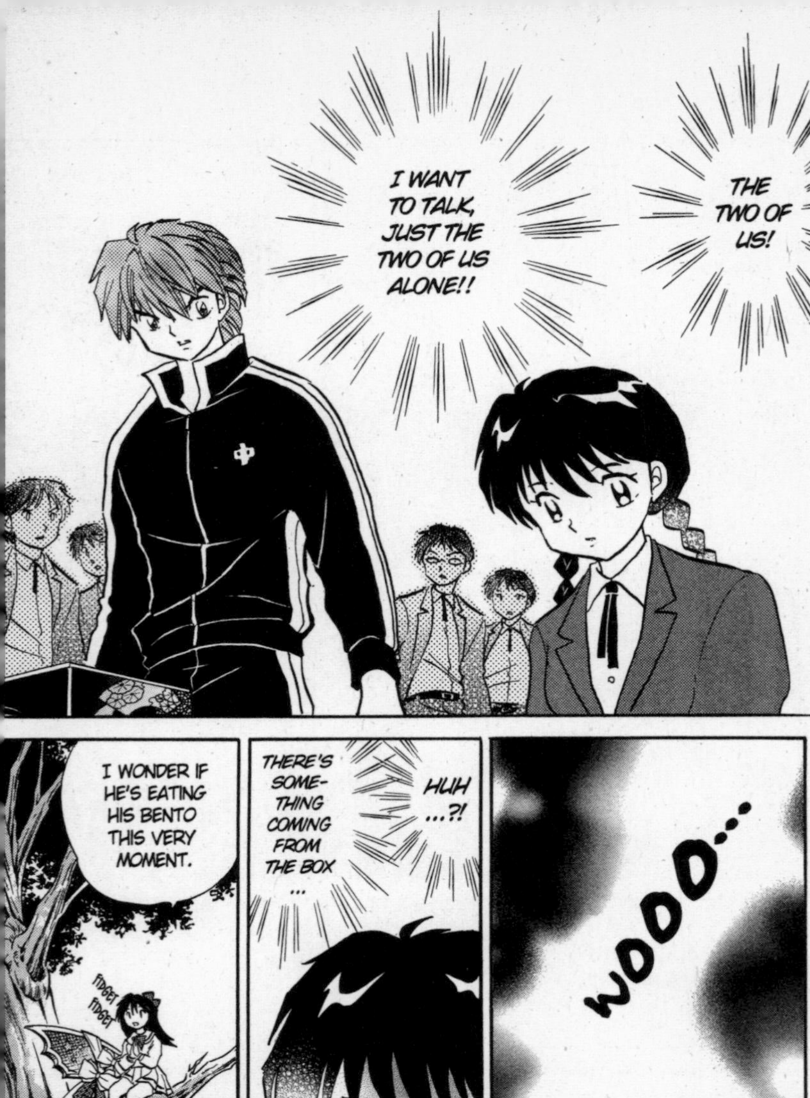
THE TWO OF US!
I WANT TO TALK, JUST THE TWO OF US ALONE!!
WOOD...
HUH ...?!
THERE'S SOME-THING COMING FROM THE BOX ...
I WONDER IF HE'S EATING HIS BENTO THIS VERY MOMENT.
FIDGET FIDGET

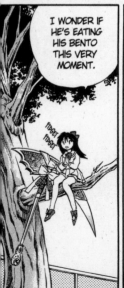

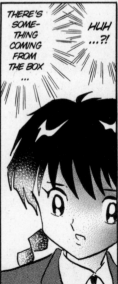

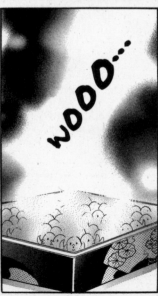

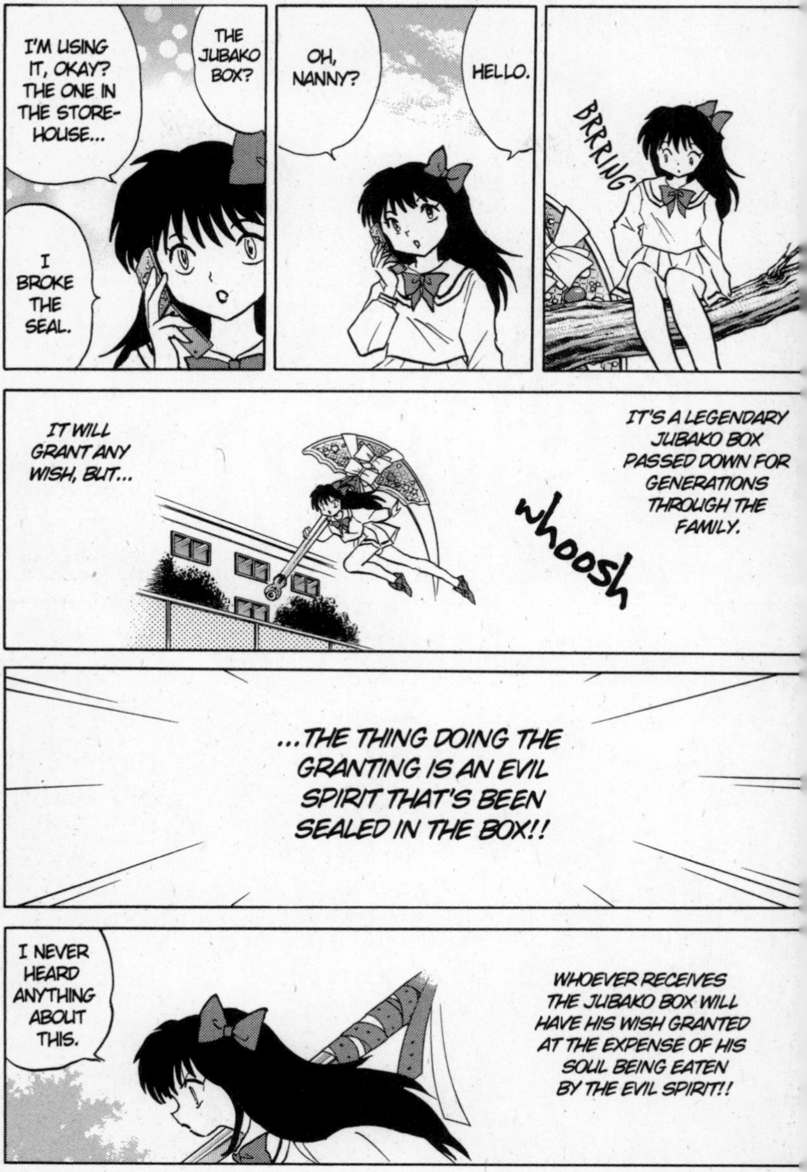
BRRRING
HELLO.
OH, NANNY?
THE JUBAKO BOX?
I'M USING IT, OKAY? THE ONE IN THE STORE-HOUSE...
I BROKE THE SEAL.
IT'S A LEGENDARY JUBAKO BOX PASSED DOWN FOR GENERATIONS THROUGH THE FAMILY.
whoosh
IT WILL GRANT ANY WISH, BUT...
...THE THING DOING THE GRANTING IS AN EVIL SPIRIT THAT'S BEEN SEALED IN THE BOX!!
WHOEVER RECEIVES THE JUBAKO BOX WILL HAVE HIS WISH GRANTED AT THE EXPENSE OF HIS SOUL BEING EATEN BY THE EVIL SPIRIT!!
I NEVER HEARD ANYTHING ABOUT THIS.

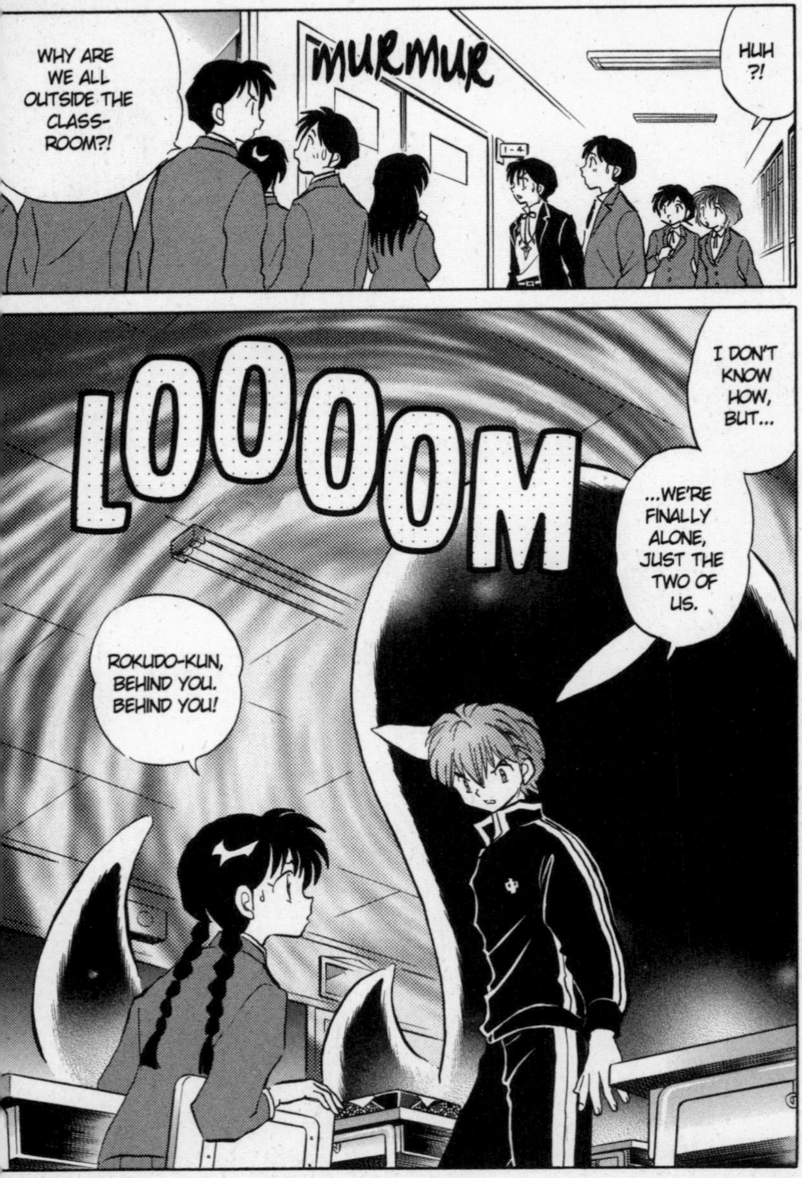
HUH ?!
MURMUR
WHY ARE WE ALL OUTSIDE THE CLASS-ROOM?!
I DON'T KNOW HOW, BUT...
LOOOOOM
...WE'RE FINALLY ALONE, JUST THE TWO OF US.
ROKUDO-KUN, BEHIND YOU. BEHIND YOU!

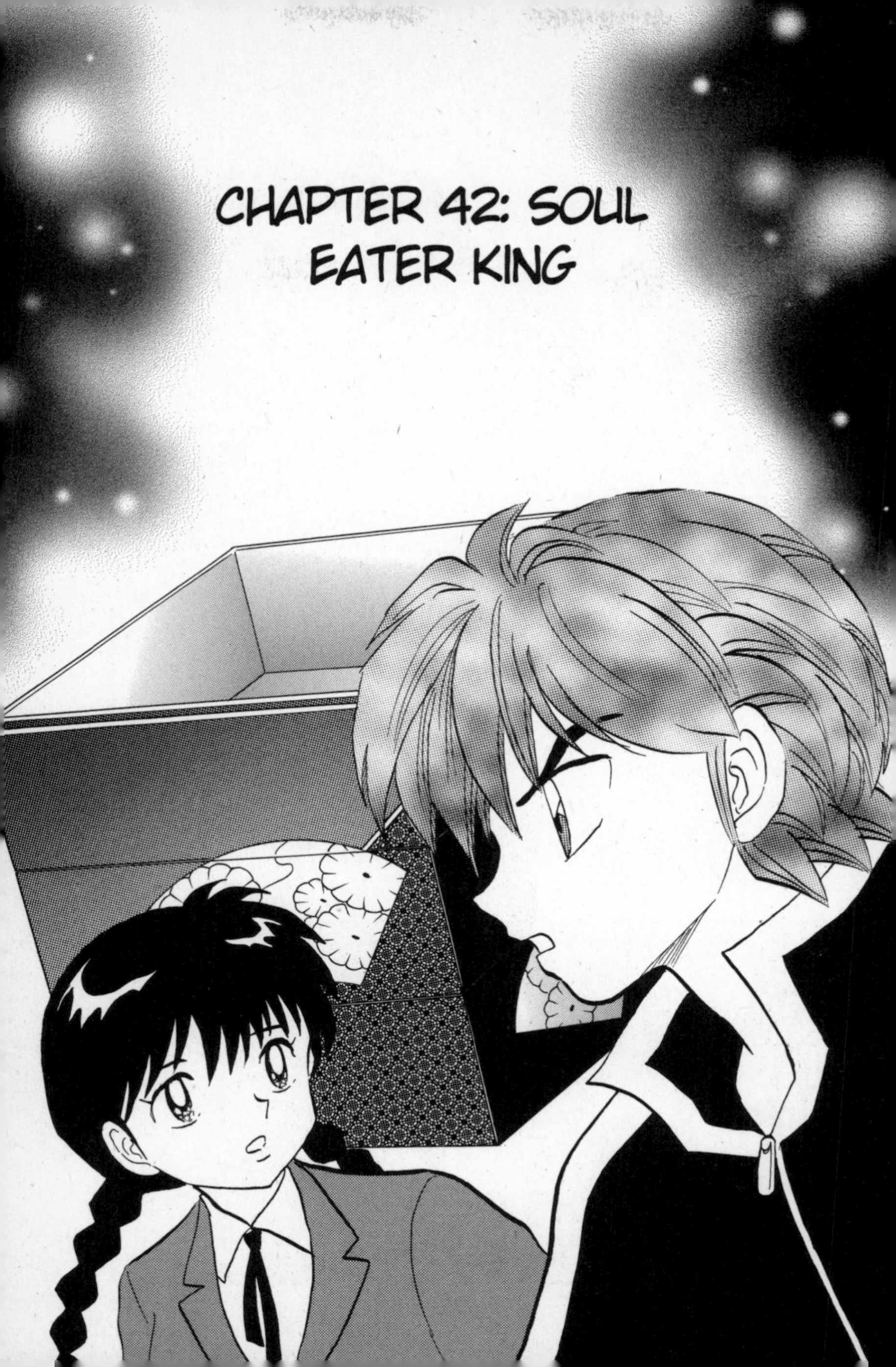
CHAPTER 42: SOUL EATER KING

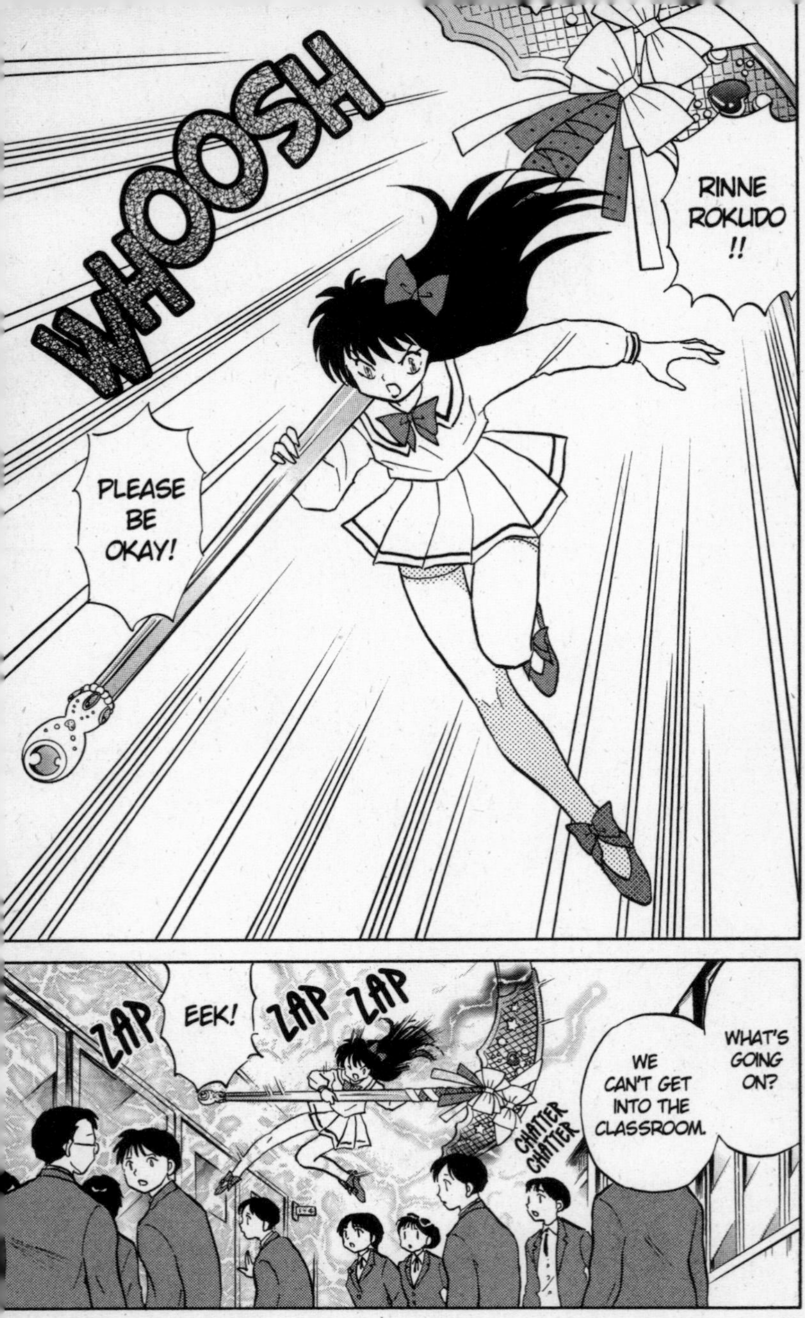
RINNE ROKUDO !!
WHOOSH
PLEASE BE OKAY!
WHAT'S GOING ON?
WE CAN'T GET INTO THE CLASSROOM.
CHATTER CHATTER
ZAP ZAP
EEK!
ZAP

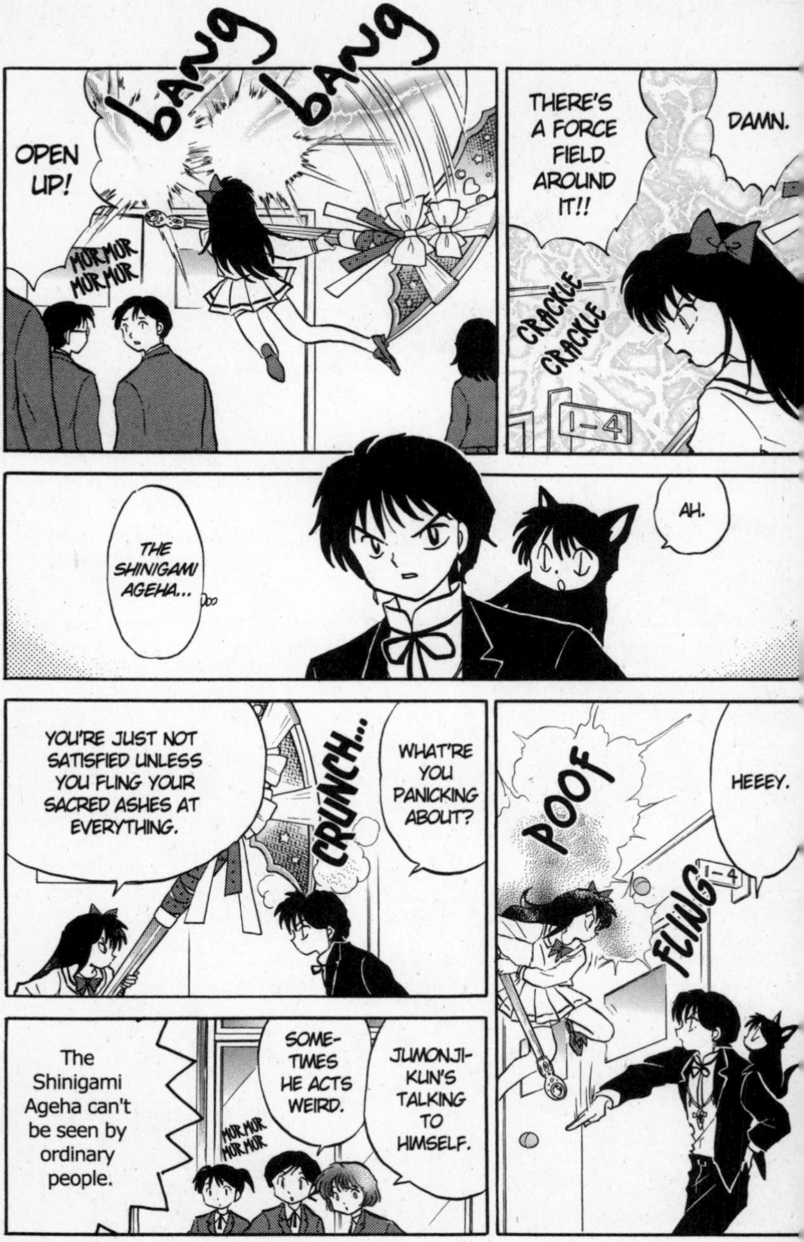
DAMN.
THERE'S A FORCE FIELD AROUND IT!!
CRACKLE CRACKLE
BANG BANG
OPEN UP!
MURMUR MURMUR
AH.
THE SHINIGAMI AGEHA...
HEEEY.
POOF
FLING
WHAT'RE YOU PANICKING ABOUT?
CRUNCH...
YOU'RE JUST NOT SATISFIED UNLESS YOU FLING YOUR SACRED ASHES AT EVERYTHING.
JUMONJI-KUN'S TALKING TO HIMSELF.
SOME-TIMES HE ACTS WEIRD.
MURMUR MURMUR
The Shinigami Ageha can't be seen by ordinary people.

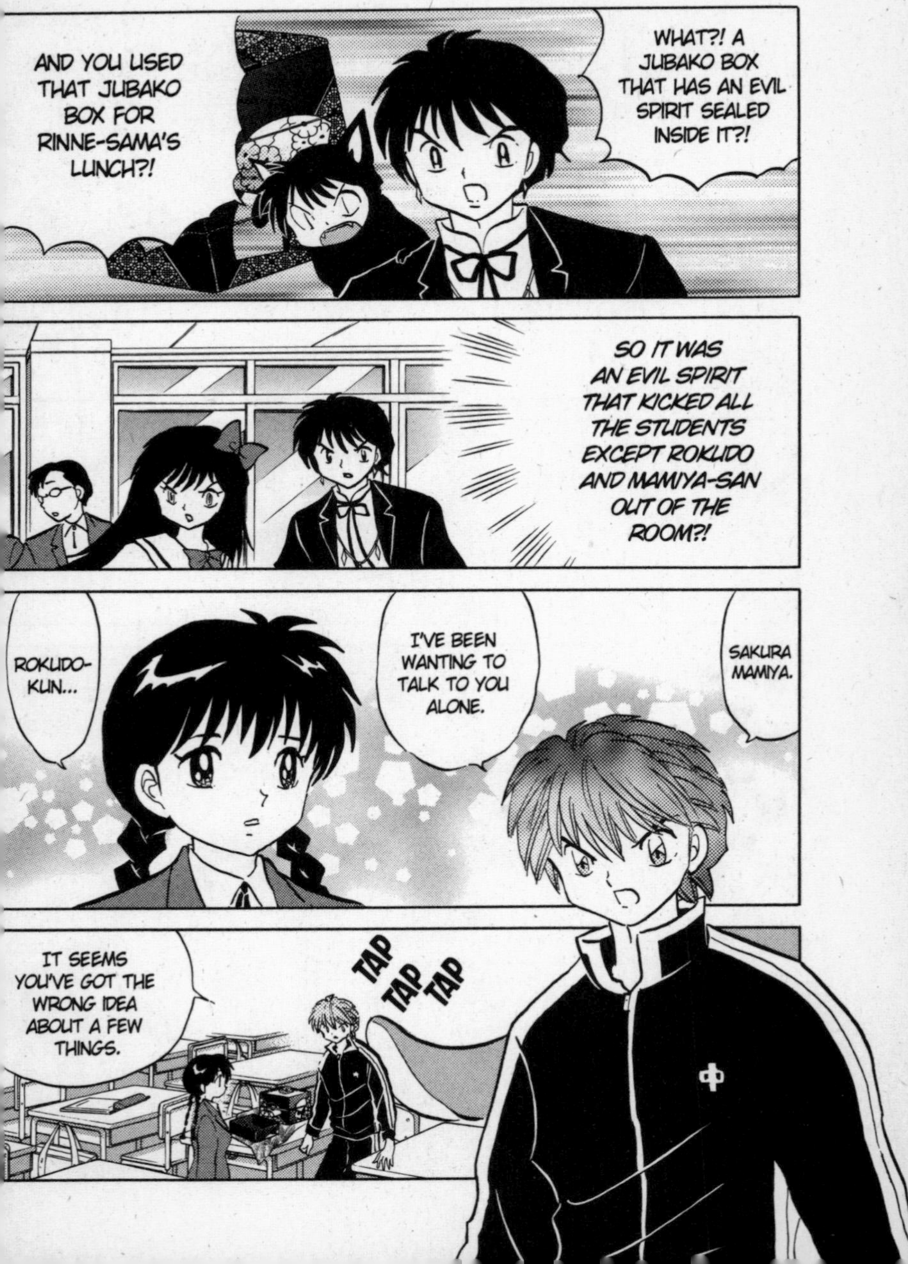
WHAT?! A JUBAKO BOX THAT HAS AN EVIL SPIRIT SEALED INSIDE IT?!
AND YOU USED THAT JUBAKO BOX FOR RINNE-SAMA'S LUNCH?!
SO IT WAS AN EVIL SPIRIT THAT KICKED ALL THE STUDENTS EXCEPT ROKUDO AND MAMIYA-SAN OUT OF THE ROOM?!
SAKURA MAMIYA.
I'VE BEEN WANTING TO TALK TO YOU ALONE.
ROKUDO-KUN...
TAP TAP TAP
IT SEEMS YOU'VE GOT THE WRONG IDEA ABOUT A FEW THINGS.

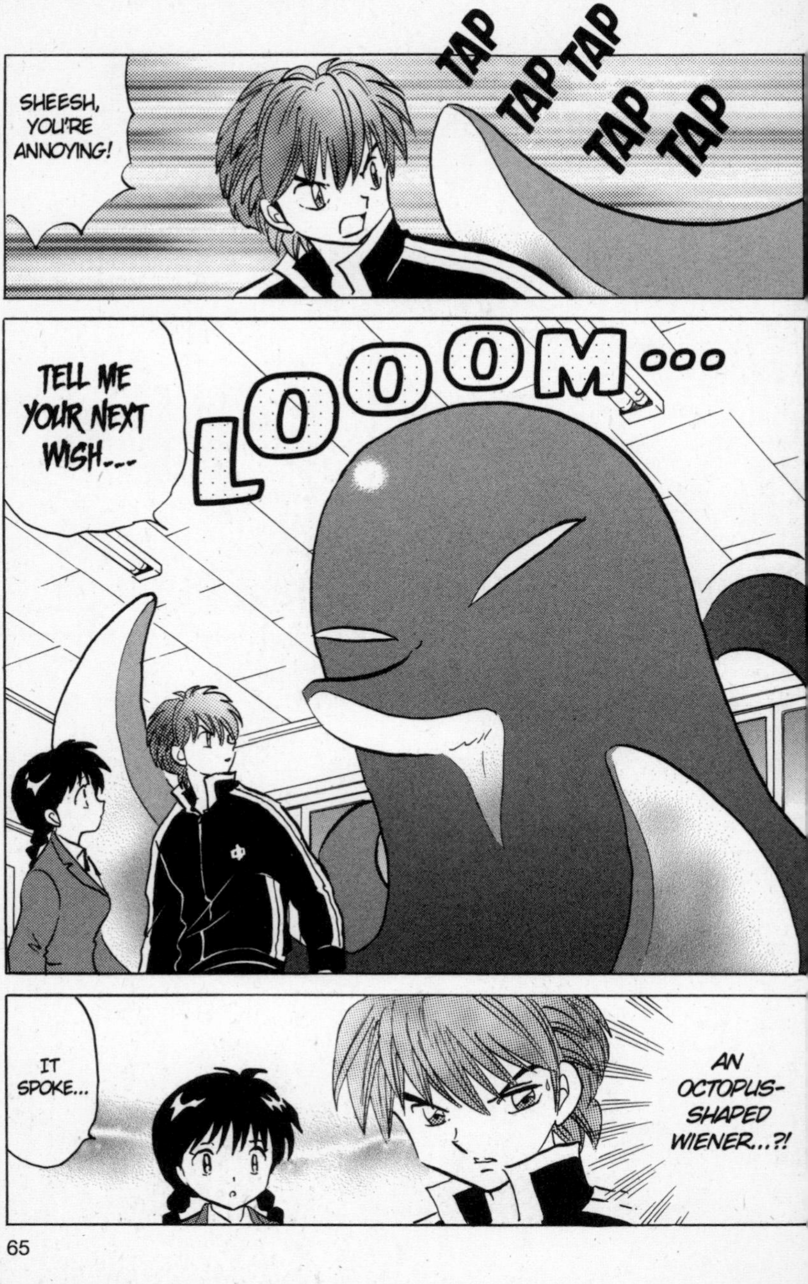

TAP TAP TAP TAP TAP TAP
SHEESH, YOU'RE ANNOYING!
LOOOM...
TELL ME YOUR NEXT WISH...
AN OCTOPUS-SHAPED WIENER...?!
IT SPOKE...

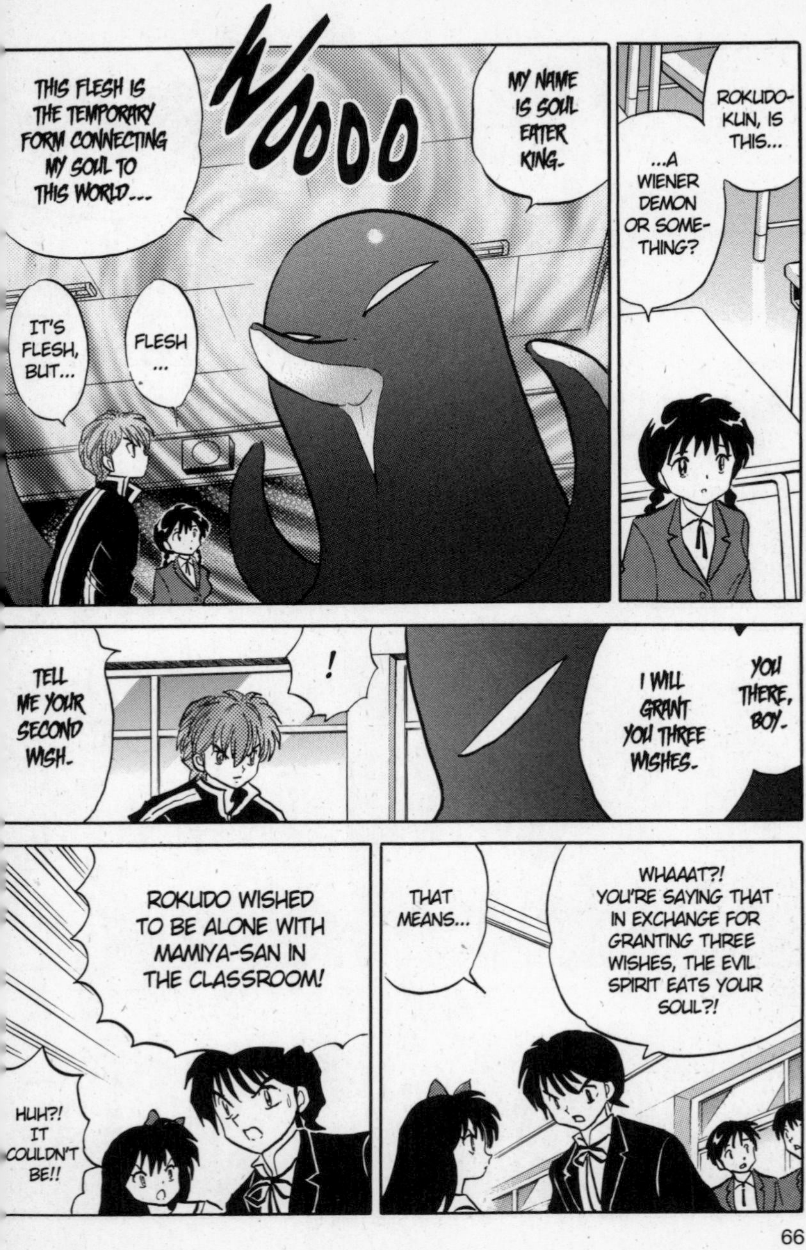
ROKUDO-KUN, IS THIS...
...A WIENER DEMON OR SOME-THING?
WOOOO
MY NAME IS SOUL EATER KING.
THIS FLESH IS THE TEMPORARY FORM CONNECTING MY SOUL TO THIS WORLD...
FLESH...
IT'S FLESH, BUT...
YOU THERE, BOY.
I WILL GRANT YOU THREE WISHES.
!
TELL ME YOUR SECOND WISH.
WHAAAT?! YOU'RE SAYING THAT IN EXCHANGE FOR GRANTING THREE WISHES, THE EVIL SPIRIT EATS YOUR SOUL?!
THAT MEANS...
ROKUDO WISHED TO BE ALONE WITH MAMIYA-SAN IN THE CLASSROOM!
HUH?! IT COULDN'T BE!!

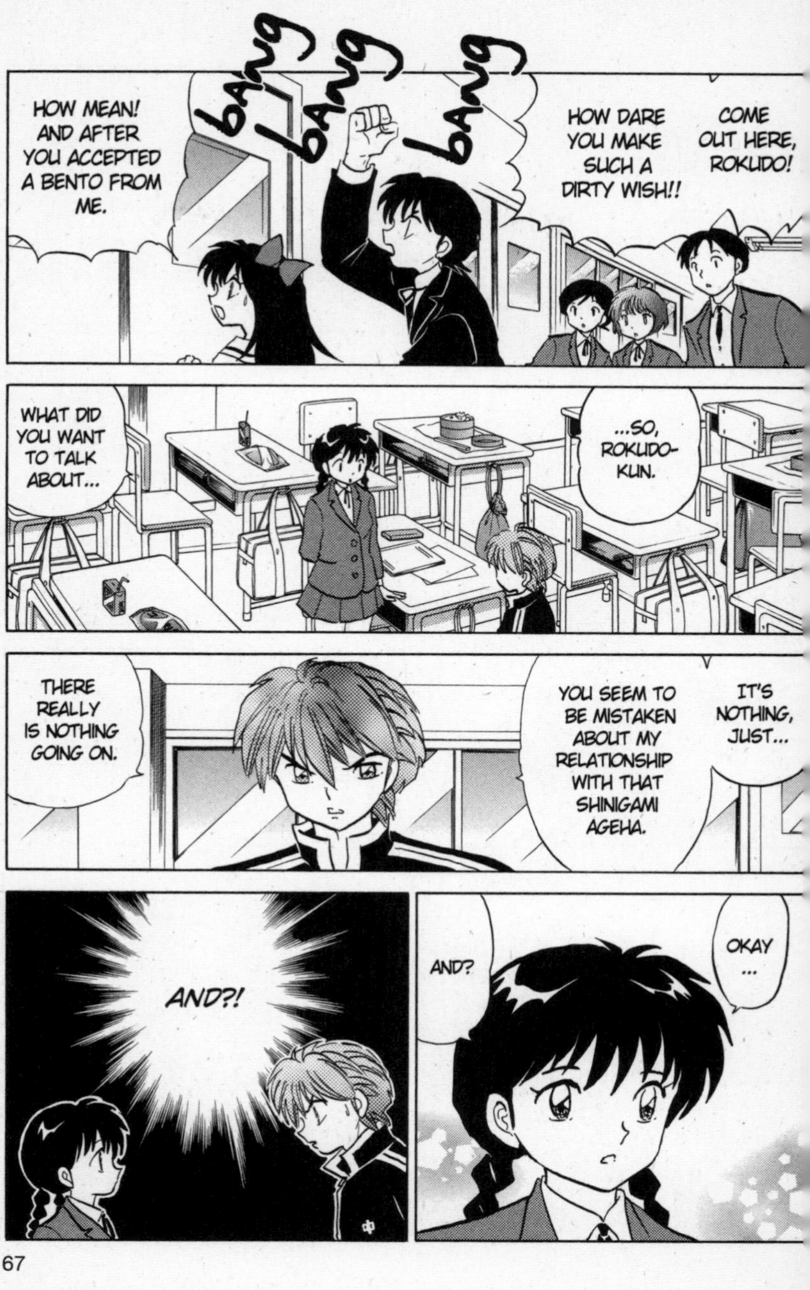
COME OUT HERE, ROKUDO!
HOW DARE YOU MAKE SUCH A DIRTY WISH!!
BANG
BANG
BANG
HOW MEAN! AND AFTER YOU ACCEPTED A BENTO FROM ME.
...SO, ROKUDO-KUN.
WHAT DID YOU WANT TO TALK ABOUT...
IT'S NOTHING, JUST...
YOU SEEM TO BE MISTAKEN ABOUT MY RELATIONSHIP WITH THAT SHINIGAMI AGEHA.
THERE REALLY IS NOTHING GOING ON.
OKAY ...
AND?
AND?!

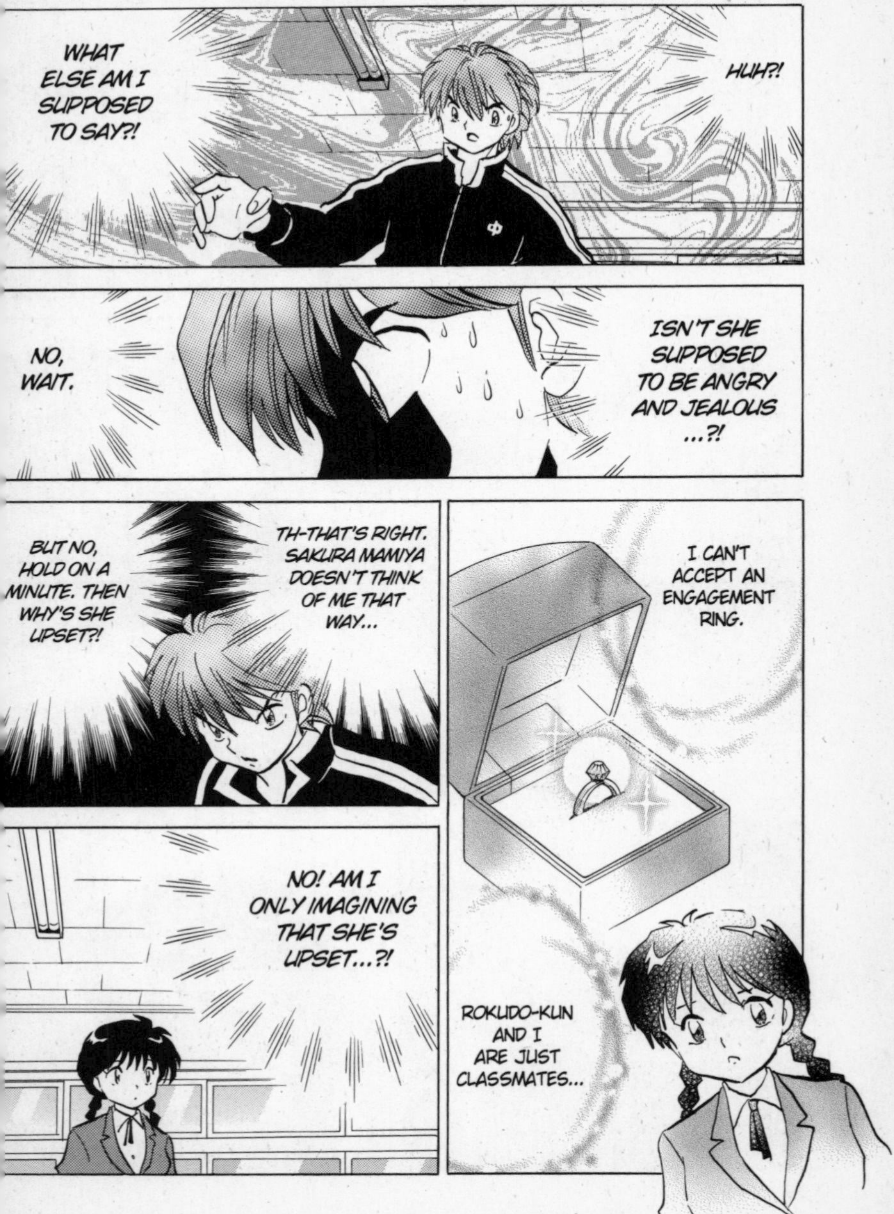
HUH?!
WHAT ELSE AM I SUPPOSED TO SAY?!
ISN'T SHE SUPPOSED TO BE ANGRY AND JEALOUS ...?!
NO, WAIT.
I CAN'T ACCEPT AN ENGAGEMENT RING.
ROKUDO-KUN AND I ARE JUST CLASSMATES...
TH-THAT'S RIGHT. SAKURA MAMIYA DOESN'T THINK OF ME THAT WAY...
BUT NO, HOLD ON A MINUTE. THEN WHY'S SHE UPSET?!
NO! AM I ONLY IMAGINING THAT SHE'S UPSET...?!

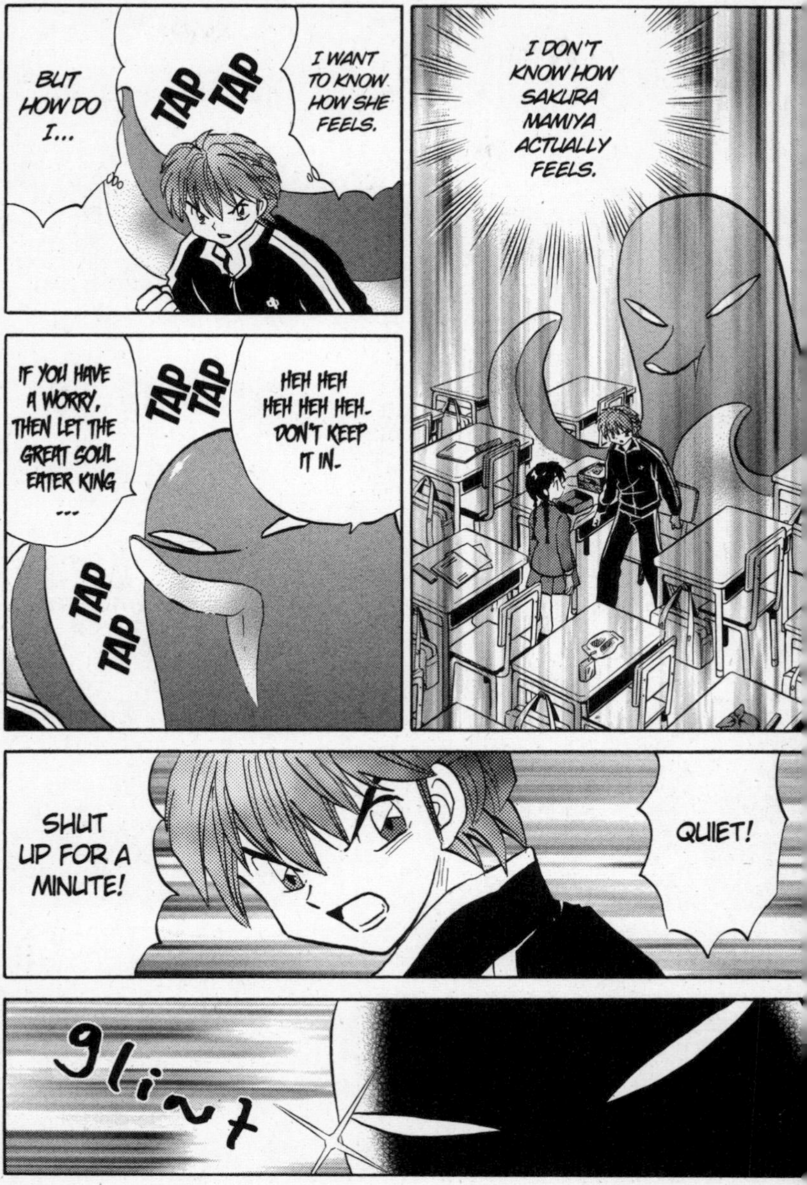
I DON'T KNOW HOW SAKURA MAMIYA ACTUALLY FEELS.
I WANT TO KNOW HOW SHE FEELS.
TAP TAP
BUT HOW DO I...
HEH HEH HEH HEH HEH. DON'T KEEP IT IN.
TAP TAP
IF YOU HAVE A WORRY, THEN LET THE GREAT SOUL EATER KING ...
TAP TAP
QUIET!
SHUT UP FOR A MINUTE!
glint

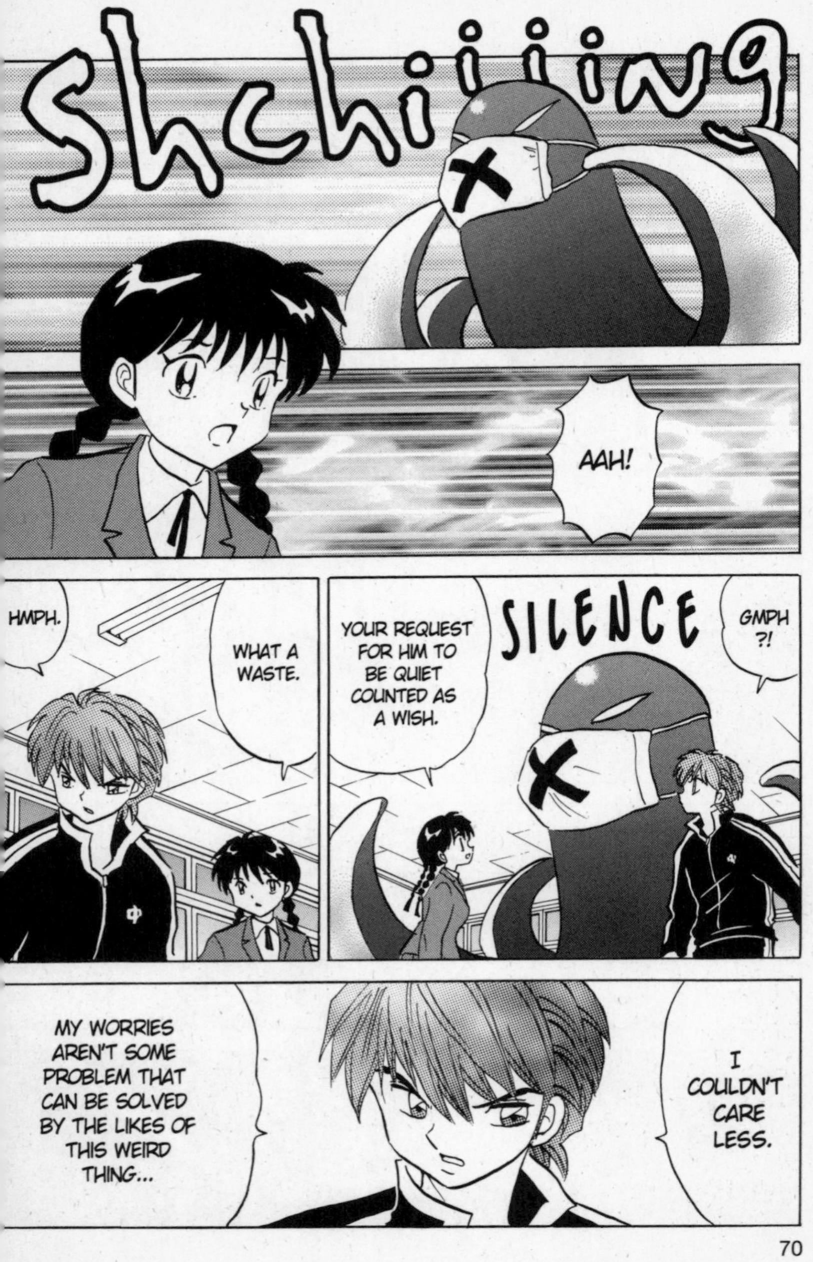
Shchiiing
AAH!
GMPH ?!
SILENCE
YOUR REQUEST FOR HIM TO BE QUIET COUNTED AS A WISH.
WHAT A WASTE.
HMPH.
I COULDN'T CARE LESS.
MY WORRIES AREN'T SOME PROBLEM THAT CAN BE SOLVED BY THE LIKES OF THIS WEIRD THING...

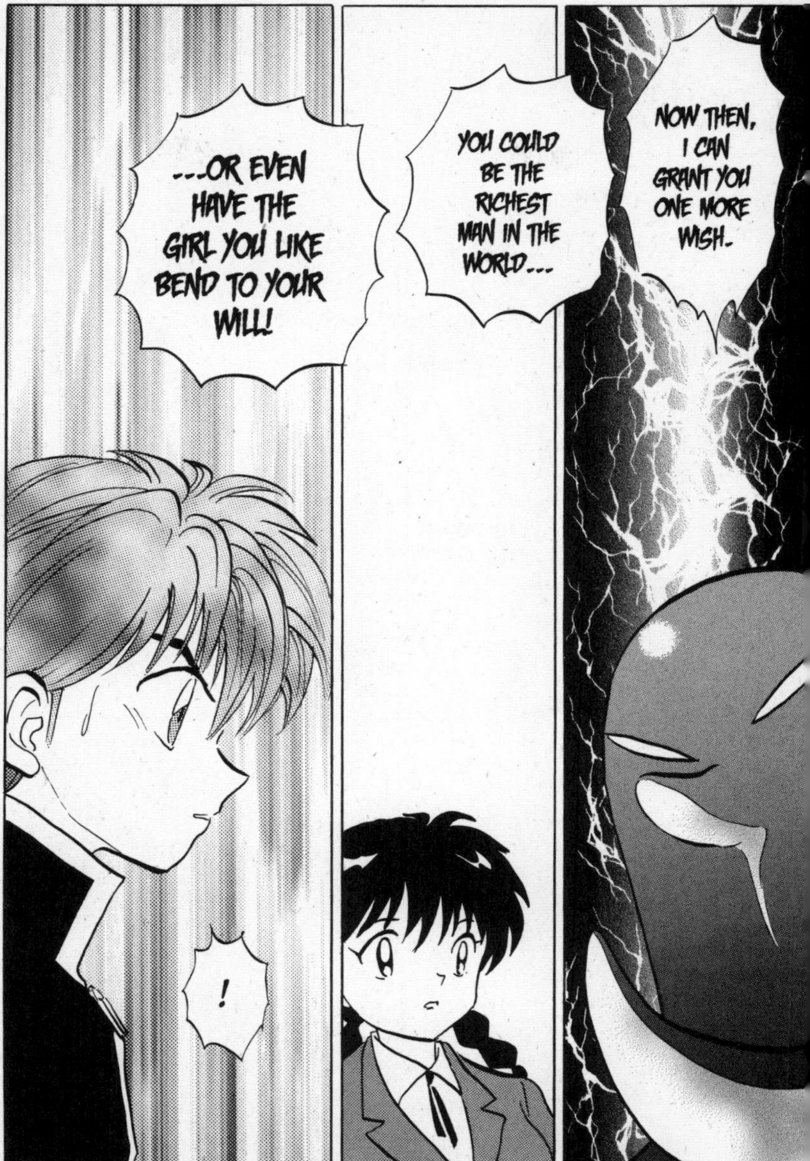
NOW THEN, I CAN GRANT YOU ONE MORE WISH.
YOU COULD BE THE RICHEST MAN IN THE WORLD...
...OR EVEN HAVE THE GIRL YOU LIKE BEND TO YOUR WILL!
!

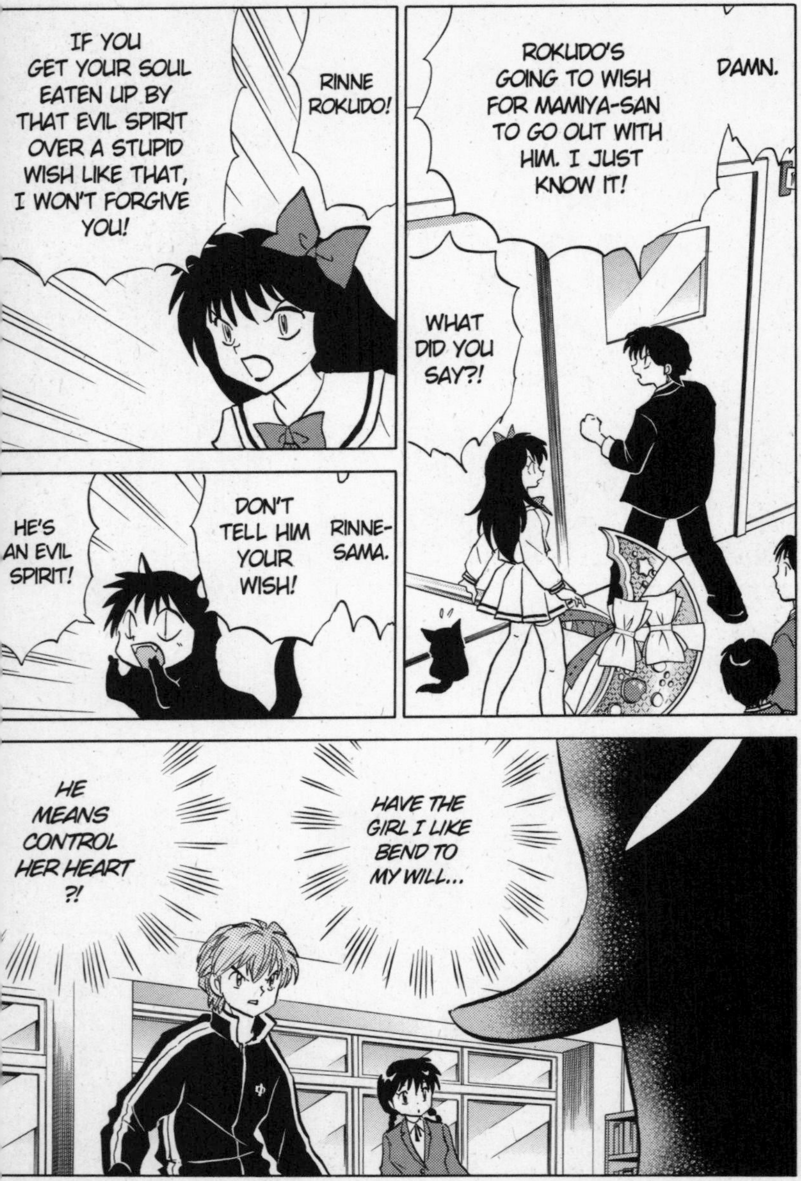
DAMN.
ROKUDO'S GOING TO WISH FOR MAMIYA-SAN TO GO OUT WITH HIM. I JUST KNOW IT!
WHAT DID YOU SAY?!
RINNE ROKUDO!
IF YOU GET YOUR SOUL EATEN UP BY THAT EVIL SPIRIT OVER A STUPID WISH LIKE THAT, I WON'T FORGIVE YOU!
RINNE-SAMA.
DON'T TELL HIM YOUR WISH!
HE'S AN EVIL SPIRIT!
HAVE THE GIRL I LIKE BEND TO MY WILL...
HE MEANS CONTROL HER HEART ?!

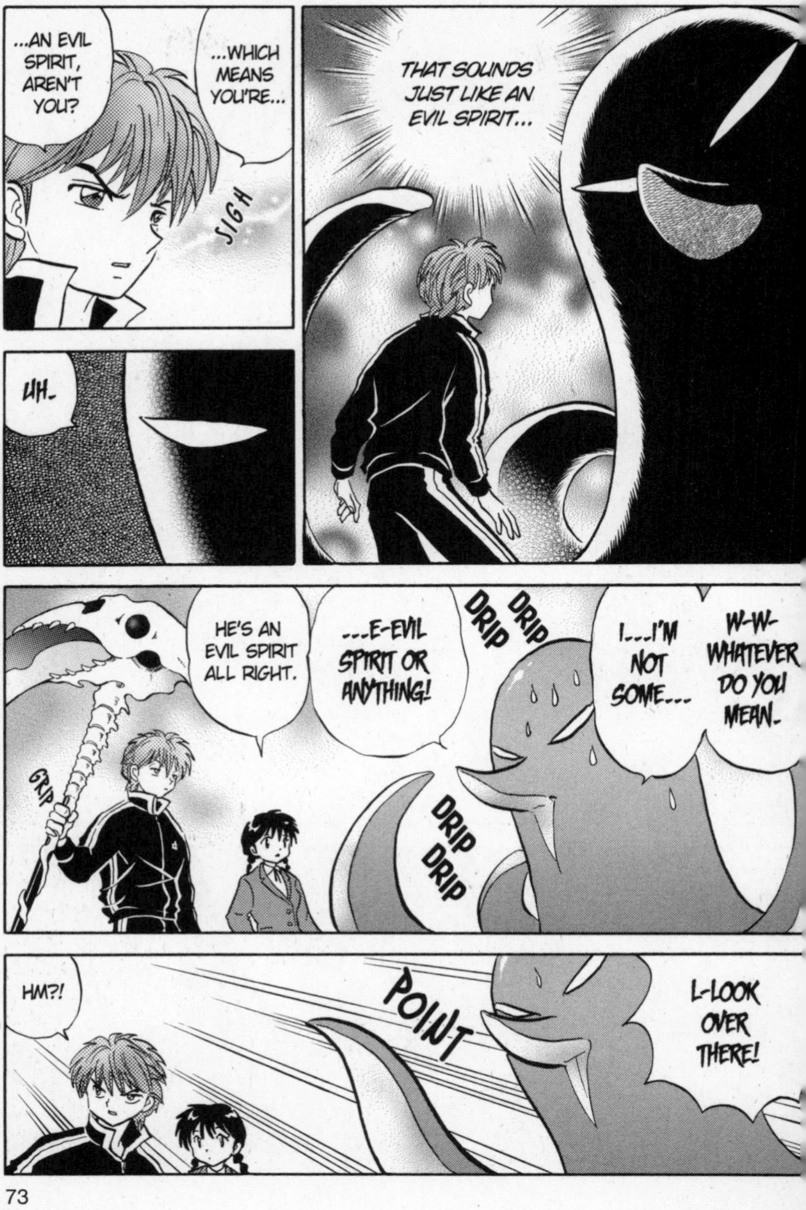
THAT SOUNDS JUST LIKE AN EVIL SPIRIT...
...WHICH MEANS YOU'RE...
...AN EVIL SPIRIT, AREN'T YOU?
SIGH
UH...
W-W-WHATEVER DO YOU MEAN...
I...I'M NOT SOME...
DRIP DRIP
...E-EVIL SPIRIT OR ANYTHING!
DRIP DRIP
HE'S AN EVIL SPIRIT ALL RIGHT.
GRIP
L-LOOK OVER THERE!
POINT
HM?!

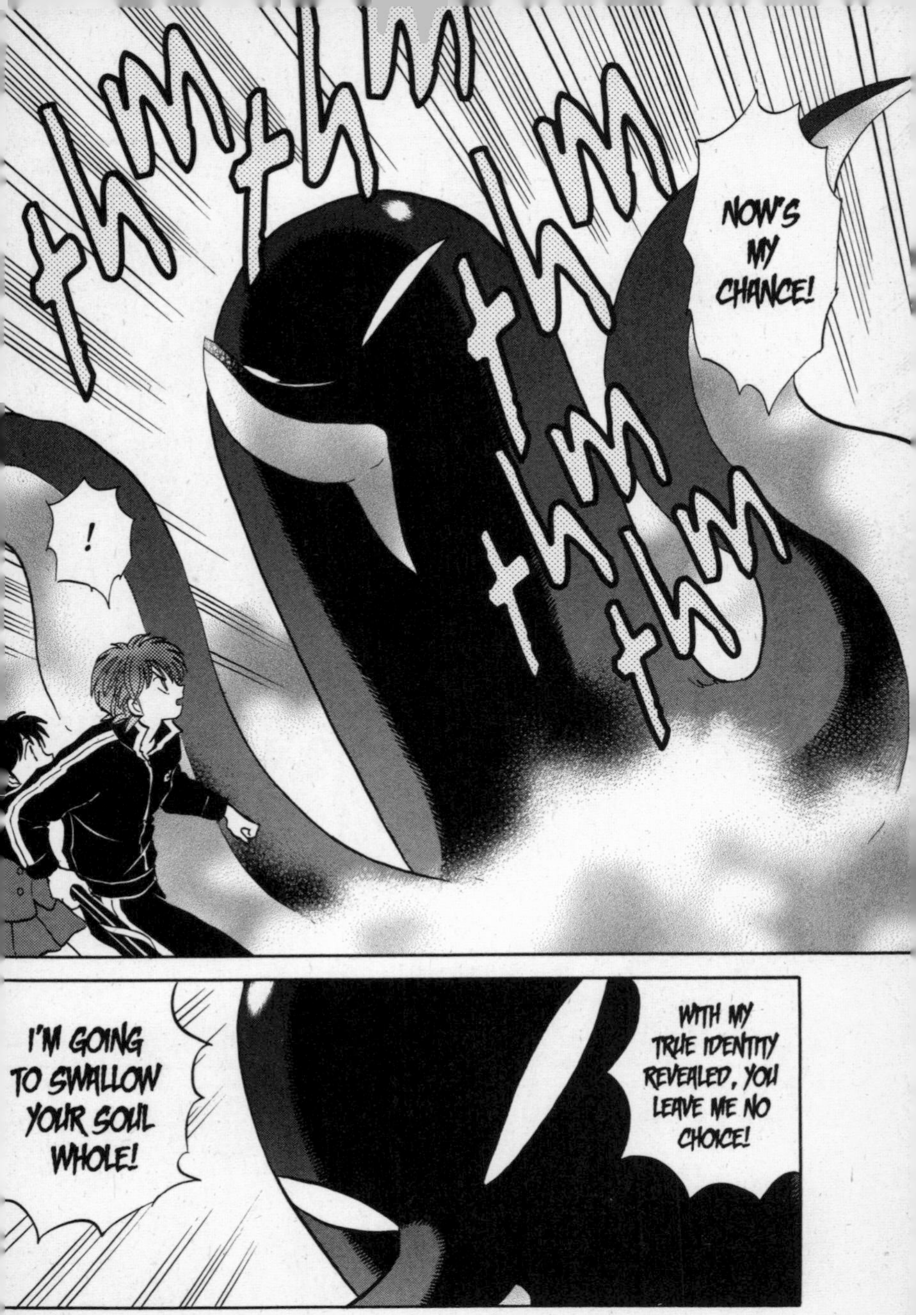
NOW'S MY CHANCE!
thm thm thm
thm thm thm
thm thm
!
WITH MY TRUE IDENTITY REVEALED, YOU LEAVE ME NO CHOICE!
I'M GOING TO SWALLOW YOUR SOUL WHOLE!

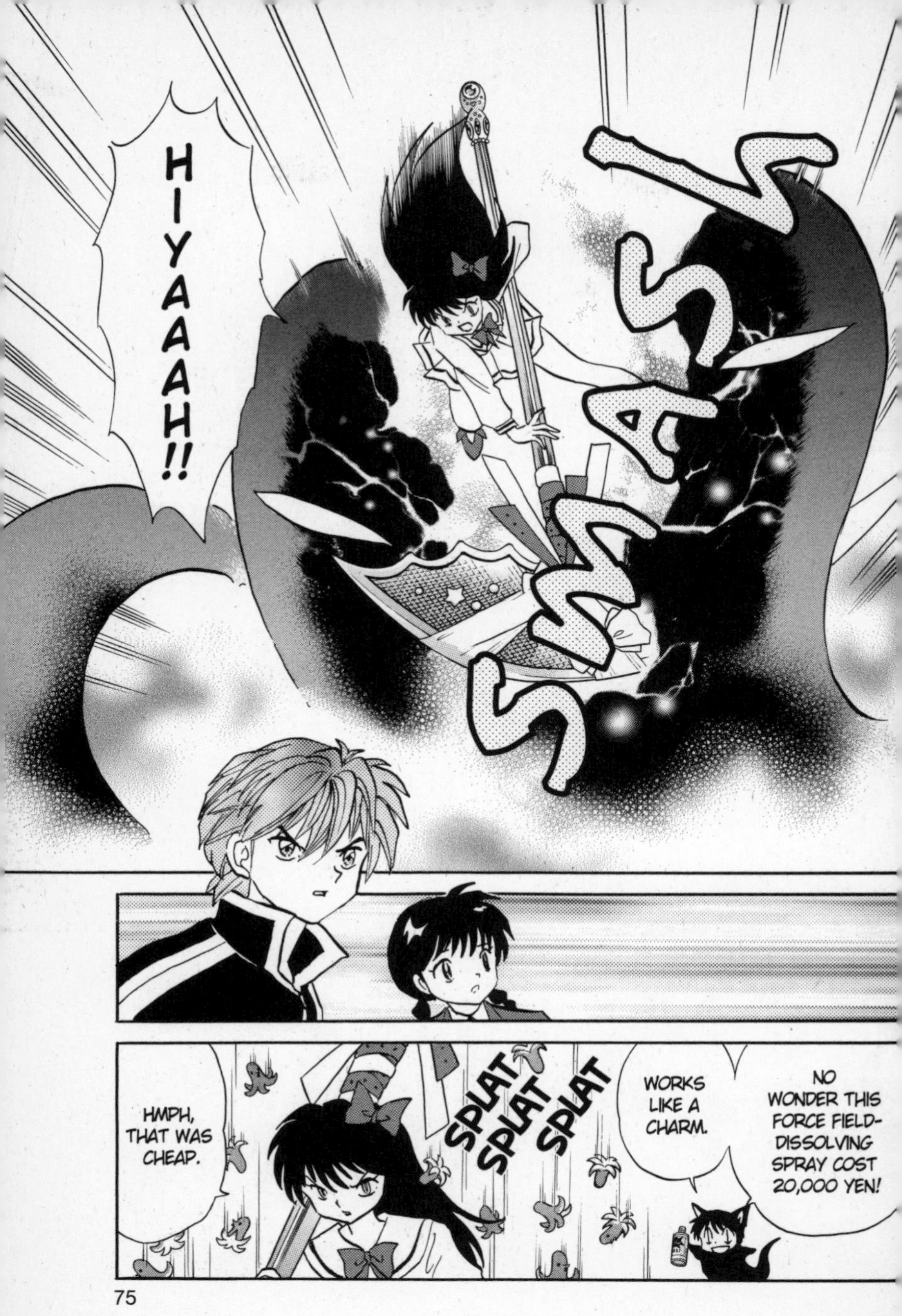
SMASH
HIYAAAAH!!
NO WONDER THIS FORCE FIELD-DISSOLVING SPRAY COST 20,000 YEN!
WORKS LIKE A CHARM.
SPLAT SPLAT SPLAT
HMPH, THAT WAS CHEAP.

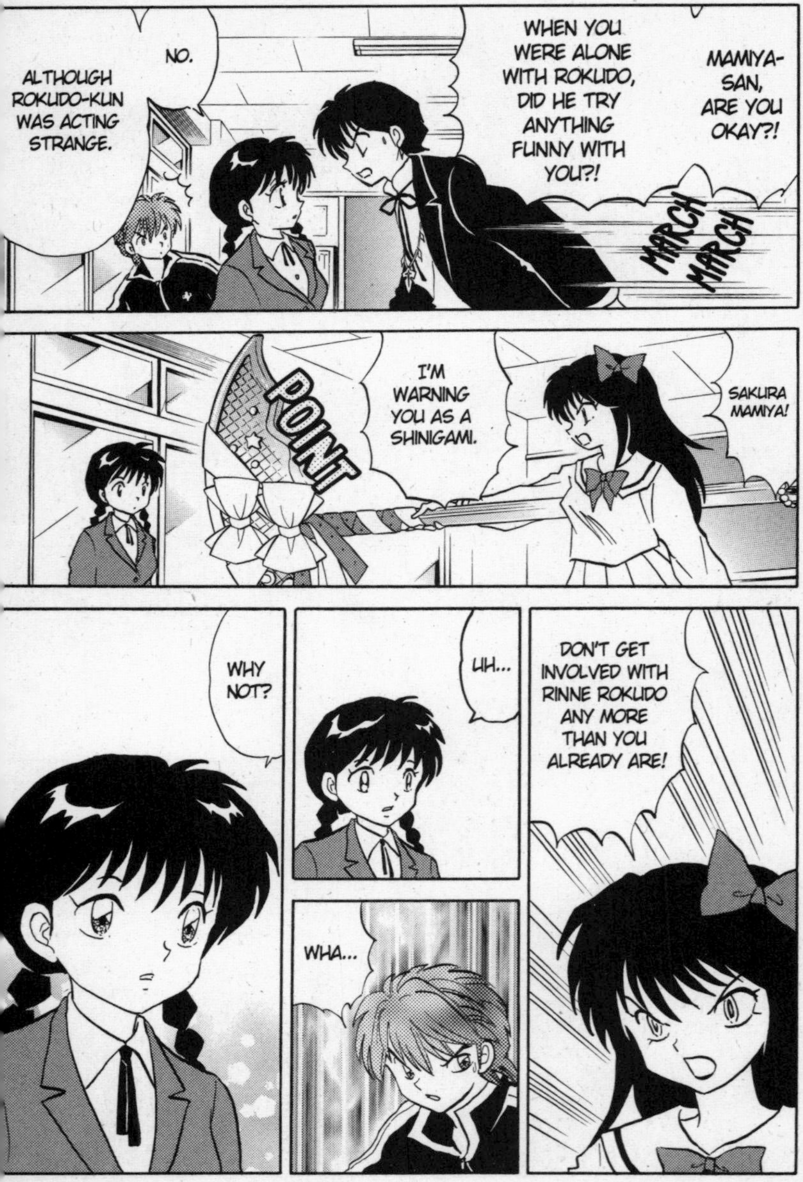
MAMIYA-SAN, ARE YOU OKAY?!
MARCH MARCH
WHEN YOU WERE ALONE WITH ROKUDO, DID HE TRY ANYTHING FUNNY WITH YOU?!
NO.
ALTHOUGH ROKUDO-KUN WAS ACTING STRANGE.
SAKURA MAMIYA!
I'M WARNING YOU AS A SHINIGAMI.
POINT
DON'T GET INVOLVED WITH RINNE ROKUDO ANY MORE THAN YOU ALREADY ARE!
UH...
WHA...
WHY NOT?

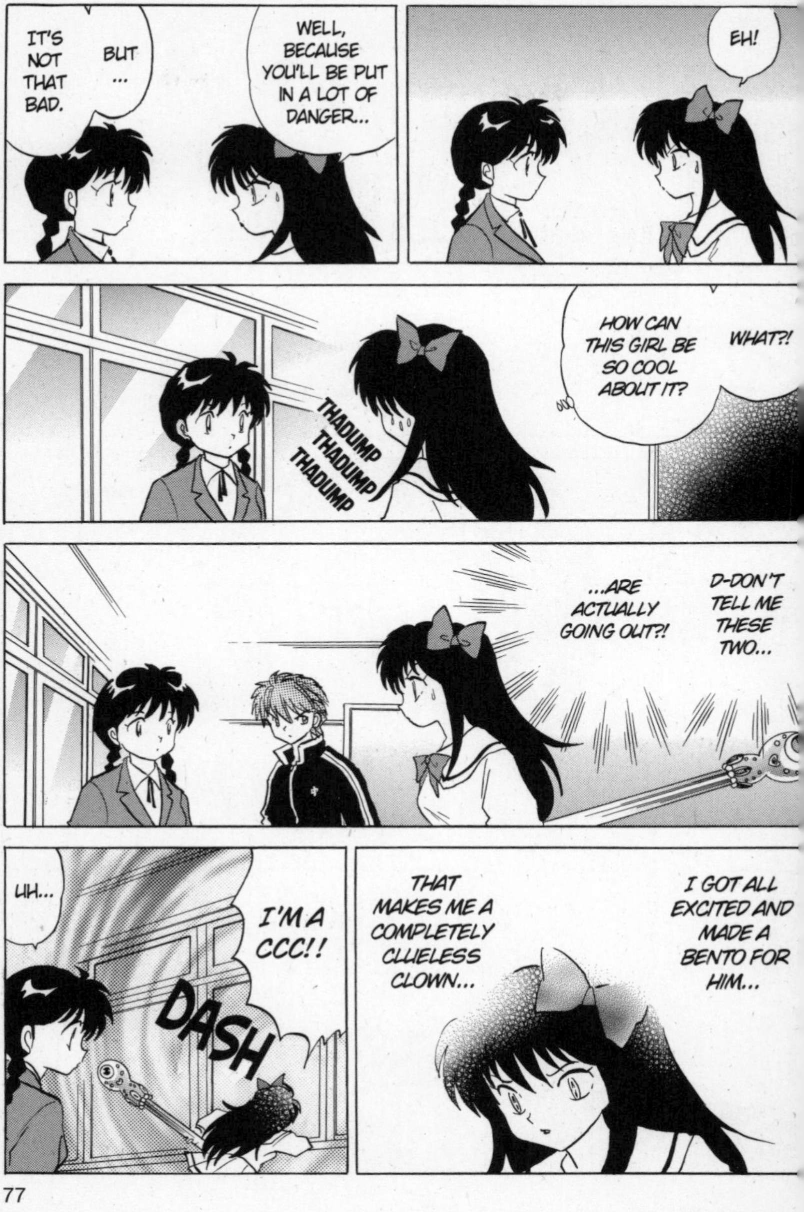
EH!
WELL, BECAUSE YOU'LL BE PUT IN A LOT OF DANGER...
IT'S NOT THAT BAD. BUT ...
WHAT?!
HOW CAN THIS GIRL BE SO COOL ABOUT IT?
THADUMP THADUMP THADUMP
D-DON'T TELL ME THESE TWO...
...ARE ACTUALLY GOING OUT?!
I GOT ALL EXCITED AND MADE A BENTO FOR HIM...
THAT MAKES ME A COMPLETELY CLUELESS CLOWN...
I'M A CCC!!
DASH
UH...

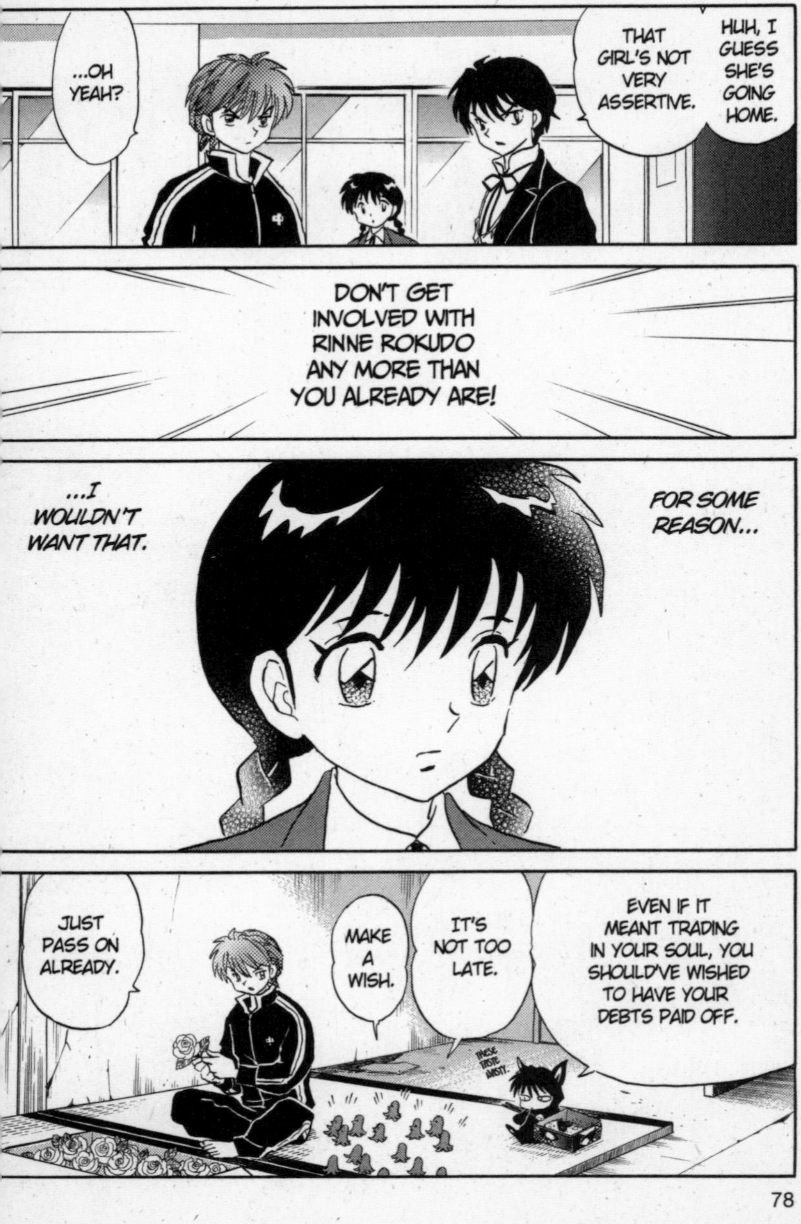
HUH, I GUESS SHE'S GOING HOME.
THAT GIRL'S NOT VERY ASSERTIVE.
...OH YEAH?
DON'T GET INVOLVED WITH RINNE ROKUDO ANY MORE THAN YOU ALREADY ARE!
FOR SOME REASON...
...I WOULDN'T WANT THAT.
EVEN IF IT MEANT TRADING IN YOUR SOUL, YOU SHOULD'VE WISHED TO HAVE YOUR DEBTS PAID OFF.
THESE TASTE NASTY.
IT'S NOT TOO LATE.
MAKE A WISH.
JUST PASS ON ALREADY.

CHAPTER 43: THE UNOPENABLE BOOKSHELVES

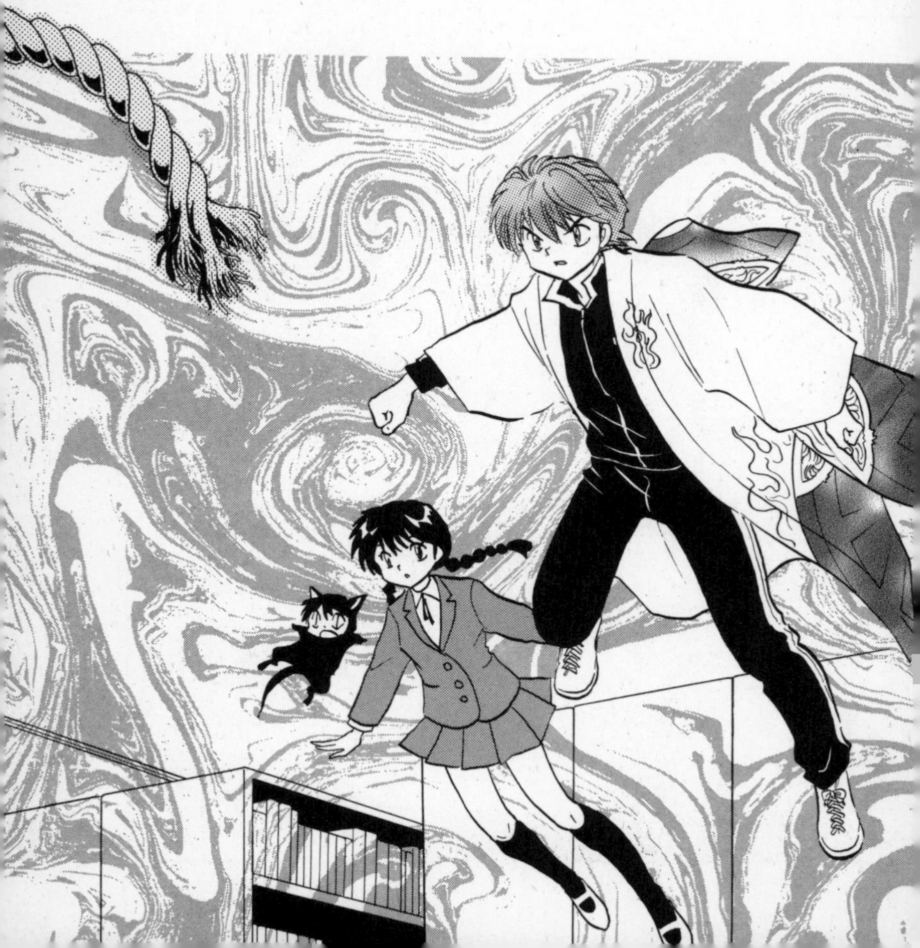

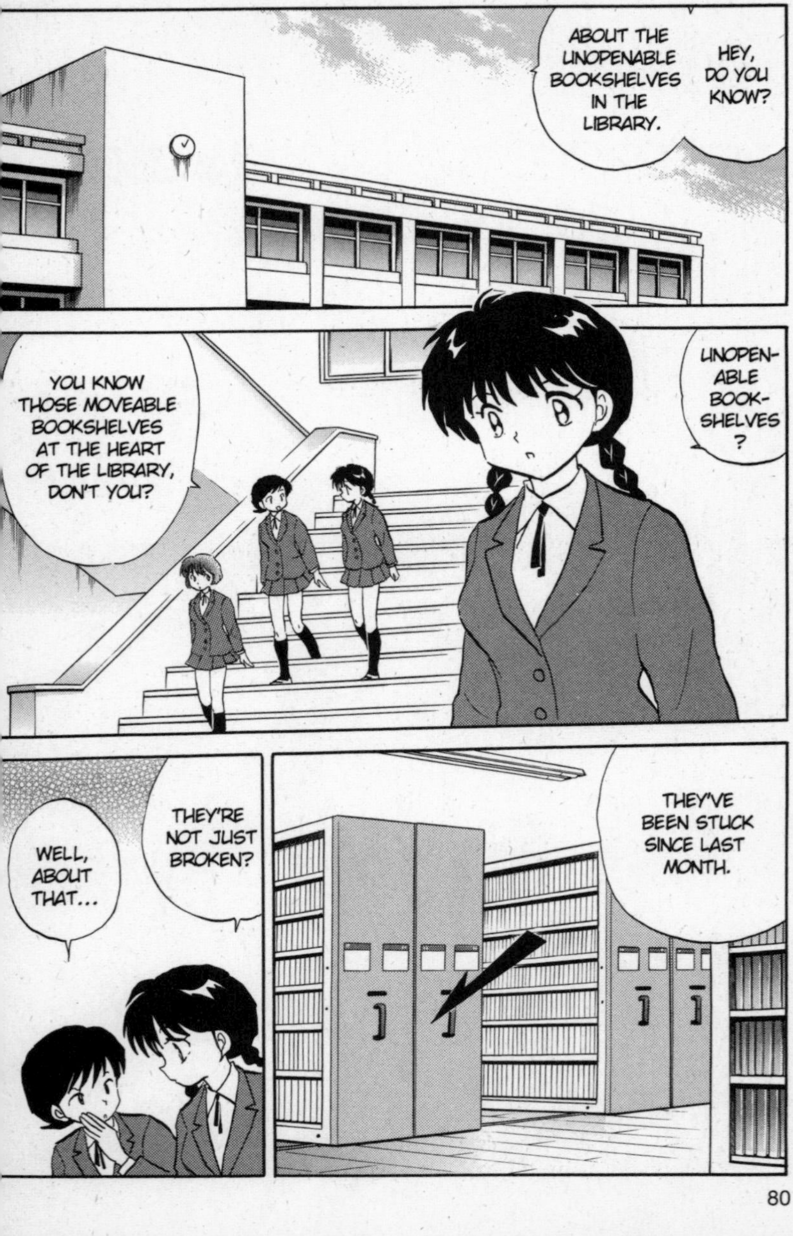
HEY, DO YOU KNOW?
ABOUT THE UNOPENABLE BOOKSHELVES IN THE LIBRARY.
UNOPEN-ABLE BOOK-SHELVES?
YOU KNOW THOSE MOVEABLE BOOKSHELVES AT THE HEART OF THE LIBRARY, DON'T YOU?
THEY'VE BEEN STUCK SINCE LAST MONTH.
THEY'RE NOT JUST BROKEN?
WELL, ABOUT THAT...

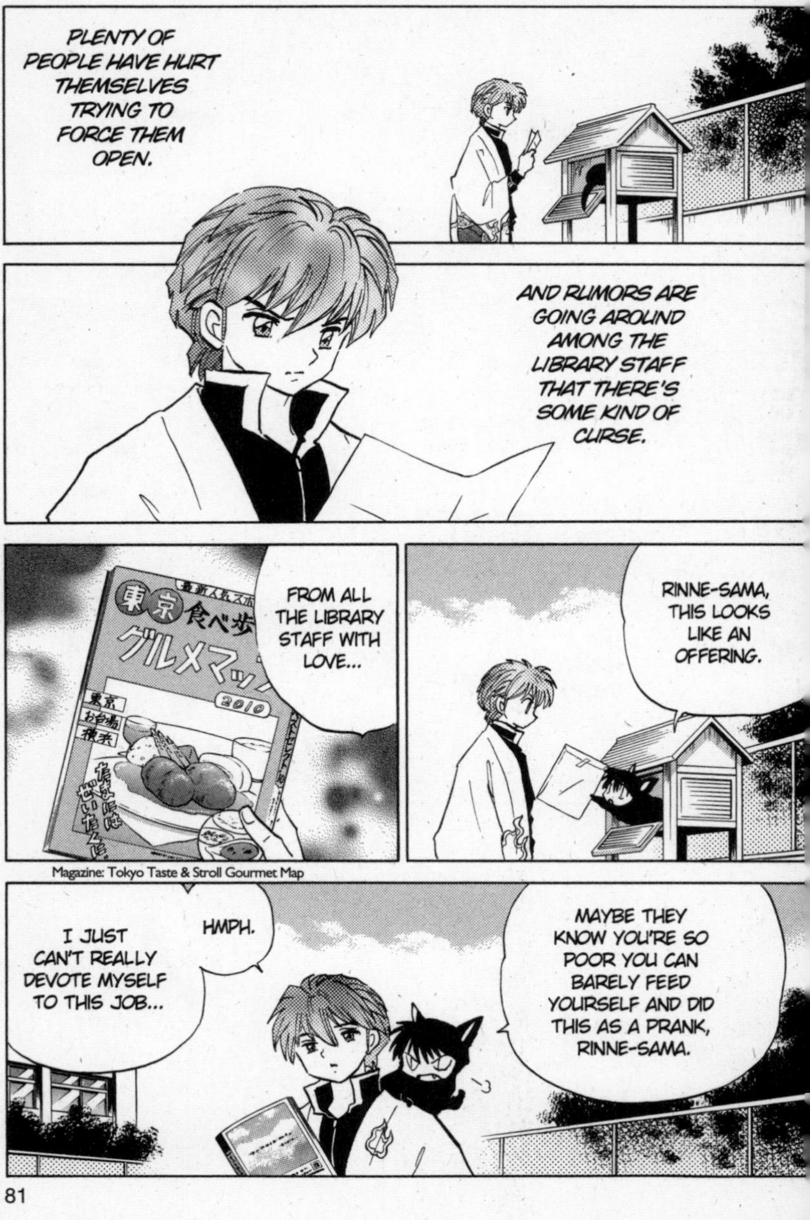
PLENTY OF PEOPLE HAVE HURT THEMSELVES TRYING TO FORCE THEM OPEN.
AND RUMORS ARE GOING AROUND AMONG THE LIBRARY STAFF THAT THERE'S SOME KIND OF CURSE.
RINNE-SAMA, THIS LOOKS LIKE AN OFFERING.
FROM ALL THE LIBRARY STAFF WITH LOVE...
MAYBE THEY KNOW YOU'RE SO POOR YOU CAN BARELY FEED YOURSELF AND DID THIS AS A PRANK, RINNE-SAMA.
HMPH.
I JUST CAN'T REALLY DEVOTE MYSELF TO THIS JOB...
Magazine: Tokyo Taste & Stroll Gourmet Map

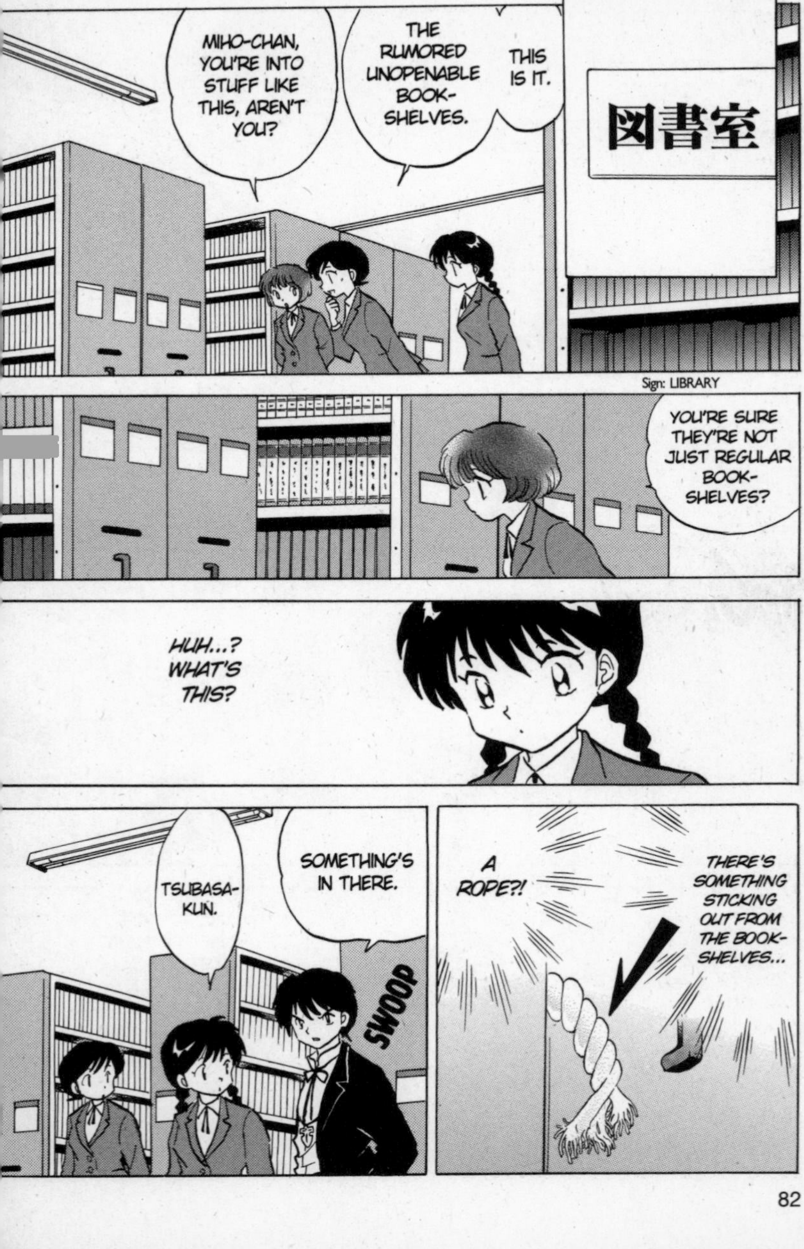
図書室
THIS IS IT.
THE RUMORED UNOPENABLE BOOK-SHELVES.
MIHO-CHAN, YOU'RE INTO STUFF LIKE THIS, AREN'T YOU?
Sign: LIBRARY
YOU'RE SURE THEY'RE NOT JUST REGULAR BOOK-SHELVES?
HUH...? WHAT'S THIS?
THERE'S SOMETHING STICKING OUT FROM THE BOOK-SHELVES...
A ROPE?!
SWOOP
SOMETHING'S IN THERE.
TSUBASA-KUN.

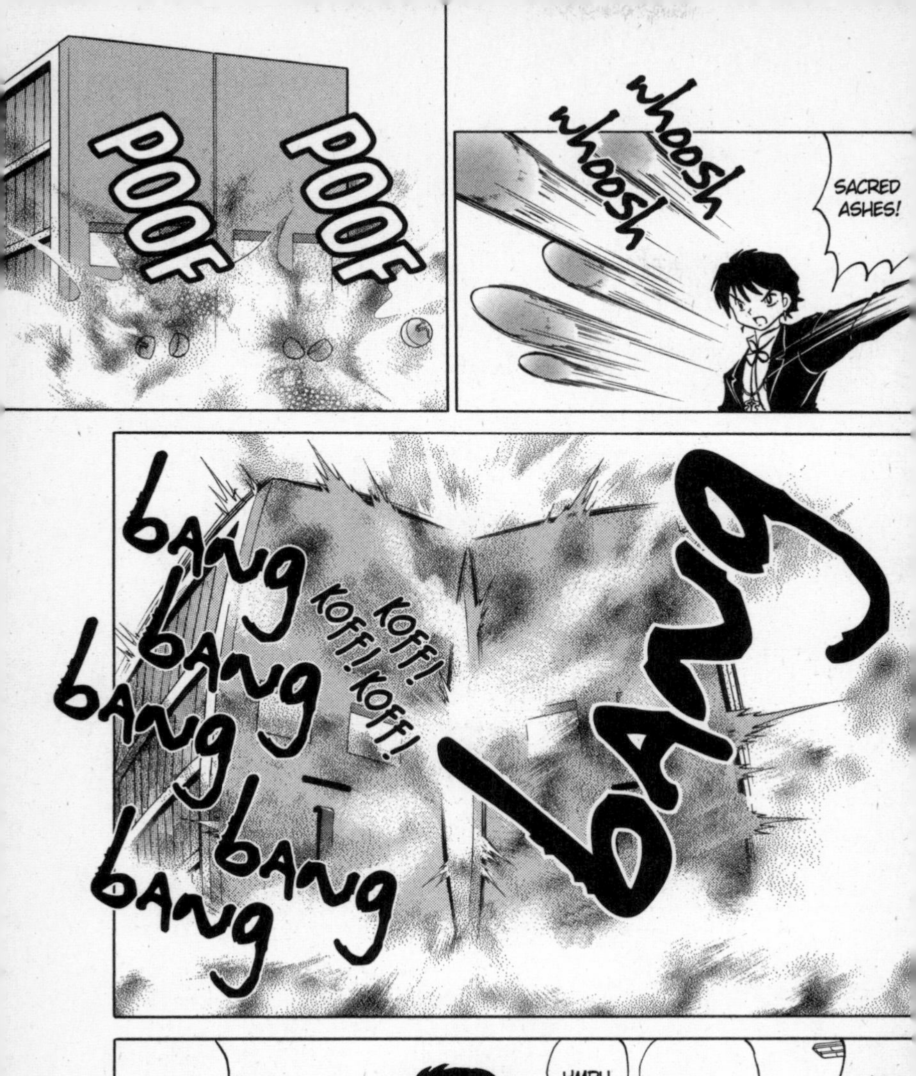
whoosh whoosh
SACRED ASHES!
POOF POOF
bang
bang bang bang bang bang
KOFF! KOFF! KOFF!
HUH ?!
WHAT, WHAT?!
HMPH.
THEY'RE IN PAIN?!

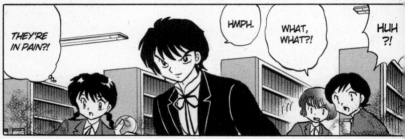

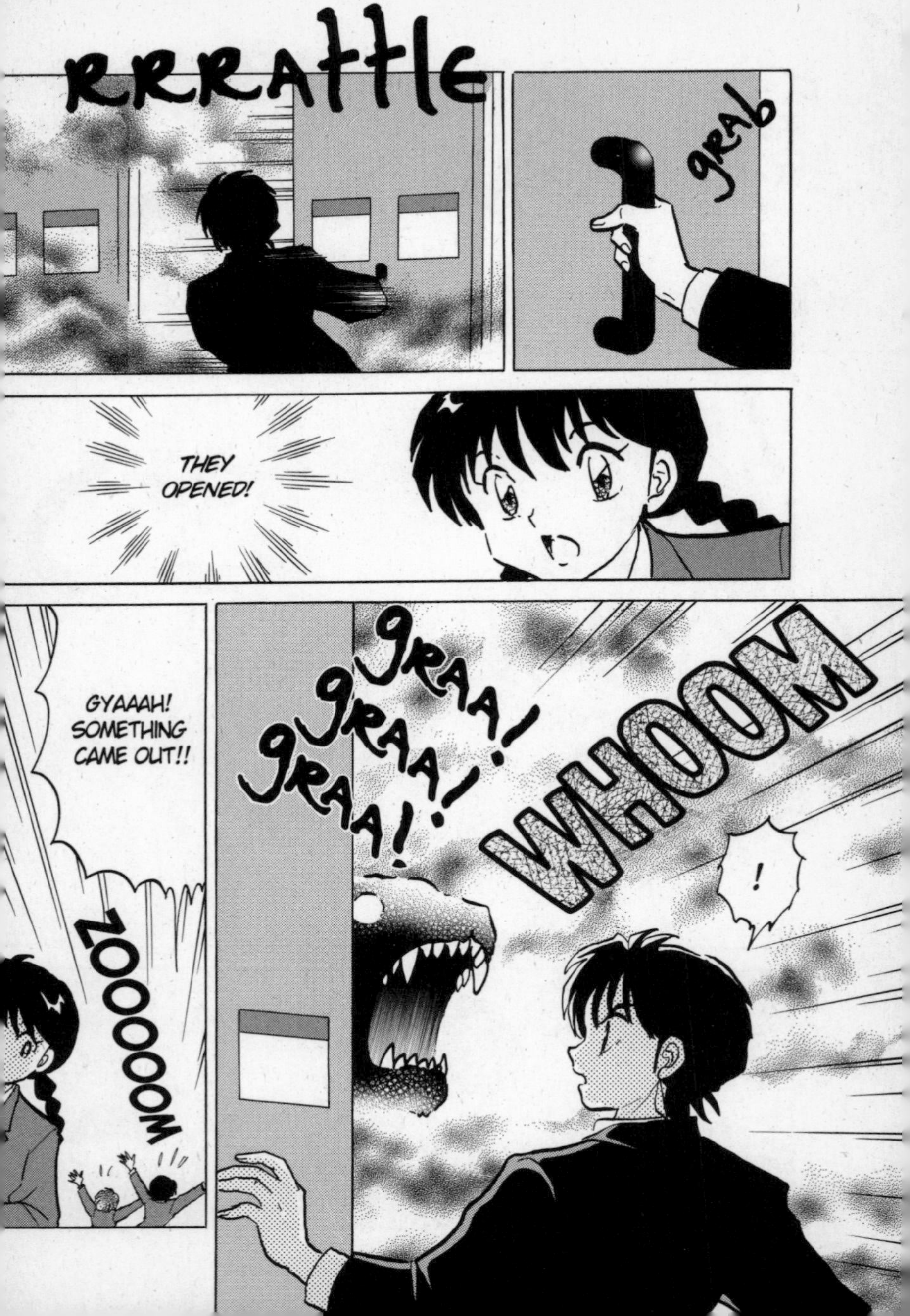
grab
RRRattle
THEY OPENED!
WHOOM
!
graa!
graa!
graa!
GYAAAH! SOMETHING CAME OUT!!
ZOOOOOM

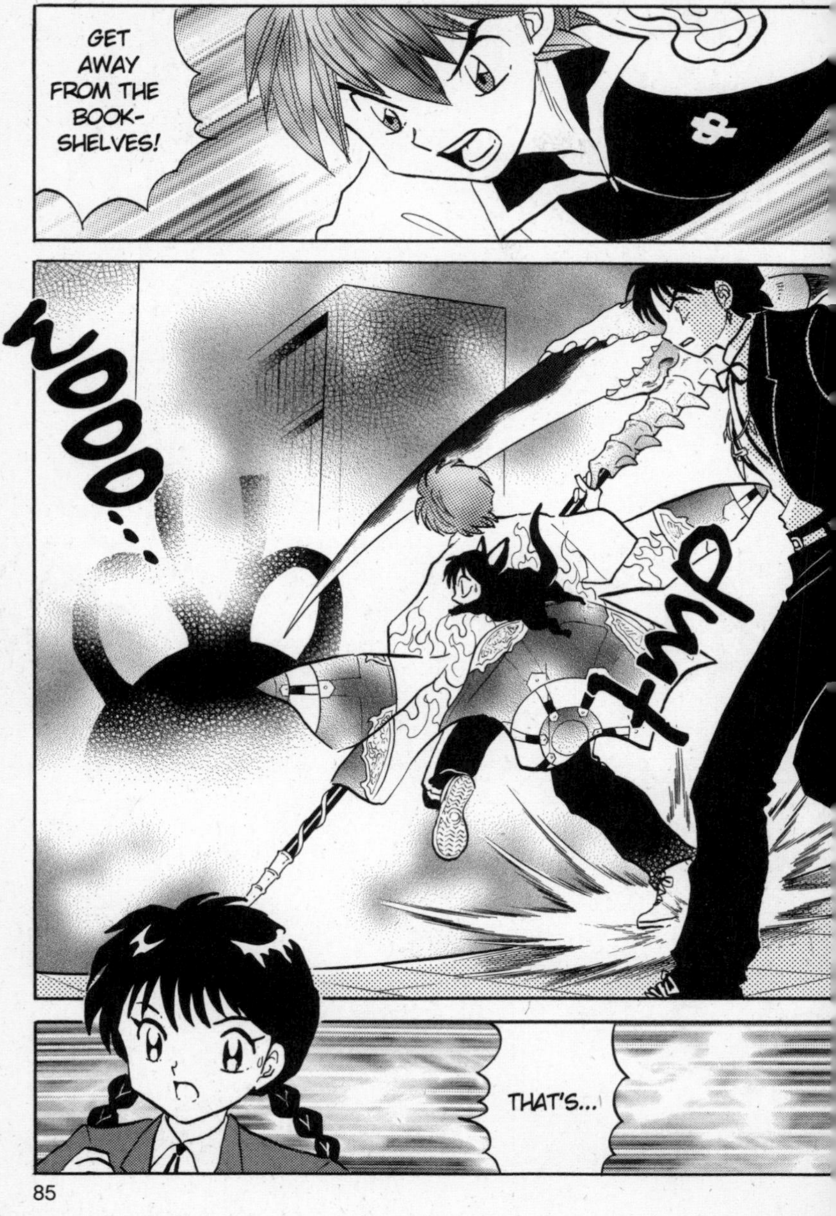
GET AWAY FROM THE BOOK-SHELVES!
WOOOO...
THMP
THAT'S...

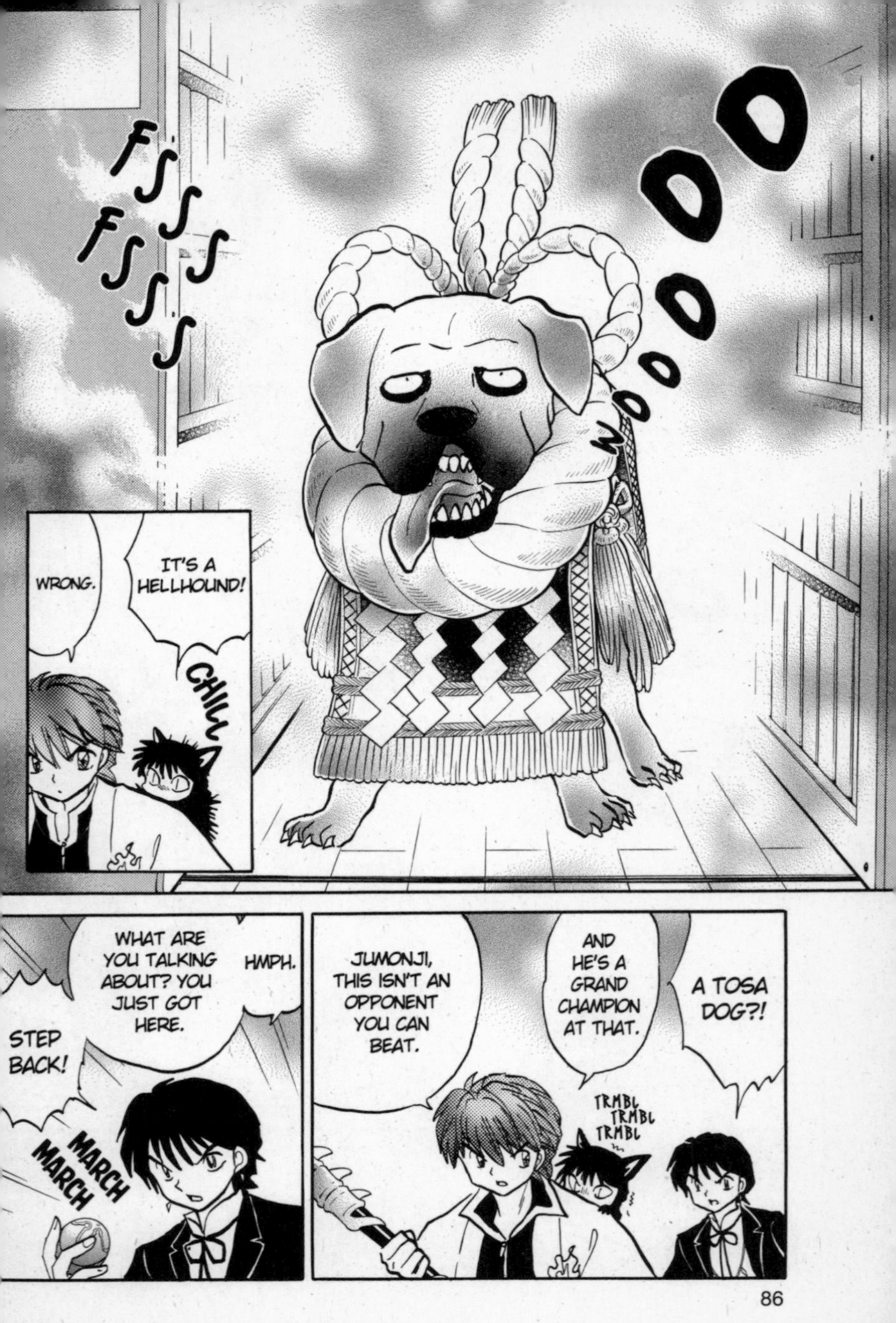
DOOOOOM
FSSS
FSSSS
IT'S A HELLHOUND!
CHILL
WRONG.
A TOSA DOG?!
TRMBL TRMBL TRMBL
AND HE'S A GRAND CHAMPION AT THAT.
JUMONJI, THIS ISN'T AN OPPONENT YOU CAN BEAT.
HMPH.
WHAT ARE YOU TALKING ABOUT? YOU JUST GOT HERE.
STEP BACK!
MARCH MARCH

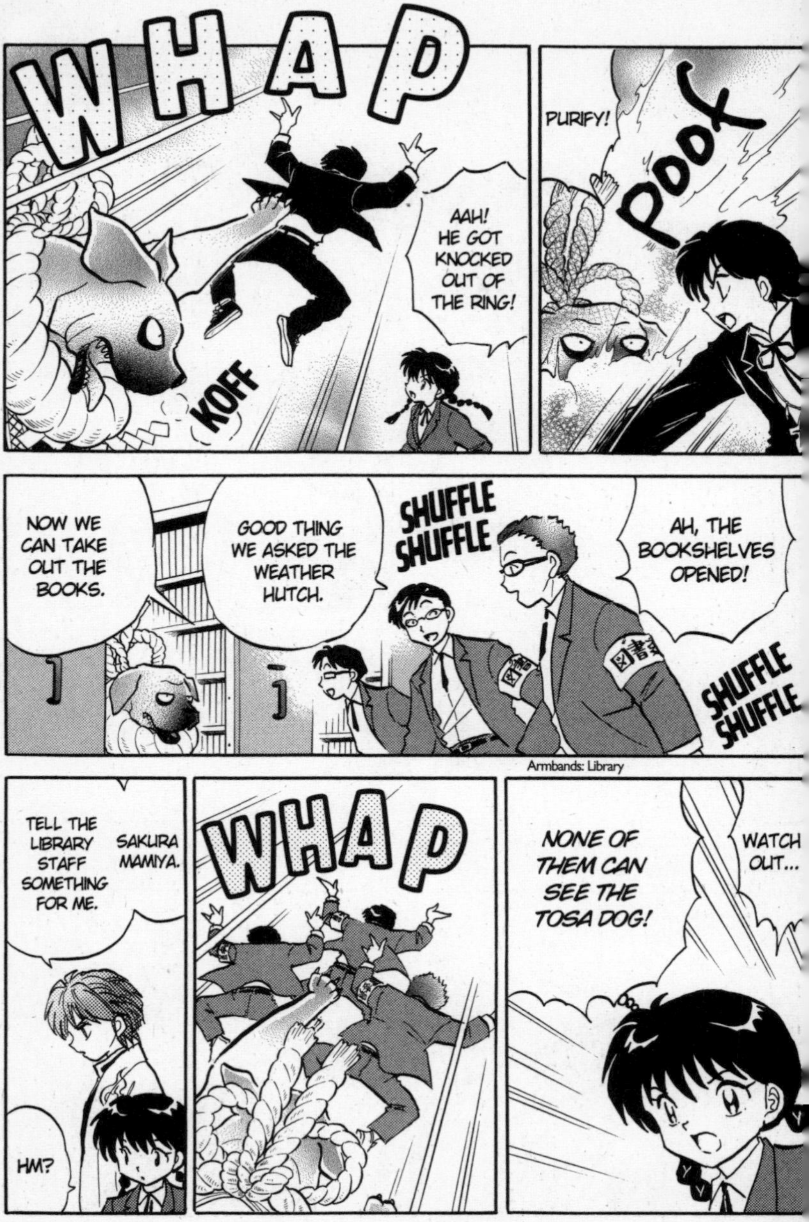
PURIFY!
POOF
WHAP
AAH! HE GOT KNOCKED OUT OF THE RING!
KOFF
AH, THE BOOKSHELVES OPENED!
SHUFFLE SHUFFLE
SHUFFLE SHUFFLE
GOOD THING WE ASKED THE WEATHER HUTCH.
NOW WE CAN TAKE OUT THE BOOKS.
Armbands: Library
WATCH OUT...
NONE OF THEM CAN SEE THE TOSA DOG!
WHAP
SAKURA MAMIYA.
TELL THE LIBRARY STAFF SOMETHING FOR ME.
HM?

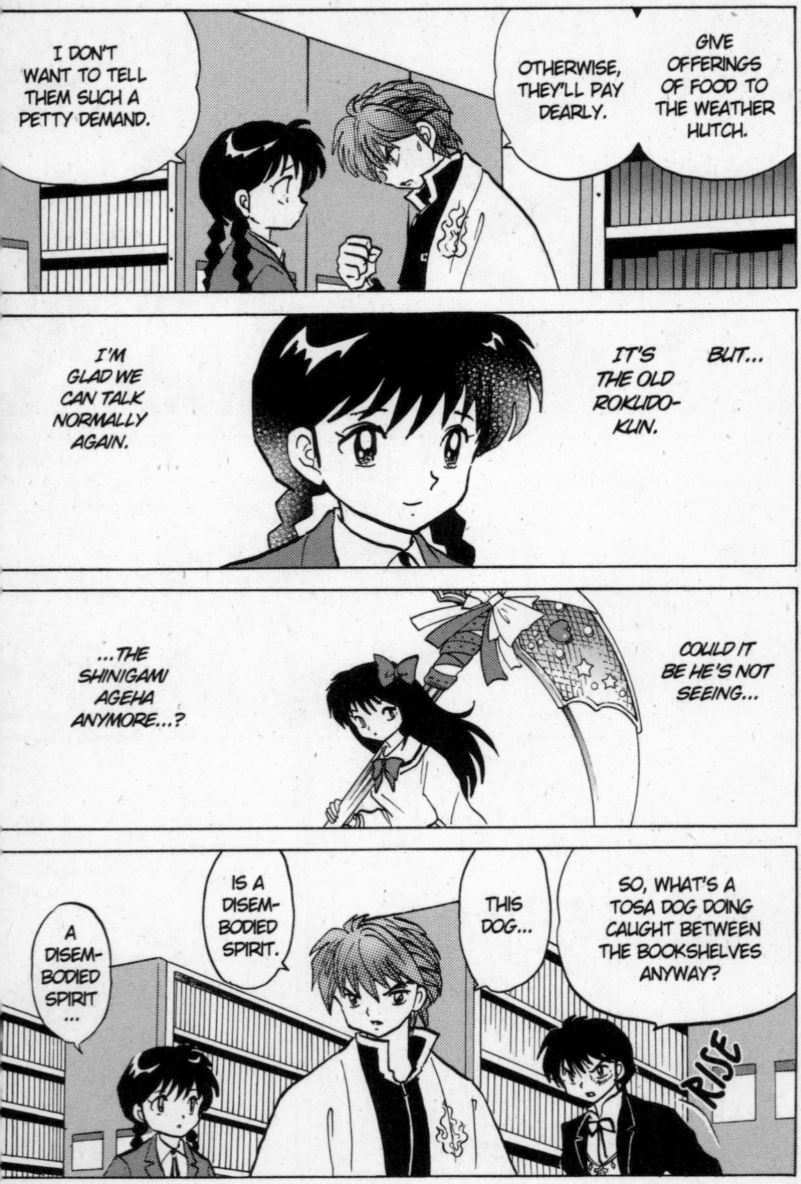
GIVE OFFERINGS OF FOOD TO THE WEATHER HUTCH.
OTHERWISE, THEY'LL PAY DEARLY.
I DON'T WANT TO TELL THEM SUCH A PETTY DEMAND.
BUT...
IT'S THE OLD ROKUDO-KUN.
I'M GLAD WE CAN TALK NORMALLY AGAIN.
COULD IT BE HE'S NOT SEEING...
...THE SHINIGAMI AGEHA ANYMORE...?
SO, WHAT'S A TOSA DOG DOING CAUGHT BETWEEN THE BOOKSHELVES ANYWAY?
RISE
THIS DOG...
IS A DISEM-BODIED SPIRIT.
A DISEM-BODIED SPIRIT...

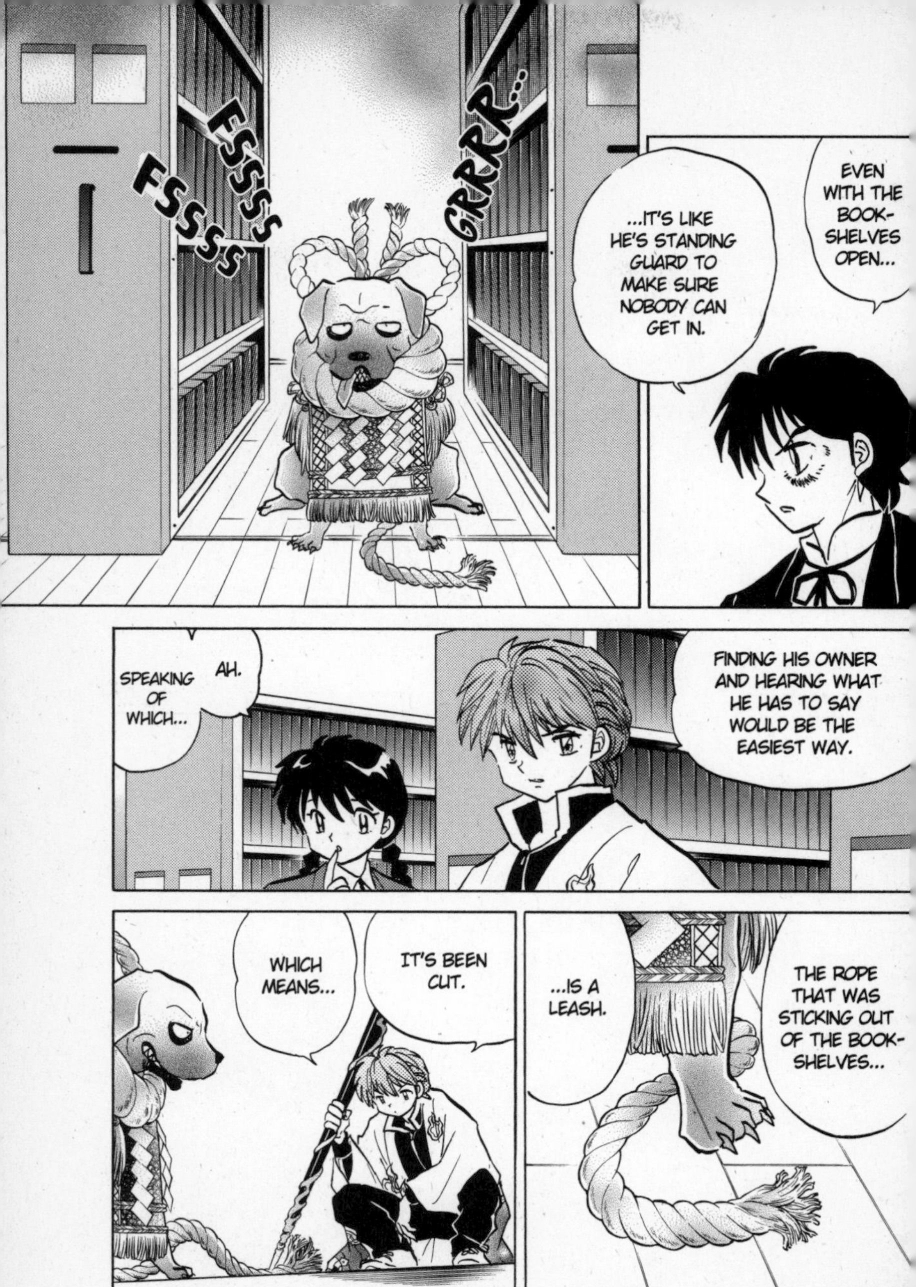
EVEN WITH THE BOOK-SHELVES OPEN...
...IT'S LIKE HE'S STANDING GUARD TO MAKE SURE NOBODY CAN GET IN.
GRRR...
FSSSS FSSSS
FINDING HIS OWNER AND HEARING WHAT HE HAS TO SAY WOULD BE THE EASIEST WAY.
AH.
SPEAKING OF WHICH...
THE ROPE THAT WAS STICKING OUT OF THE BOOK-SHELVES...
...IS A LEASH.
IT'S BEEN CUT.
WHICH MEANS...

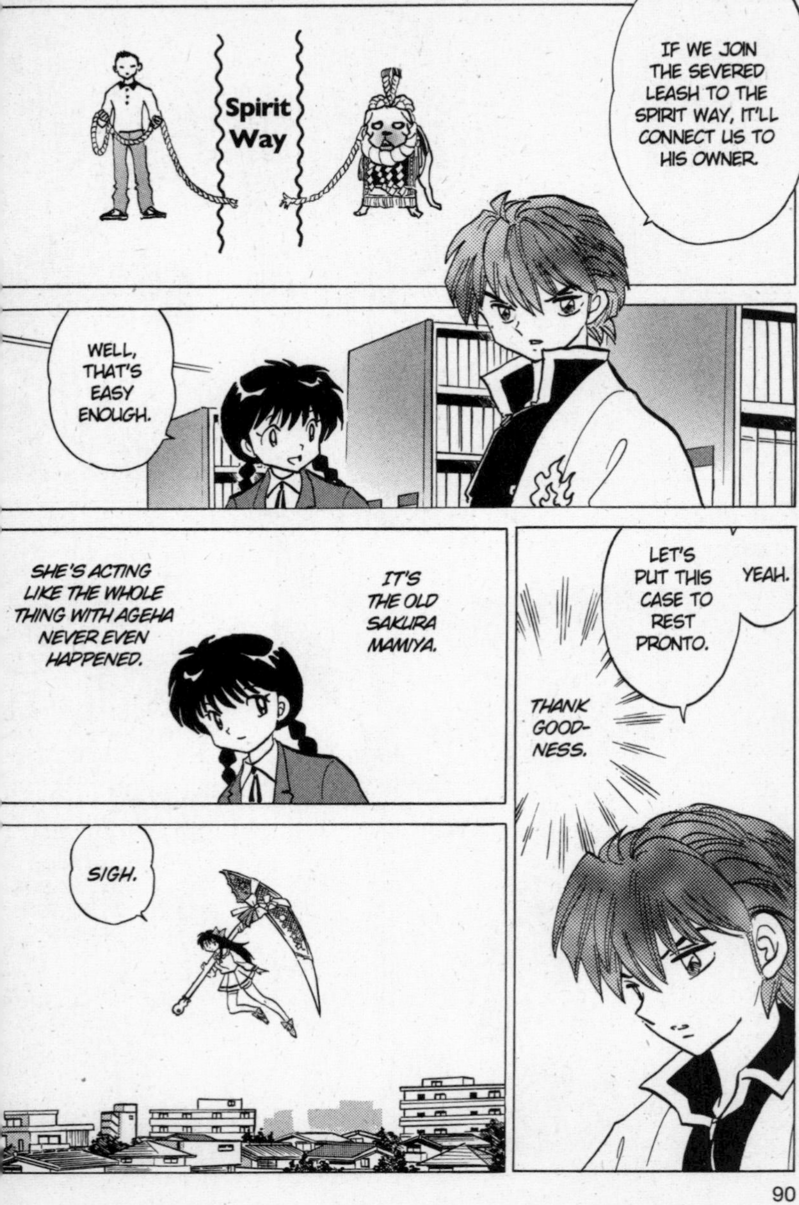

IF WE JOIN THE SEVERED LEASH TO THE SPIRIT WAY, IT'LL CONNECT US TO HIS OWNER.
Spirit Way
WELL, THAT'S EASY ENOUGH.
LET'S PUT THIS CASE TO REST PRONTO.
YEAH.
THANK GOODNESS.
IT'S THE OLD SAKURA MAMIYA.
SHE'S ACTING LIKE THE WHOLE THING WITH AGEHA NEVER EVEN HAPPENED.
SIGH.

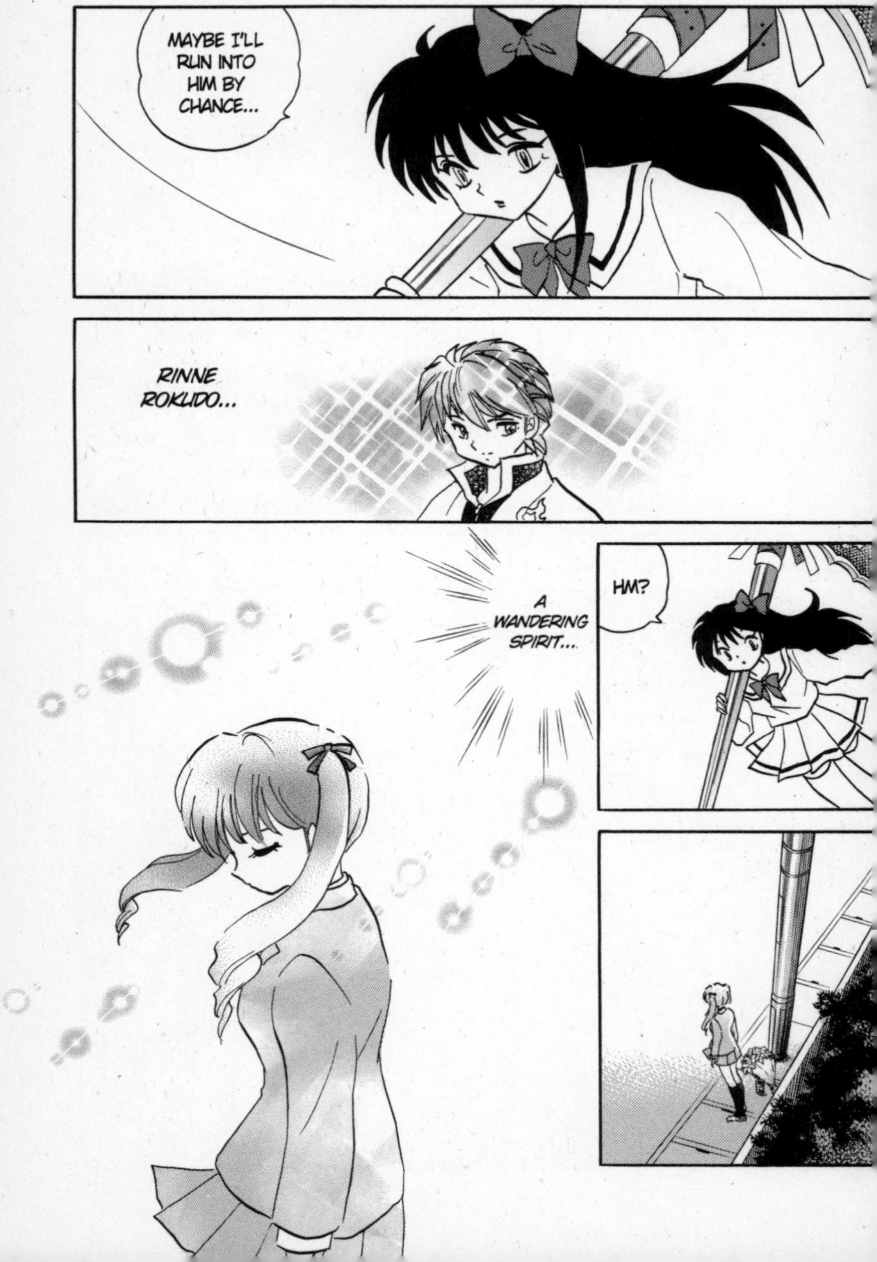
MAYBE I'LL RUN INTO HIM BY CHANCE...
RINNE ROKUDO...
HM?
A WANDERING SPIRIT...

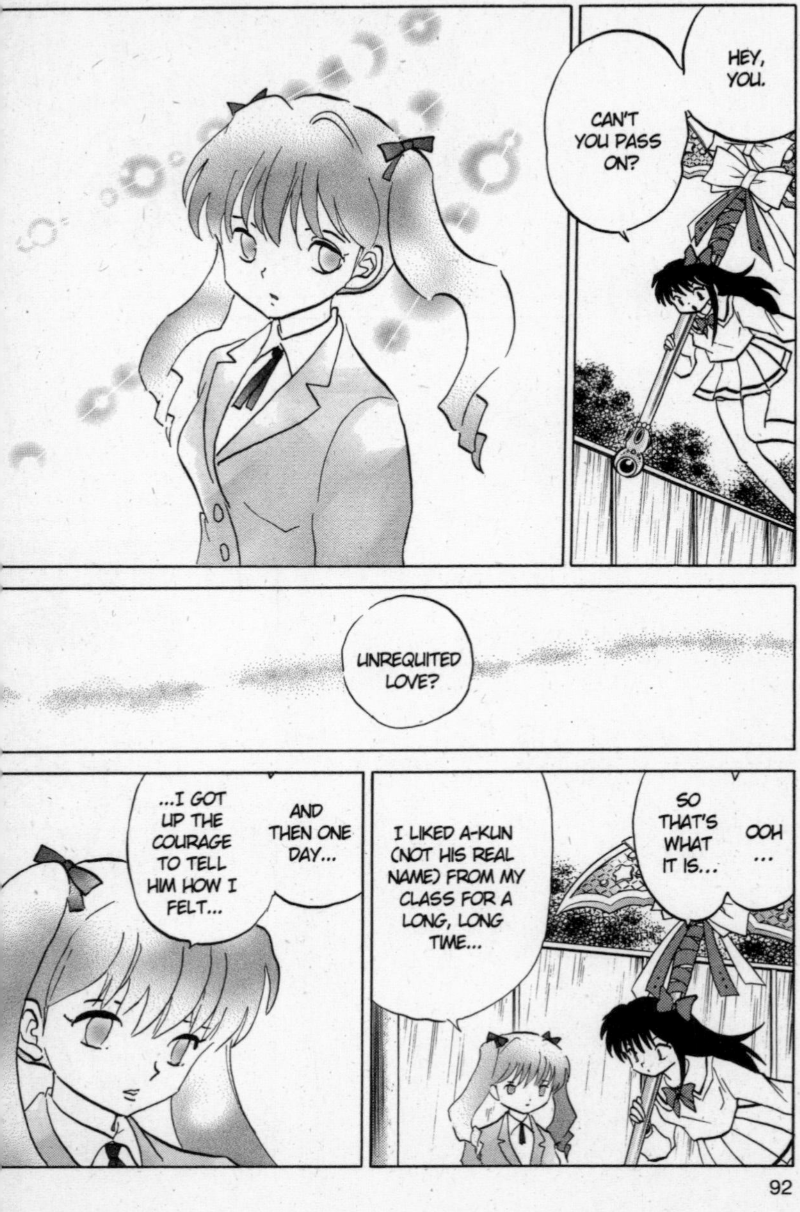
HEY, YOU.
CAN'T YOU PASS ON?
UNREQUITED LOVE?
OOH ...
SO THAT'S WHAT IT IS...
I LIKED A-KUN (NOT HIS REAL NAME) FROM MY CLASS FOR A LONG, LONG TIME...
AND THEN ONE DAY...
...I GOT UP THE COURAGE TO TELL HIM HOW I FELT...

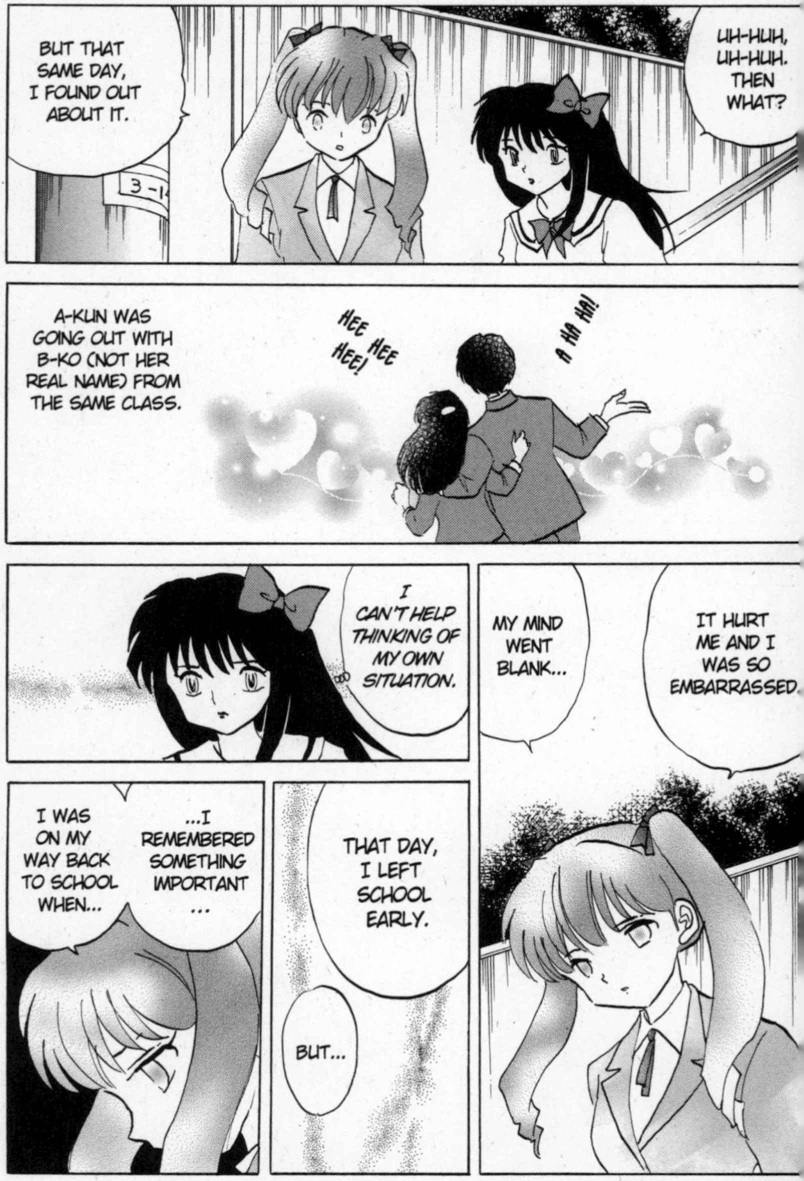
UH-HUH, UH-HUH. THEN WHAT?
BUT THAT SAME DAY, I FOUND OUT ABOUT IT.
A HA HA!
HEE HEE HEE!
A-KUN WAS GOING OUT WITH B-KO (NOT HER REAL NAME) FROM THE SAME CLASS.
IT HURT ME AND I WAS SO EMBARRASSED.
MY MIND WENT BLANK...
I CAN'T HELP THINKING OF MY OWN SITUATION.
THAT DAY, I LEFT SCHOOL EARLY.
BUT...
...I REMEMBERED SOMETHING IMPORTANT ...
I WAS ON MY WAY BACK TO SCHOOL WHEN...

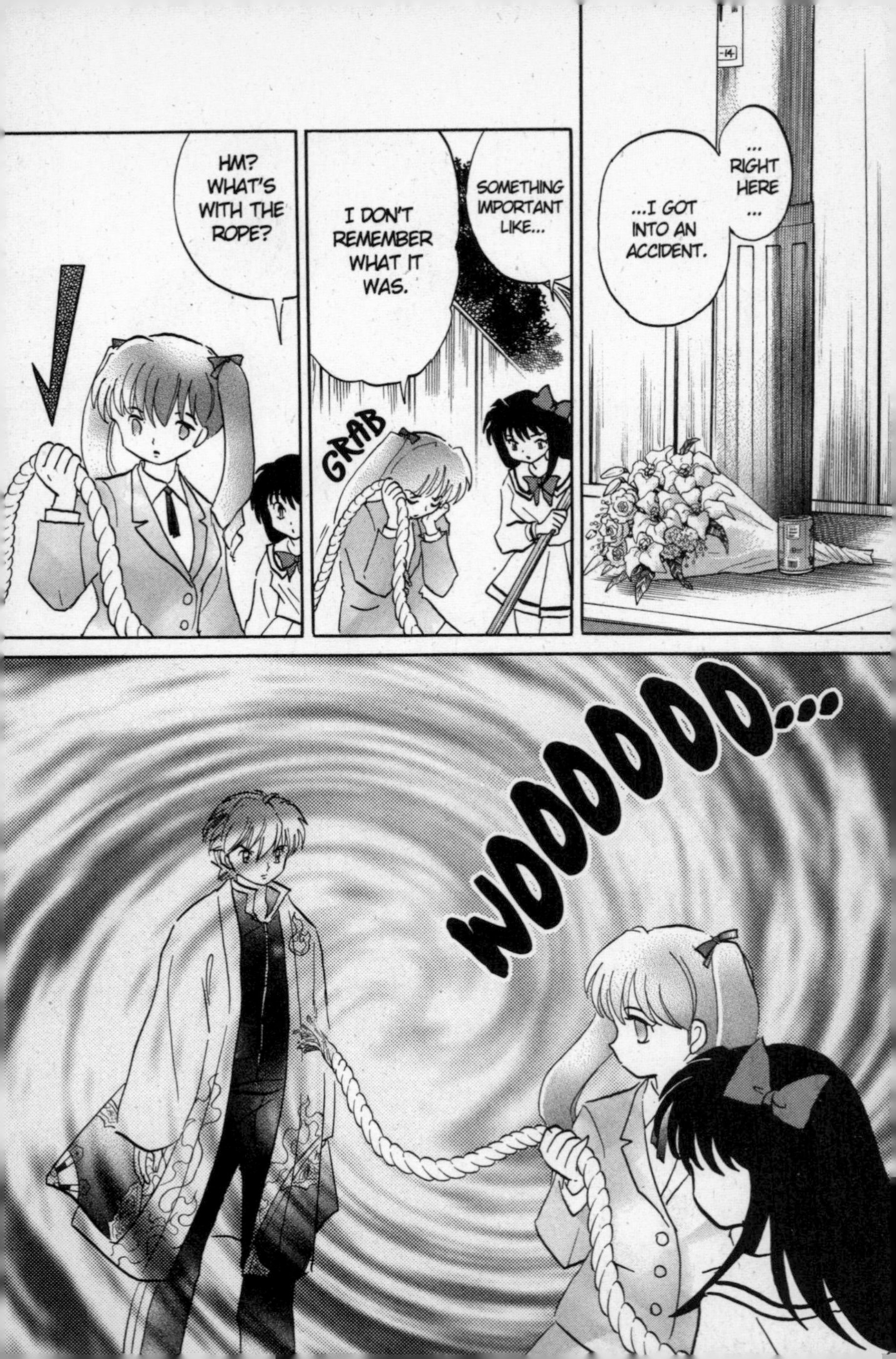
... RIGHT HERE ...
...I GOT INTO AN ACCIDENT.
SOMETHING IMPORTANT LIKE...
I DON'T REMEMBER WHAT IT WAS.
GRAB
HM? WHAT'S WITH THE ROPE?
WOOOOOO...

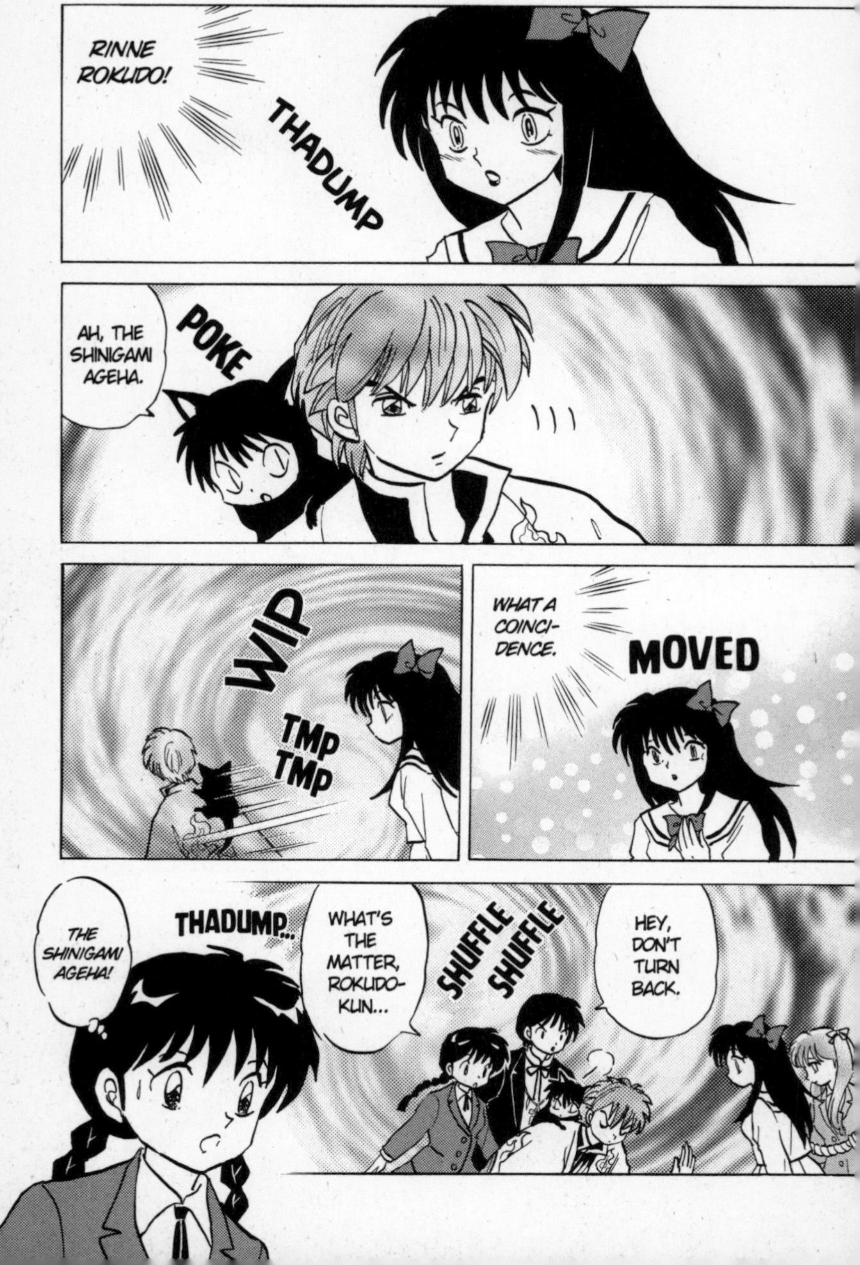
RINNE ROKUDO!
THADUMP
AH, THE SHINIGAMI AGEHA.
POKE
WHAT A COINCIDENCE.
MOVED
WIP
TMP TMP
HEY, DON'T TURN BACK.
SHUFFLE SHUFFLE
WHAT'S THE MATTER, ROKUDO-KUN...
THADUMP...
THE SHINIGAMI AGEHA!

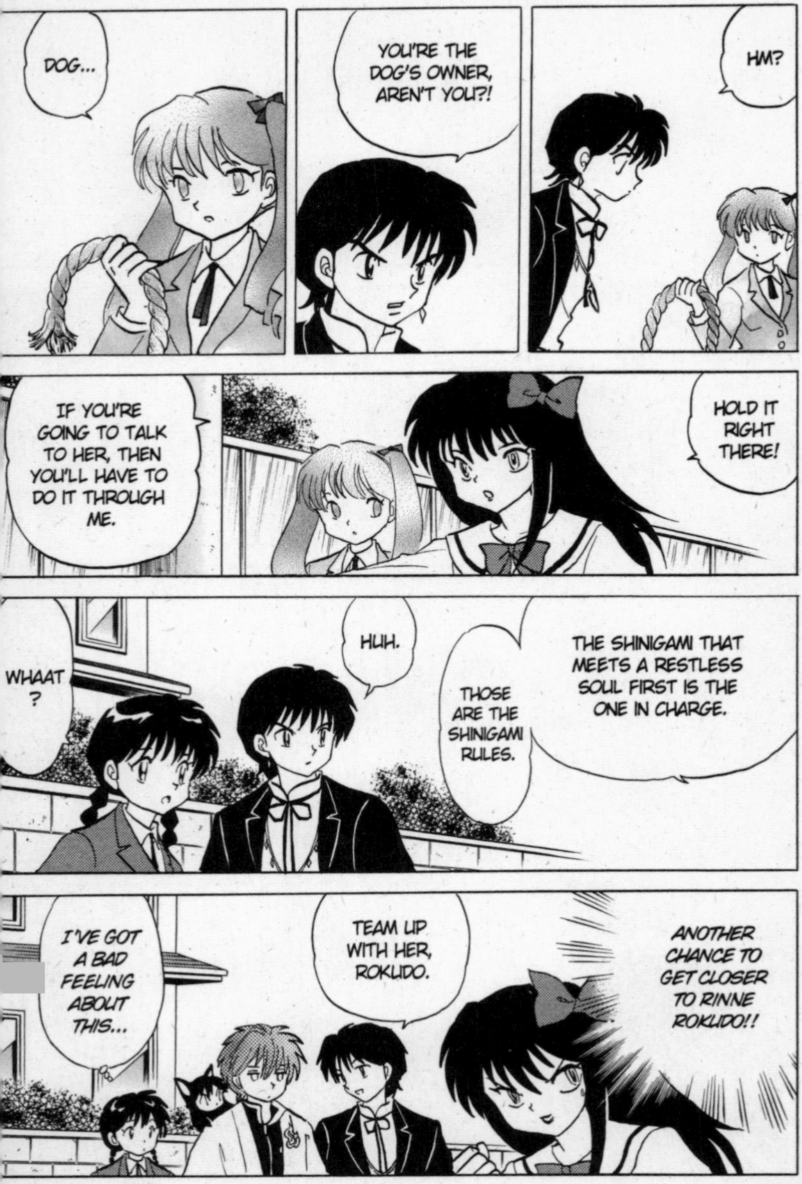
HM?
YOU'RE THE DOG'S OWNER, AREN'T YOU?!
DOG...
HOLD IT RIGHT THERE!
IF YOU'RE GOING TO TALK TO HER, THEN YOU'LL HAVE TO DO IT THROUGH ME.
THE SHINIGAMI THAT MEETS A RESTLESS SOUL FIRST IS THE ONE IN CHARGE.
THOSE ARE THE SHINIGAMI RULES.
HUH.
WHAAT?
ANOTHER CHANCE TO GET CLOSER TO RINNE ROKUDO!!
TEAM UP WITH HER, ROKUDO.
I'VE GOT A BAD FEELING ABOUT THIS...

CHAPTER 44: ROSES AND SOY SAUCE

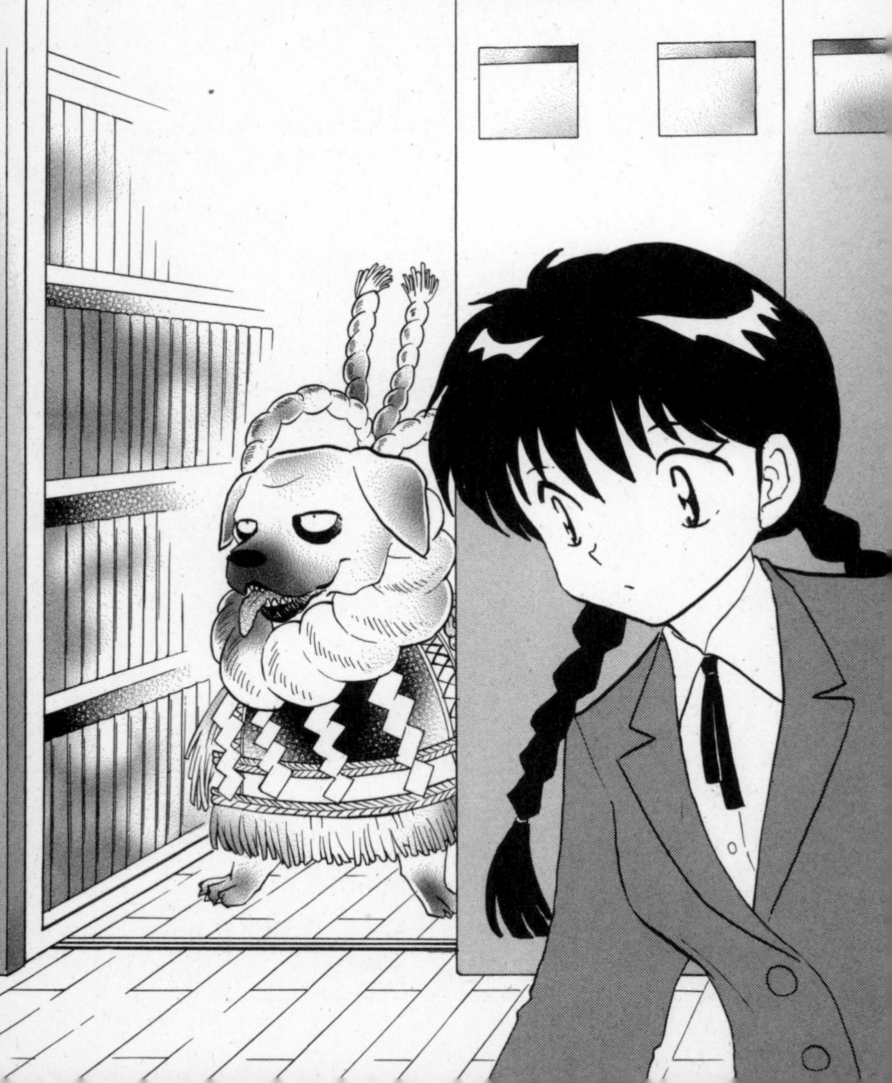

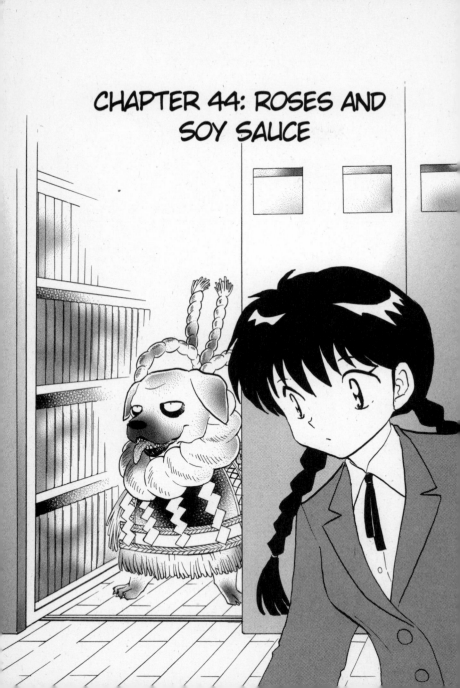

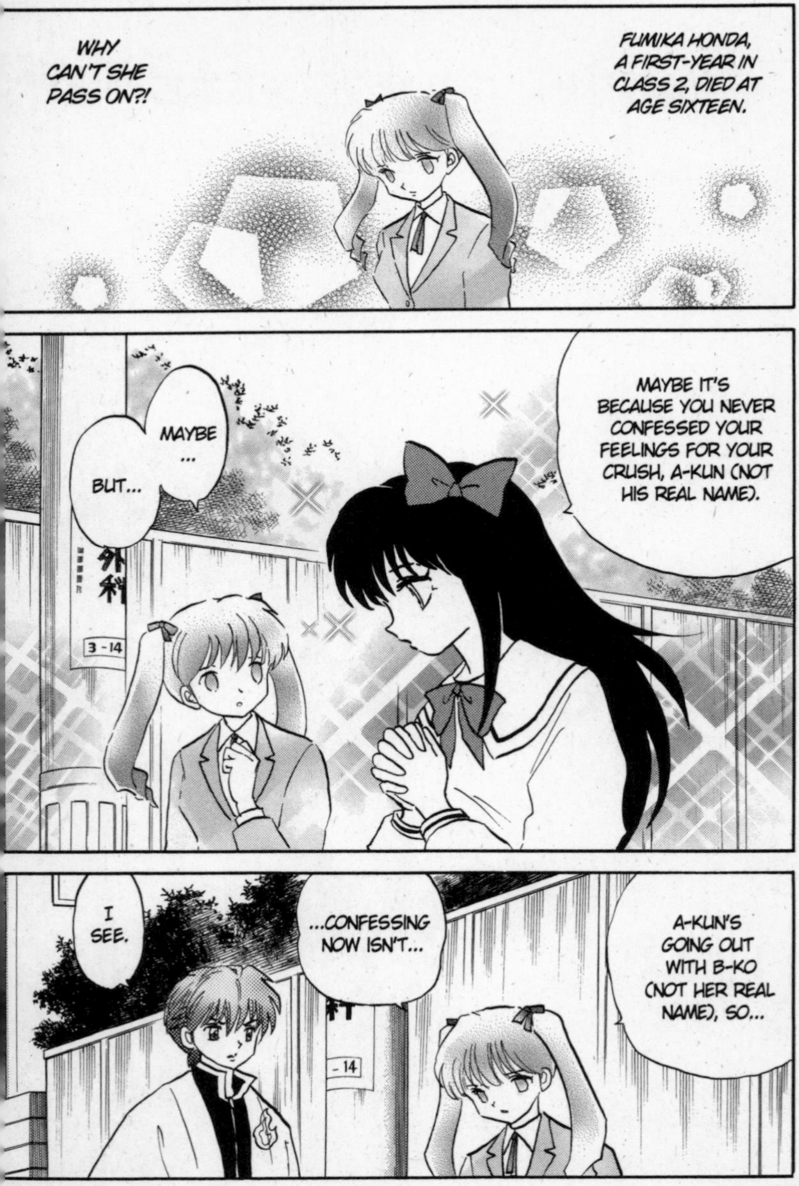
FUMIKA HONDA, A FIRST-YEAR IN CLASS 2, DIED AT AGE SIXTEEN.
WHY CAN'T SHE PASS ON?!
MAYBE IT'S BECAUSE YOU NEVER CONFESSED YOUR FEELINGS FOR YOUR CRUSH, A-KUN (NOT HIS REAL NAME).
MAYBE ... BUT...
A-KUN'S GOING OUT WITH B-KO (NOT HER REAL NAME), SO...
...CONFESSING NOW ISN'T...
I SEE.

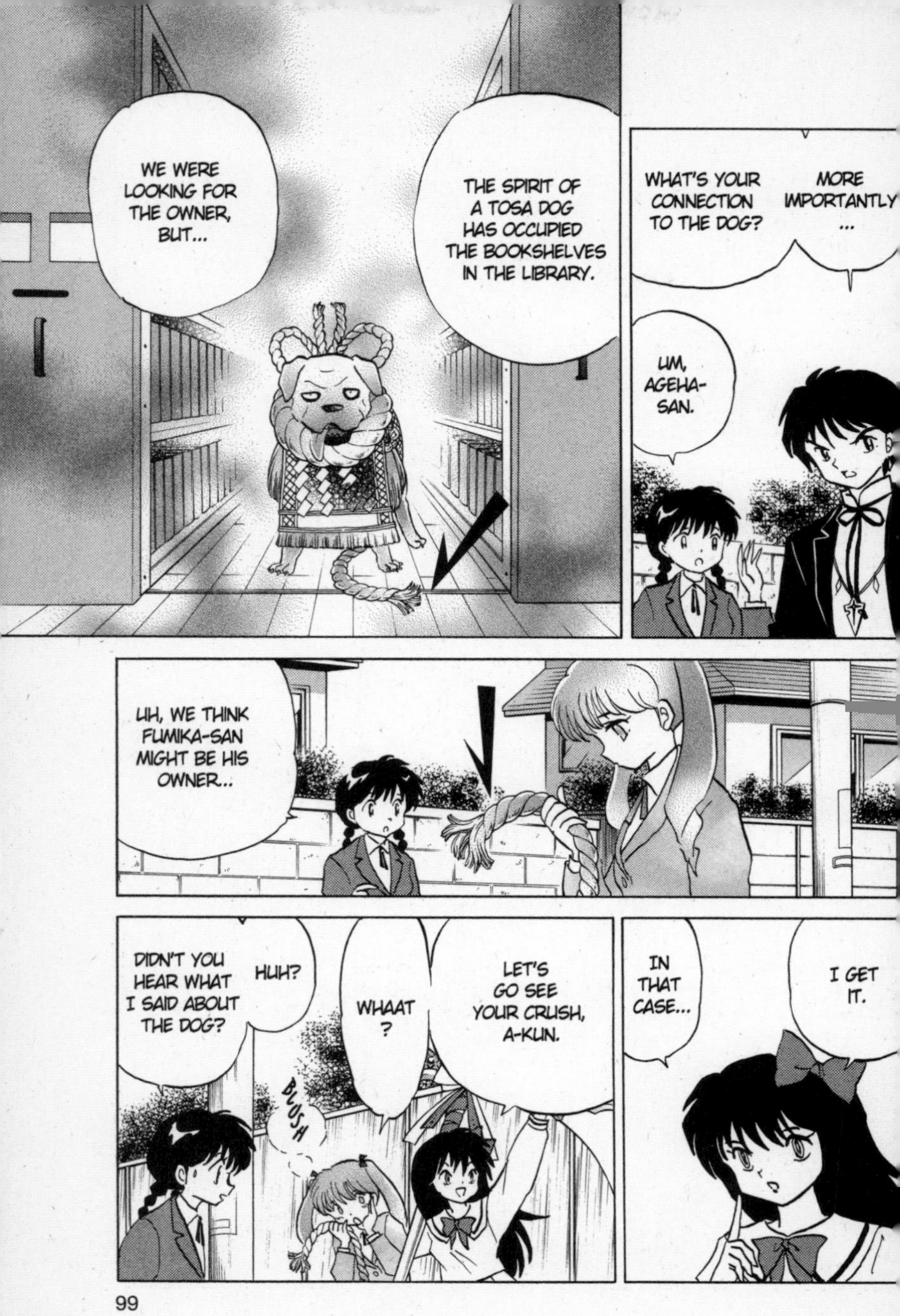
MORE IMPORTANTLY ...
WHAT'S YOUR CONNECTION TO THE DOG?
UM, AGEHA-SAN.
THE SPIRIT OF A TOSA DOG HAS OCCUPIED THE BOOKSHELVES IN THE LIBRARY.
WE WERE LOOKING FOR THE OWNER, BUT...
UH, WE THINK FUMIKA-SAN MIGHT BE HIS OWNER...
I GET IT.
IN THAT CASE...
LET'S GO SEE YOUR CRUSH, A-KUN.
WHAAT?
BLUSH
HUH?
DIDN'T YOU HEAR WHAT I SAID ABOUT THE DOG?

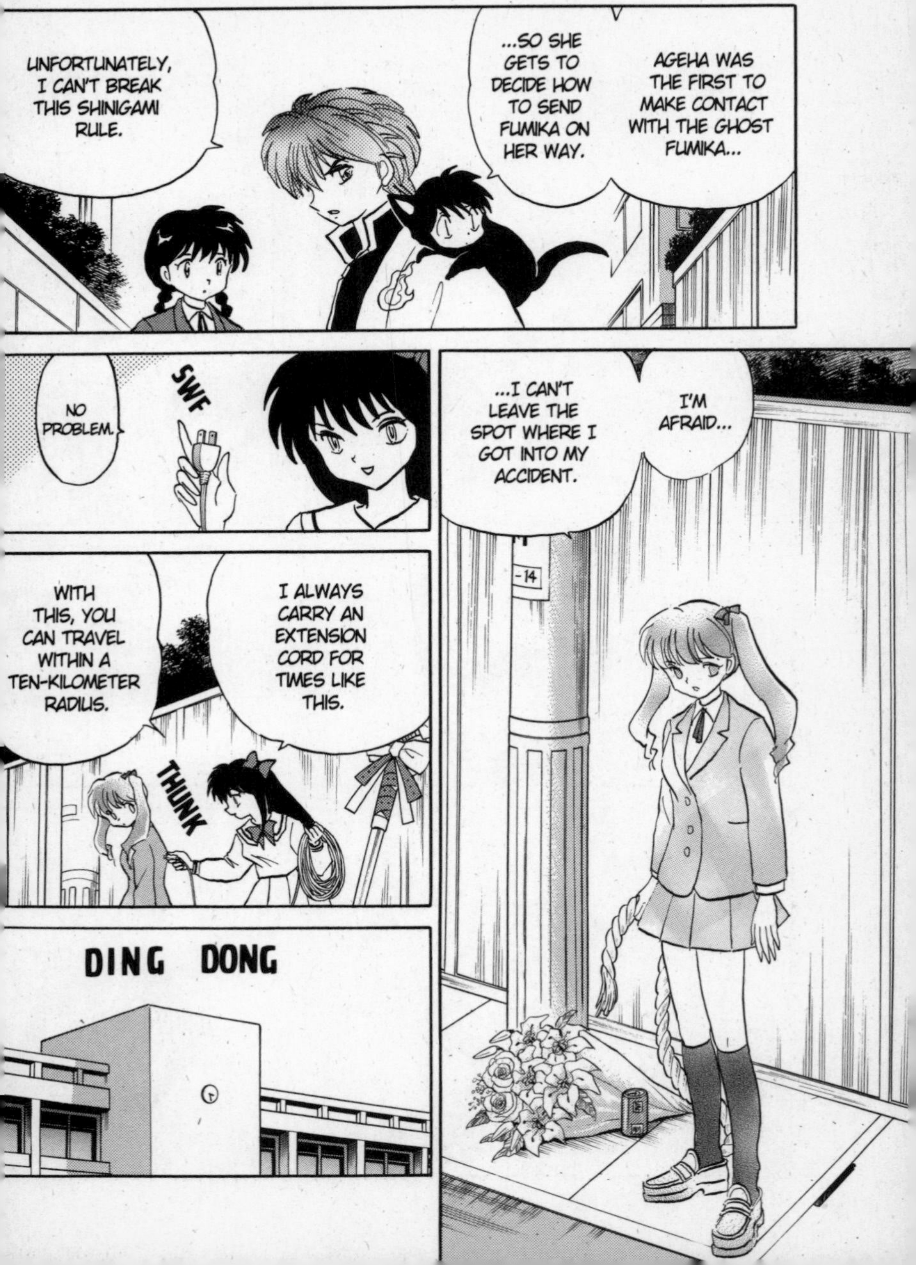
AGEHA WAS THE FIRST TO MAKE CONTACT WITH THE GHOST FUMIKA...
...SO SHE GETS TO DECIDE HOW TO SEND FUMIKA ON HER WAY.
UNFORTUNATELY, I CAN'T BREAK THIS SHINIGAMI RULE.
I'M AFRAID...
...I CAN'T LEAVE THE SPOT WHERE I GOT INTO MY ACCIDENT.
-14
SWF
NO PROBLEM.
I ALWAYS CARRY AN EXTENSION CORD FOR TIMES LIKE THIS.
WITH THIS, YOU CAN TRAVEL WITHIN A TEN-KILOMETER RADIUS.
THUNK
DING DONG

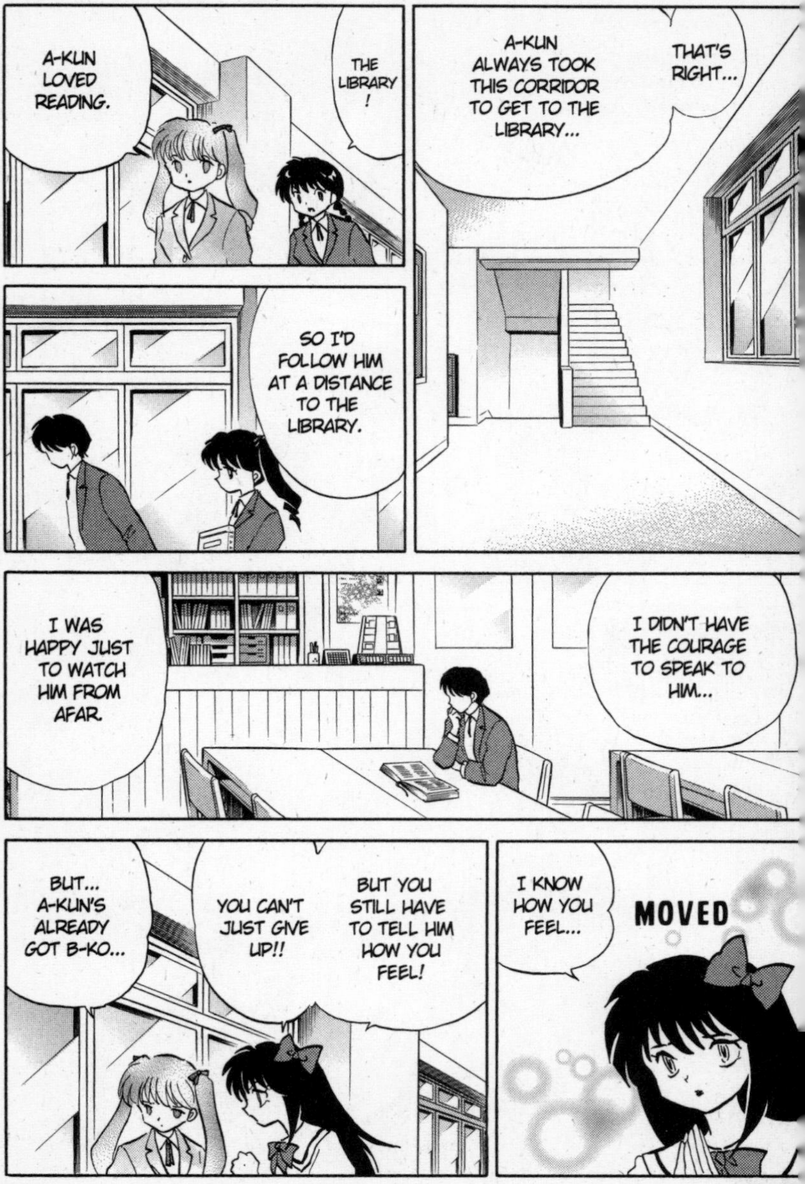
THAT'S RIGHT...
A-KUN ALWAYS TOOK THIS CORRIDOR TO GET TO THE LIBRARY...
THE LIBRARY!
A-KUN LOVED READING.
SO I'D FOLLOW HIM AT A DISTANCE TO THE LIBRARY.
I DIDN'T HAVE THE COURAGE TO SPEAK TO HIM...
I WAS HAPPY JUST TO WATCH HIM FROM AFAR.
I KNOW HOW YOU FEEL...
MOVED
YOU CAN'T JUST GIVE UP!!
BUT YOU STILL HAVE TO TELL HIM HOW YOU FEEL!
BUT... A-KUN'S ALREADY GOT B-KO...

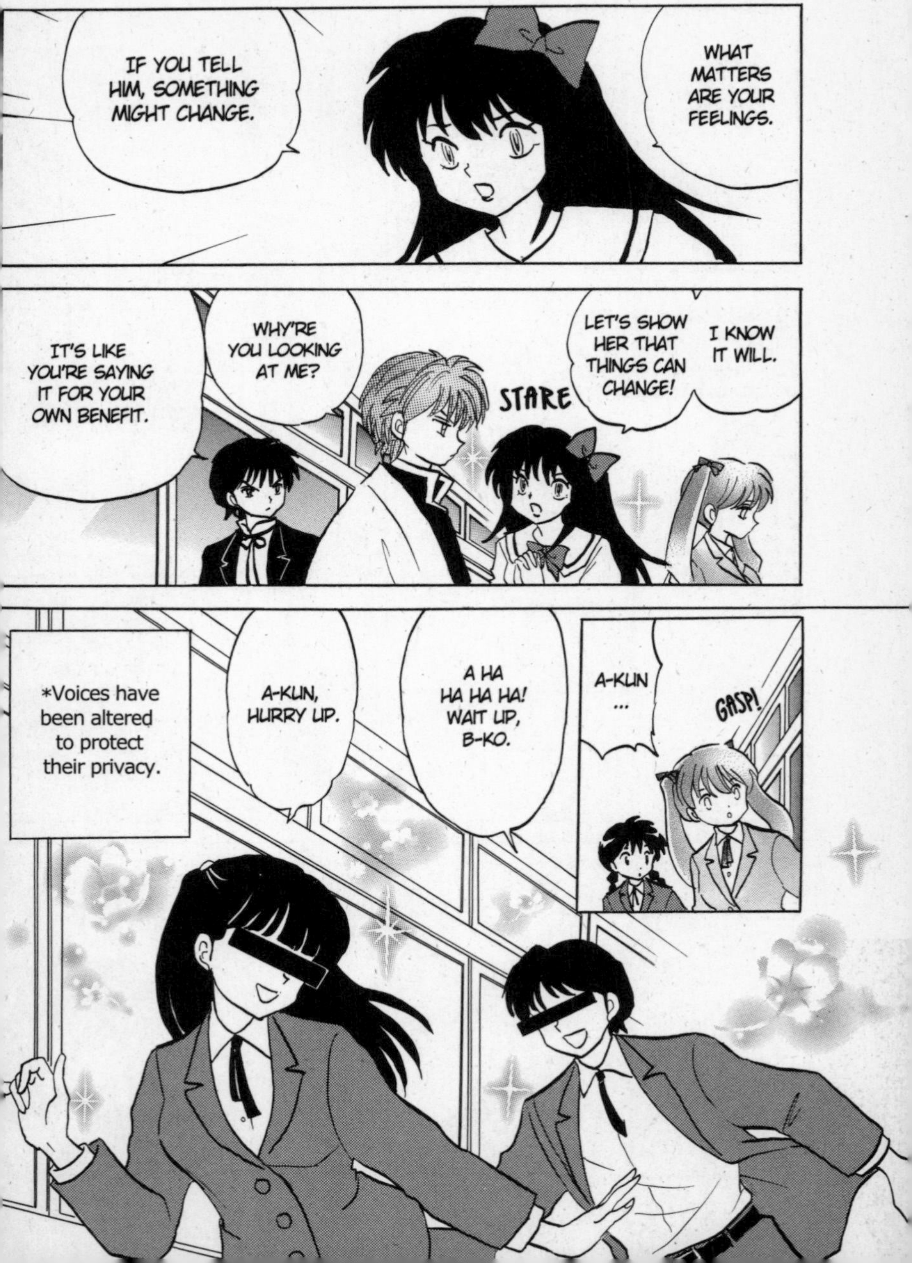
WHAT MATTERS ARE YOUR FEELINGS.
IF YOU TELL HIM, SOMETHING MIGHT CHANGE.
I KNOW IT WILL.
LET'S SHOW HER THAT THINGS CAN CHANGE!
STARE
WHY'RE YOU LOOKING AT ME?
IT'S LIKE YOU'RE SAYING IT FOR YOUR OWN BENEFIT.
GASP!
A-KUN ...
A HA HA HA HA! WAIT UP, B-KO.
A-KUN, HURRY UP.
*Voices have been altered to protect their privacy.

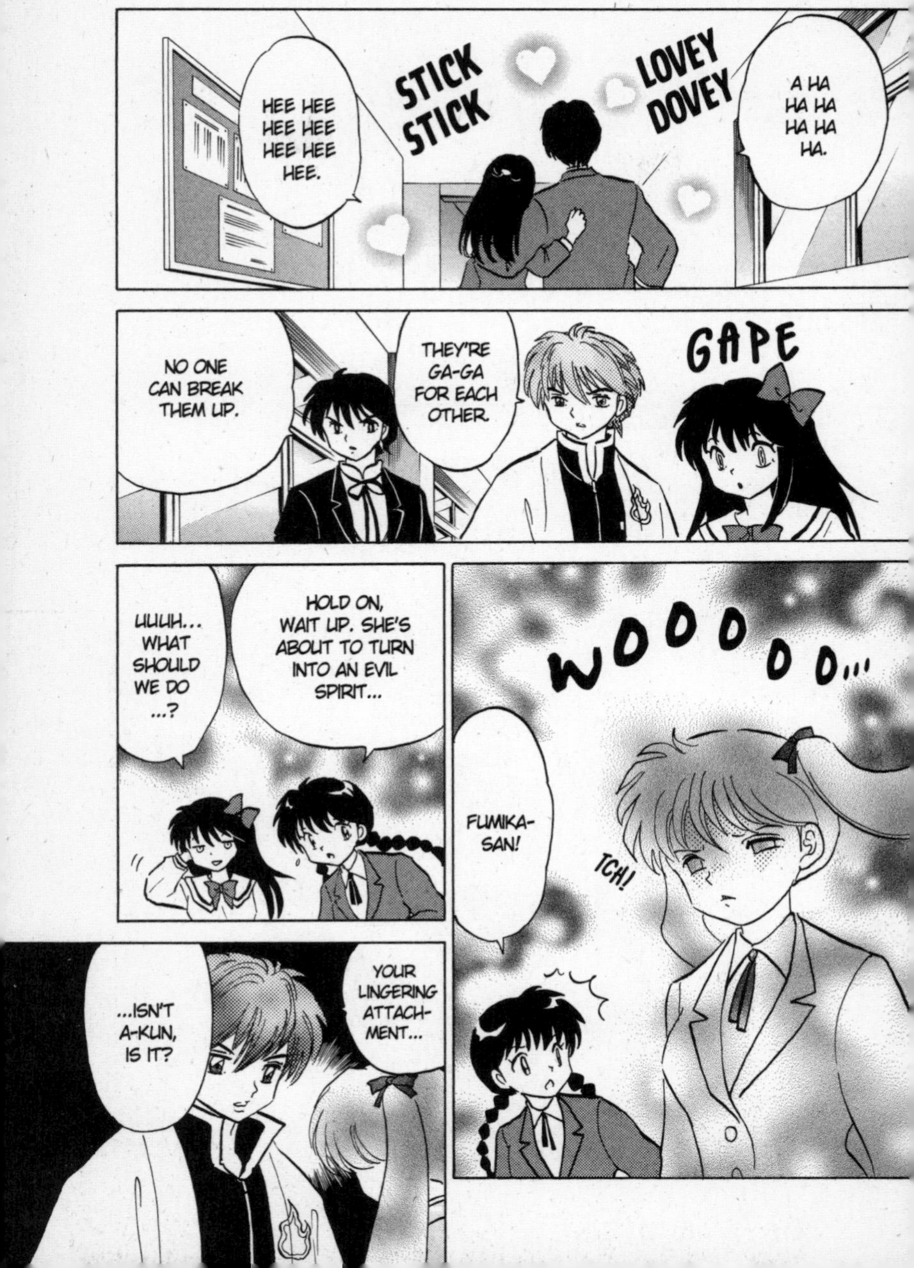
A HA HA HA HA HA HA.
LOVEY DOVEY
STICK STICK
HEE HEE HEE HEE HEE HEE HEE.
GAPE
THEY'RE GA-GA FOR EACH OTHER.
NO ONE CAN BREAK THEM UP.
WOOOOO...
FUMIKA-SAN!
TCH!
HOLD ON, WAIT UP. SHE'S ABOUT TO TURN INTO AN EVIL SPIRIT...
UUUH... WHAT SHOULD WE DO ...?
YOUR LINGERING ATTACHMENT...
...ISN'T A-KUN, IS IT?

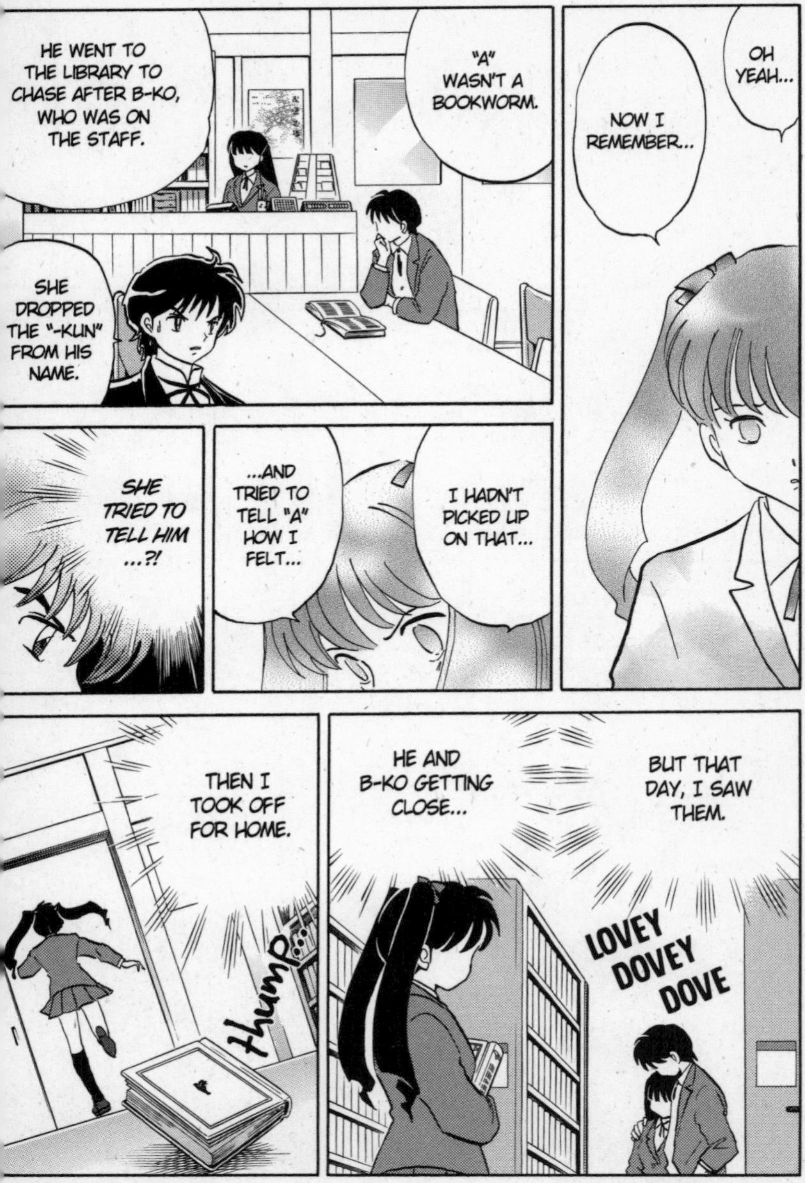

OH YEAH...
NOW I REMEMBER...
"A" WASN'T A BOOKWORM.
HE WENT TO THE LIBRARY TO CHASE AFTER B-KO, WHO WAS ON THE STAFF.
SHE DROPPED THE "-KUN" FROM HIS NAME.
I HADN'T PICKED UP ON THAT...
...AND TRIED TO TELL "A" HOW I FELT...
SHE TRIED TO TELL HIM ...?!
BUT THAT DAY, I SAW THEM.
HE AND B-KO GETTING CLOSE...
LOVEY DOVEY DOVE
THEN I TOOK OFF FOR HOME.
THUMP

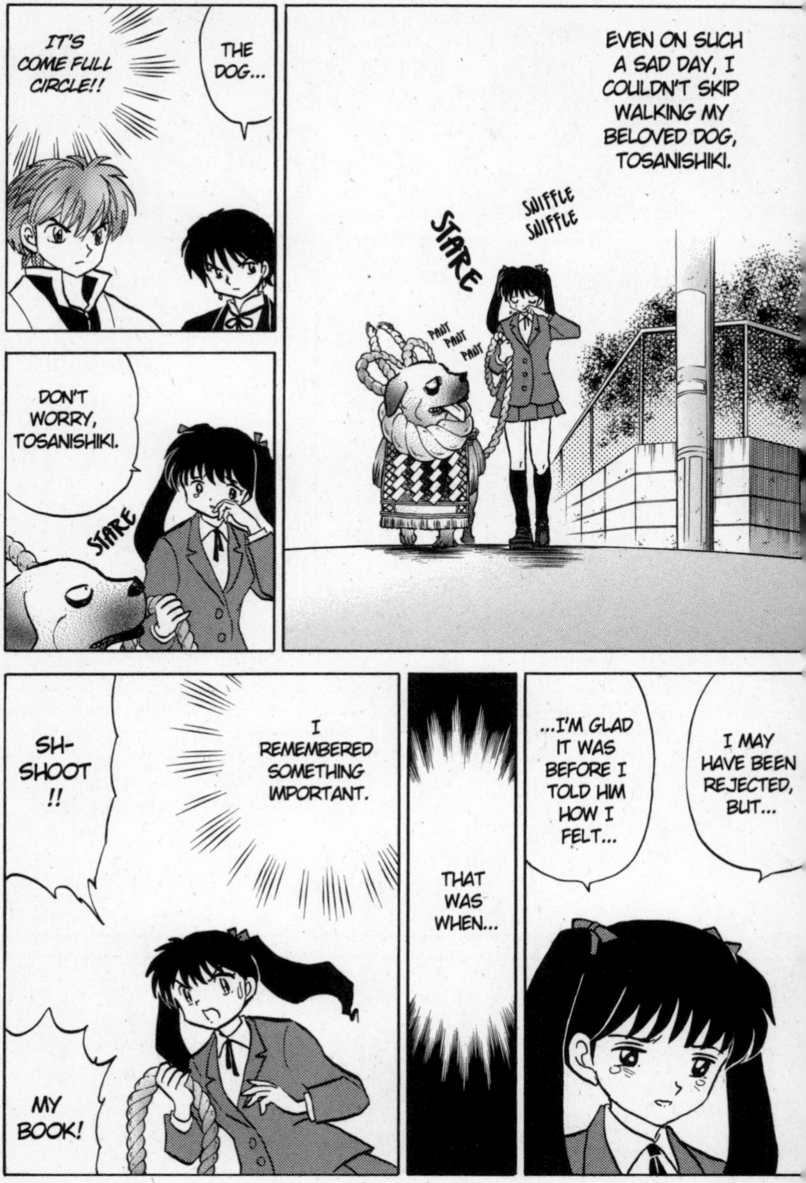
EVEN ON SUCH A SAD DAY, I COULDN'T SKIP WALKING MY BELOVED DOG, TOSANISHIKI.
SNIFFLE SNIFFLE
STARE
PANT PANT PANT
THE DOG...
IT'S COME FULL CIRCLE!!
DON'T WORRY, TOSANISHIKI.
STARE
I MAY HAVE BEEN REJECTED, BUT...
...I'M GLAD IT WAS BEFORE I TOLD HIM HOW I FELT...
THAT WAS WHEN...
I REMEMBERED SOMETHING IMPORTANT.
SH-SHOOT!!
MY BOOK!

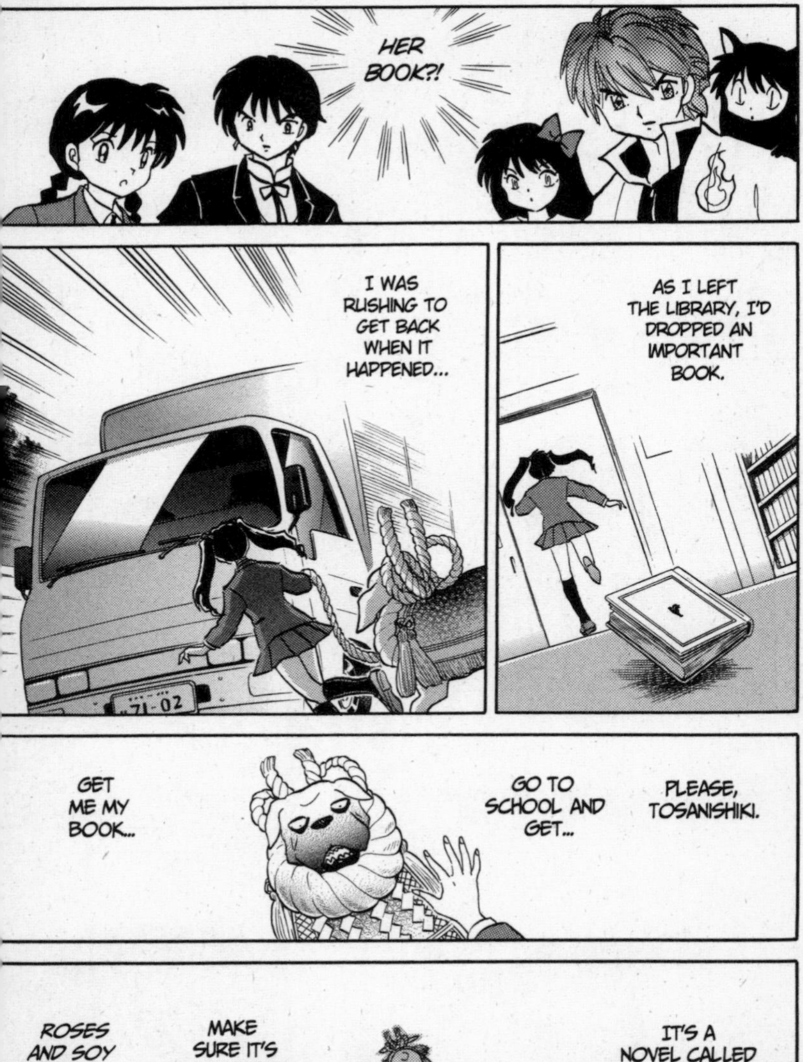
HER BOOK?!
AS I LEFT THE LIBRARY, I'D DROPPED AN IMPORTANT BOOK.
I WAS RUSHING TO GET BACK WHEN IT HAPPENED...
PLEASE, TOSANISHIKI.
GO TO SCHOOL AND GET...
GET ME MY BOOK...
IT'S A NOVEL CALLED ROSES AND SOY SAUCE.
MAKE SURE IT'S THE RIGHT BOOK...
ROSES AND SOY SAUCE...

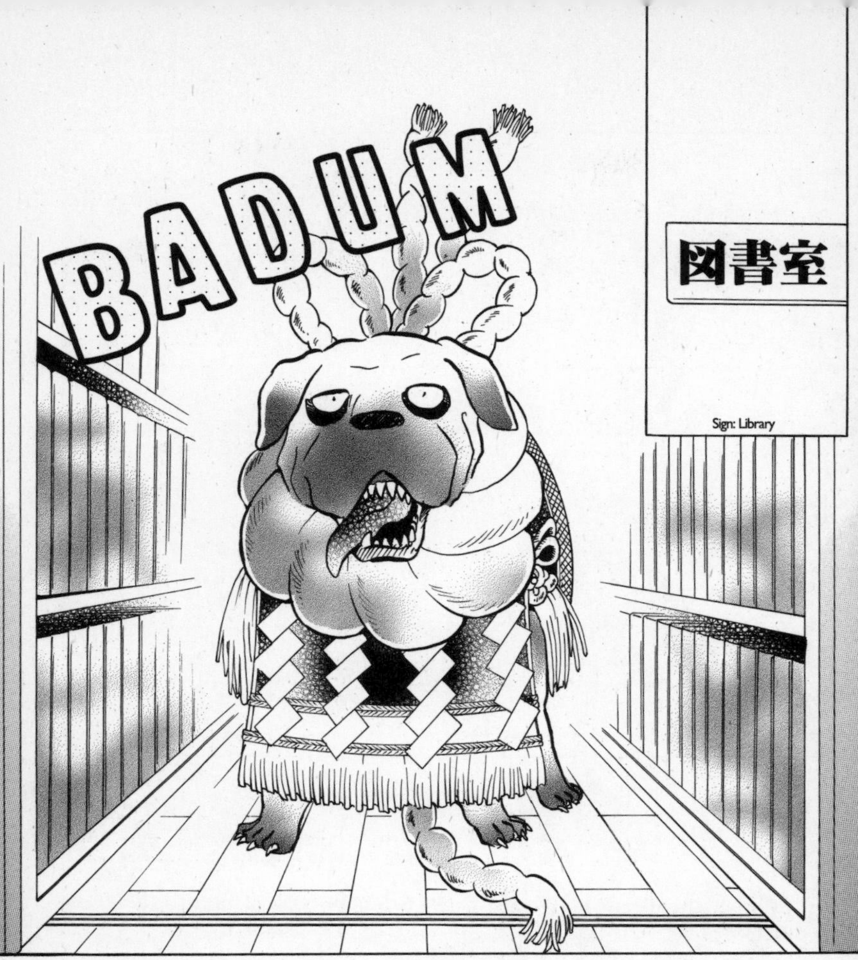
図書室
Sign: Library
BADUM
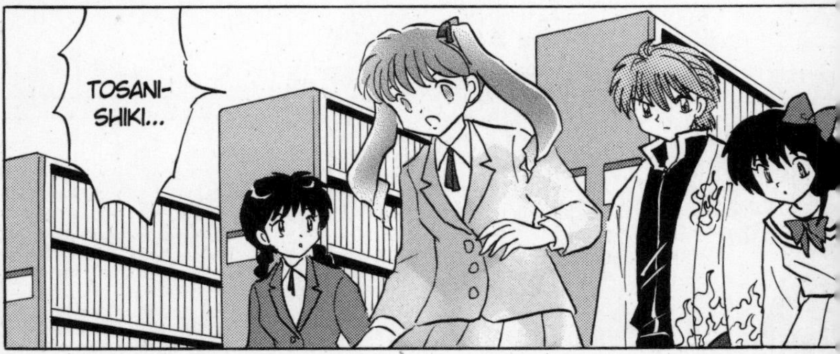
TOSANI-
SHIKI...

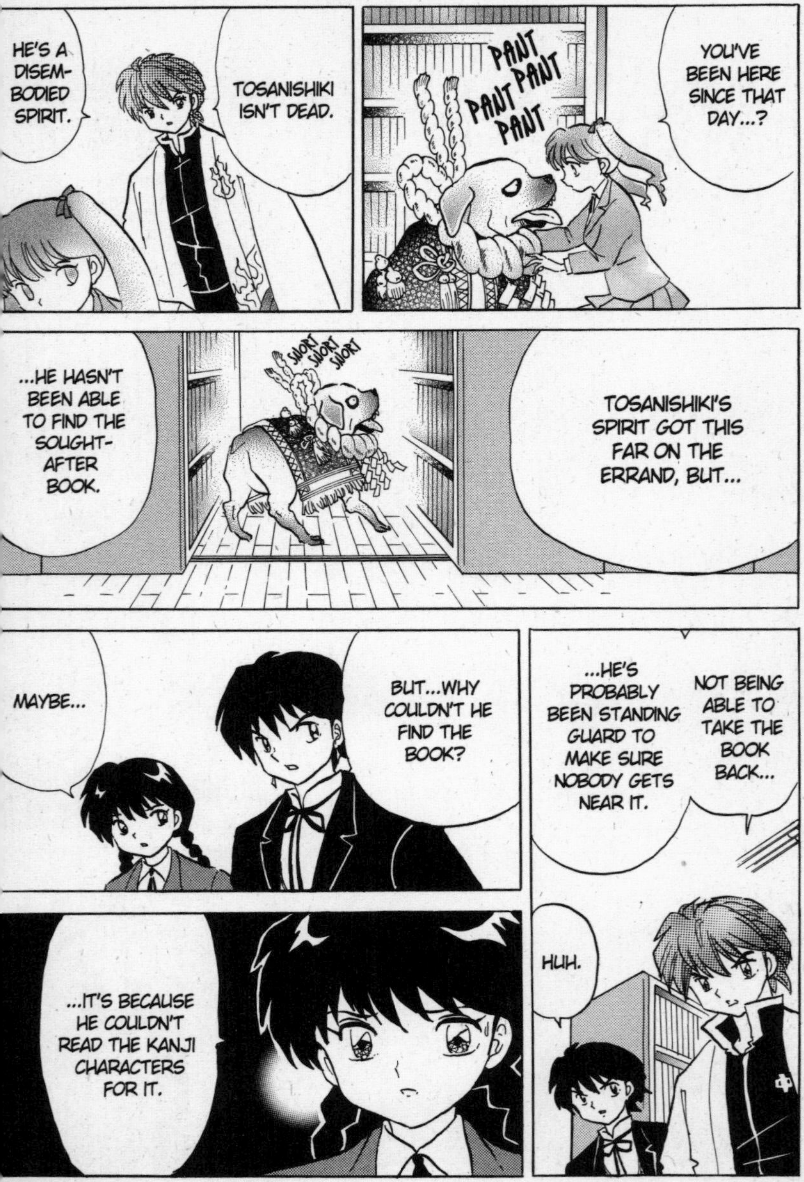

YOU'VE BEEN HERE SINCE THAT DAY...?
PANT PANT PANT PANT
TOSANISHIKI ISN'T DEAD.
HE'S A DISEMBODIED SPIRIT.
TOSANISHIKI'S SPIRIT GOT THIS FAR ON THE ERRAND, BUT...
SNORT SNORT SNORT
...HE HASN'T BEEN ABLE TO FIND THE SOUGHT-AFTER BOOK.
NOT BEING ABLE TO TAKE THE BOOK BACK...
...HE'S PROBABLY BEEN STANDING GUARD TO MAKE SURE NOBODY GETS NEAR IT.
BUT...WHY COULDN'T HE FIND THE BOOK?
MAYBE...
...IT'S BECAUSE HE COULDN'T READ THE KANJI CHARACTERS FOR IT.
HUH.

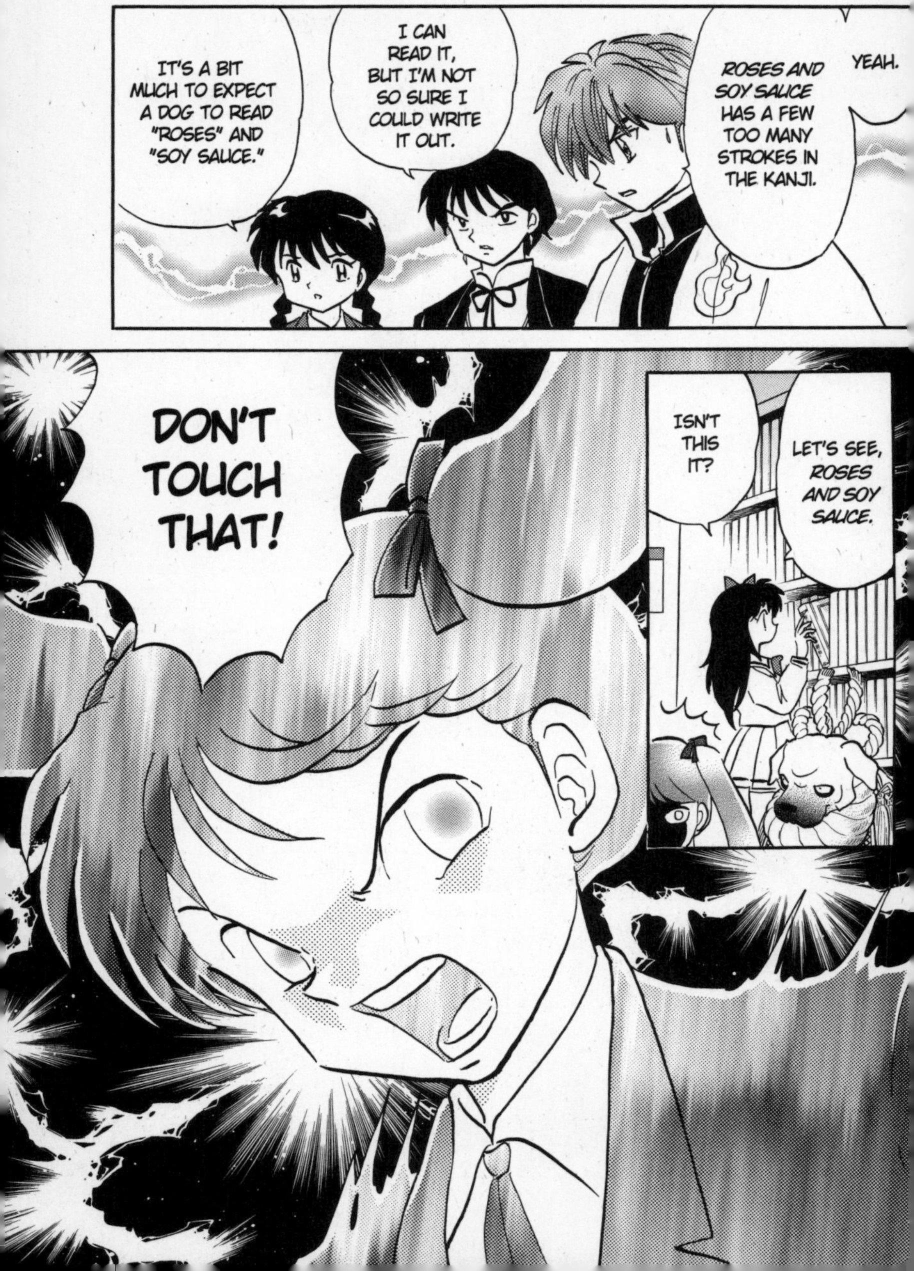
YEAH.
ROSES AND SOY SAUCE HAS A FEW TOO MANY STROKES IN THE KANJI.
I CAN READ IT, BUT I'M NOT SO SURE I COULD WRITE IT OUT.
IT'S A BIT MUCH TO EXPECT A DOG TO READ "ROSES" AND "SOY SAUCE."
LET'S SEE, ROSES AND SOY SAUCE.
ISN'T THIS IT?
DON'T TOUCH THAT!

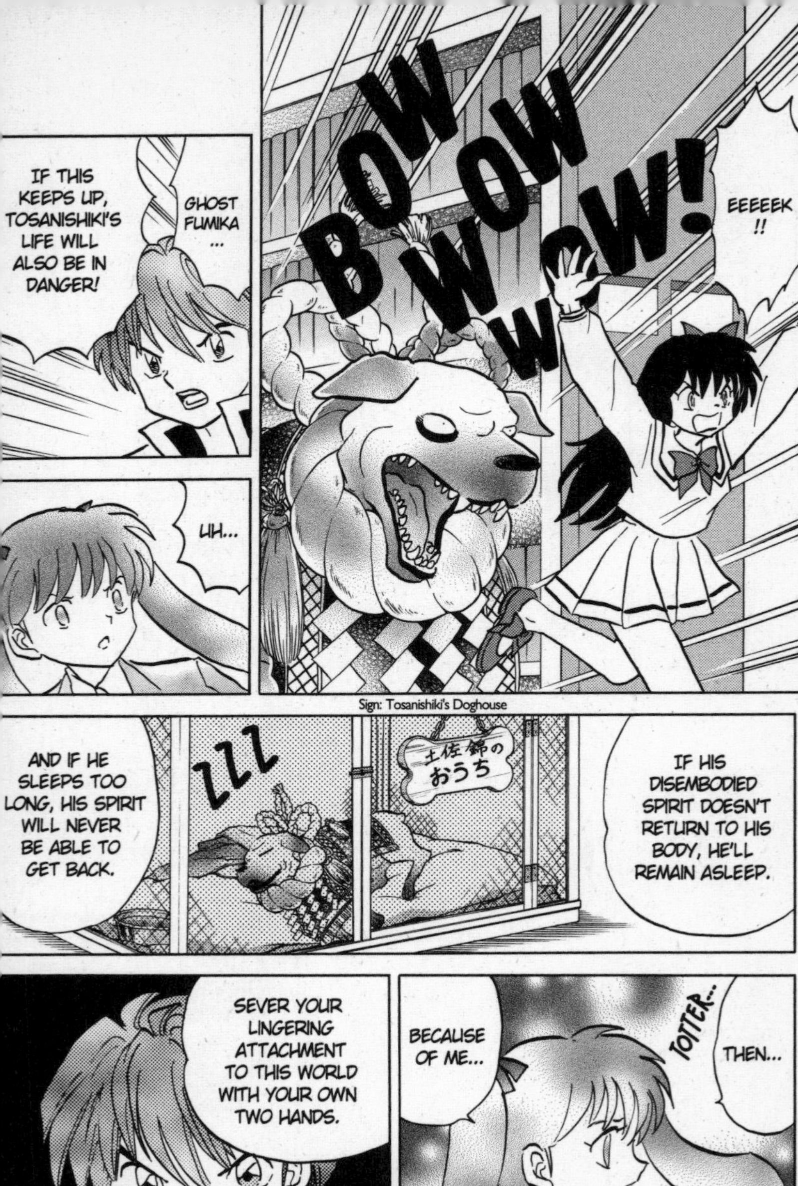
BOW WOW WOW!
EEEEEK !!
GHOST FUMIKA ...
IF THIS KEEPS UP, TOSANISHIKI'S LIFE WILL ALSO BE IN DANGER!
UH...
Sign: Tosanishiki's Doghouse
IF HIS DISEMBODIED SPIRIT DOESN'T RETURN TO HIS BODY, HE'LL REMAIN ASLEEP.
土佐錦のおうち
ZZZ
AND IF HE SLEEPS TOO LONG, HIS SPIRIT WILL NEVER BE ABLE TO GET BACK.
THEN...
TOTTER...
BECAUSE OF ME...
SEVER YOUR LINGERING ATTACHMENT TO THIS WORLD WITH YOUR OWN TWO HANDS.

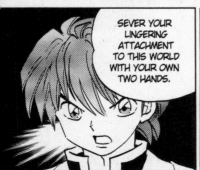

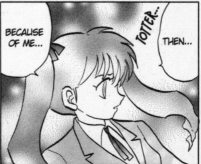

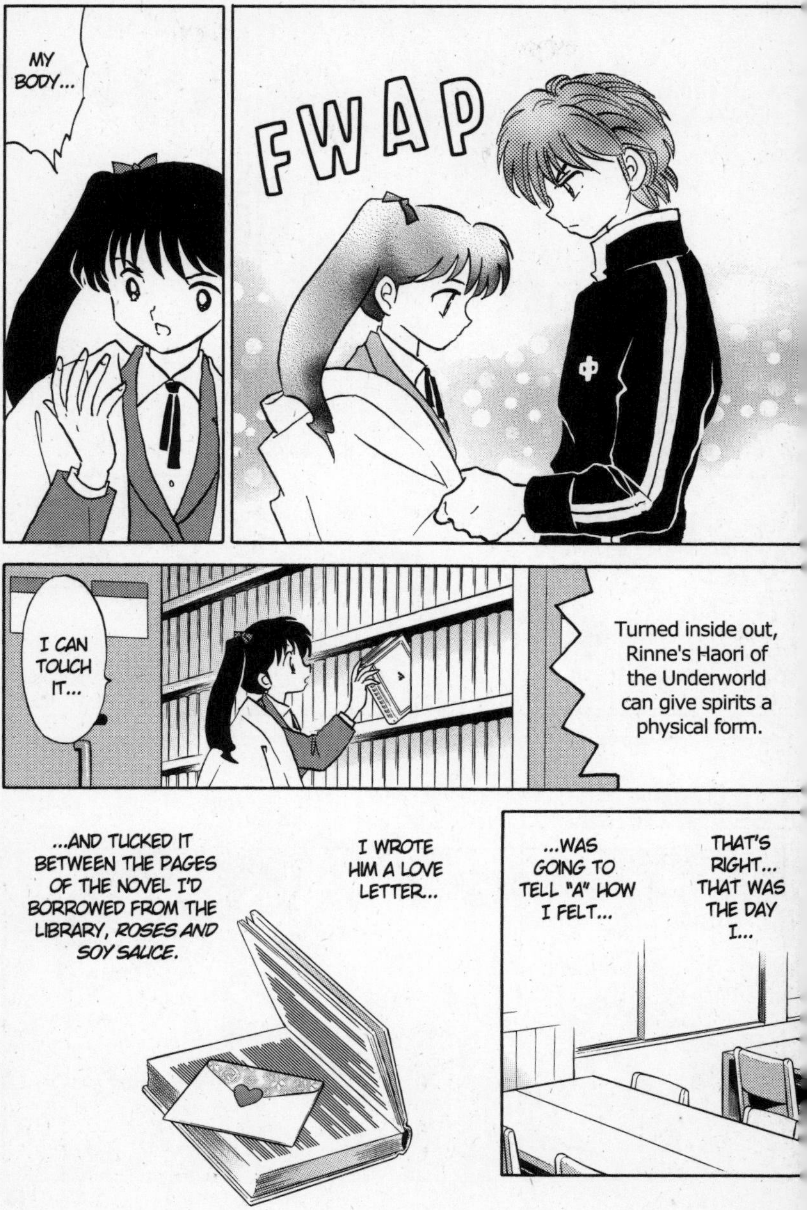
FWAP
MY BODY...
Turned inside out, Rinne's Haori of the Underworld can give spirits a physical form.
I CAN TOUCH IT...
THAT'S RIGHT... THAT WAS THE DAY I...
...WAS GOING TO TELL "A" HOW I FELT...
I WROTE HIM A LOVE LETTER...
...AND TUCKED IT BETWEEN THE PAGES OF THE NOVEL I'D BORROWED FROM THE LIBRARY, *ROSES AND SOY SAUCE*.

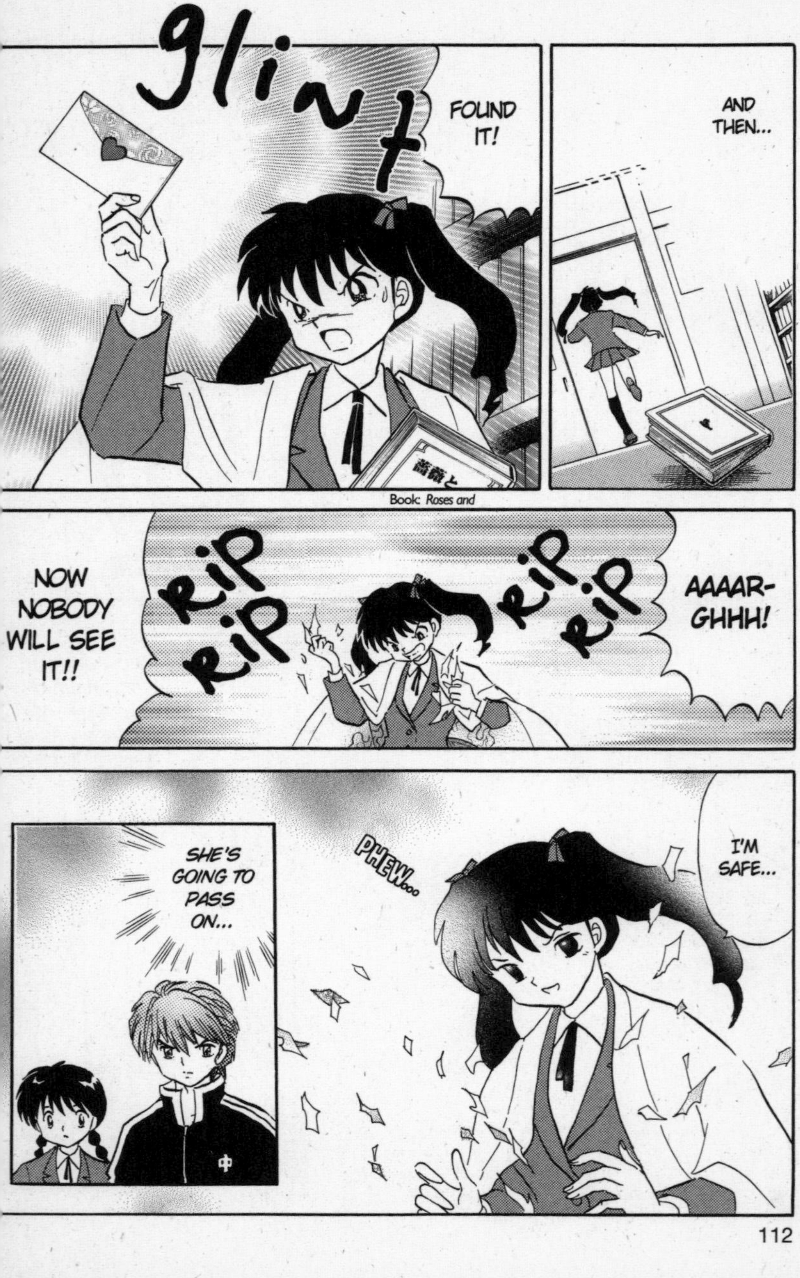
AND THEN...
glint
FOUND IT!
Book: Roses and
AAAAR-GHHH!
RIP RIP
RIP RIP
NOW NOBODY WILL SEE IT!!
I'M SAFE...
PHEW...
SHE'S GOING TO PASS ON...

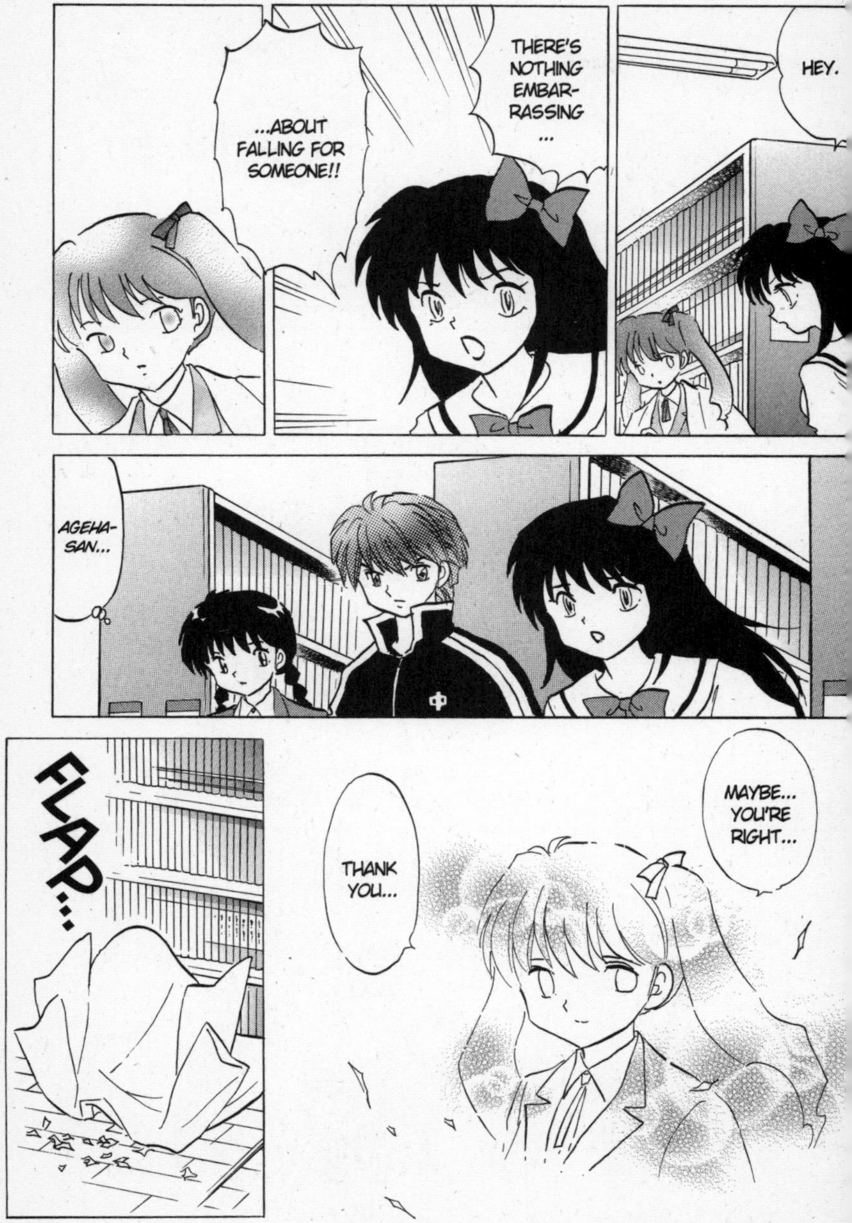
HEY.
THERE'S NOTHING EMBAR-RASSING ...
...ABOUT FALLING FOR SOMEONE!!
AGEHA-SAN...
MAYBE... YOU'RE RIGHT...
THANK YOU...
FLAP...

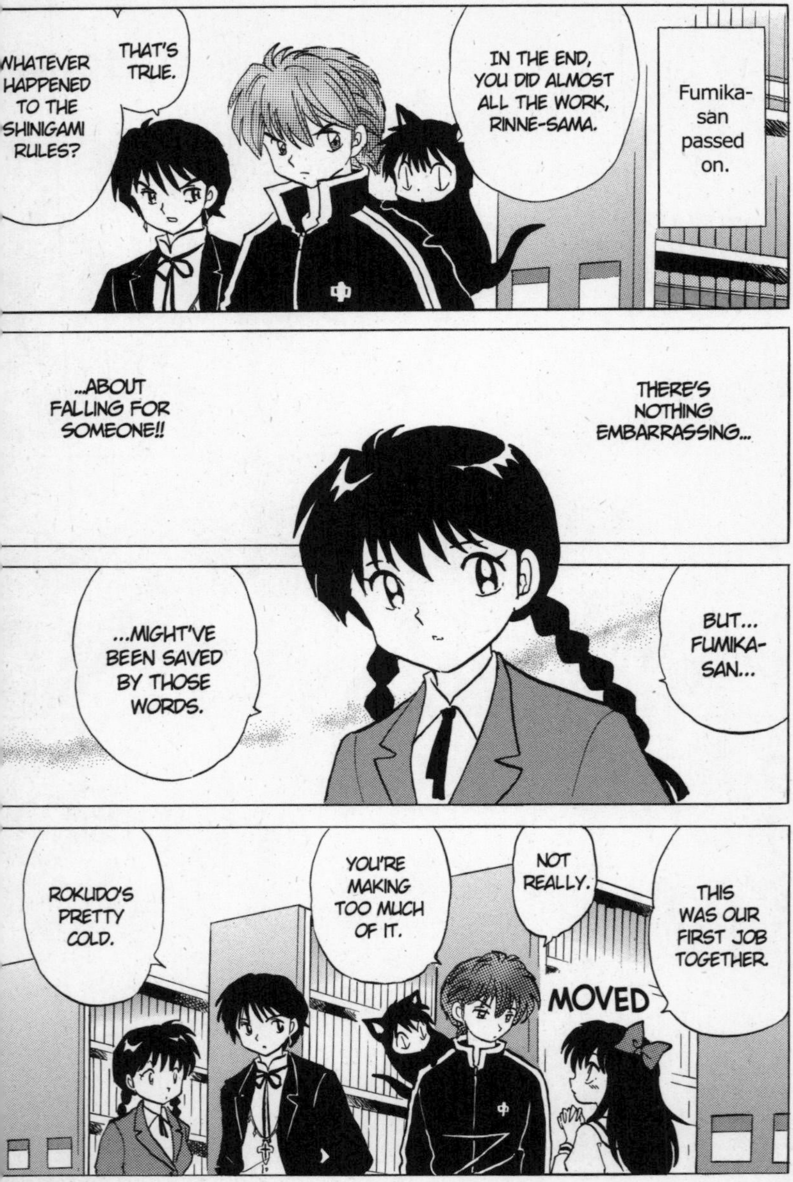
Fumika-san passed on.
IN THE END, YOU DID ALMOST ALL THE WORK, RINNE-SAMA.
THAT'S TRUE.
WHATEVER HAPPENED TO THE SHINIGAMI RULES?
THERE'S NOTHING EMBARRASSING...
...ABOUT FALLING FOR SOMEONE!!
BUT... FUMIKA-SAN...
...MIGHT'VE BEEN SAVED BY THOSE WORDS.
THIS WAS OUR FIRST JOB TOGETHER.
MOVED
NOT REALLY.
YOU'RE MAKING TOO MUCH OF IT.
ROKUDO'S PRETTY COLD.

CHAPTER 45: THE CURSED TRACK STAR

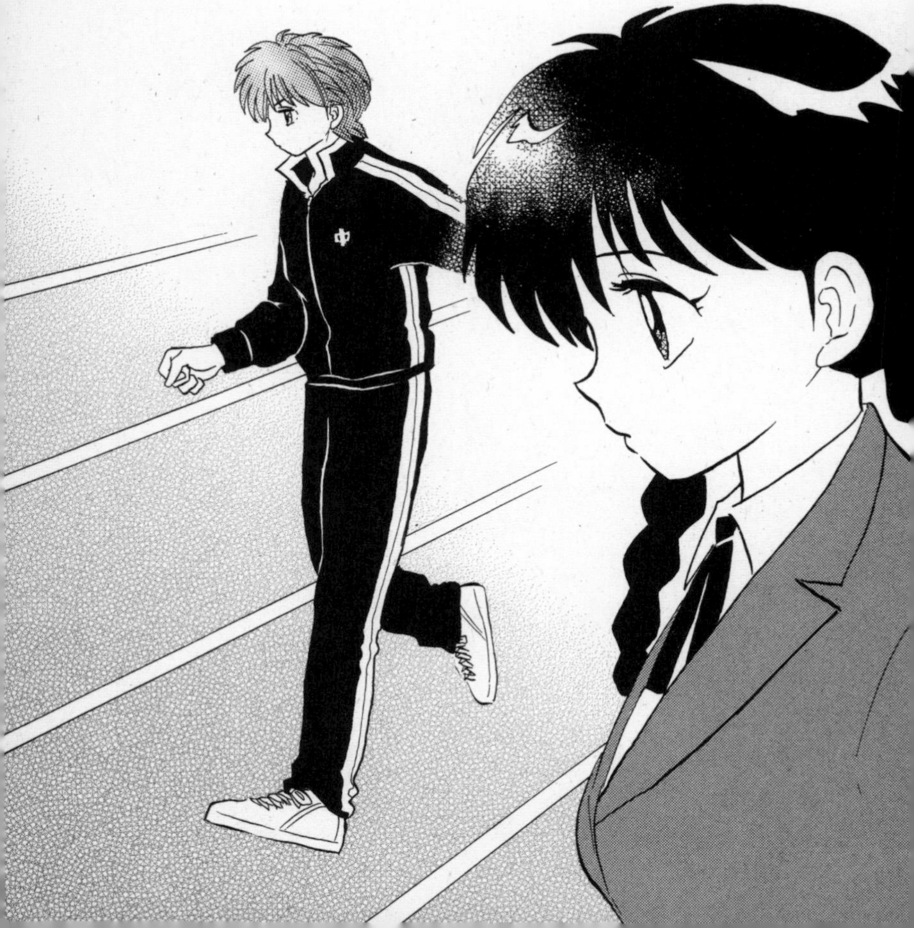

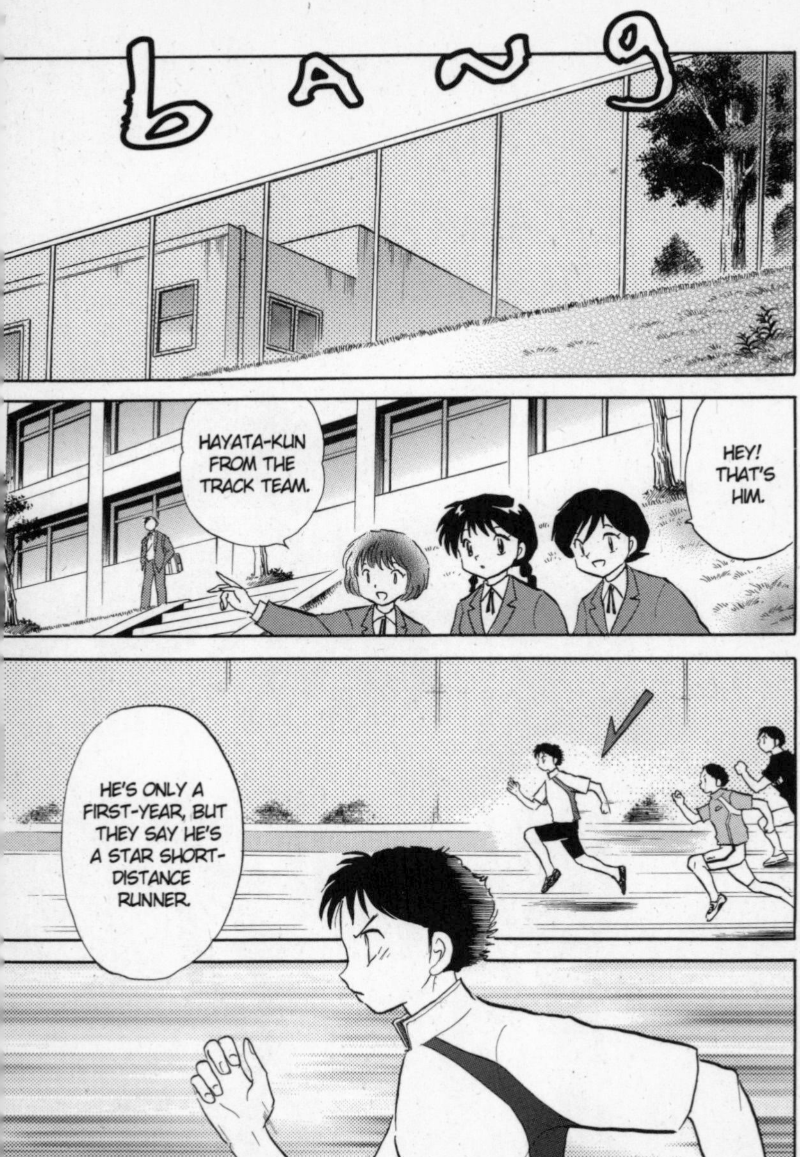
bang
HEY! THAT'S HIM.
HAYATA-KUN FROM THE TRACK TEAM.
HE'S ONLY A FIRST-YEAR, BUT THEY SAY HE'S A STAR SHORT-DISTANCE RUNNER.

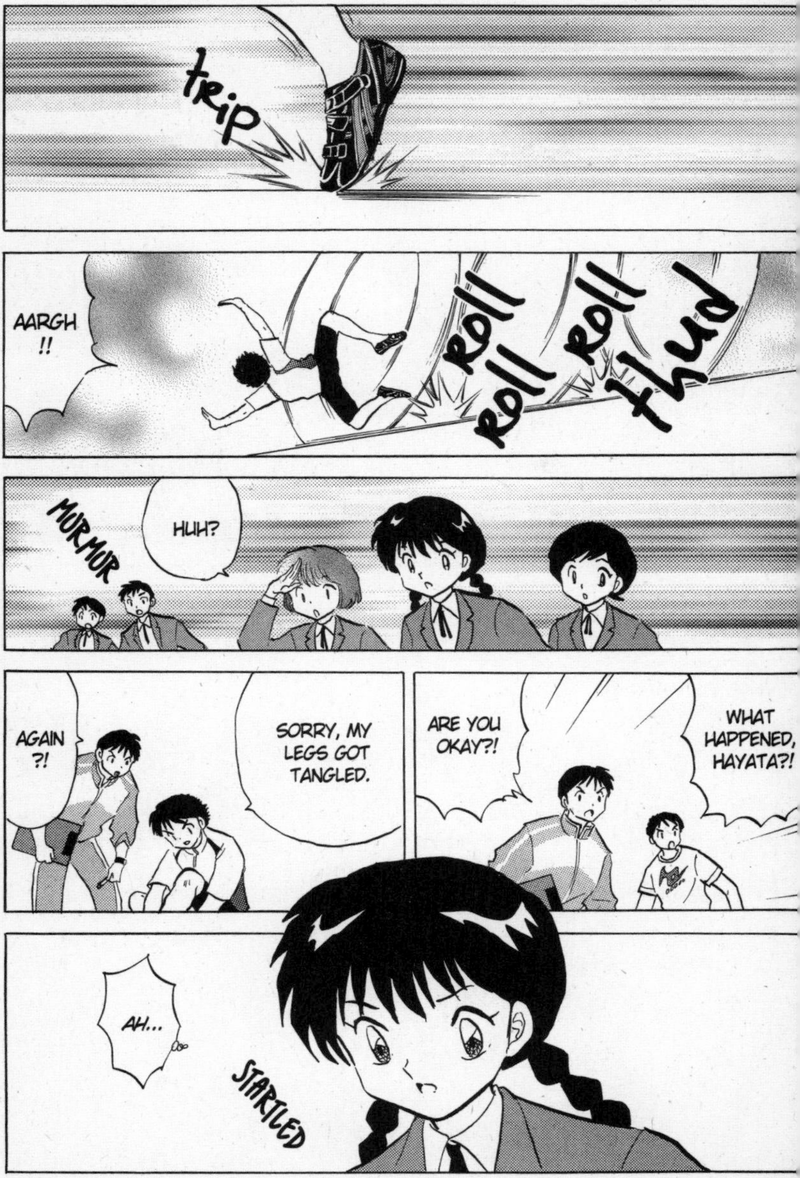
trip
thud
roll
roll roll
AARGH !!
HUH?
MURMUR
WHAT HAPPENED, HAYATA?!
ARE YOU OKAY?!
SORRY, MY LEGS GOT TANGLED.
AGAIN ?!
AH...
STARTLED

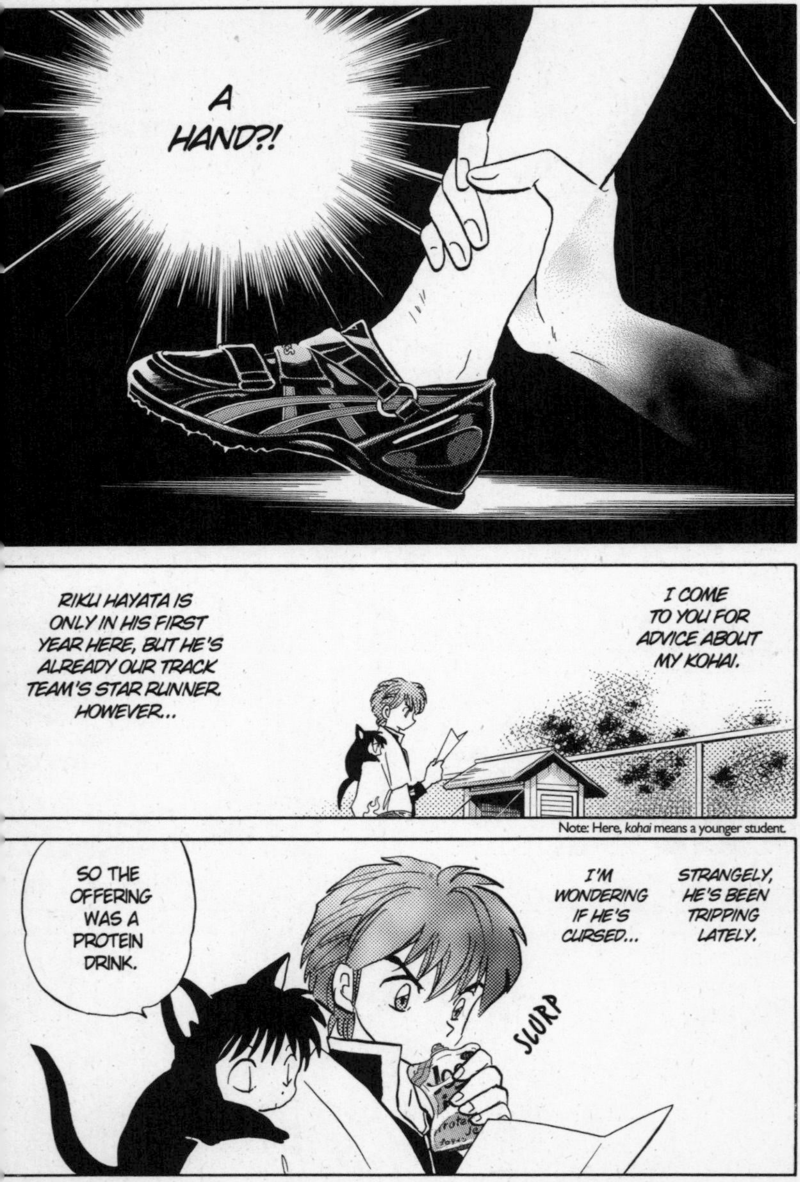
A HAND?!
I COME TO YOU FOR ADVICE ABOUT MY KOHAI.
RIKU HAYATA IS ONLY IN HIS FIRST YEAR HERE, BUT HE'S ALREADY OUR TRACK TEAM'S STAR RUNNER. HOWEVER...
STRANGELY, HE'S BEEN TRIPPING LATELY.
I'M WONDERING IF HE'S CURSED...
SLURP
SO THE OFFERING WAS A PROTEIN DRINK.

Note: Here, *kohai* means a younger student.

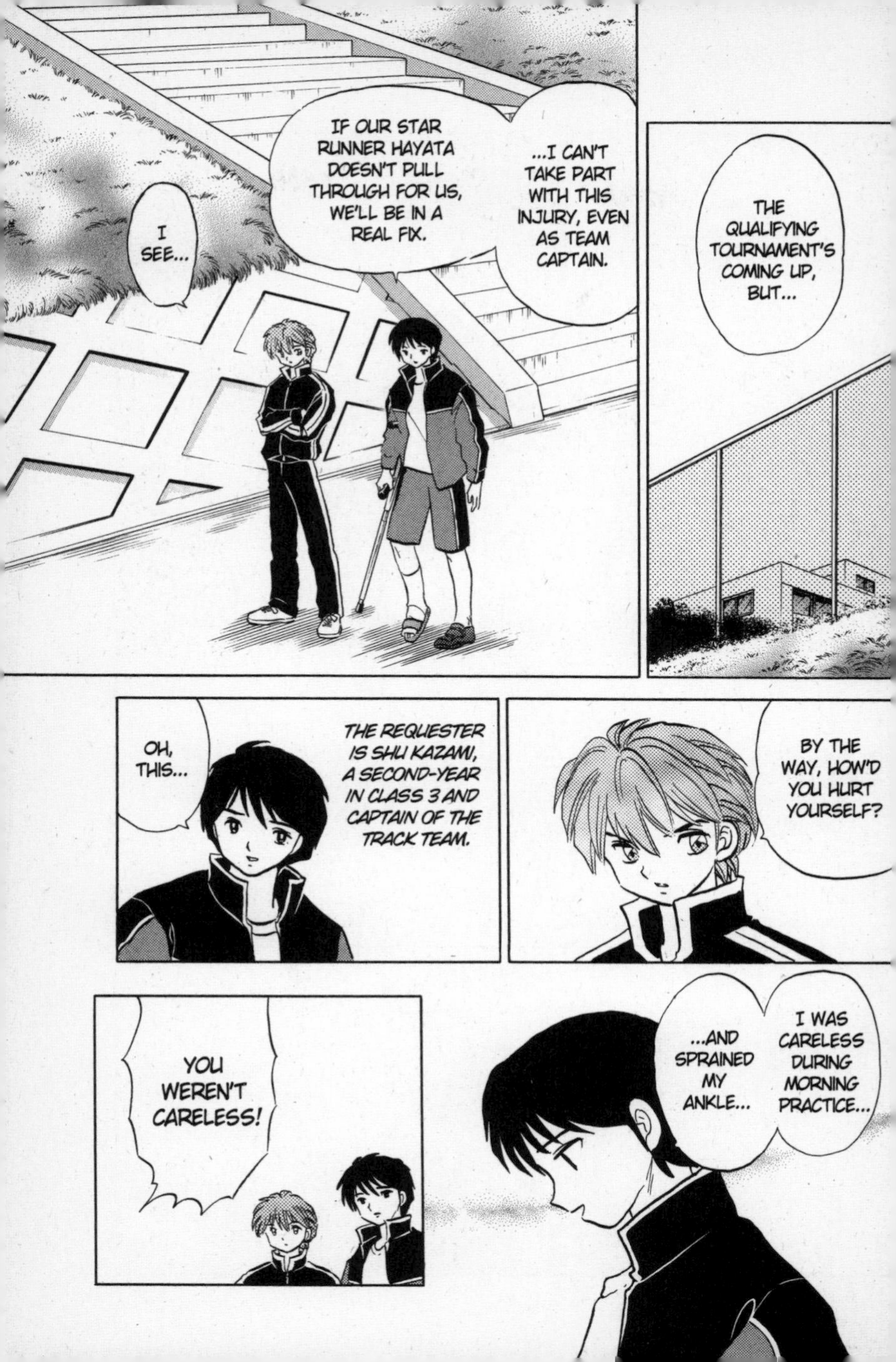
THE QUALIFYING TOURNAMENT'S COMING UP, BUT...
...I CAN'T TAKE PART WITH THIS INJURY, EVEN AS TEAM CAPTAIN.
IF OUR STAR RUNNER HAYATA DOESN'T PULL THROUGH FOR US, WE'LL BE IN A REAL FIX.
I SEE...
BY THE WAY, HOW'D YOU HURT YOURSELF?
THE REQUESTER IS SHU KAZAMI, A SECOND-YEAR IN CLASS 3 AND CAPTAIN OF THE TRACK TEAM.
OH, THIS...
I WAS CARELESS DURING MORNING PRACTICE...
...AND SPRAINED MY ANKLE...
YOU WEREN'T CARELESS!

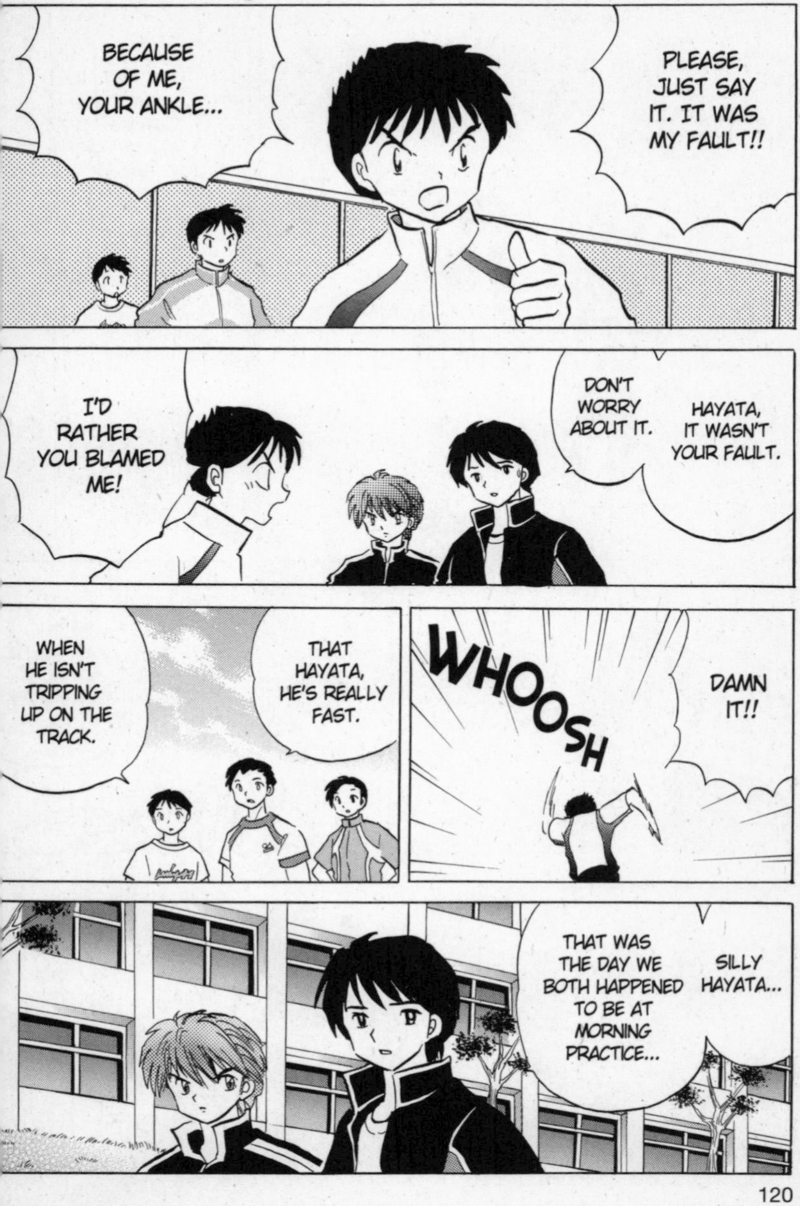
PLEASE, JUST SAY IT. IT WAS MY FAULT!!
BECAUSE OF ME, YOUR ANKLE...
HAYATA, IT WASN'T YOUR FAULT.
DON'T WORRY ABOUT IT.
I'D RATHER YOU BLAMED ME!
DAMN IT!!
WHOOSH
THAT HAYATA, HE'S REALLY FAST.
WHEN HE ISN'T TRIPPING UP ON THE TRACK.
SILLY HAYATA...
THAT WAS THE DAY WE BOTH HAPPENED TO BE AT MORNING PRACTICE...

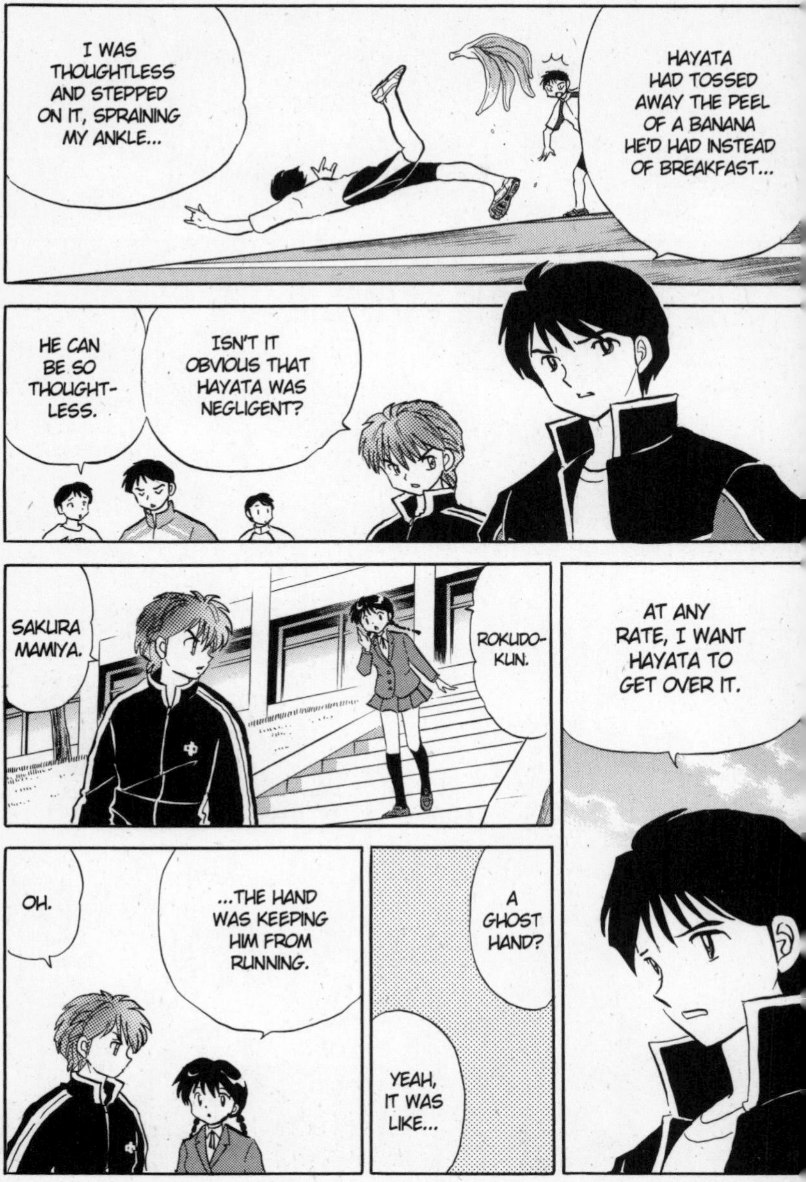

HAYATA HAD TOSSED AWAY THE PEEL OF A BANANA HE'D HAD INSTEAD OF BREAKFAST...
I WAS THOUGHTLESS AND STEPPED ON IT, SPRAINING MY ANKLE...
ISN'T IT OBVIOUS THAT HAYATA WAS NEGLIGENT?
HE CAN BE SO THOUGHT-LESS.
AT ANY RATE, I WANT HAYATA TO GET OVER IT.
ROKUDO-KUN.
SAKURA MAMIYA.
A GHOST HAND?
YEAH, IT WAS LIKE...
...THE HAND WAS KEEPING HIM FROM RUNNING.
OH.

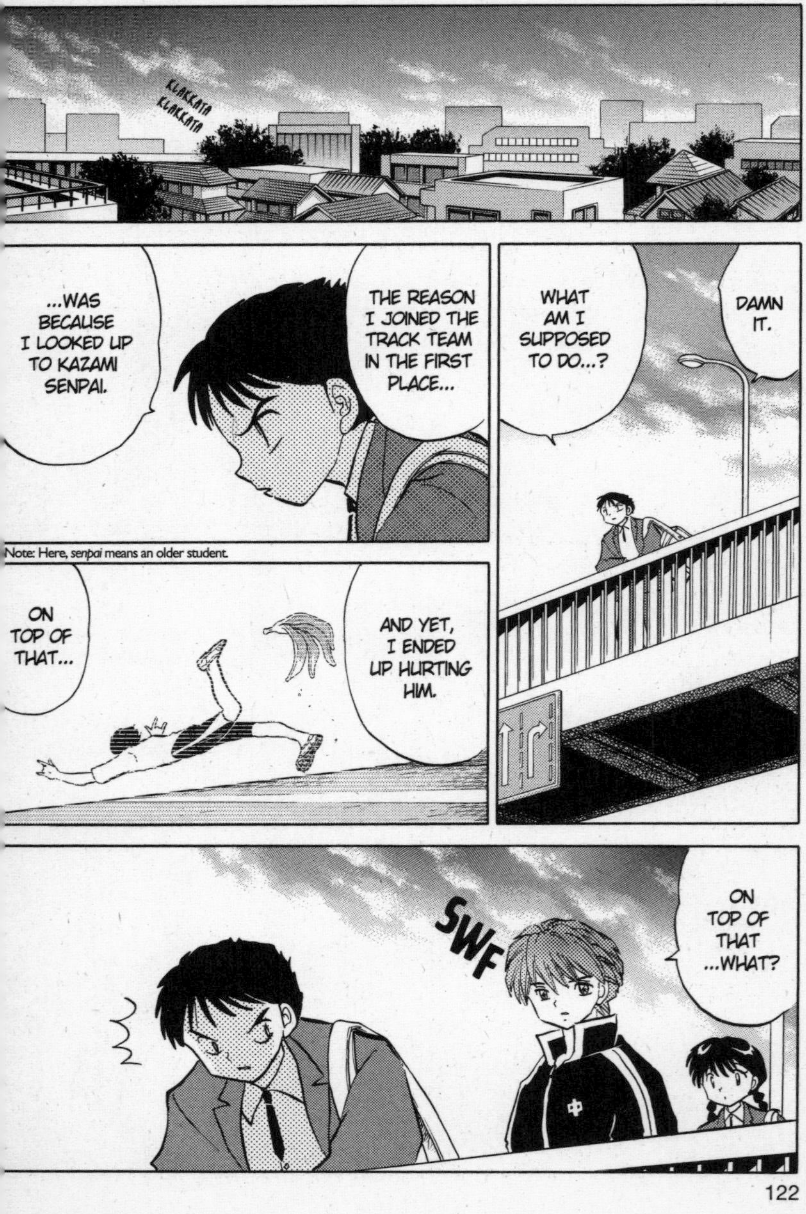
KLAKKATA KLAKKATA
DAMN IT.
WHAT AM I SUPPOSED TO DO...?
THE REASON I JOINED THE TRACK TEAM IN THE FIRST PLACE...
...WAS BECAUSE I LOOKED UP TO KAZAMI SENPAI.
AND YET, I ENDED UP HURTING HIM.
ON TOP OF THAT...
ON TOP OF THAT ...WHAT?
SWF

Note: Here, *senpai* means an older student.

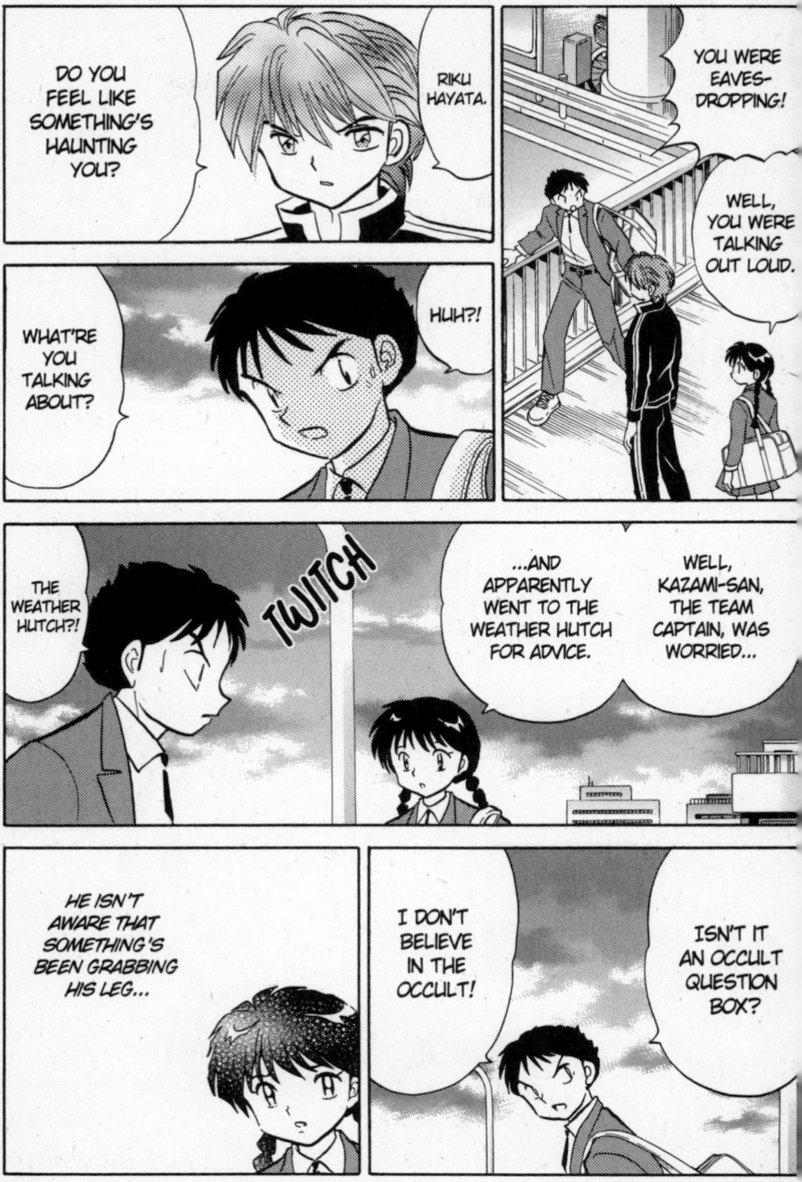
YOU WERE EAVES-DROPPING!
WELL, YOU WERE TALKING OUT LOUD.
RIKU HAYATA.
DO YOU FEEL LIKE SOMETHING'S HAUNTING YOU?
HUH?!
WHAT'RE YOU TALKING ABOUT?
WELL, KAZAMI-SAN, THE TEAM CAPTAIN, WAS WORRIED...
...AND APPARENTLY WENT TO THE WEATHER HUTCH FOR ADVICE.
TWITCH
THE WEATHER HUTCH?!
ISN'T IT AN OCCULT QUESTION BOX?
I DON'T BELIEVE IN THE OCCULT!
HE ISN'T AWARE THAT SOMETHING'S BEEN GRABBING HIS LEG...

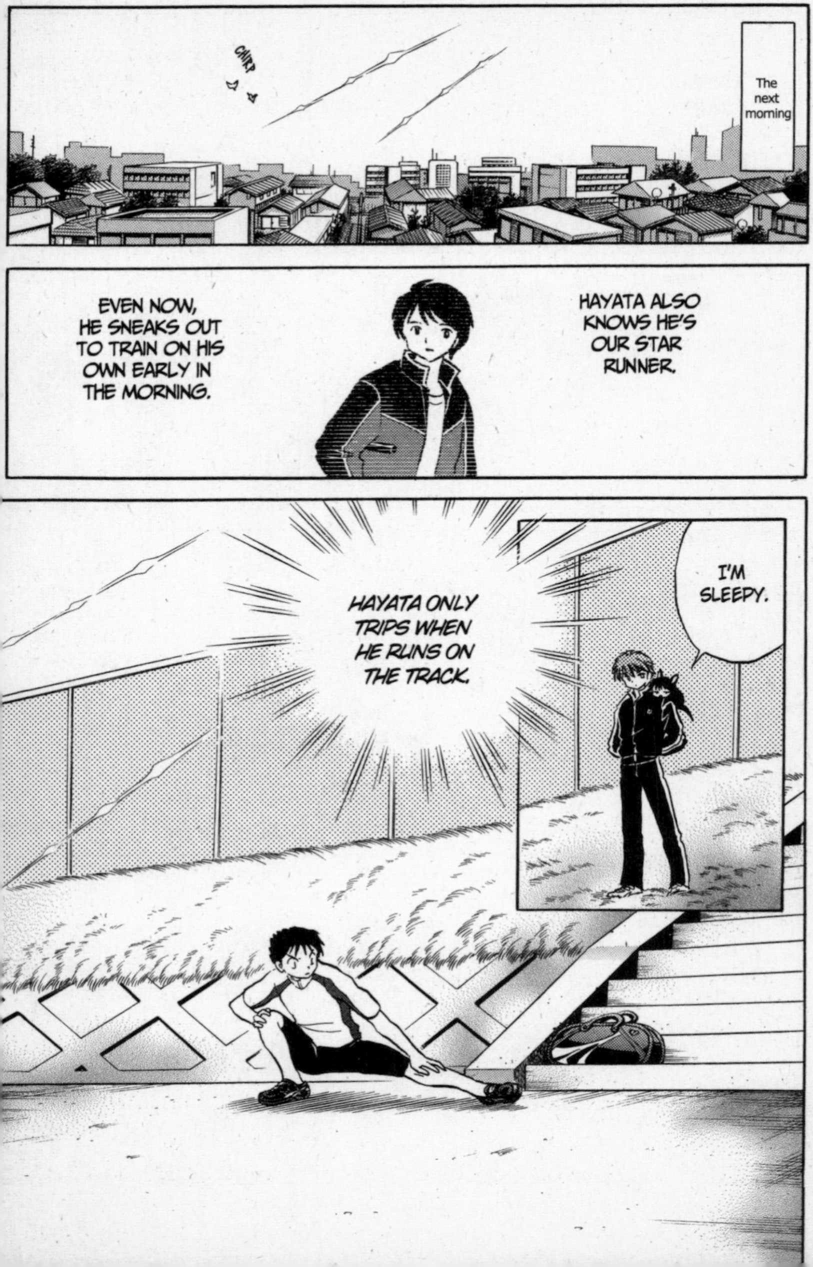
The next morning
CHIRP
HAYATA ALSO KNOWS HE'S OUR STAR RUNNER.
EVEN NOW, HE SNEAKS OUT TO TRAIN ON HIS OWN EARLY IN THE MORNING.
I'M SLEEPY.
HAYATA ONLY TRIPS WHEN HE RUNS ON THE TRACK.

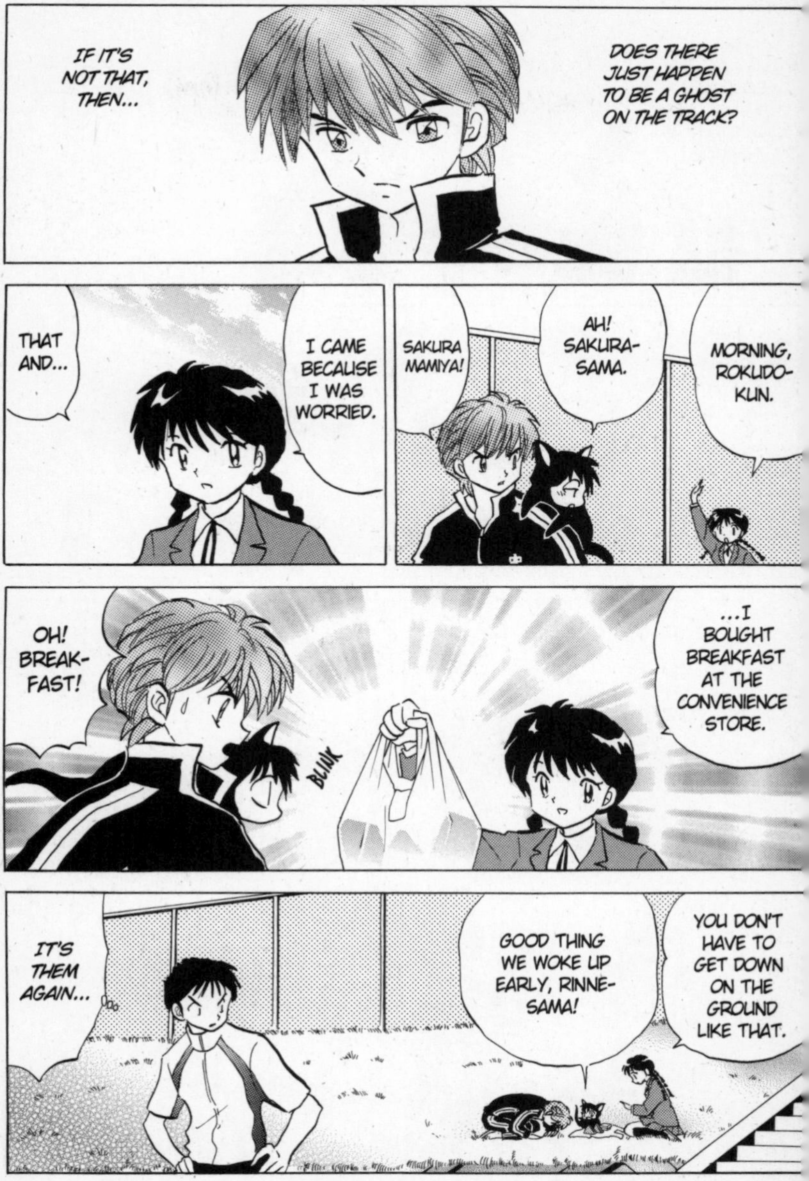
DOES THERE JUST HAPPEN TO BE A GHOST ON THE TRACK?
IF IT'S NOT THAT, THEN...
MORNING, ROKUDO-KUN.
AH! SAKURA-SAMA.
SAKURA MAMIYA!
I CAME BECAUSE I WAS WORRIED.
THAT AND...
...I BOUGHT BREAKFAST AT THE CONVENIENCE STORE.
BLINK
OH! BREAK-FAST!
YOU DON'T HAVE TO GET DOWN ON THE GROUND LIKE THAT.
GOOD THING WE WOKE UP EARLY, RINNE-SAMA!
IT'S THEM AGAIN...

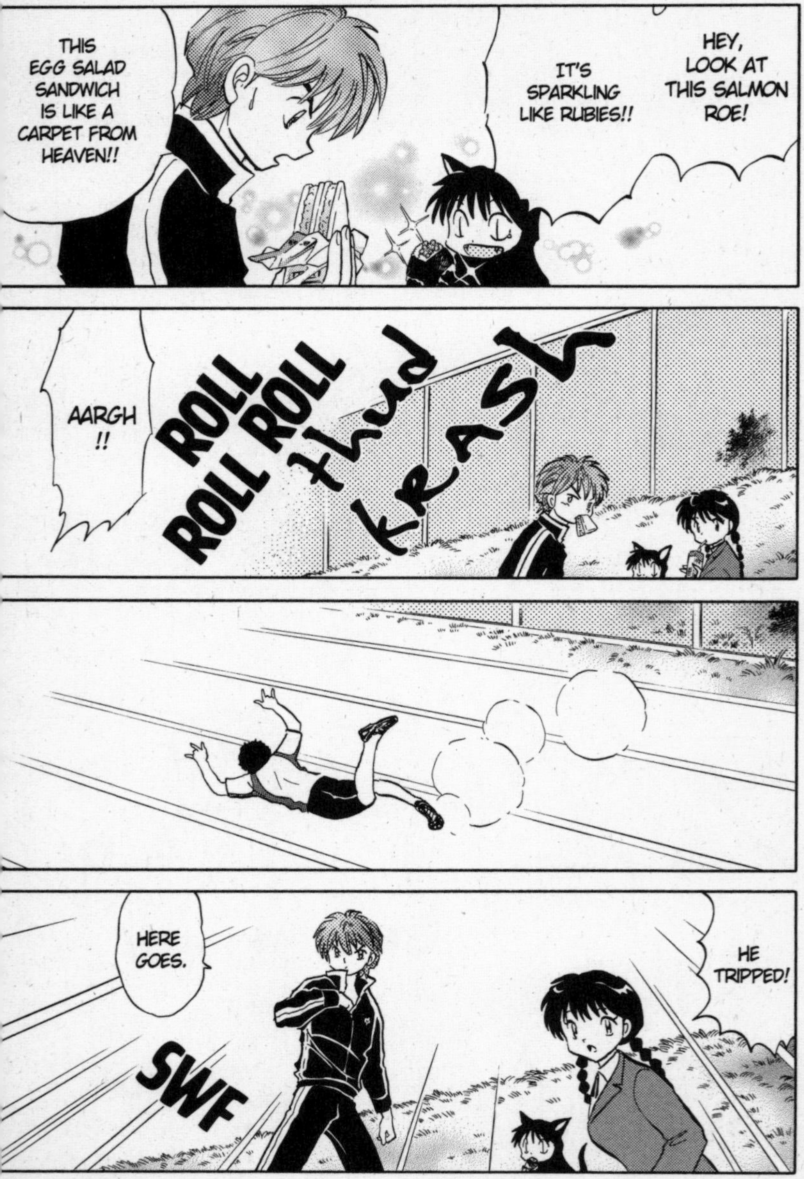
HEY, LOOK AT THIS SALMON ROE!
IT'S SPARKLING LIKE RUBIES!!
THIS EGG SALAD SANDWICH IS LIKE A CARPET FROM HEAVEN!!
krash
thud
ROLL ROLL ROLL ROLL
AARGH!!
HE TRIPPED!
SWF
HERE GOES.

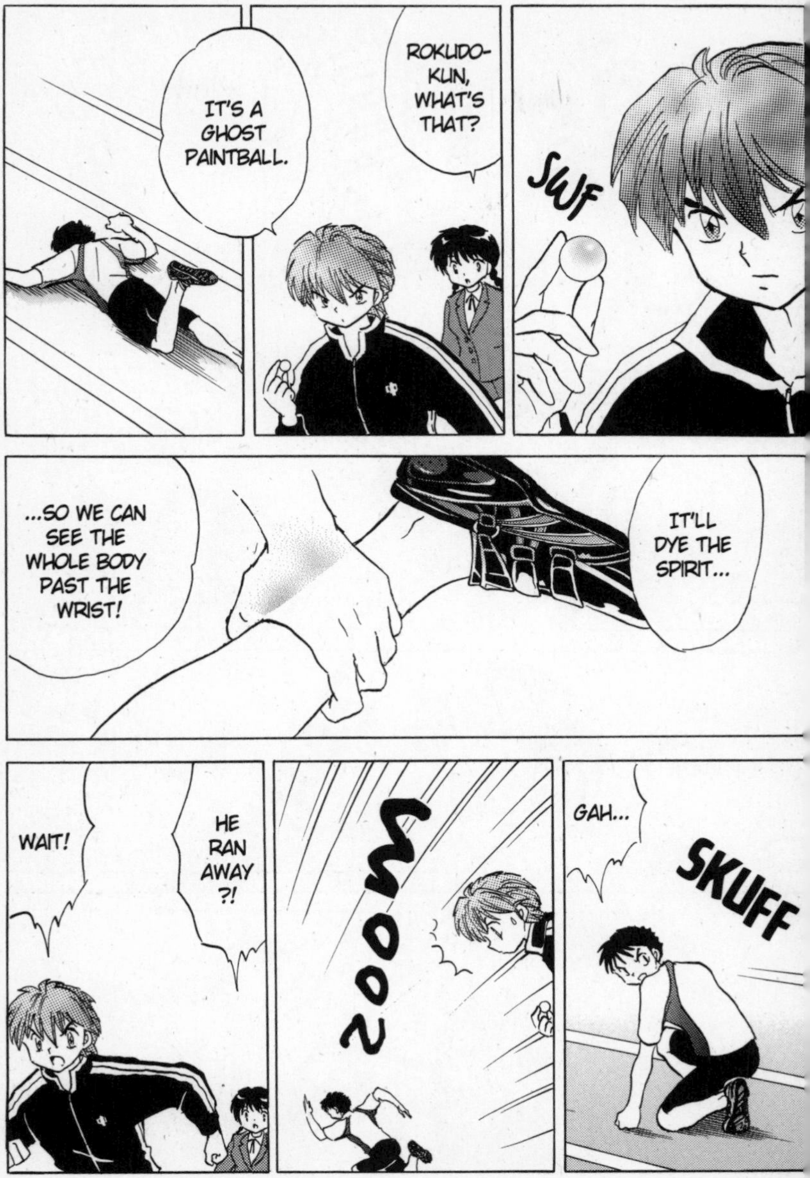
SWF
ROKUDO-KUN, WHAT'S THAT?
IT'S A GHOST PAINTBALL.
IT'LL DYE THE SPIRIT...
...SO WE CAN SEE THE WHOLE BODY PAST THE WRIST!
GAH...
SKUFF
ZOOM
HE RAN AWAY?!
WAIT!

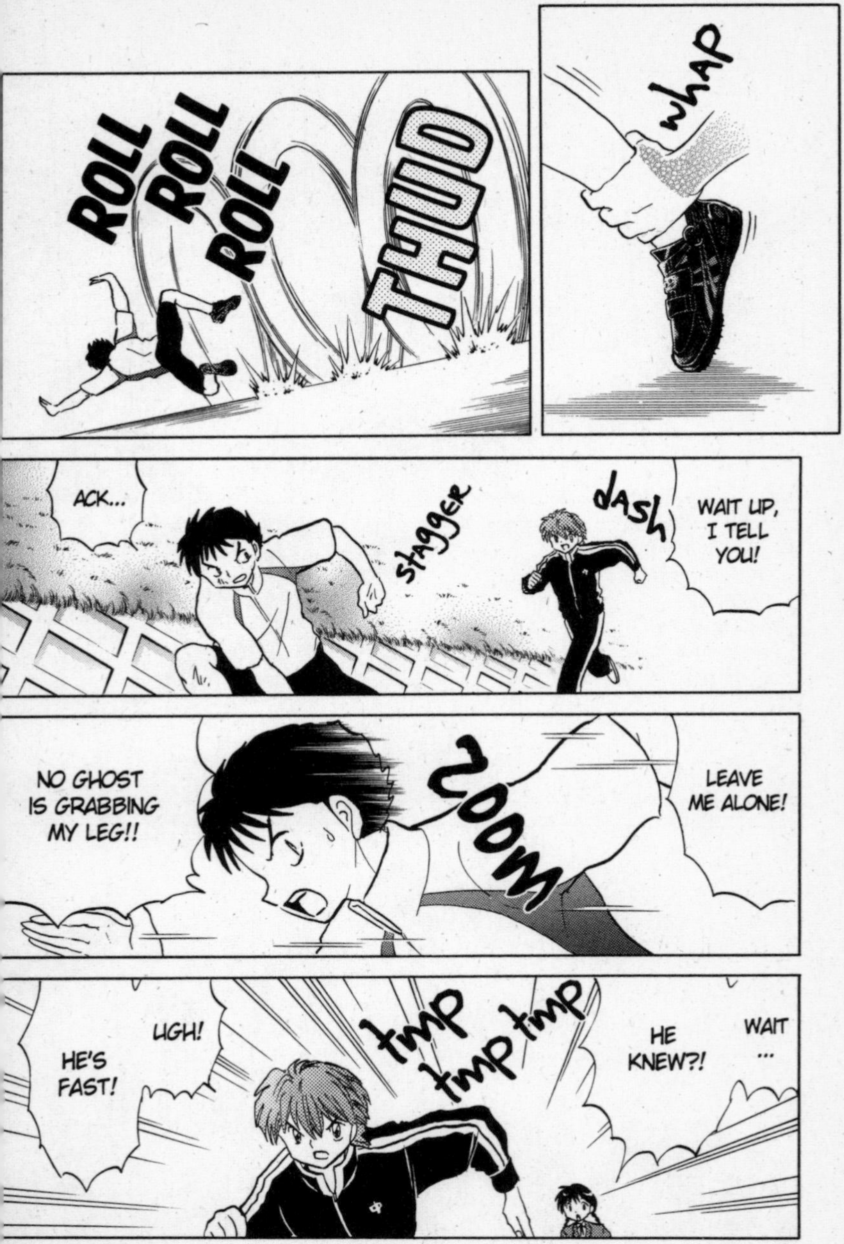
whap
ROLL ROLL ROLL
THUD
WAIT UP, I TELL YOU!
dash
stagger
ACK...
LEAVE ME ALONE!
ZOOM
NO GHOST IS GRABBING MY LEG!!
WAIT ...
HE KNEW?!
tmp tmp tmp tmp
UGH!
HE'S FAST!

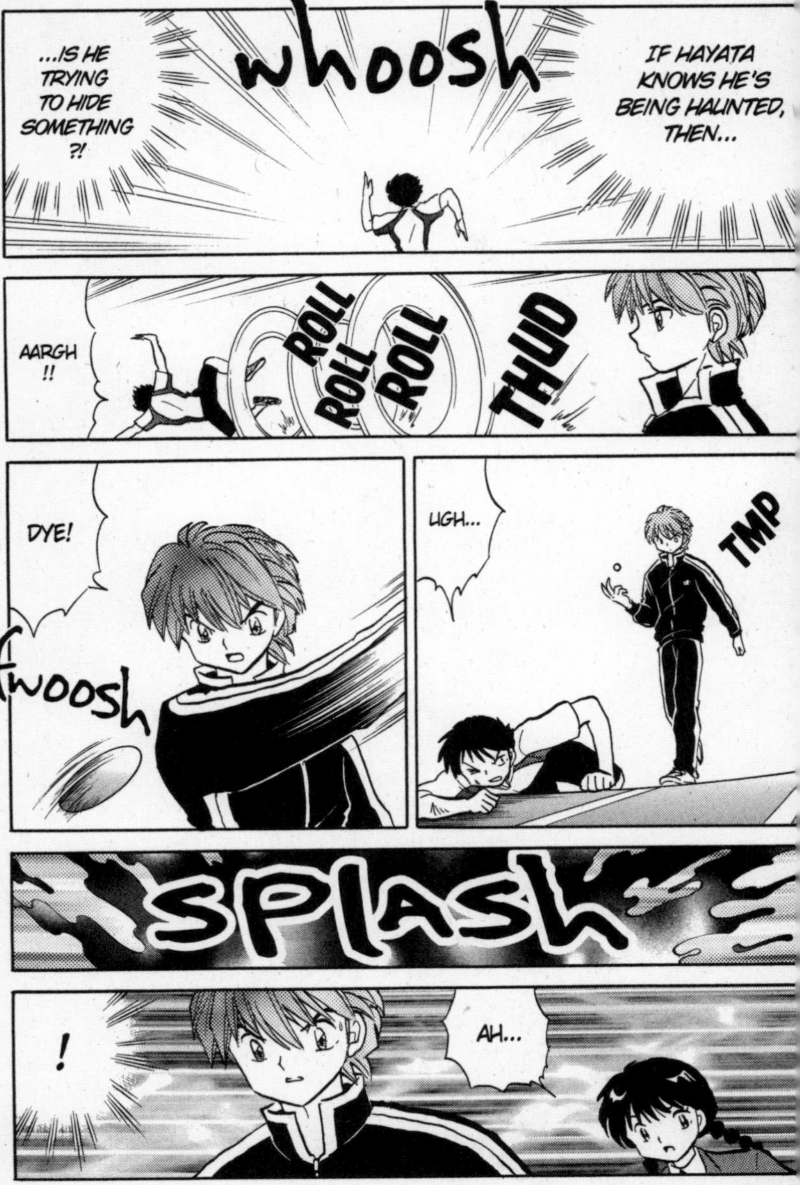
IF HAYATA KNOWS HE'S BEING HAUNTED, THEN...
whoosh
...IS HE TRYING TO HIDE SOMETHING ?!
THUD
ROLL
ROLL
ROLL
AARGH !!
TMP
UGH...
DYE!
fwoosh
splash
AH...
!

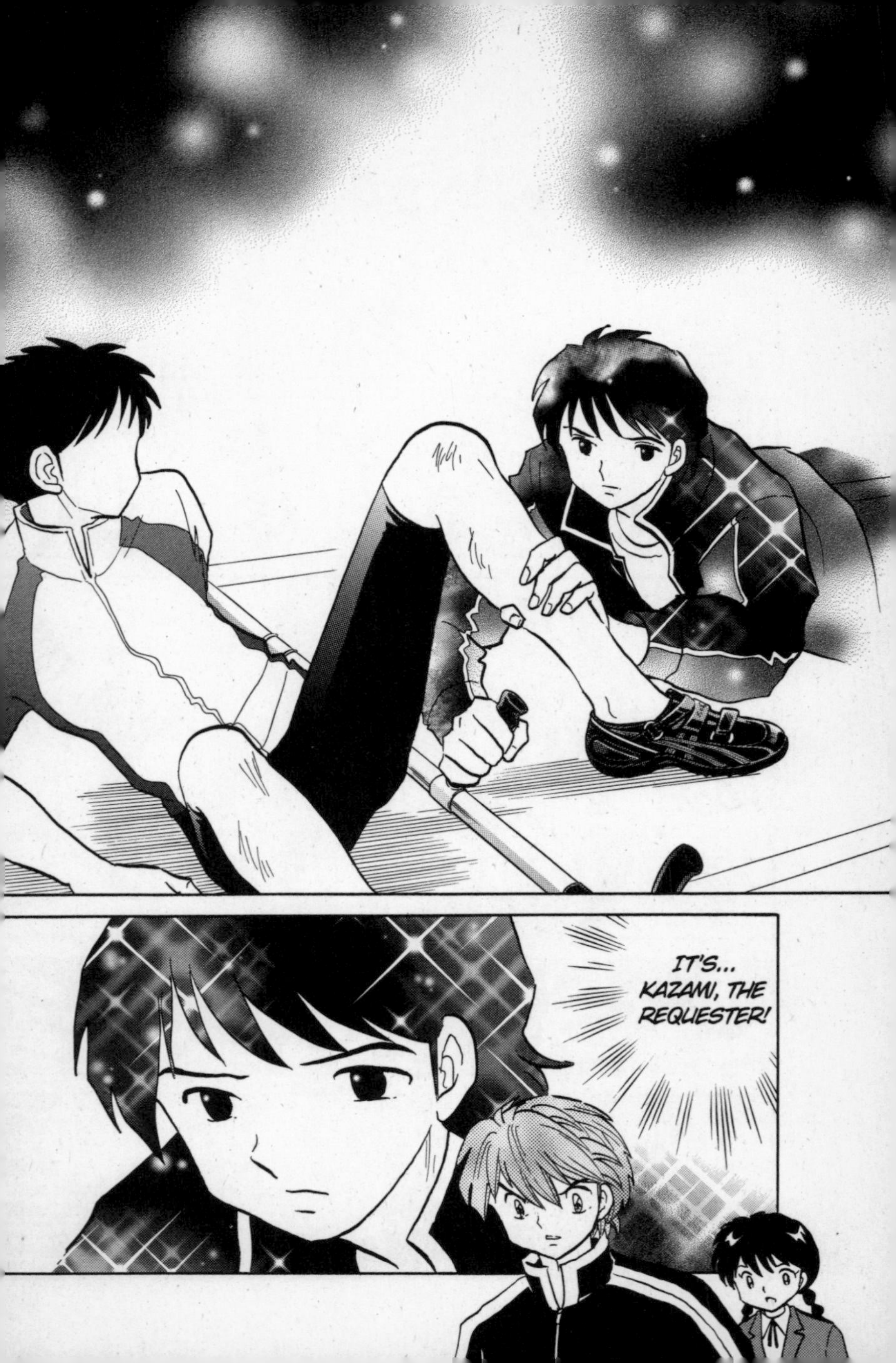
IT'S... KAZAMI, THE REQUESTER!

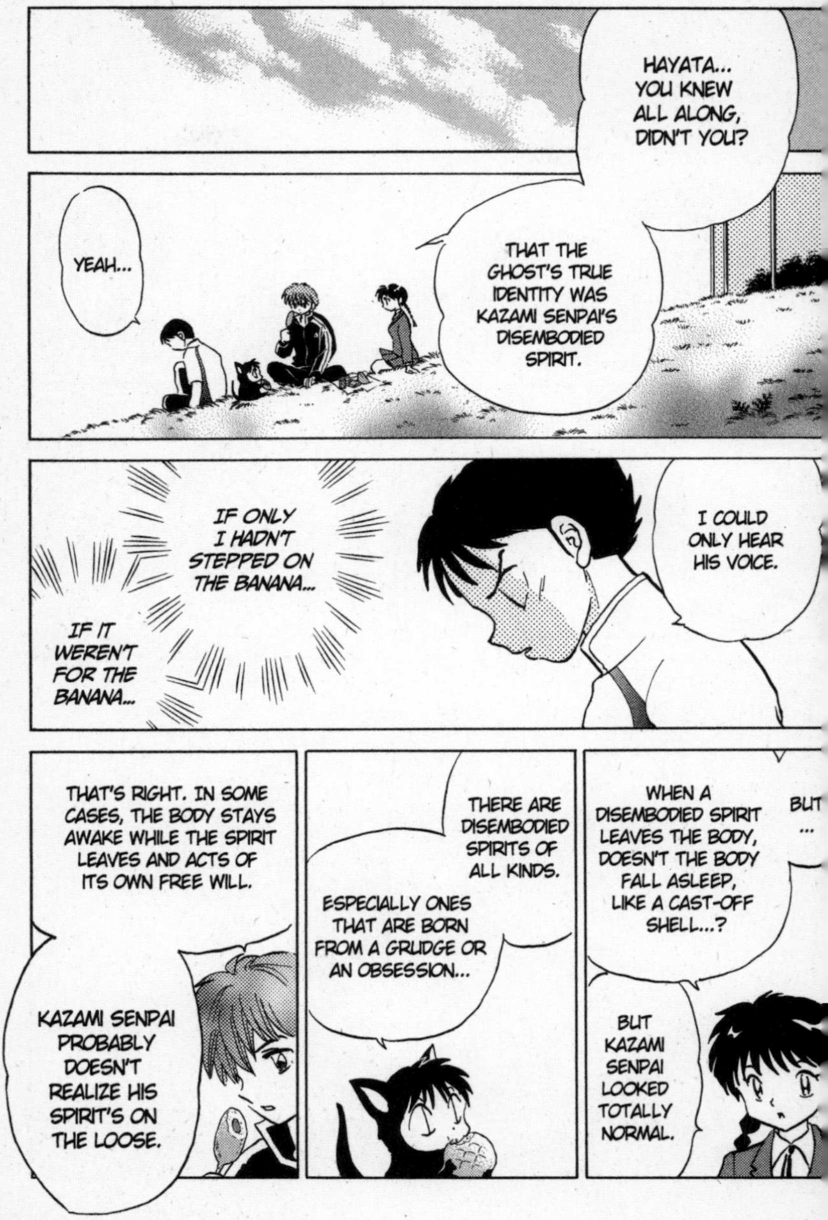
HAYATA... YOU KNEW ALL ALONG, DIDN'T YOU?
THAT THE GHOST'S TRUE IDENTITY WAS KAZAMI SENPAI'S DISEMBODIED SPIRIT.
YEAH...
I COULD ONLY HEAR HIS VOICE.
IF ONLY I HADN'T STEPPED ON THE BANANA...
IF IT WEREN'T FOR THE BANANA...
BUT ...
WHEN A DISEMBODIED SPIRIT LEAVES THE BODY, DOESN'T THE BODY FALL ASLEEP, LIKE A CAST-OFF SHELL...?
BUT KAZAMI SENPAI LOOKED TOTALLY NORMAL.
THERE ARE DISEMBODIED SPIRITS OF ALL KINDS.
ESPECIALLY ONES THAT ARE BORN FROM A GRUDGE OR AN OBSESSION...
THAT'S RIGHT. IN SOME CASES, THE BODY STAYS AWAKE WHILE THE SPIRIT LEAVES AND ACTS OF ITS OWN FREE WILL.
KAZAMI SENPAI PROBABLY DOESN'T REALIZE HIS SPIRIT'S ON THE LOOSE.

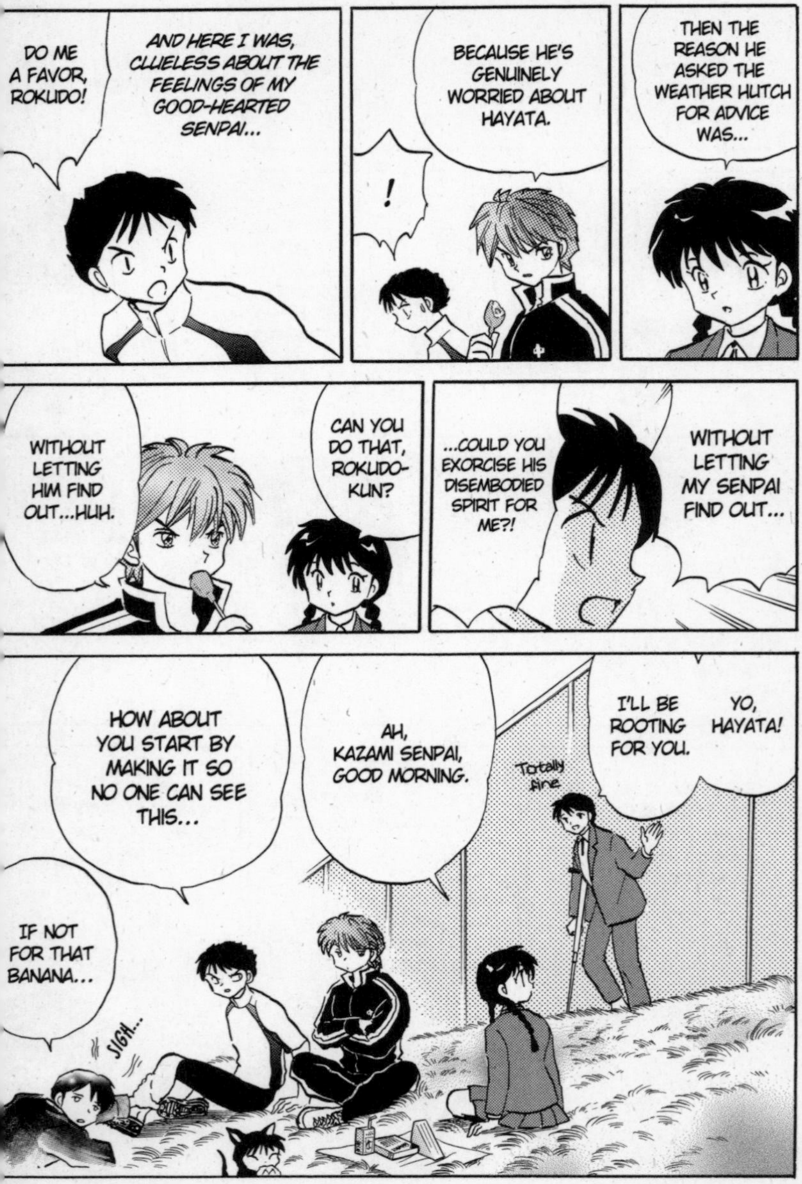
THEN THE REASON HE ASKED THE WEATHER HUTCH FOR ADVICE WAS...
BECAUSE HE'S GENUINELY WORRIED ABOUT HAYATA.
!
AND HERE I WAS, CLUELESS ABOUT THE FEELINGS OF MY GOOD-HEARTED SENPAI...
DO ME A FAVOR, ROKUDO!
WITHOUT LETTING MY SENPAI FIND OUT...
...COULD YOU EXORCISE HIS DISEMBODIED SPIRIT FOR ME?!
CAN YOU DO THAT, ROKUDO-KUN?
WITHOUT LETTING HIM FIND OUT...HUH.
YO, HAYATA!
I'LL BE ROOTING FOR YOU.
Totally fine
AH, KAZAMI SENPAI, GOOD MORNING.
HOW ABOUT YOU START BY MAKING IT SO NO ONE CAN SEE THIS...
IF NOT FOR THAT BANANA...
SIGH...

RIN-NE

WOOOOO

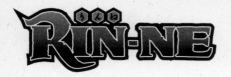

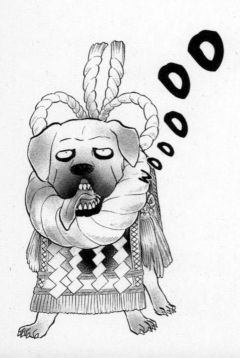

CHAPTER 46: I DON'T WANT HIM TO KNOW

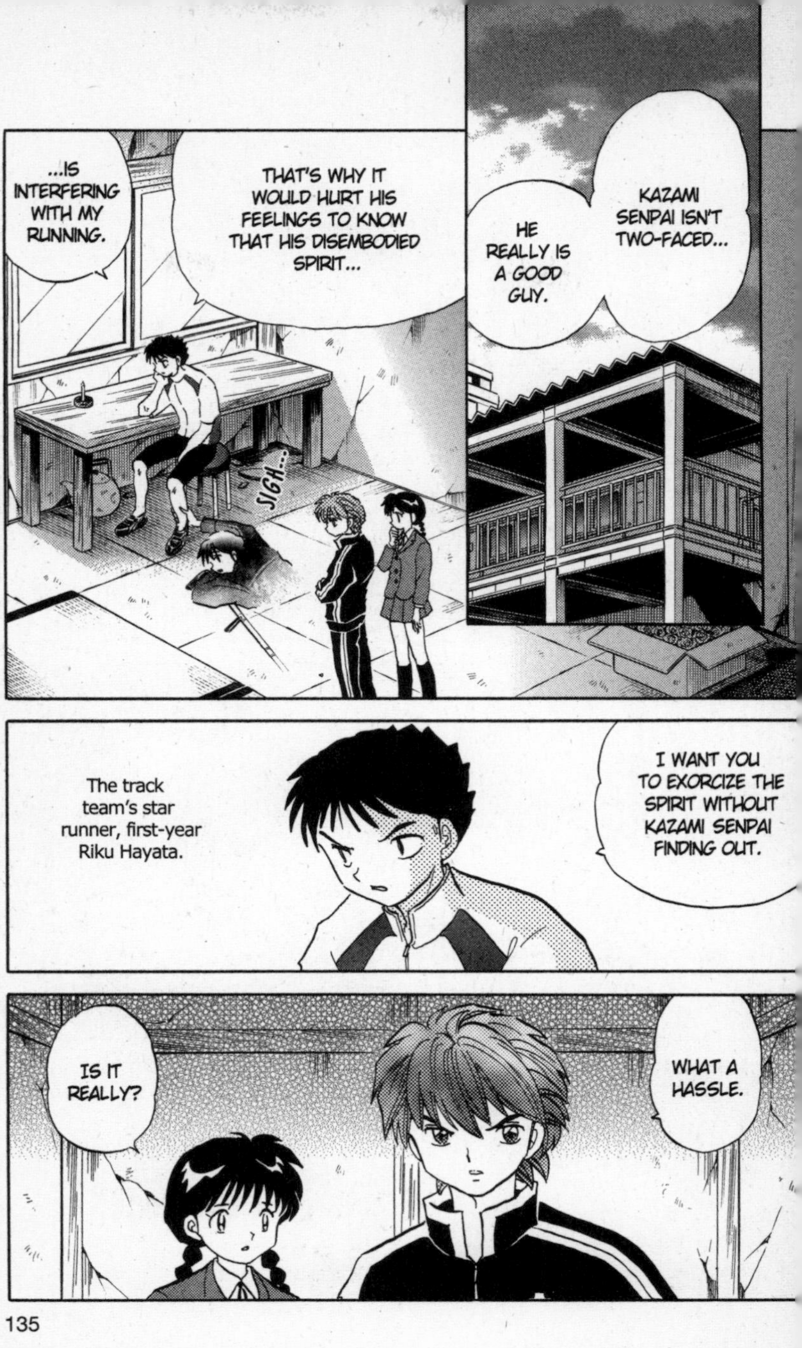
KAZAMI SENPAI ISN'T TWO-FACED...
HE REALLY IS A GOOD GUY.
THAT'S WHY IT WOULD HURT HIS FEELINGS TO KNOW THAT HIS DISEMBODIED SPIRIT...
...IS INTERFERING WITH MY RUNNING.
SIGH...
I WANT YOU TO EXORCIZE THE SPIRIT WITHOUT KAZAMI SENPAI FINDING OUT.
The track team's star runner, first-year Riku Hayata.
WHAT A HASSLE.
IS IT REALLY?

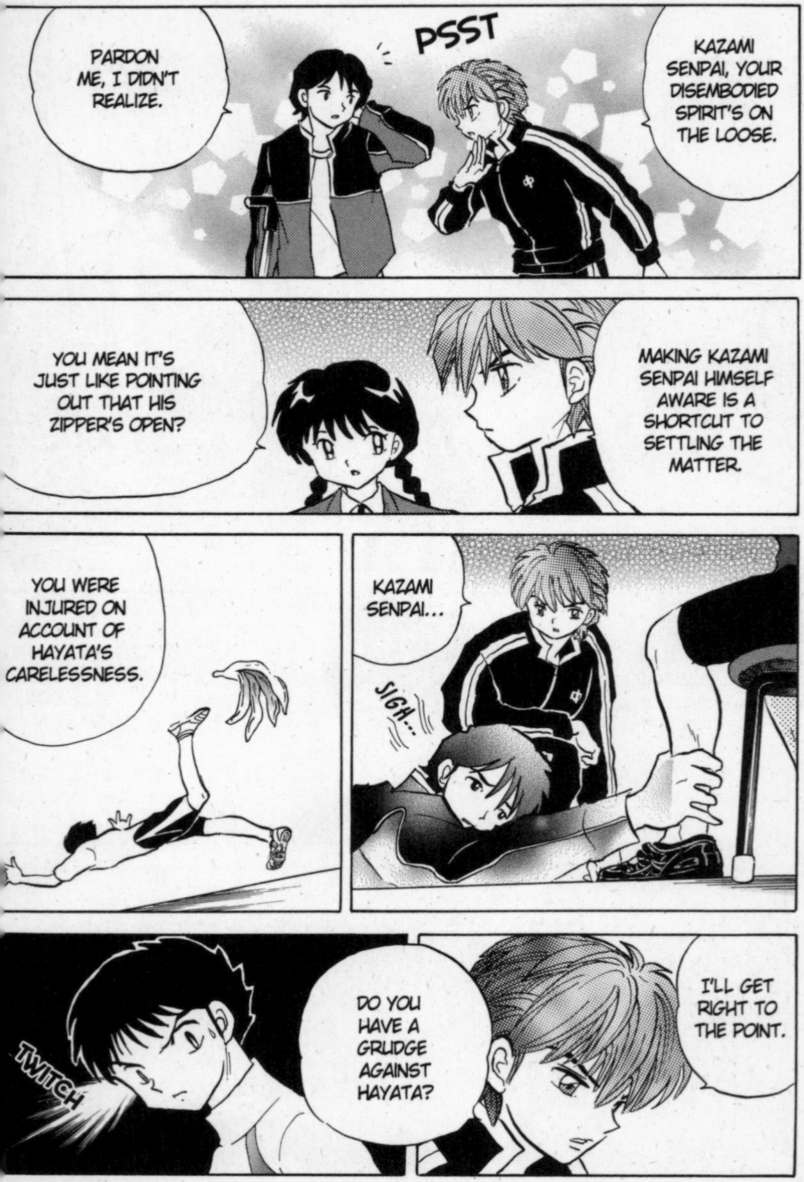
PSST
KAZAMI SENPAI, YOUR DISEMBODIED SPIRIT'S ON THE LOOSE.
PARDON ME, I DIDN'T REALIZE.
MAKING KAZAMI SENPAI HIMSELF AWARE IS A SHORTCUT TO SETTLING THE MATTER.
YOU MEAN IT'S JUST LIKE POINTING OUT THAT HIS ZIPPER'S OPEN?
KAZAMI SENPAI...
SIGH...
YOU WERE INJURED ON ACCOUNT OF HAYATA'S CARELESSNESS.
I'LL GET RIGHT TO THE POINT.
DO YOU HAVE A GRUDGE AGAINST HAYATA?
TWITCH

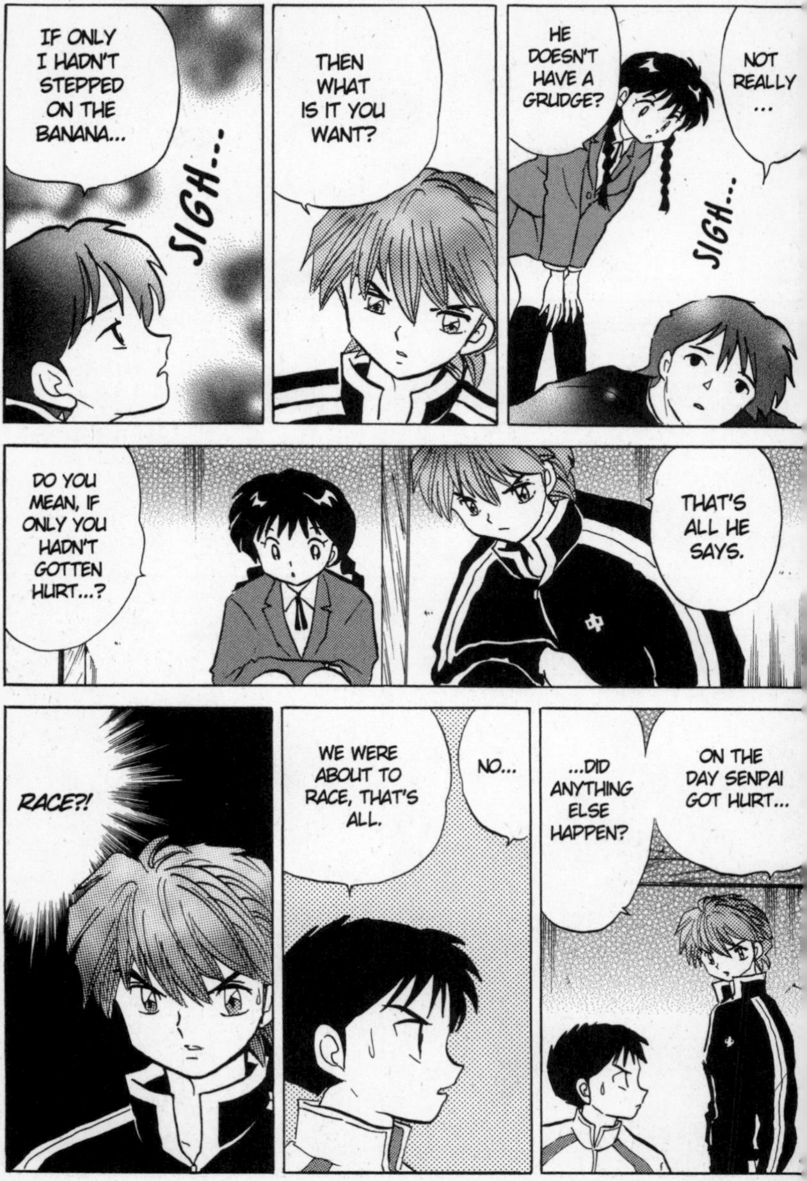
NOT REALLY...
HE DOESN'T HAVE A GRUDGE?
SIGH...
THEN WHAT IS IT YOU WANT?
IF ONLY I HADN'T STEPPED ON THE BANANA...
SIGH...
THAT'S ALL HE SAYS.
DO YOU MEAN, IF ONLY YOU HADN'T GOTTEN HURT...?
ON THE DAY SENPAI GOT HURT...
...DID ANYTHING ELSE HAPPEN?
NO...
WE WERE ABOUT TO RACE, THAT'S ALL.
RACE?!

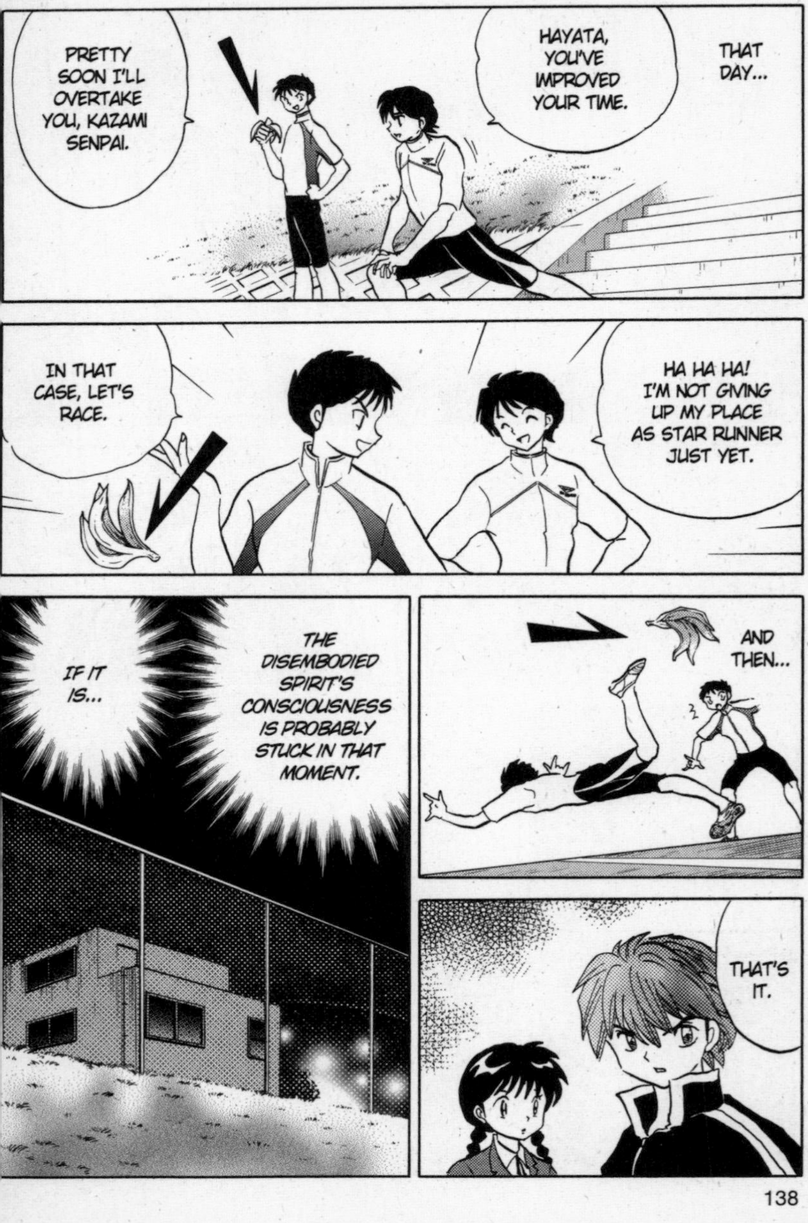
THAT DAY...
HAYATA, YOU'VE IMPROVED YOUR TIME.
PRETTY SOON I'LL OVERTAKE YOU, KAZAMI SENPAI.
HA HA HA! I'M NOT GIVING UP MY PLACE AS STAR RUNNER JUST YET.
IN THAT CASE, LET'S RACE.
AND THEN...
THAT'S IT.
THE DISEMBODIED SPIRIT'S CONSCIOUSNESS IS PROBABLY STUCK IN THAT MOMENT.
IF IT IS...

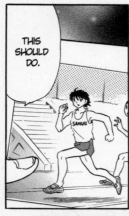

WHAT'RE YOU GOING TO DO WITH THE TRACK TEAM'S PHOTO ALBUM, OF ALL THINGS?
JUST GIVE IT TO ME.
I NEED A PHOTO OF KAZAMI SENPAI WHEN HE WASN'T INJURED.
THIS SHOULD DO.
SANKAI
RINNE-SAMA, I BOUGHT THESE.
A SCANNER AND A CHANNELING DOLL.
WARP
GOOD.
A channeling doll is a doll that houses a ghost or disembodied spirit temporarily.
Paper ¥10
Straw ¥100
Vinyl ¥1000
THIS IS THE MOST EXPENSIVE MODEL, MADE OF VINYL.
THIS THING.
VRRR
I SCAN THE PHOTO AND SEND SENPAI'S FORM TO THE DOLL...

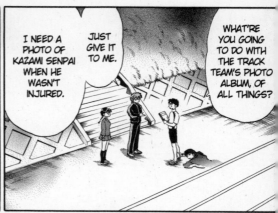

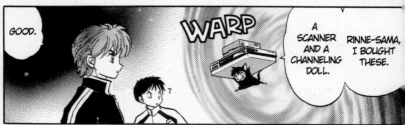

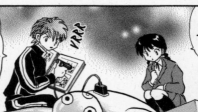

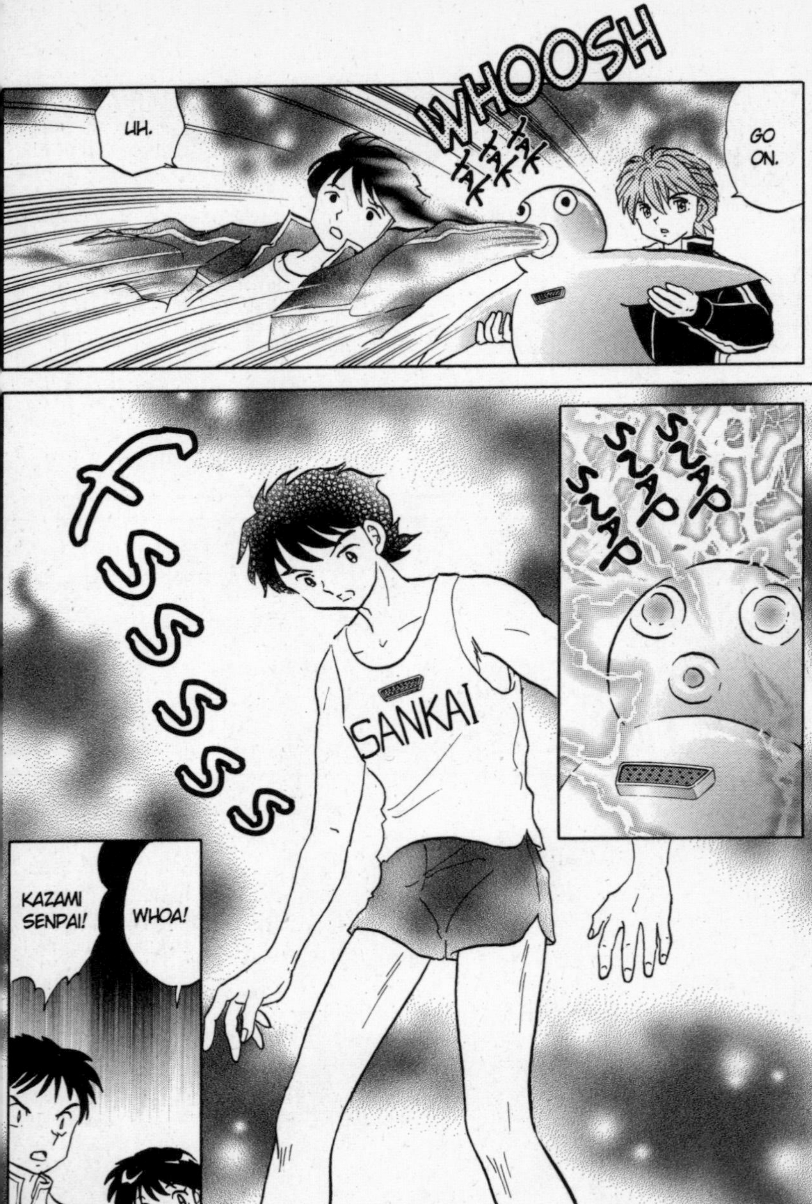
WHOOSH
GO ON.
tak tak tak
UH.
SNAP SNAP SNAP
fssssss
WHOA!
KAZAMI SENPAI!

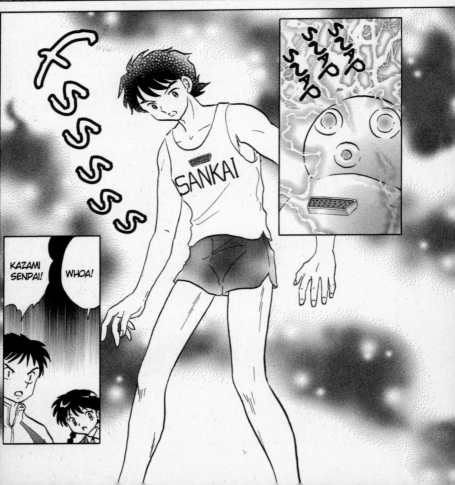

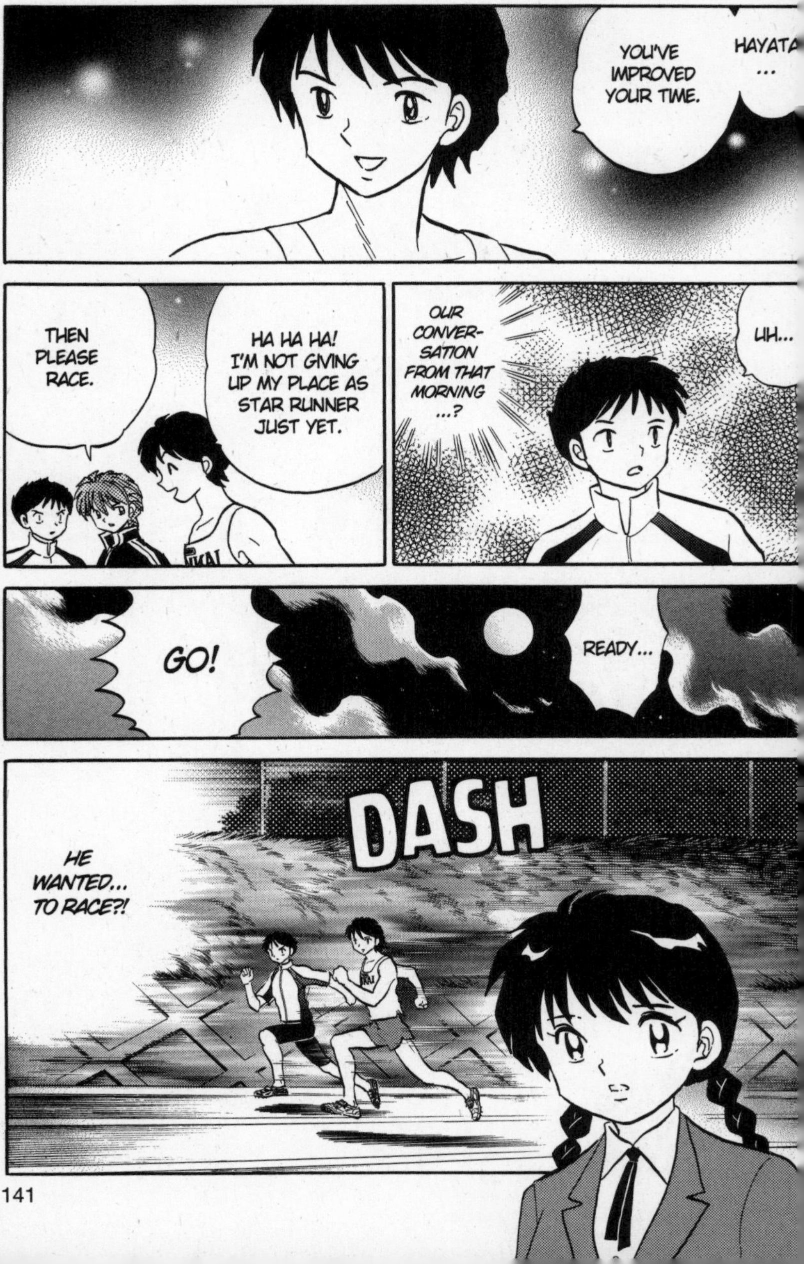

HAYATA...
YOU'VE IMPROVED YOUR TIME.
UH...
OUR CONVERSATION FROM THAT MORNING...?
HA HA HA! I'M NOT GIVING UP MY PLACE AS STAR RUNNER JUST YET.
THEN PLEASE RACE.
READY...
GO!
DASH
HE WANTED... TO RACE?!

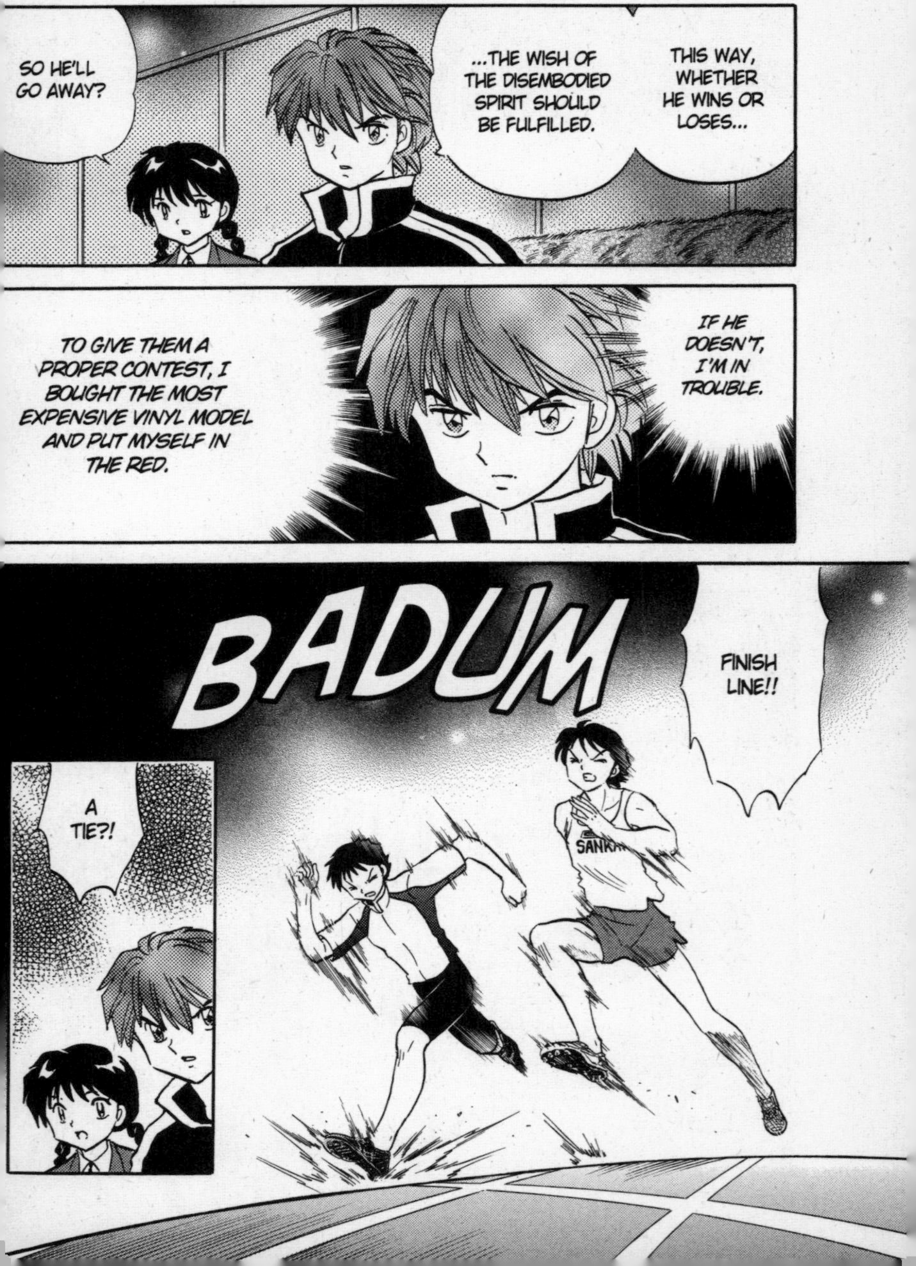
THIS WAY, WHETHER HE WINS OR LOSES...
...THE WISH OF THE DISEMBODIED SPIRIT SHOULD BE FULFILLED.
SO HE'LL GO AWAY?
IF HE DOESN'T, I'M IN TROUBLE.
TO GIVE THEM A PROPER CONTEST, I BOUGHT THE MOST EXPENSIVE VINYL MODEL AND PUT MYSELF IN THE RED.
FINISH LINE!!
BADUM
A TIE?!

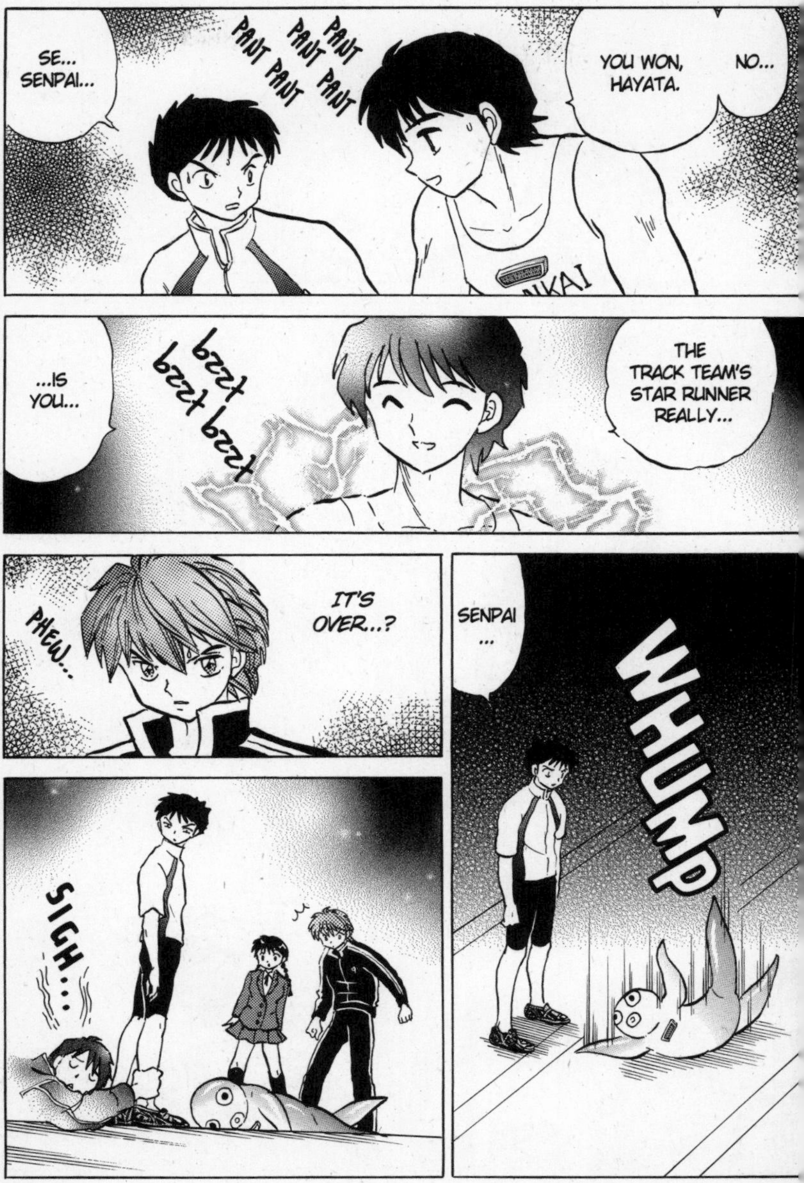
YOU WON, HAYATA. NO...
PANT PANT PANT PANT PANT
SE... SENPAI...
THE TRACK TEAM'S STAR RUNNER REALLY...
bzzt bzzt bzzt
...IS YOU...
SENPAI ...
WHUMP
IT'S OVER...?
PHEW...
SIGH...

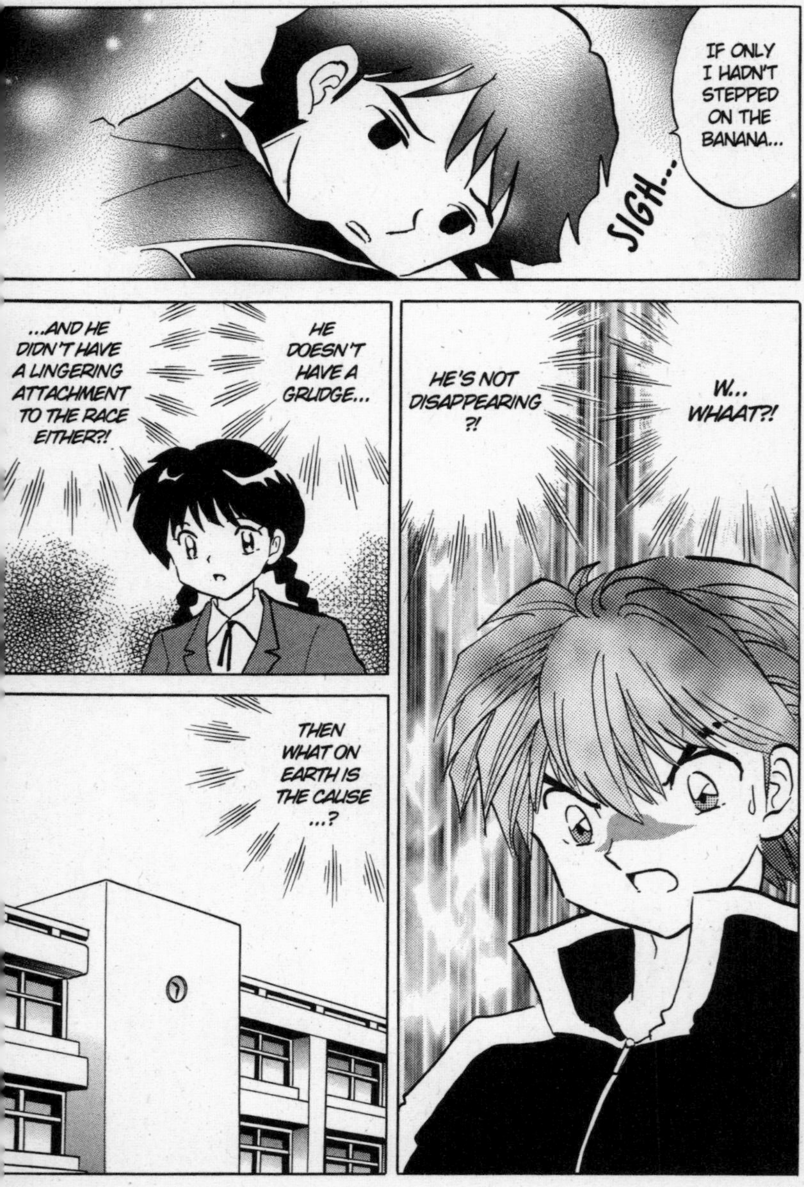
IF ONLY I HADN'T STEPPED ON THE BANANA...
SIGH...
W... WHAAT?!
HE'S NOT DISAPPEARING?!
HE DOESN'T HAVE A GRUDGE...
...AND HE DIDN'T HAVE A LINGERING ATTACHMENT TO THE RACE EITHER?!
THEN WHAT ON EARTH IS THE CAUSE...?

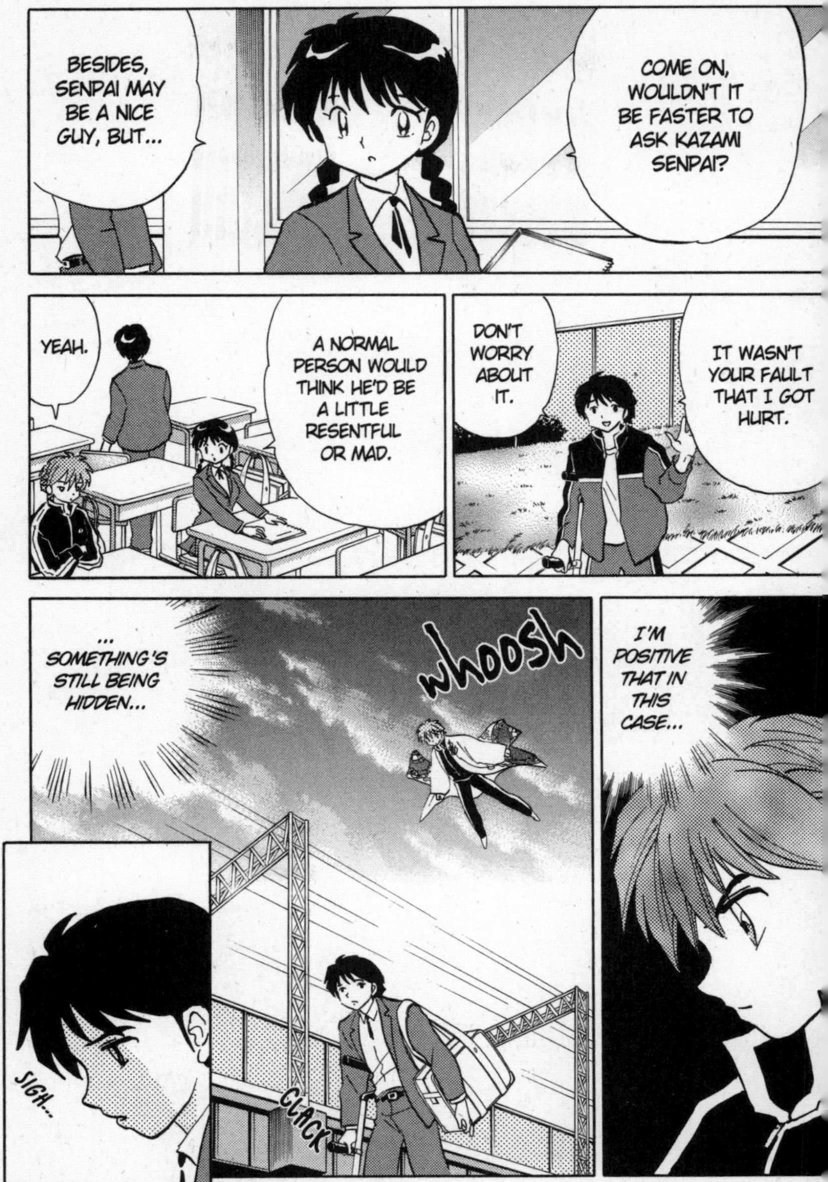
COME ON, WOULDN'T IT BE FASTER TO ASK KAZAMI SENPAI?
BESIDES, SENPAI MAY BE A NICE GUY, BUT...
IT WASN'T YOUR FAULT THAT I GOT HURT.
DON'T WORRY ABOUT IT.
A NORMAL PERSON WOULD THINK HE'D BE A LITTLE RESENTFUL OR MAD.
YEAH.
I'M POSITIVE THAT IN THIS CASE...
whoosh
... SOMETHING'S STILL BEING HIDDEN...
CLACK
SIGH...

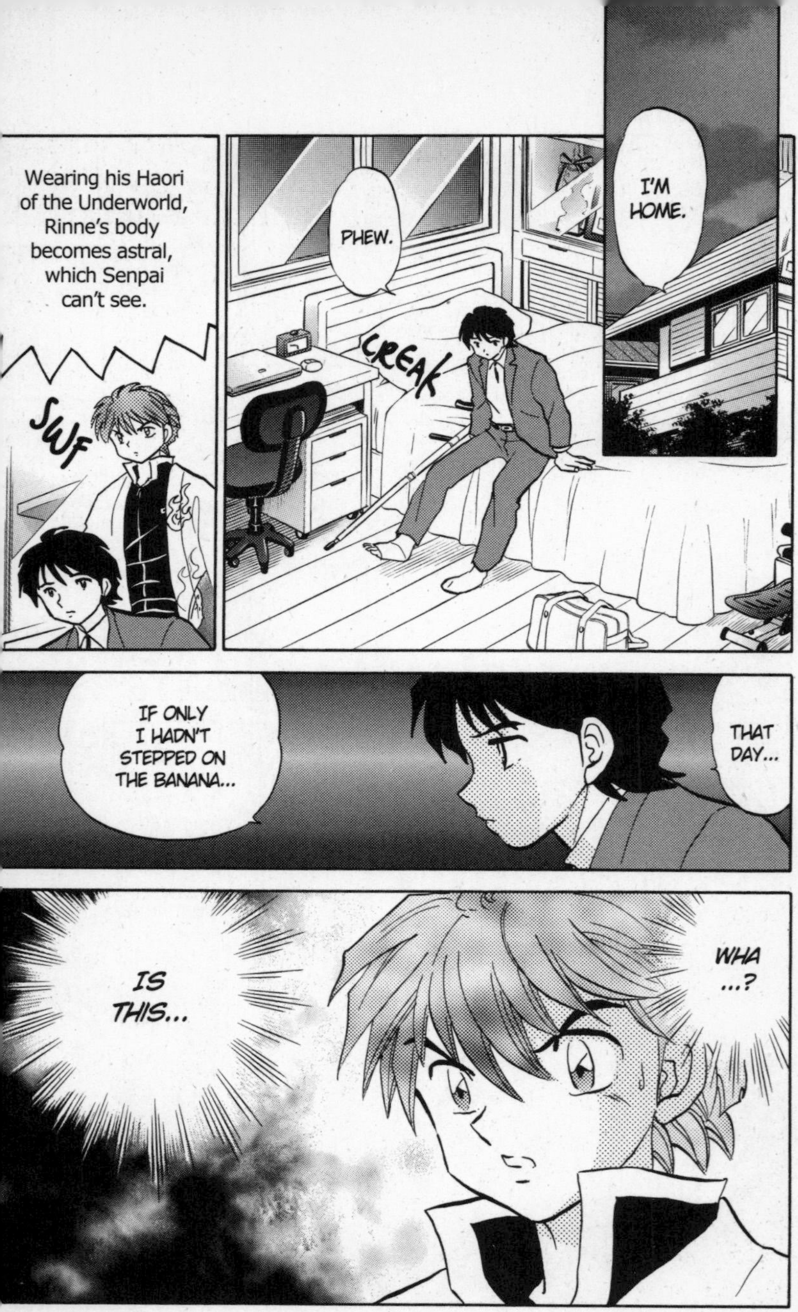
I'M HOME.
PHEW.
CREAK
Wearing his Haori of the Underworld, Rinne's body becomes astral, which Senpai can't see.
SWF
THAT DAY...
IF ONLY I HADN'T STEPPED ON THE BANANA...
WHA ...?
IS THIS...

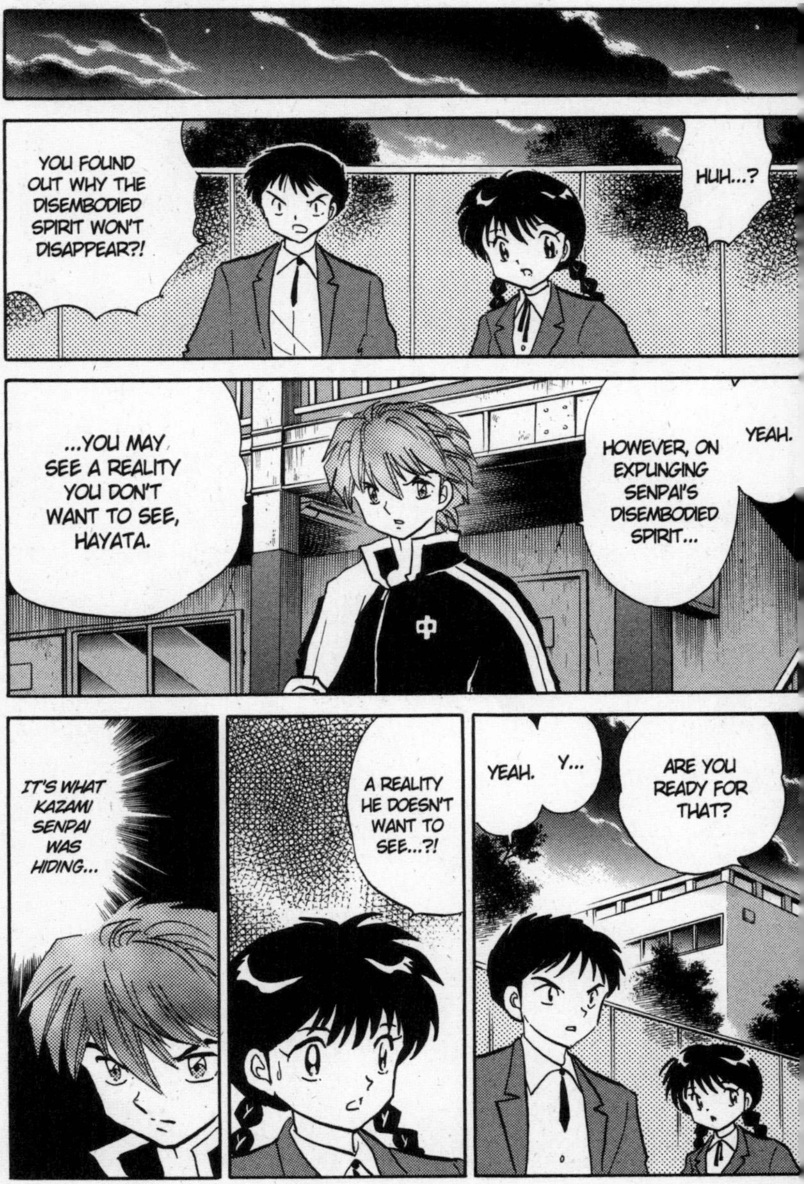
HUH...?
YOU FOUND OUT WHY THE DISEMBODIED SPIRIT WON'T DISAPPEAR?!
YEAH.
HOWEVER, ON EXPUNGING SENPAI'S DISEMBODIED SPIRIT...
...YOU MAY SEE A REALITY YOU DON'T WANT TO SEE, HAYATA.
ARE YOU READY FOR THAT?
Y...
YEAH.
A REALITY HE DOESN'T WANT TO SEE...?!
IT'S WHAT KAZAMI SENPAI WAS HIDING...

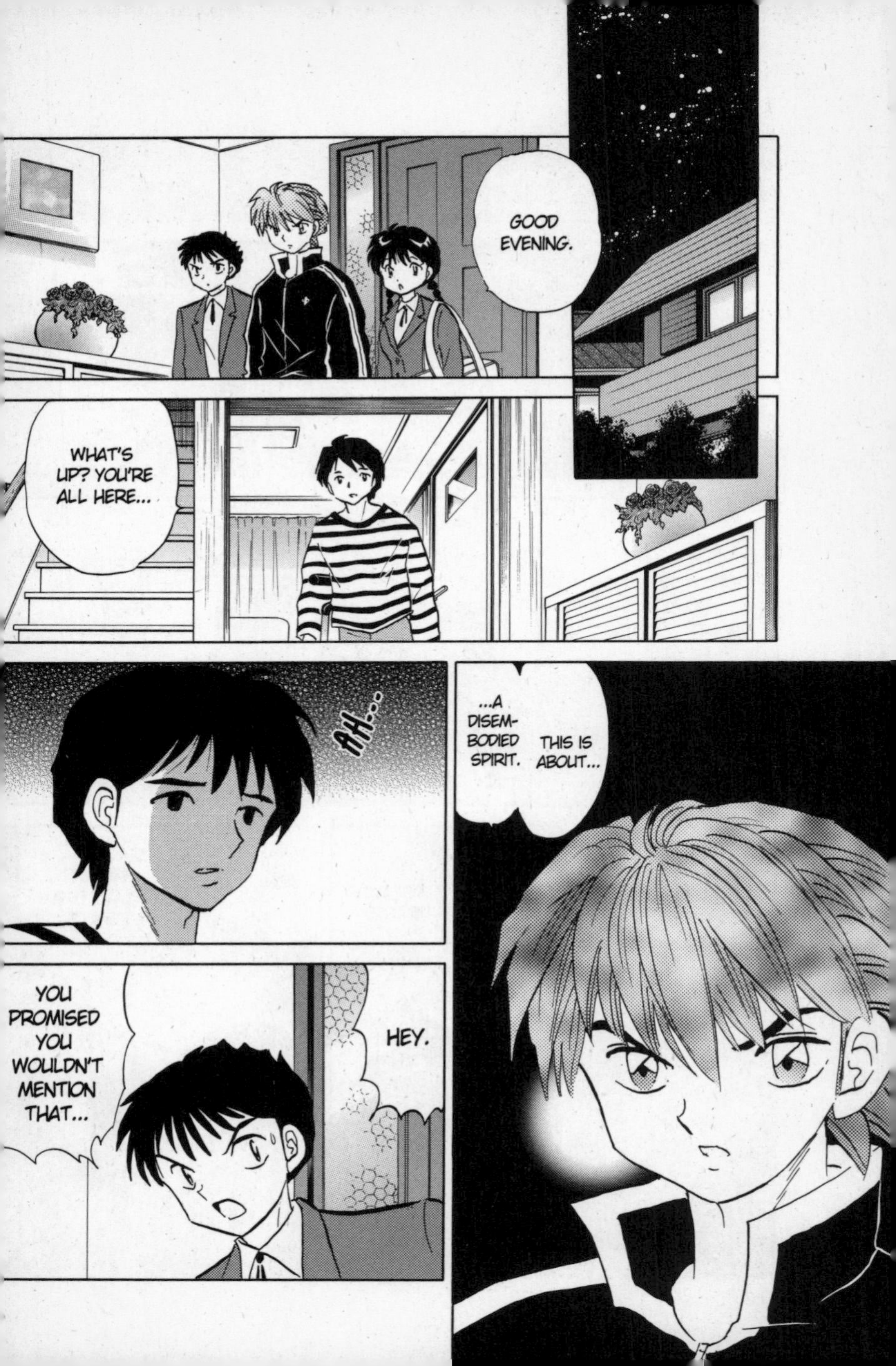
GOOD EVENING.
WHAT'S UP? YOU'RE ALL HERE...
THIS IS ABOUT...
...A DISEMBODIED SPIRIT.
AH...
HEY.
YOU PROMISED YOU WOULDN'T MENTION THAT...

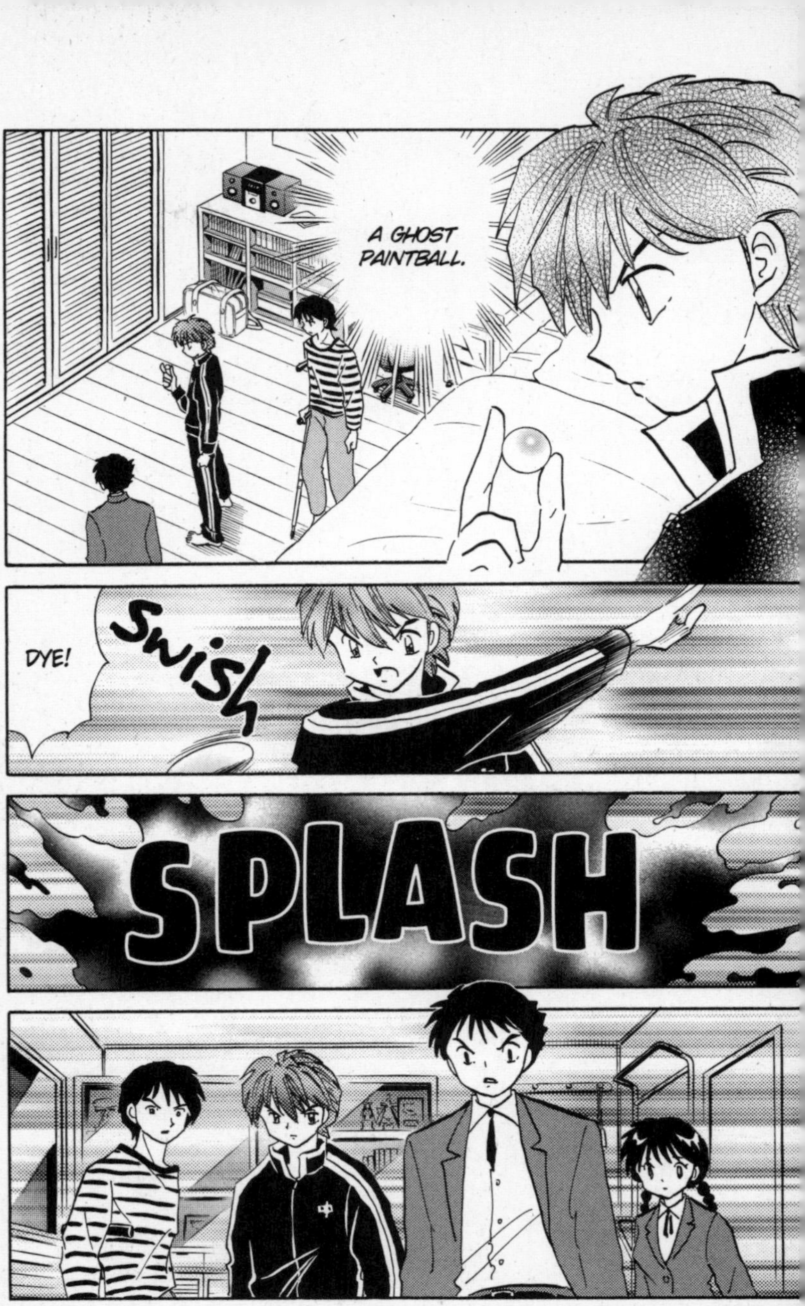
A GHOST PAINTBALL.
DYE!
SWISH
SPLASH

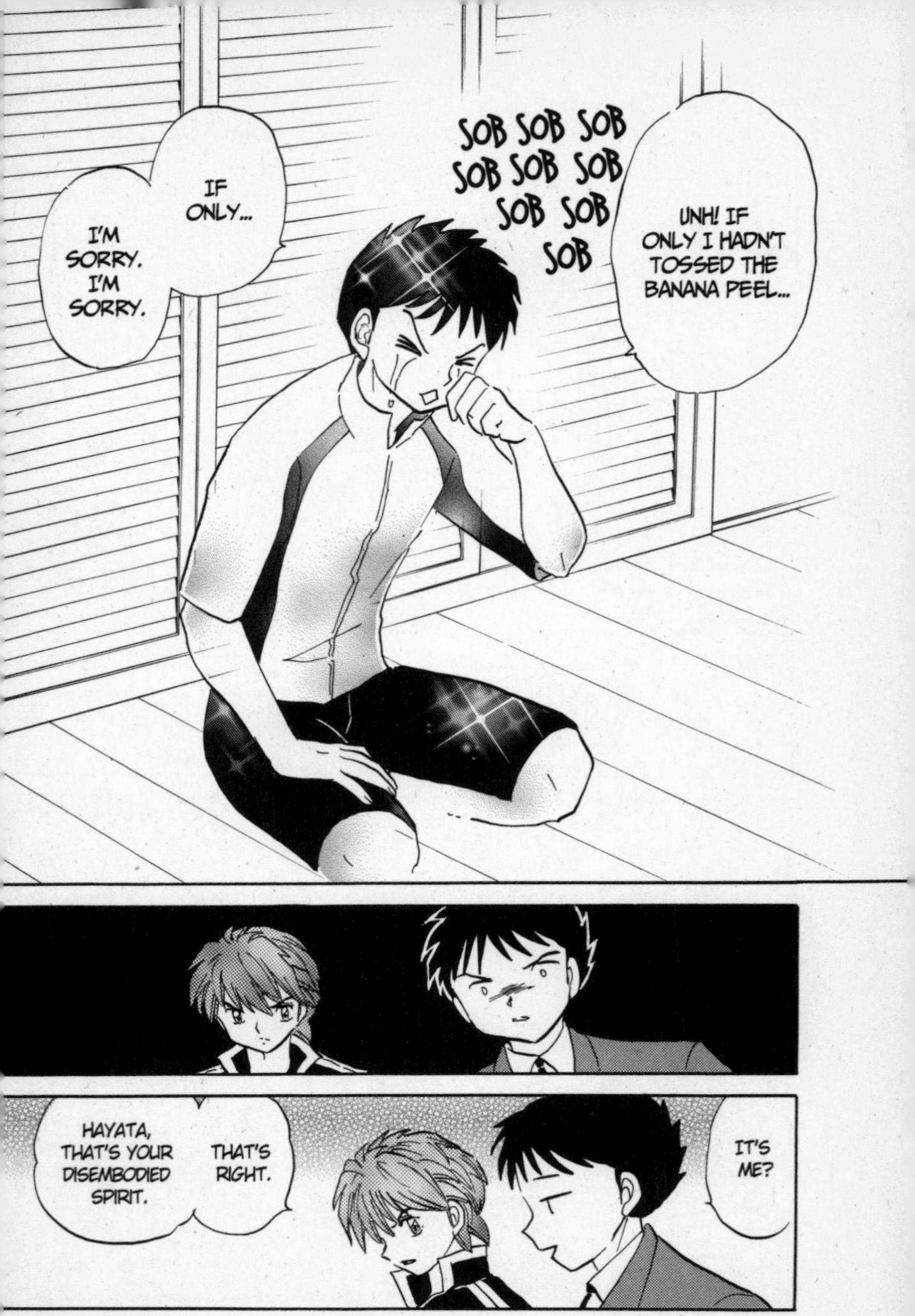
UNH! IF ONLY I HADN'T TOSSED THE BANANA PEEL...
SOB SOB SOB SOB SOB SOB SOB SOB SOB
IF ONLY...
I'M SORRY. I'M SORRY.
IT'S ME?
THAT'S RIGHT.
HAYATA, THAT'S YOUR DISEMBODIED SPIRIT.

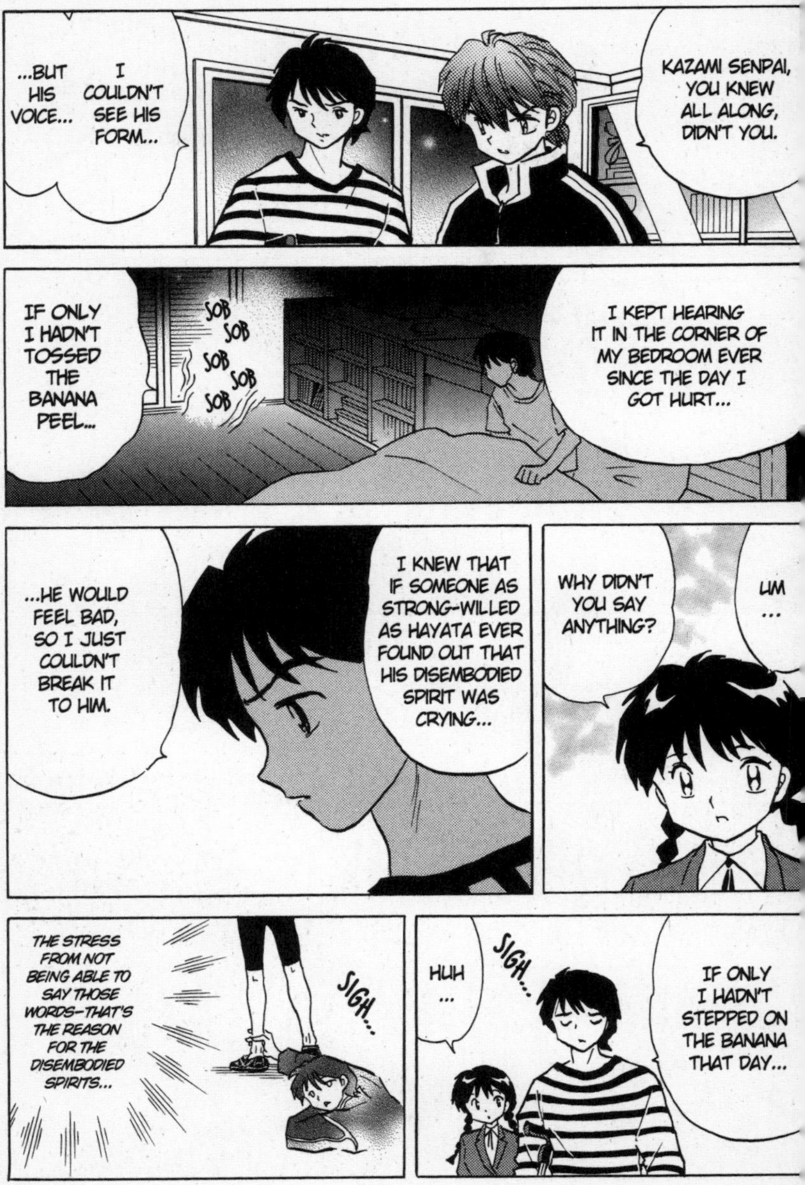
KAZAMI SENPAI, YOU KNEW ALL ALONG, DIDN'T YOU.
I COULDN'T SEE HIS FORM...
...BUT HIS VOICE...
I KEPT HEARING IT IN THE CORNER OF MY BEDROOM EVER SINCE THE DAY I GOT HURT...
SOB SOB SOB SOB SOB
IF ONLY I HADN'T TOSSED THE BANANA PEEL...
UM ...
WHY DIDN'T YOU SAY ANYTHING?
I KNEW THAT IF SOMEONE AS STRONG-WILLED AS HAYATA EVER FOUND OUT THAT HIS DISEMBODIED SPIRIT WAS CRYING...
...HE WOULD FEEL BAD, SO I JUST COULDN'T BREAK IT TO HIM.
IF ONLY I HADN'T STEPPED ON THE BANANA THAT DAY...
SIGH...
HUH ...
SIGH...
THE STRESS FROM NOT BEING ABLE TO SAY THOSE WORDS—THAT'S THE REASON FOR THE DISEMBODIED SPIRITS...

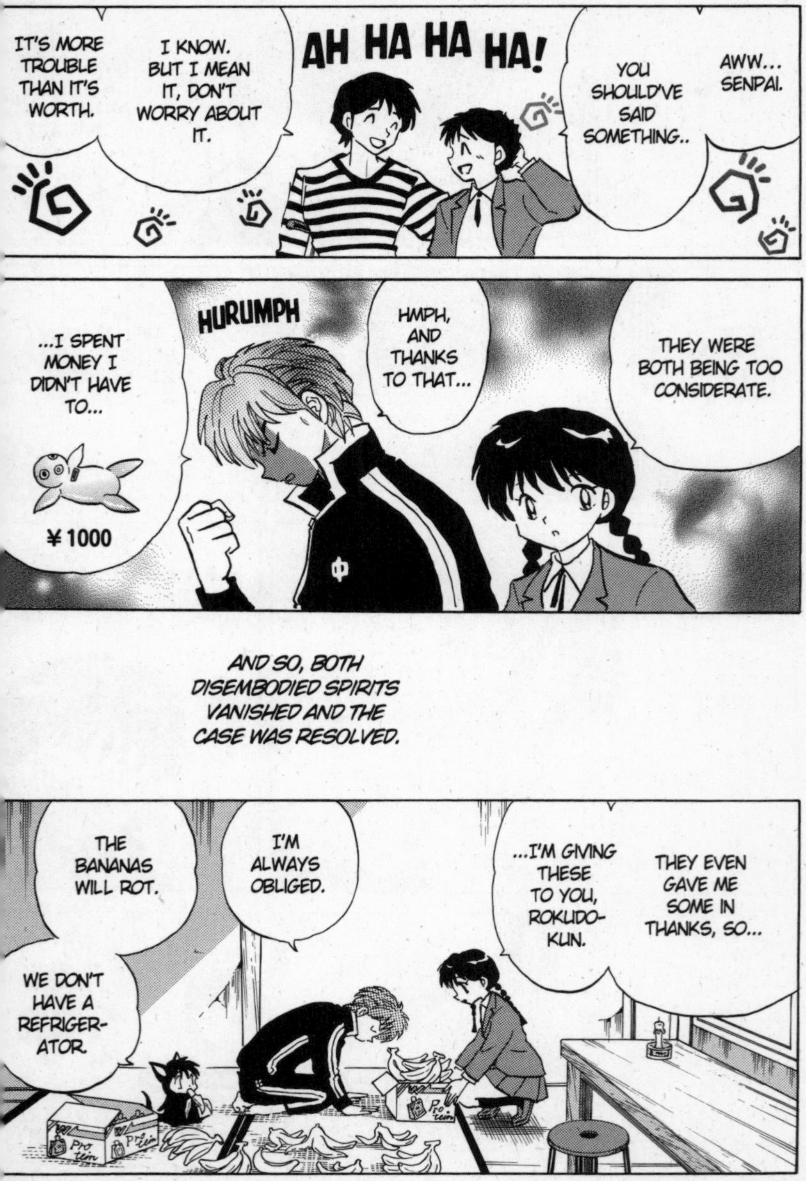
AWW... SENPAI.
YOU SHOULD'VE SAID SOMETHING..
AH HA HA HA!
I KNOW. BUT I MEAN IT, DON'T WORRY ABOUT IT.
IT'S MORE TROUBLE THAN IT'S WORTH.
THEY WERE BOTH BEING TOO CONSIDERATE.
HMPH, AND THANKS TO THAT...
HURUMPH
...I SPENT MONEY I DIDN'T HAVE TO...
¥1000
AND SO, BOTH DISEMBODIED SPIRITS VANISHED AND THE CASE WAS RESOLVED.
THEY EVEN GAVE ME SOME IN THANKS, SO...
...I'M GIVING THESE TO YOU, ROKUDO-KUN.
I'M ALWAYS OBLIGED.
THE BANANAS WILL ROT.
WE DON'T HAVE A REFRIGERATOR.

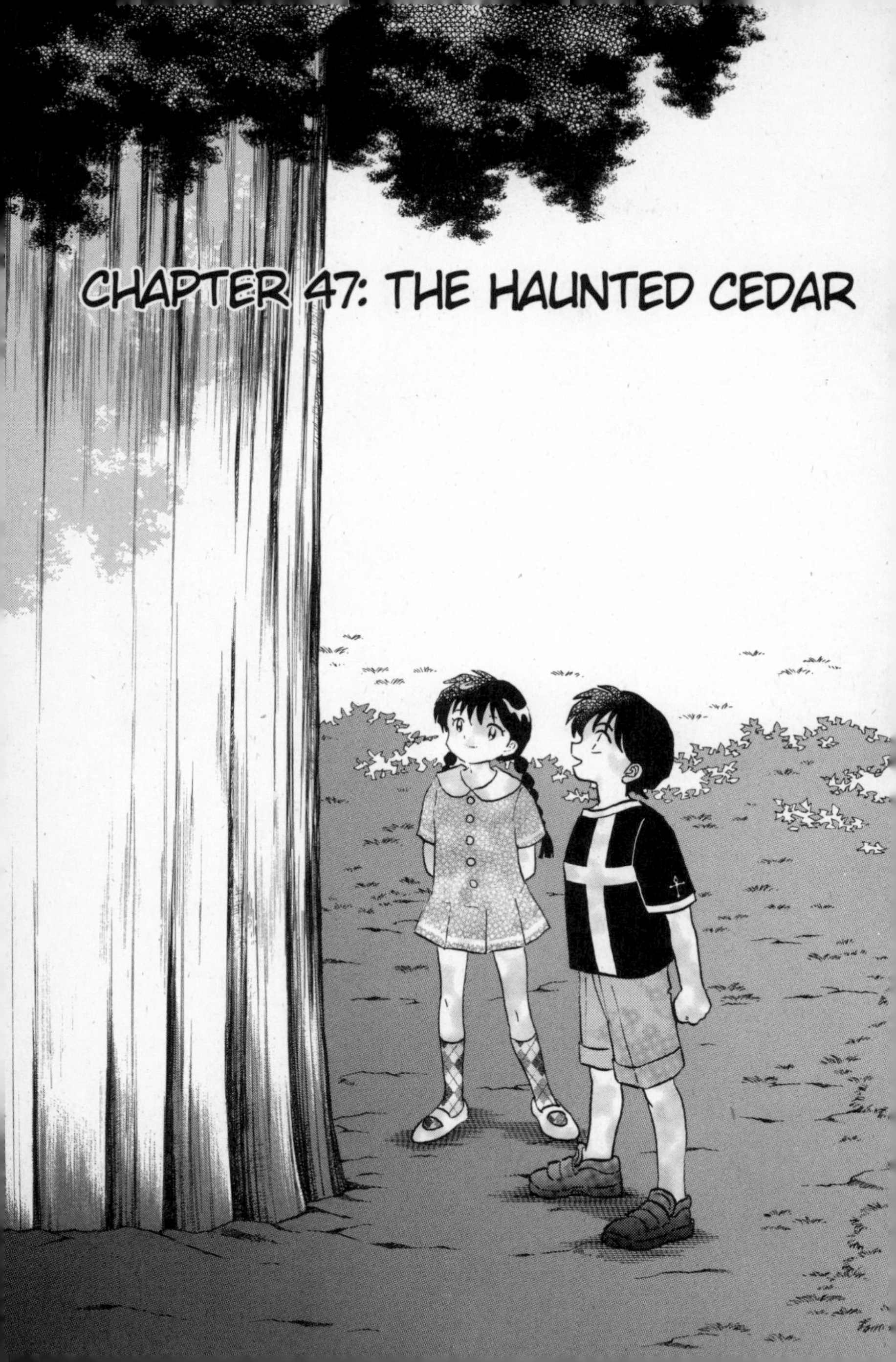
CHAPTER 47: THE HAUNTED CEDAR

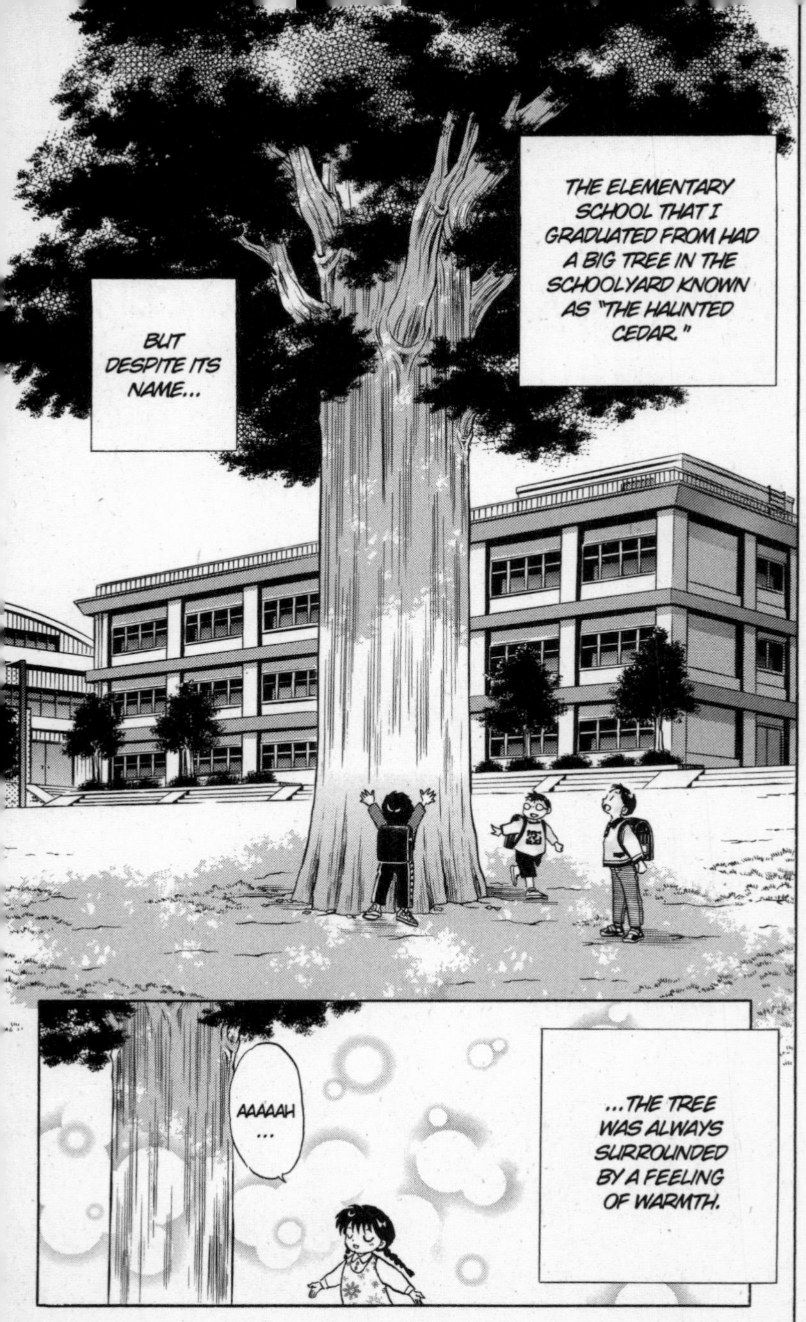
THE ELEMENTARY SCHOOL THAT I GRADUATED FROM HAD A BIG TREE IN THE SCHOOLYARD KNOWN AS "THE HAUNTED CEDAR."
BUT DESPITE ITS NAME...
...THE TREE WAS ALWAYS SURROUNDED BY A FEELING OF WARMTH.
AAAAAH...

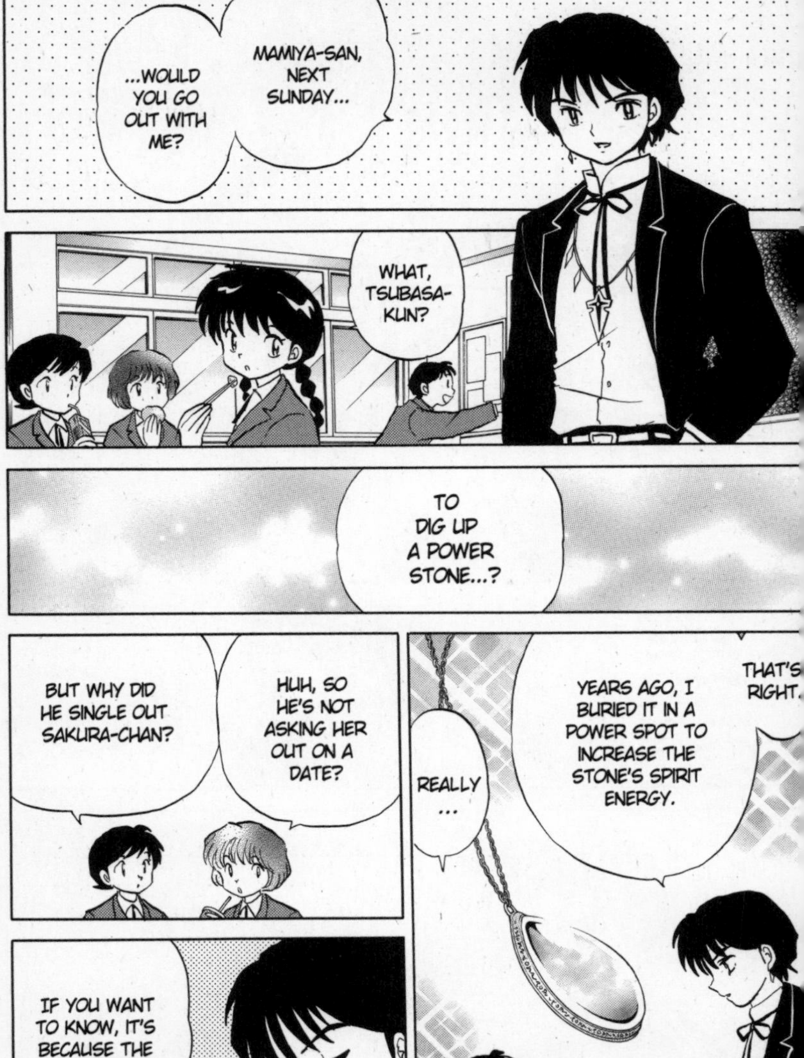
MAMIYA-SAN, NEXT SUNDAY...
...WOULD YOU GO OUT WITH ME?
WHAT, TSUBASA-KUN?
TO DIG UP A POWER STONE...?
THAT'S RIGHT.
YEARS AGO, I BURIED IT IN A POWER SPOT TO INCREASE THE STONE'S SPIRIT ENERGY.
REALLY...
HUH, SO HE'S NOT ASKING HER OUT ON A DATE?
BUT WHY DID HE SINGLE OUT SAKURA-CHAN?
IF YOU WANT TO KNOW, IT'S BECAUSE THE POWER SPOT...

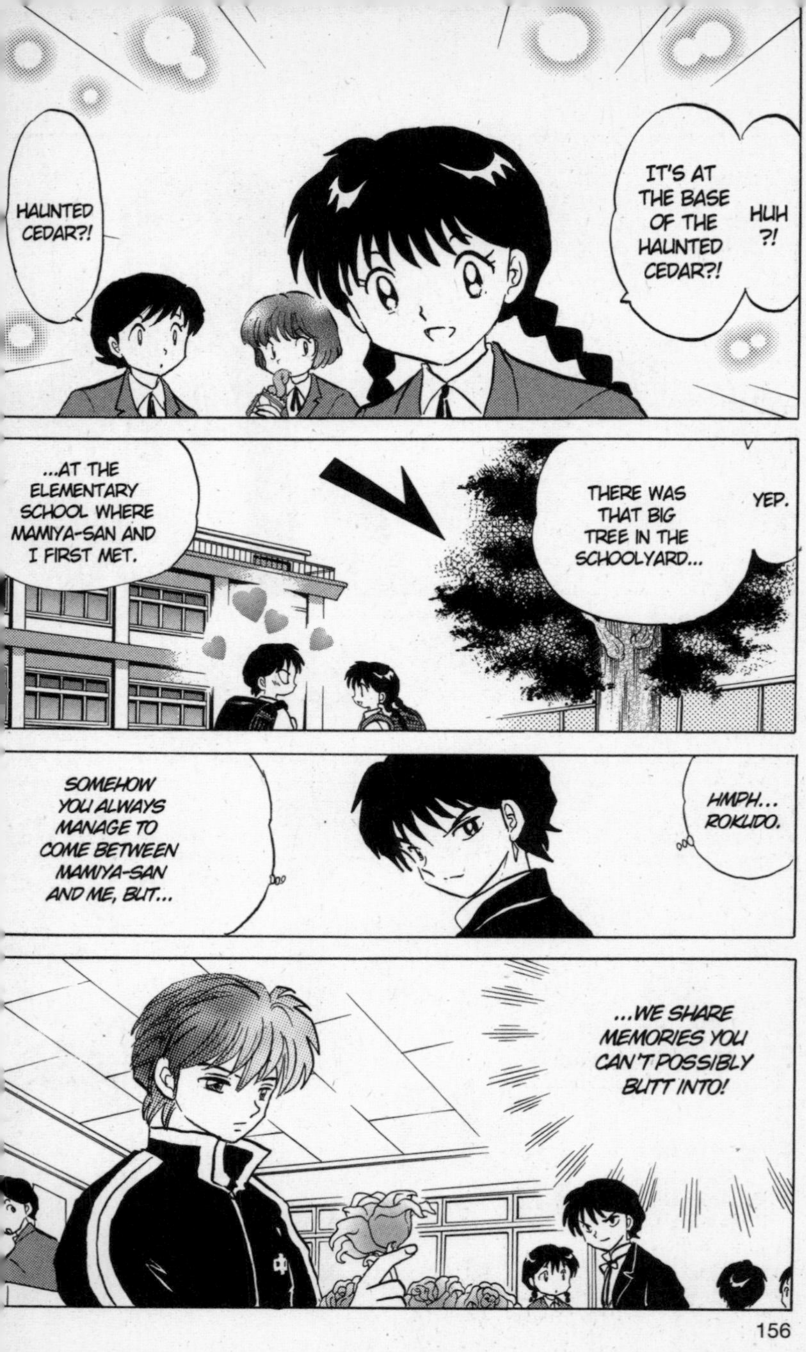
IT'S AT THE BASE OF THE HAUNTED CEDAR?!
HUH ?!
HAUNTED CEDAR?!
YEP.
THERE WAS THAT BIG TREE IN THE SCHOOLYARD...
...AT THE ELEMENTARY SCHOOL WHERE MAMIYA-SAN AND I FIRST MET.
HMPH... ROKUDO.
SOMEHOW YOU ALWAYS MANAGE TO COME BETWEEN MAMIYA-SAN AND ME, BUT...
...WE SHARE MEMORIES YOU CAN'T POSSIBLY BUTT INTO!

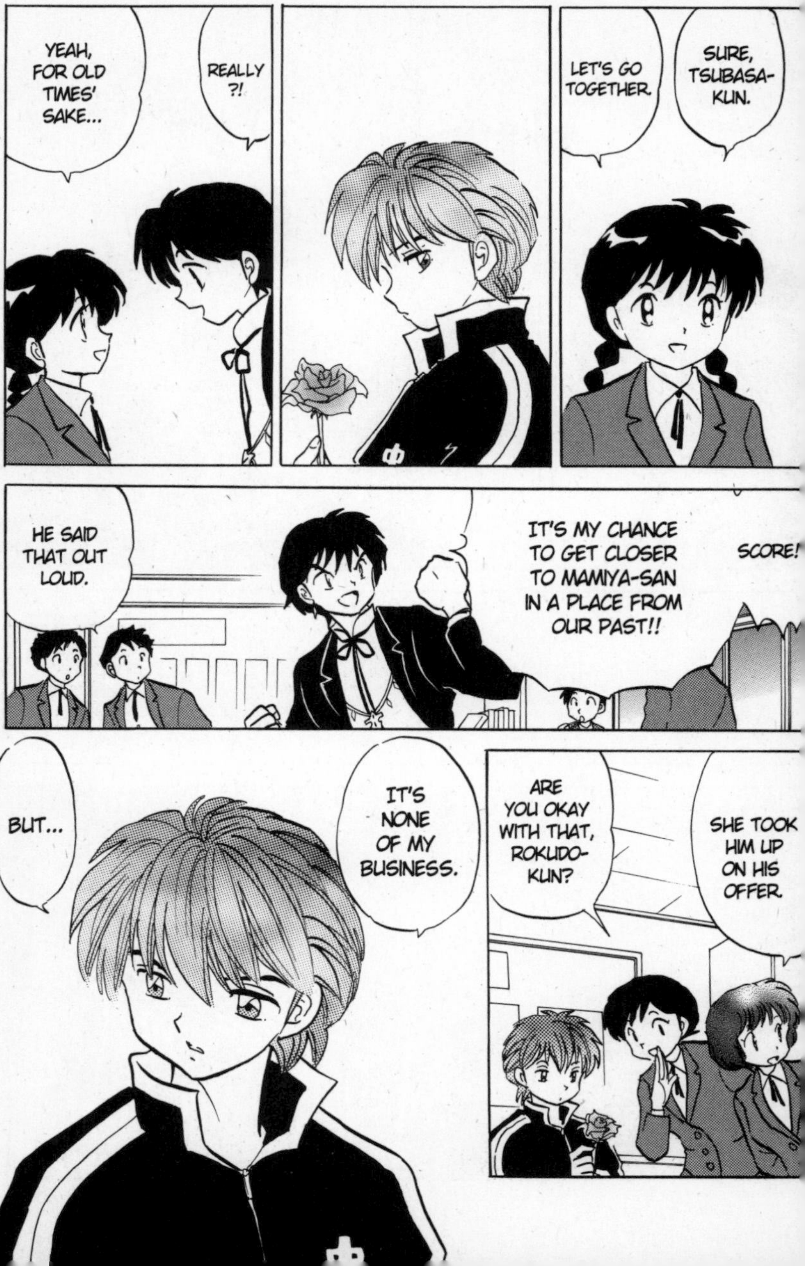
SURE, TSUBASA-KUN.
LET'S GO TOGETHER.
REALLY?!
YEAH, FOR OLD TIMES' SAKE...
SCORE!
IT'S MY CHANCE TO GET CLOSER TO MAMIYA-SAN IN A PLACE FROM OUR PAST!!
HE SAID THAT OUT LOUD.
SHE TOOK HIM UP ON HIS OFFER.
ARE YOU OKAY WITH THAT, ROKUDO-KUN?
IT'S NONE OF MY BUSINESS.
BUT...

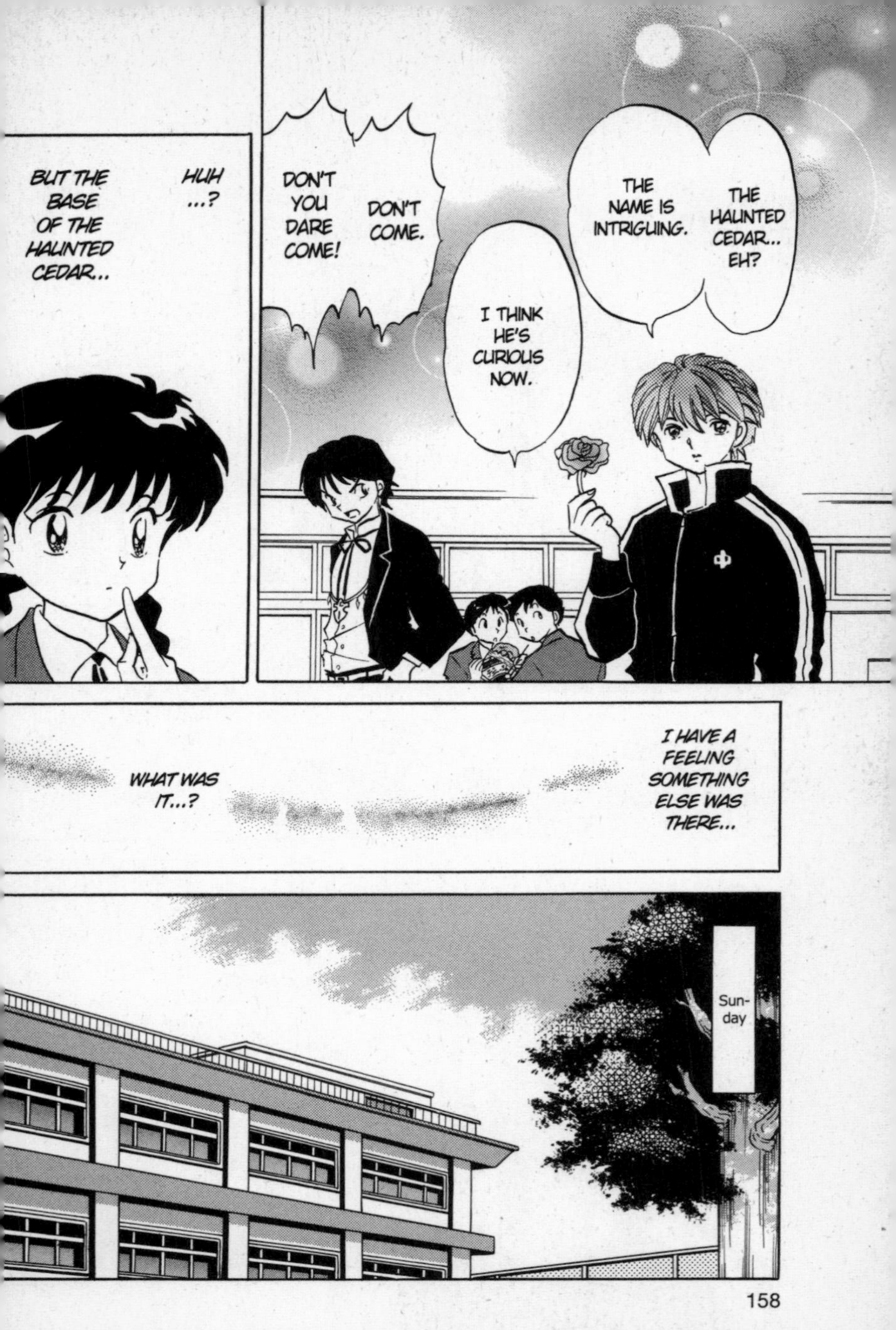
THE HAUNTED CEDAR... EH?
THE NAME IS INTRIGUING.
I THINK HE'S CURIOUS NOW.
DON'T COME.
DON'T YOU DARE COME!
HUH ...?
BUT THE BASE OF THE HAUNTED CEDAR...
I HAVE A FEELING SOMETHING ELSE WAS THERE...
WHAT WAS IT...?
Sunday

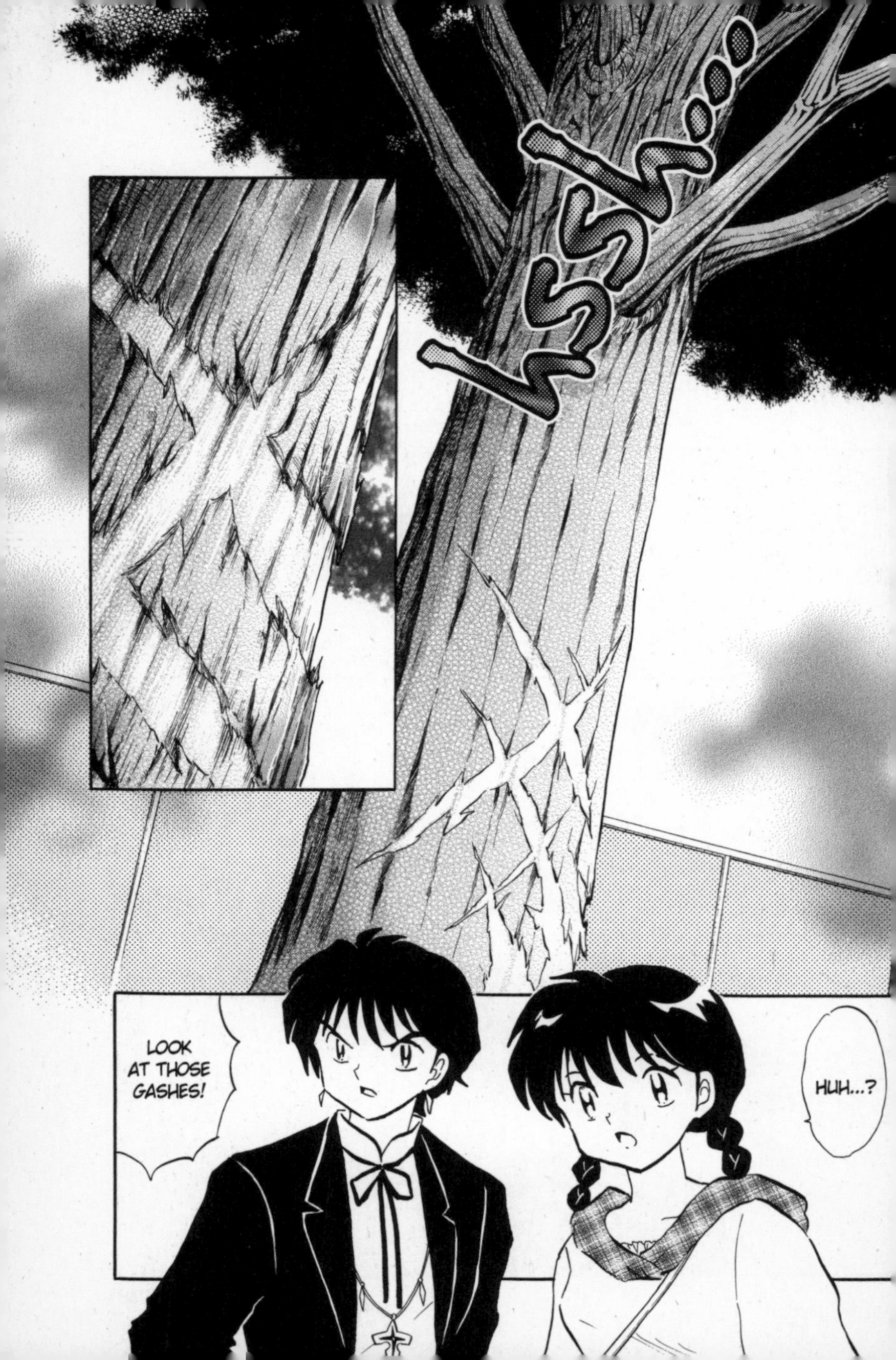
HUH...?
LOOK AT THOSE GASHES!

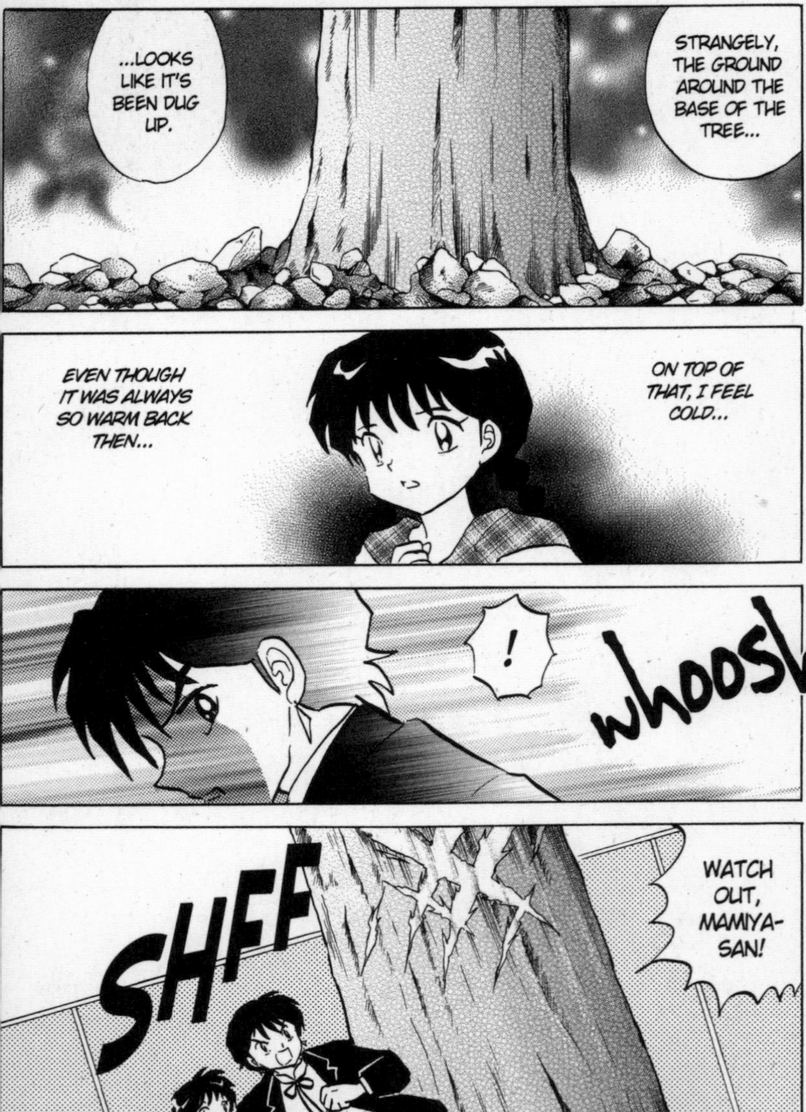
STRANGELY, THE GROUND AROUND THE BASE OF THE TREE...
...LOOKS LIKE IT'S BEEN DUG UP.
ON TOP OF THAT, I FEEL COLD...
EVEN THOUGH IT WAS ALWAYS SO WARM BACK THEN...
!
whoosh
WATCH OUT, MAMIYA-SAN!
SHFF

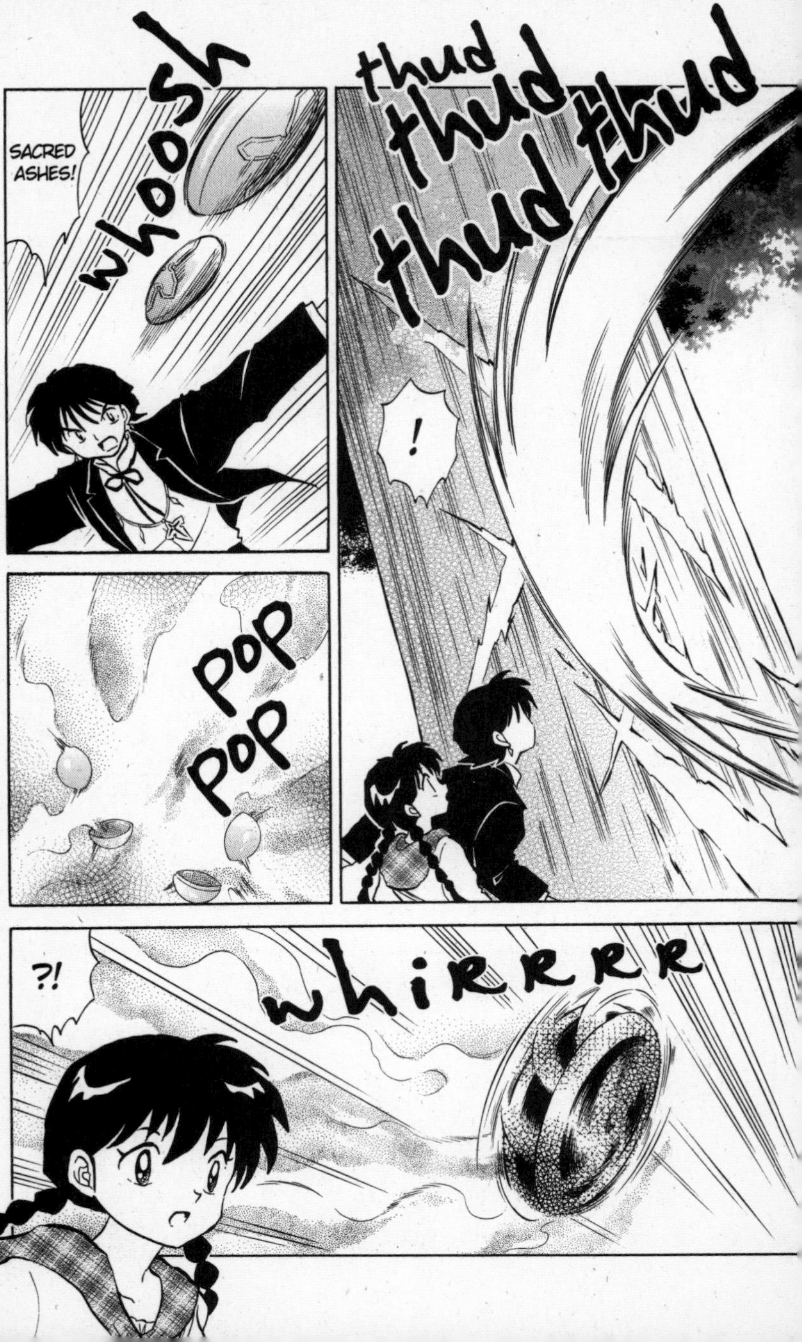
thud thud thud thud
!
whoosh
SACRED ASHES!
POP POP
whiRRRR
?!

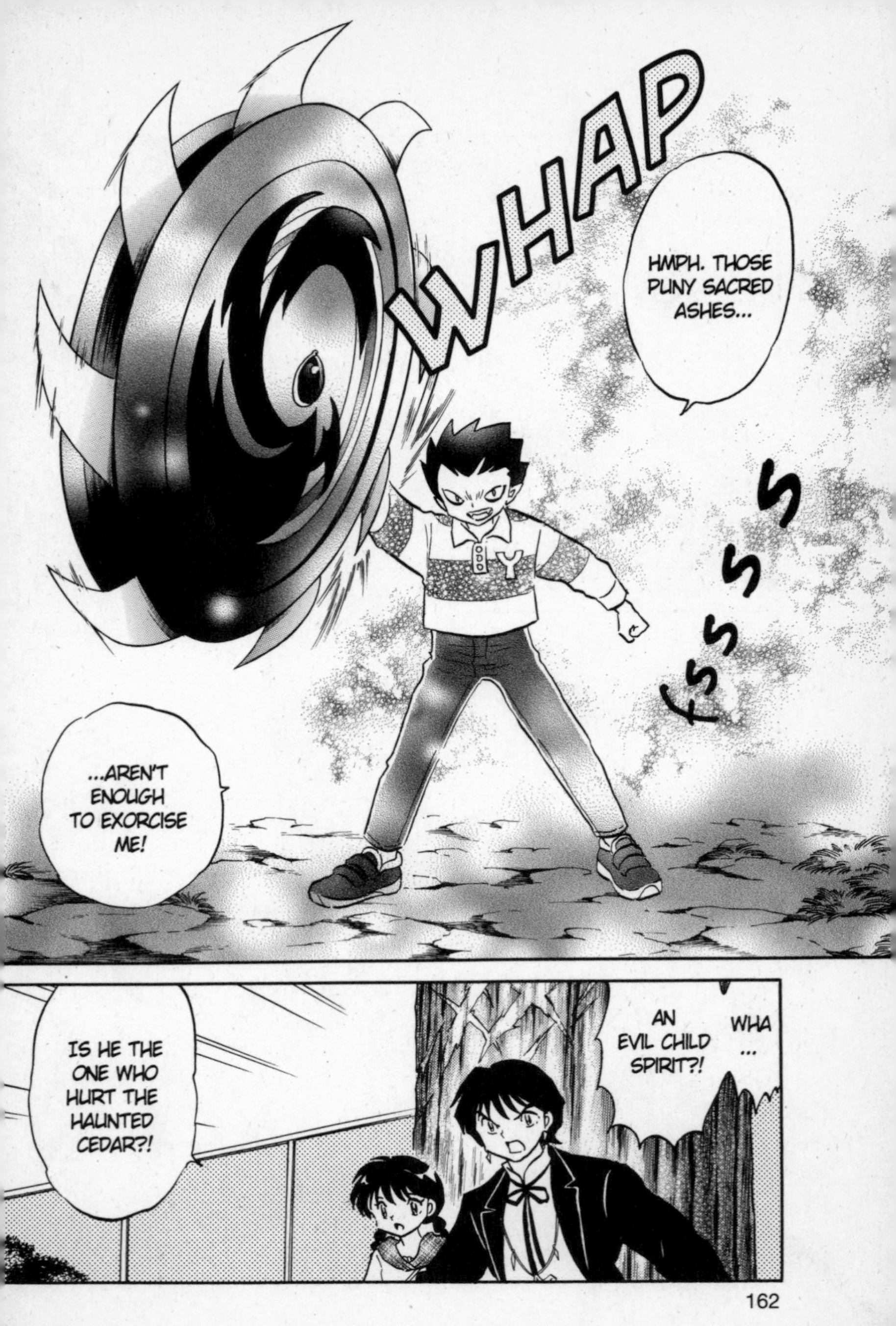
WHAP
HMPH. THOSE PUNY SACRED ASHES...
fsssss
...AREN'T ENOUGH TO EXORCISE ME!
WHA ...
AN EVIL CHILD SPIRIT?!
IS HE THE ONE WHO HURT THE HAUNTED CEDAR?!

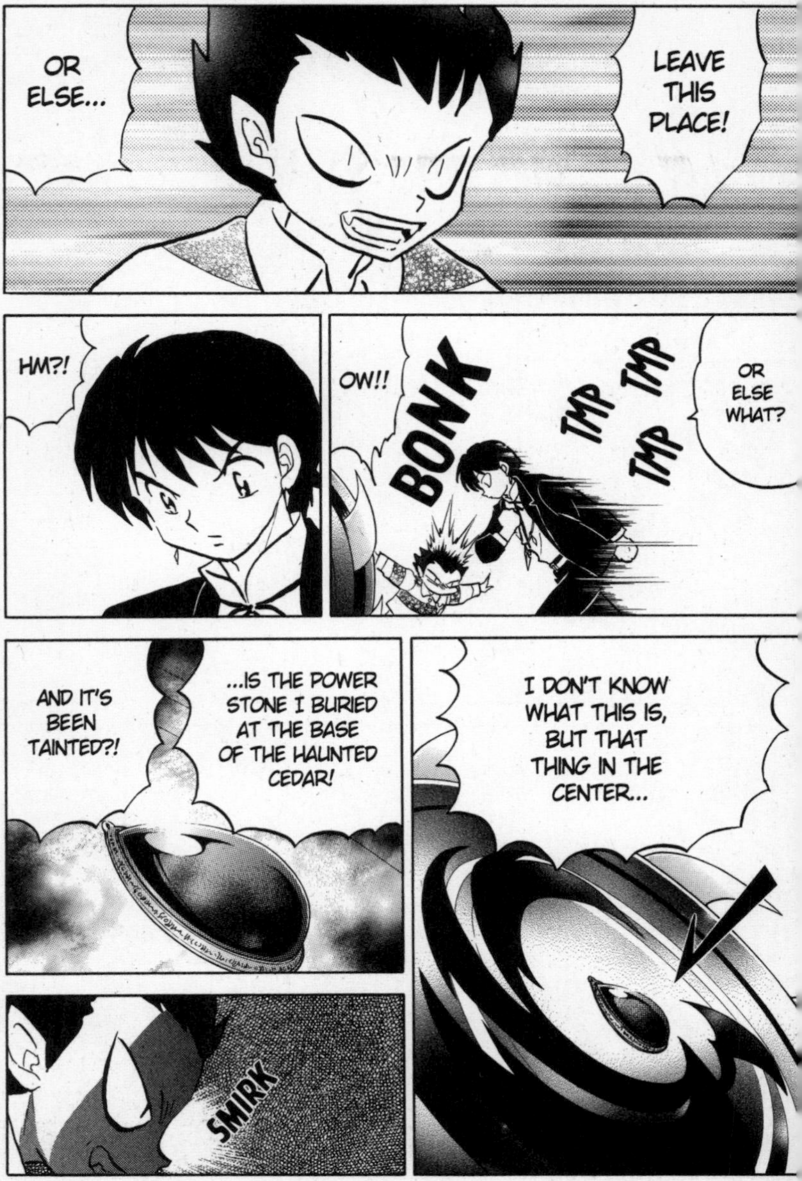
LEAVE THIS PLACE!
OR ELSE...
OR ELSE WHAT?
TMP TMP TMP
BONK
OW!!
HM?!
I DON'T KNOW WHAT THIS IS, BUT THAT THING IN THE CENTER...
...IS THE POWER STONE I BURIED AT THE BASE OF THE HAUNTED CEDAR!
AND IT'S BEEN TAINTED?!
SMIRK

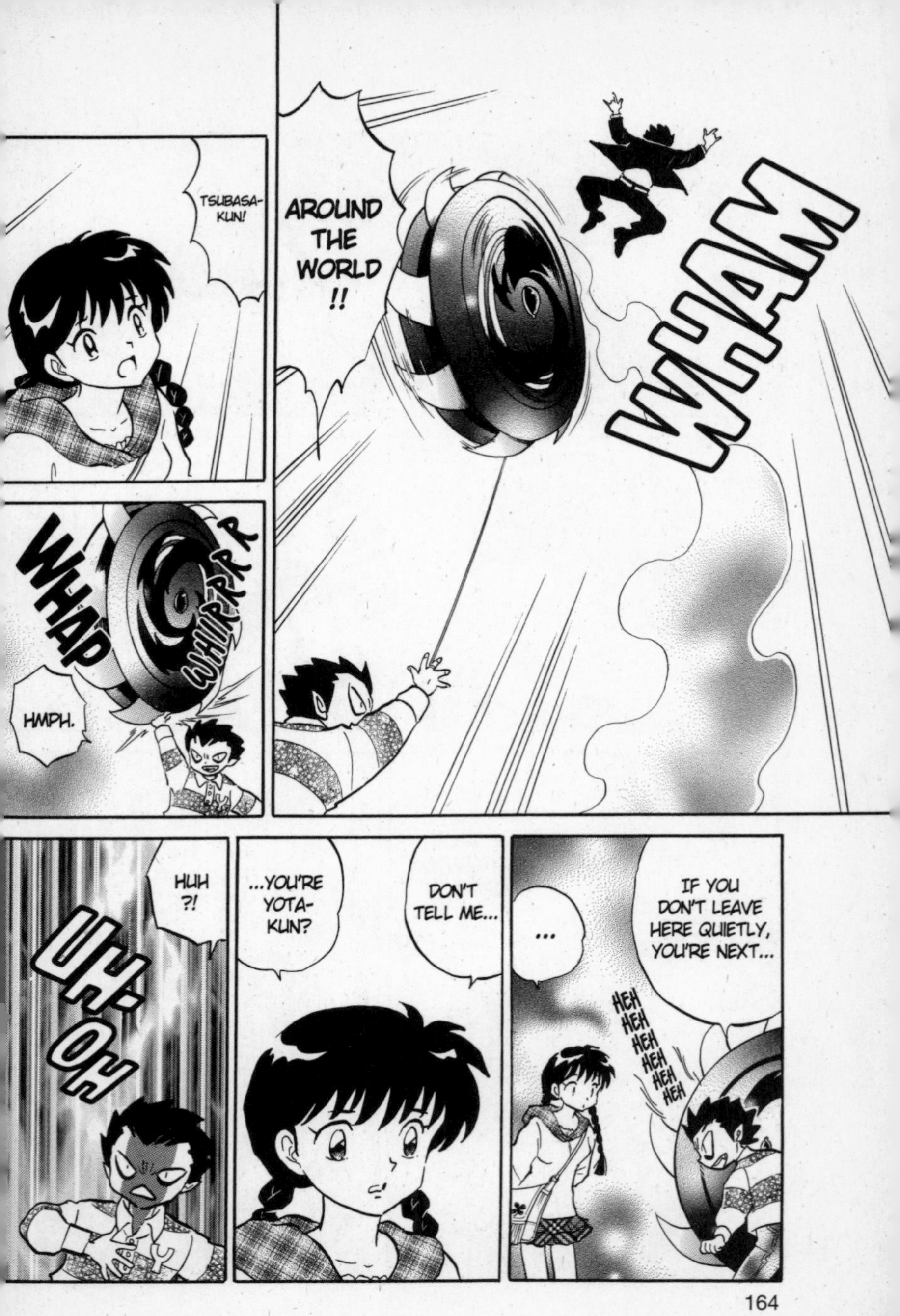
AROUND THE WORLD !!
WHAM
TSUBASA-KUN!
WHAP
WHIPPPR
HMPH.
IF YOU DON'T LEAVE HERE QUIETLY, YOU'RE NEXT...
...
HEH HEH HEH HEH HEH HEH HEH
DON'T TELL ME...
...YOU'RE YOTA-KUN?
HUH ?!
UH-OH

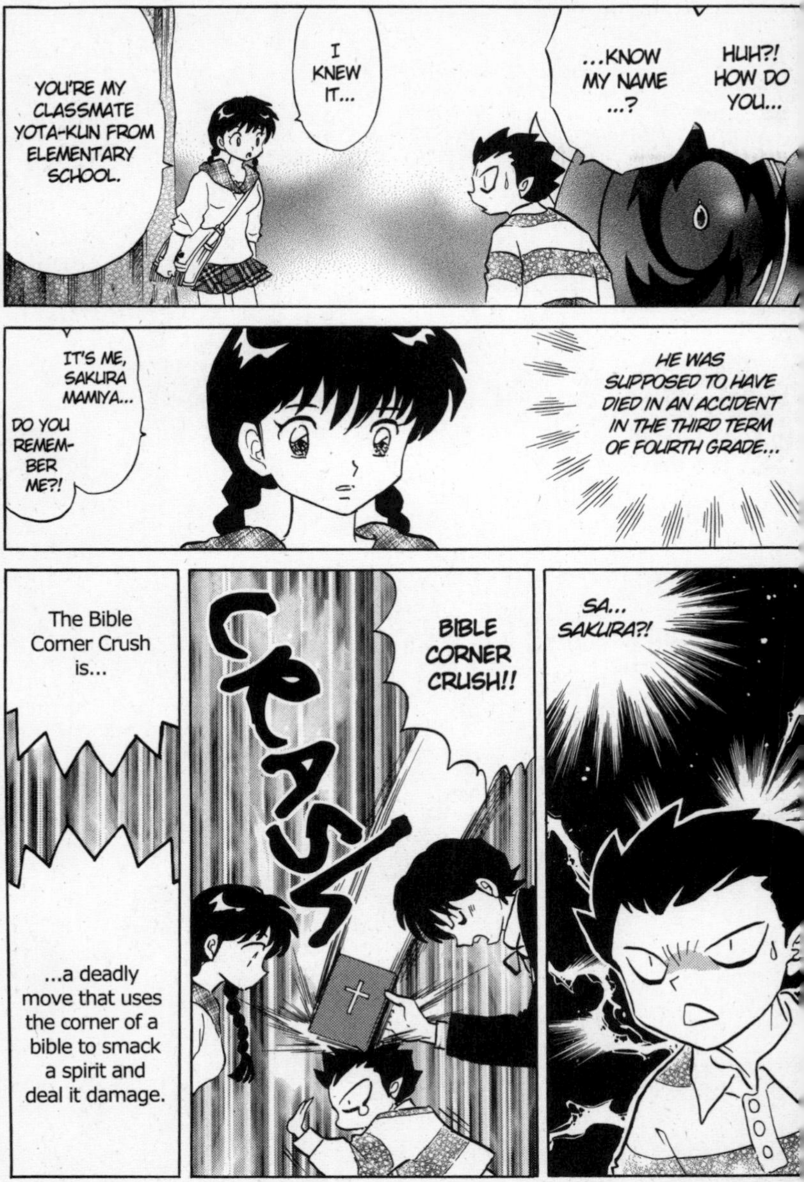
HUH?! HOW DO YOU...
...KNOW MY NAME ...?
I KNEW IT...
YOU'RE MY CLASSMATE YOTA-KUN FROM ELEMENTARY SCHOOL.
HE WAS SUPPOSED TO HAVE DIED IN AN ACCIDENT IN THE THIRD TERM OF FOURTH GRADE...
IT'S ME, SAKURA MAMIYA...
DO YOU REMEMBER ME?!
SA... SAKURA?!
BIBLE CORNER CRUSH!!
CRASH
The Bible Corner Crush is...
...a deadly move that uses the corner of a bible to smack a spirit and deal it damage.

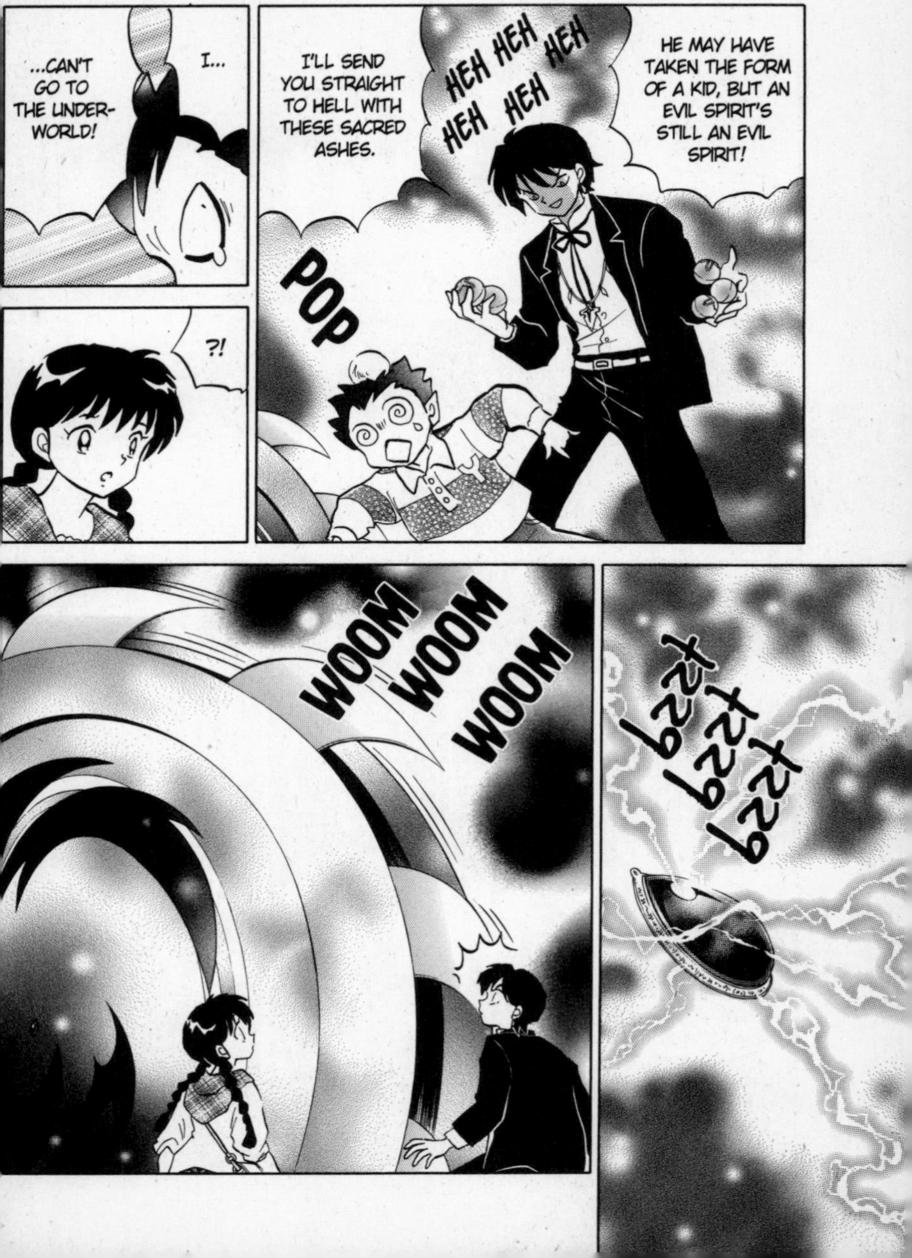
HE MAY HAVE TAKEN THE FORM OF A KID, BUT AN EVIL SPIRIT'S STILL AN EVIL SPIRIT!
HEH HEH HEH HEH HEH
I'LL SEND YOU STRAIGHT TO HELL WITH THESE SACRED ASHES.
POP
I...
...CAN'T GO TO THE UNDER-WORLD!
?!
BZZT BZZT BZZT
WOOM WOOM WOOM

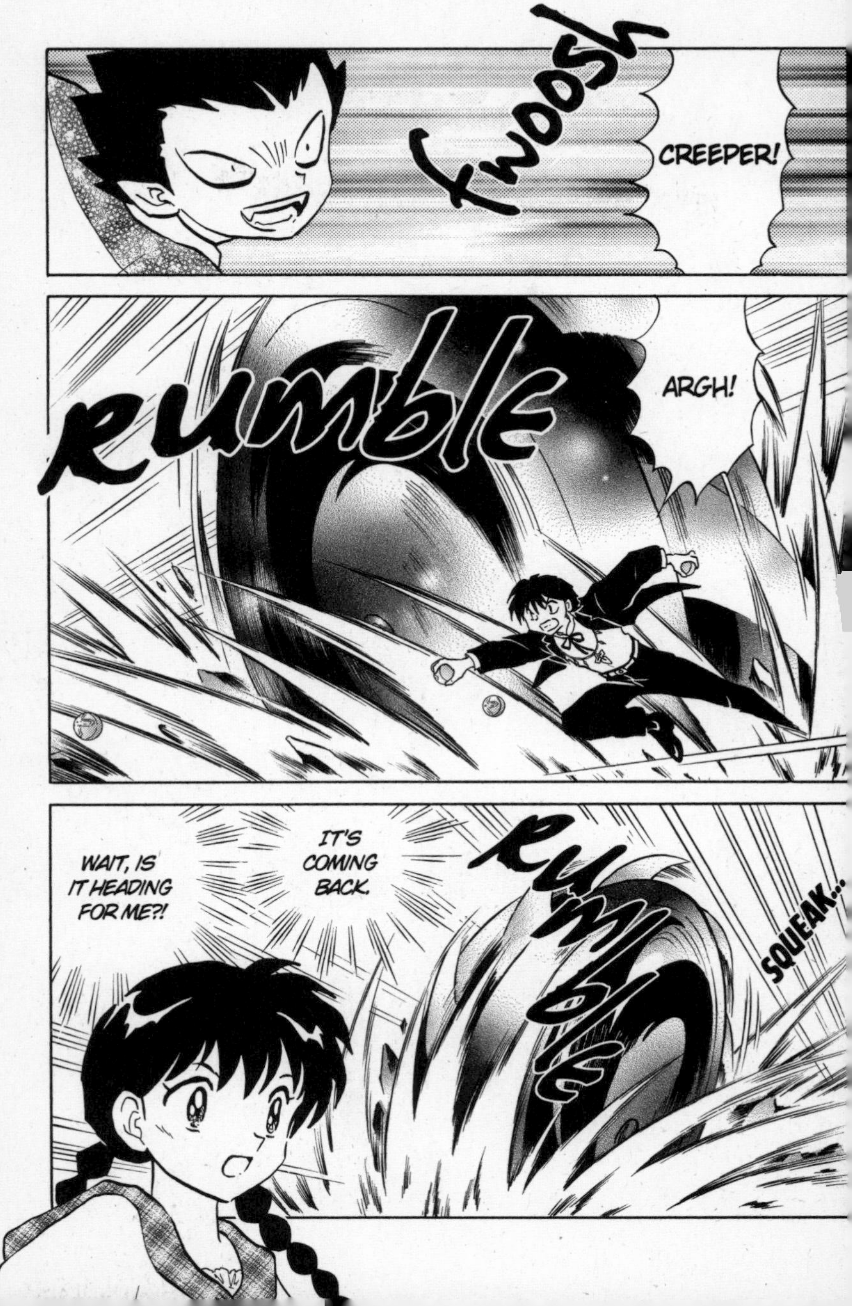
twoosh
CREEPER!
rumble
ARGH!
SQUEAK...
rumble
IT'S COMING BACK.
WAIT, IS IT HEADING FOR ME?!

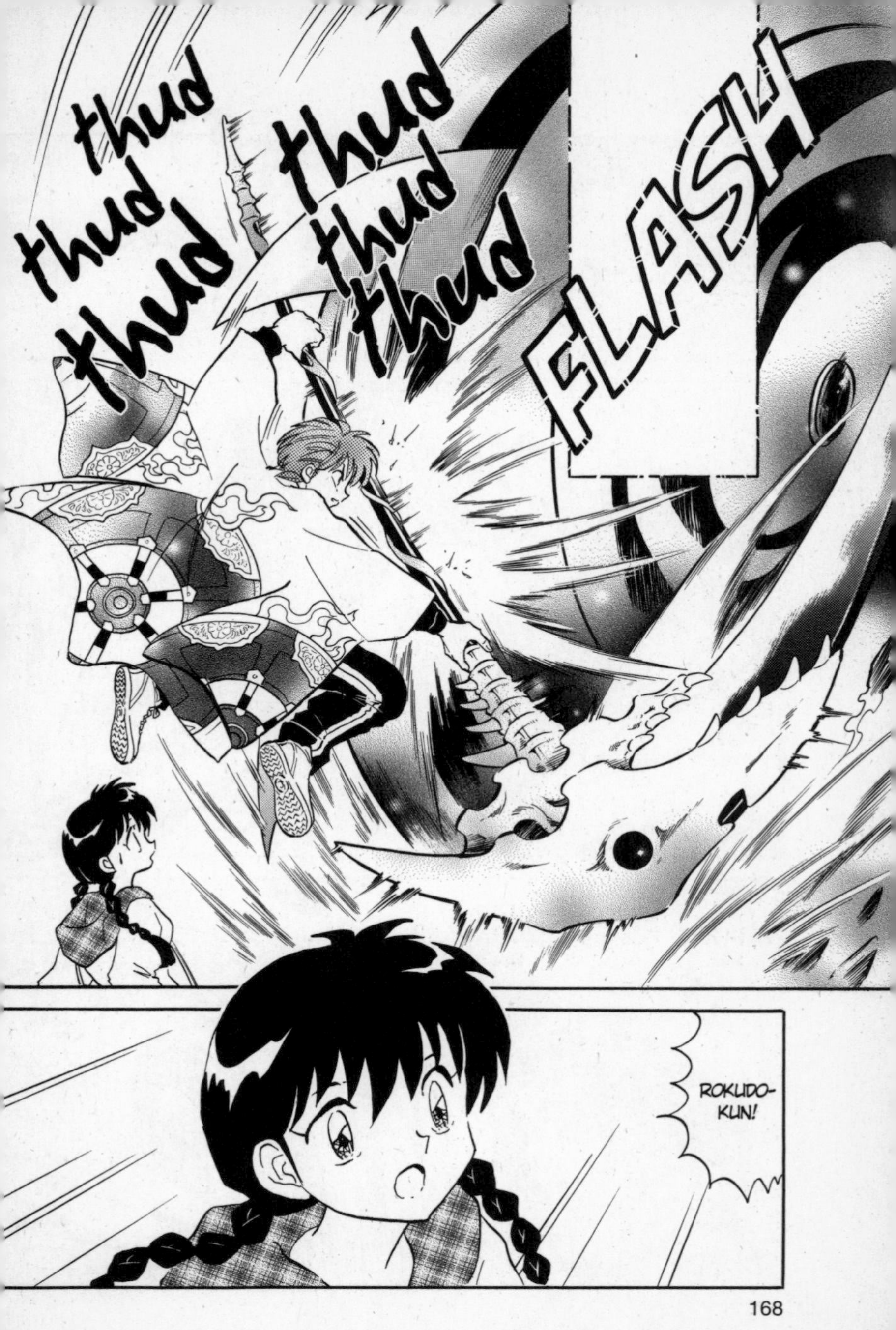
thud thud thud
thud thud thud
FLASH
ROKUDO-KUN!

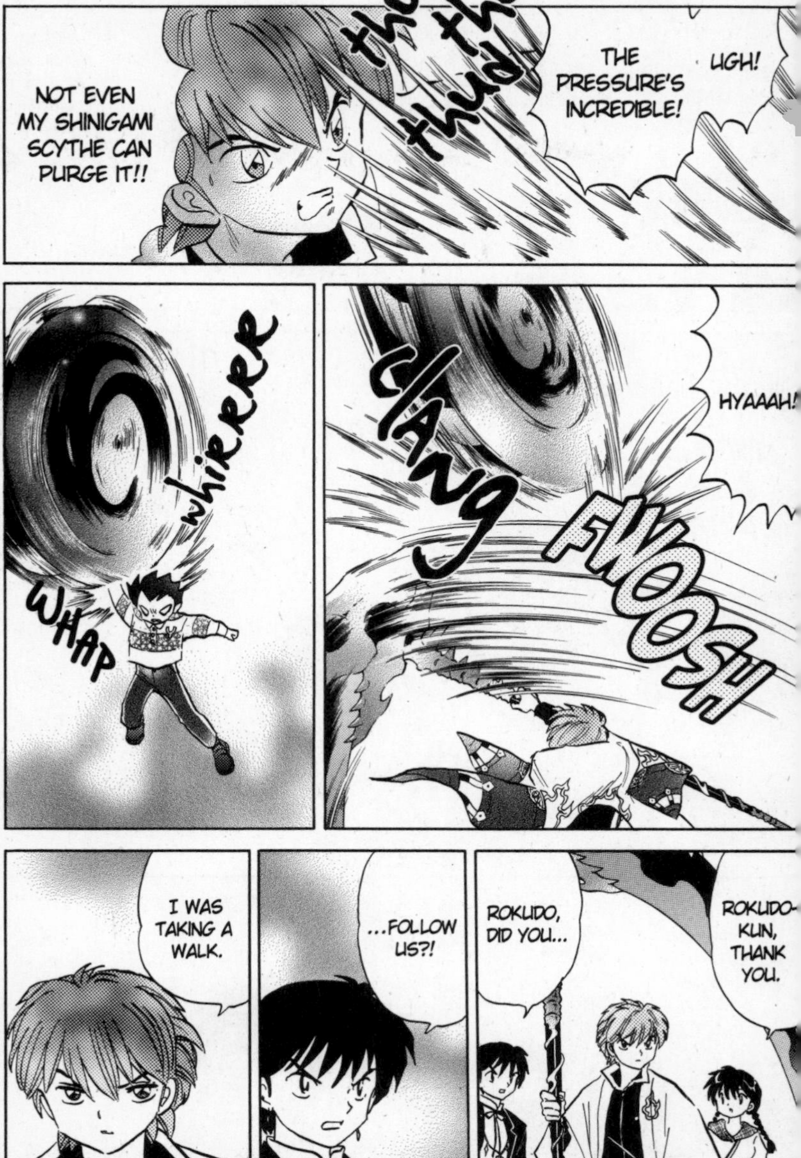
UGH!
THE PRESSURE'S INCREDIBLE!
thud thud thud
NOT EVEN MY SHINIGAMI SCYTHE CAN PURGE IT!!
HYAAAH!
clang
FWOOSH
whirrrr
WHAP
ROKUDO-KUN, THANK YOU.
ROKUDO, DID YOU...
...FOLLOW US?!
I WAS TAKING A WALK.

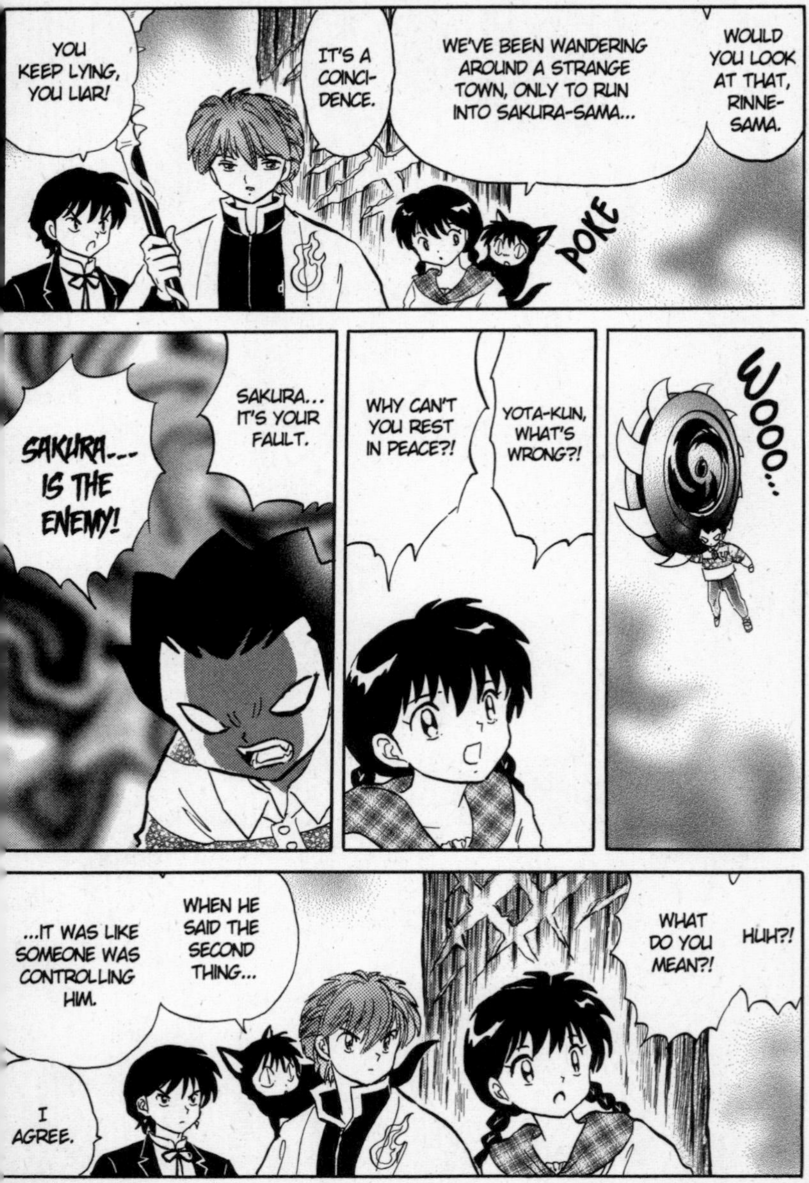

WOULD YOU LOOK AT THAT, RINNE-SAMA.
WE'VE BEEN WANDERING AROUND A STRANGE TOWN, ONLY TO RUN INTO SAKURA-SAMA...
IT'S A COINCIDENCE.
YOU KEEP LYING, YOU LIAR!
POKE
WOOOO...
YOTA-KUN, WHAT'S WRONG?!
WHY CAN'T YOU REST IN PEACE?!
SAKURA... IT'S YOUR FAULT.
SAKURA... IS THE ENEMY!
HUH?!
WHAT DO YOU MEAN?!
WHEN HE SAID THE SECOND THING...
...IT WAS LIKE SOMEONE WAS CONTROLLING HIM.
I AGREE.

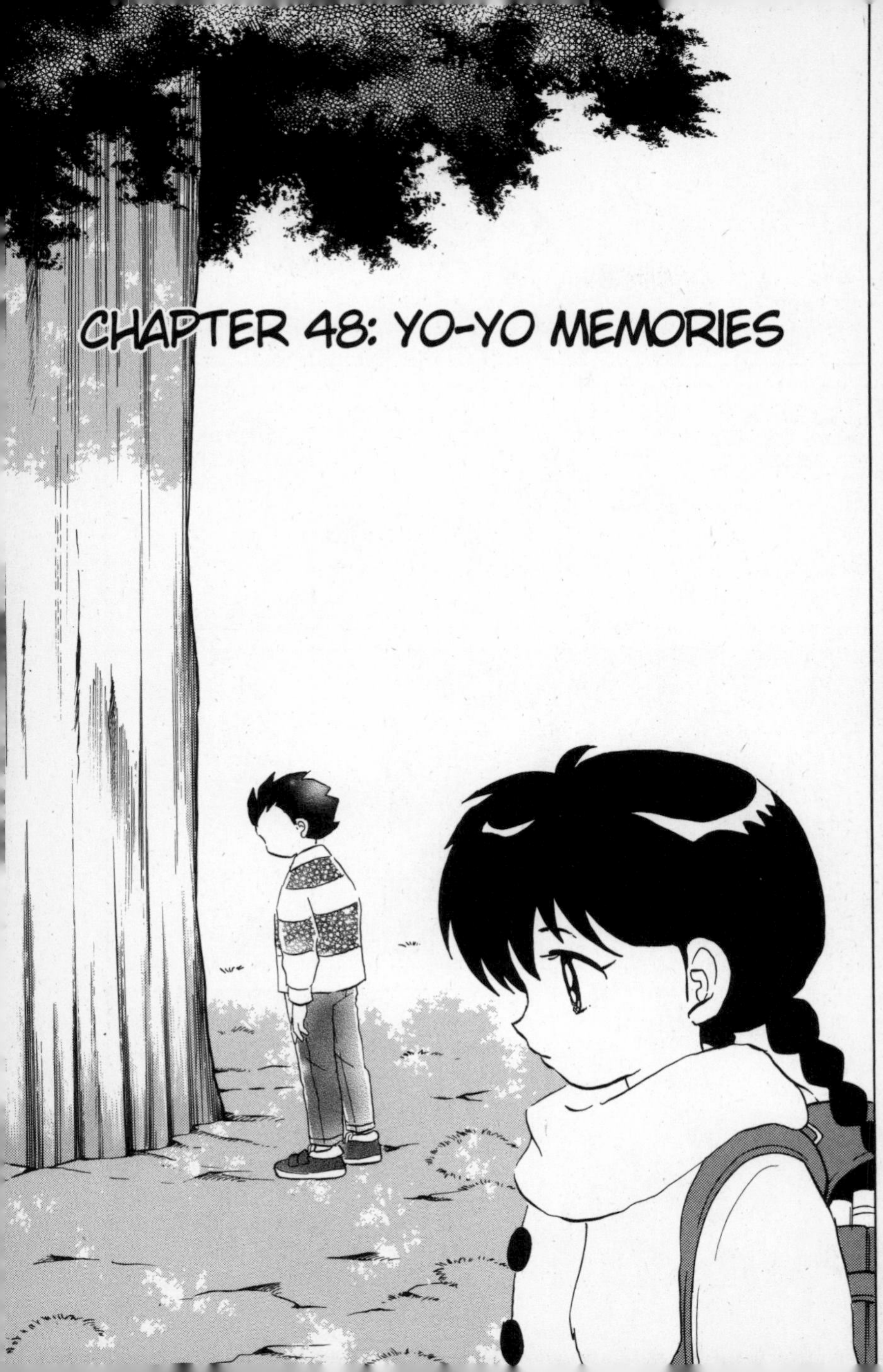
CHAPTER 48: YO-YO MEMORIES

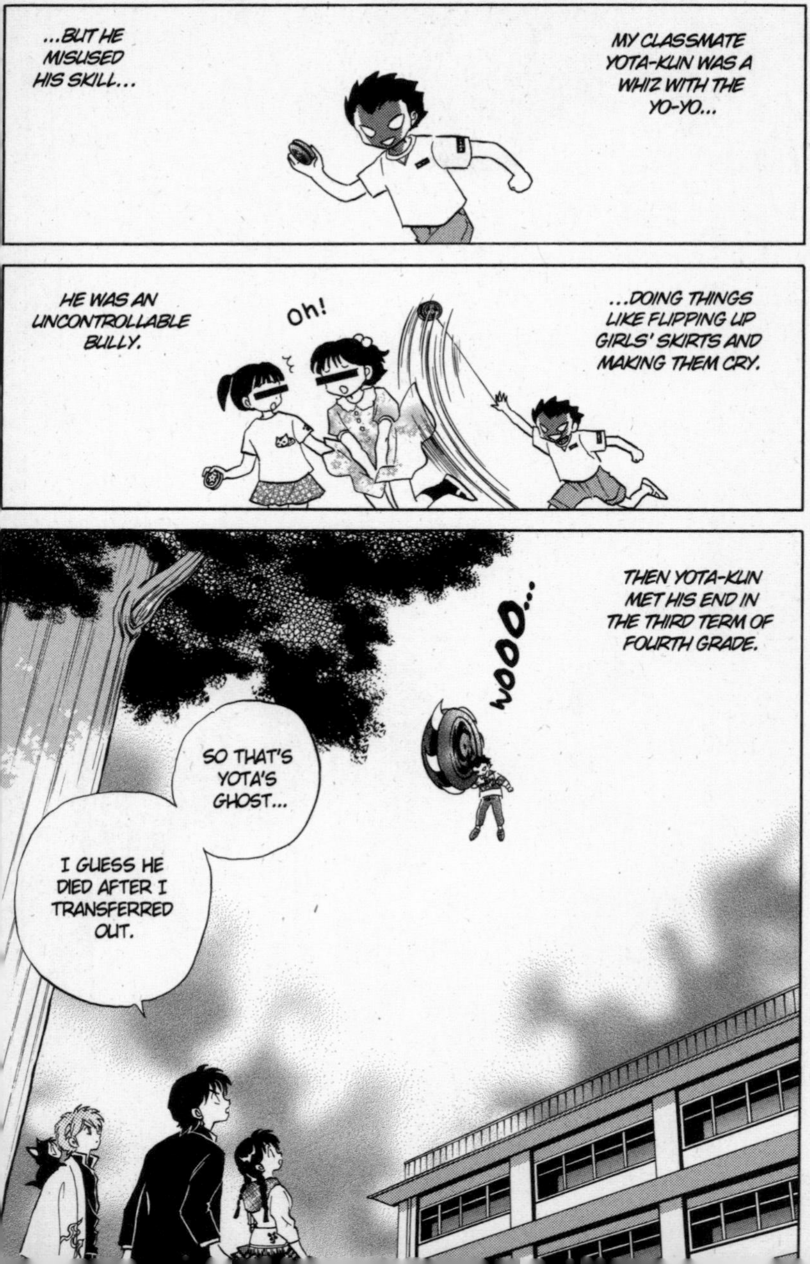
MY CLASSMATE YOTA-KUN WAS A WHIZ WITH THE YO-YO...
...BUT HE MISUSED HIS SKILL...
...DOING THINGS LIKE FLIPPING UP GIRLS' SKIRTS AND MAKING THEM CRY.
Oh!
HE WAS AN UNCONTROLLABLE BULLY.
THEN YOTA-KUN MET HIS END IN THE THIRD TERM OF FOURTH GRADE.
WOOOO...
SO THAT'S YOTA'S GHOST...
I GUESS HE DIED AFTER I TRANSFERRED OUT.

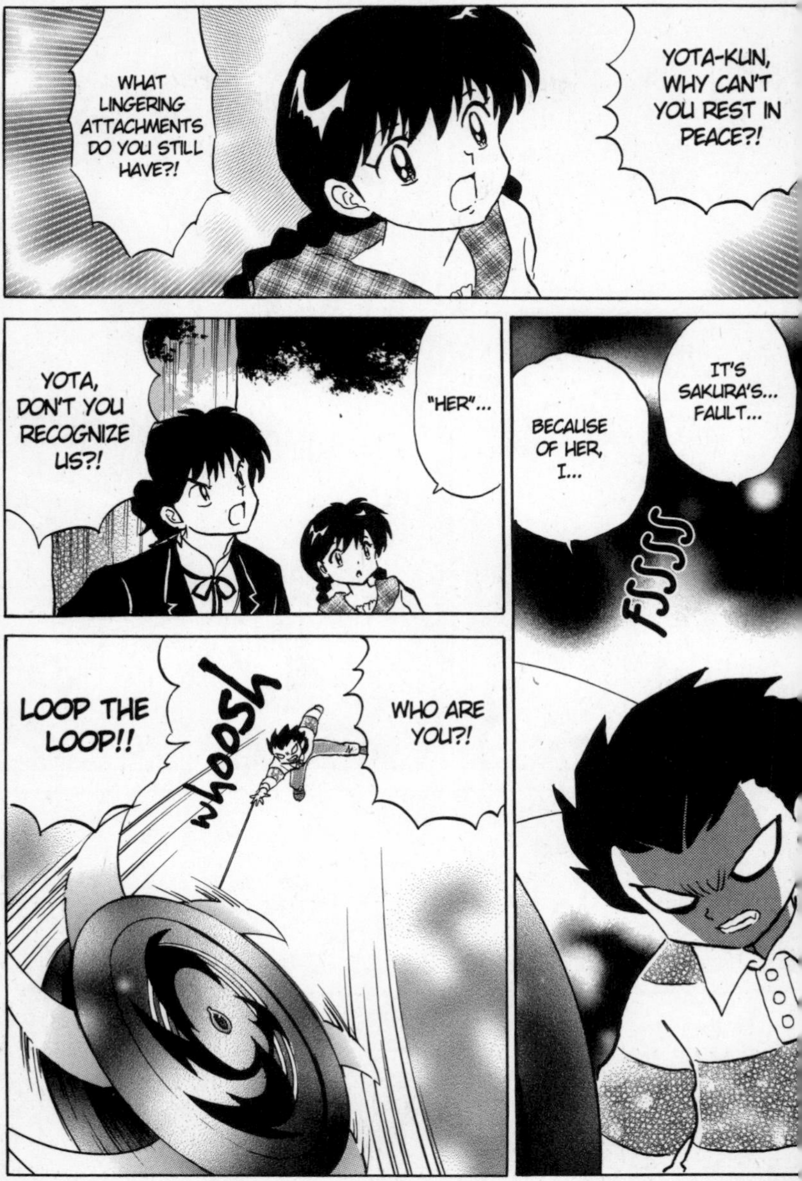
YOTA-KUN, WHY CAN'T YOU REST IN PEACE?!
WHAT LINGERING ATTACHMENTS DO YOU STILL HAVE?!
IT'S SAKURA'S... FAULT...
BECAUSE OF HER, I...
FSSSS
"HER"...
YOTA, DON'T YOU RECOGNIZE US?!
WHO ARE YOU?!
whoosh
LOOP THE LOOP!!

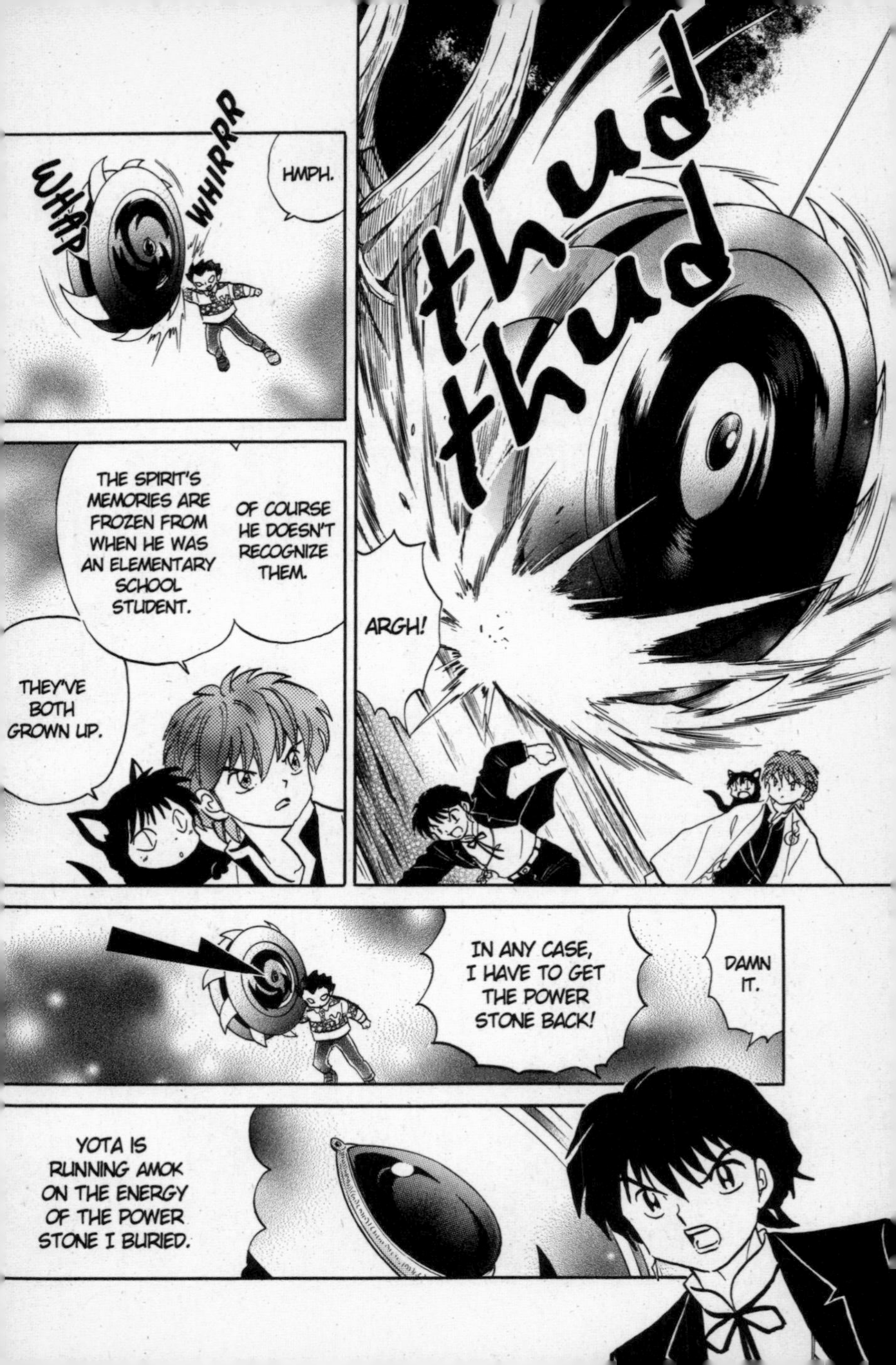
thud thud
ARGH!
HMPH.
WHIRRR
WHAP
OF COURSE HE DOESN'T RECOGNIZE THEM.
THE SPIRIT'S MEMORIES ARE FROZEN FROM WHEN HE WAS AN ELEMENTARY SCHOOL STUDENT.
THEY'VE BOTH GROWN UP.
DAMN IT.
IN ANY CASE, I HAVE TO GET THE POWER STONE BACK!
YOTA IS RUNNING AMOK ON THE ENERGY OF THE POWER STONE I BURIED.

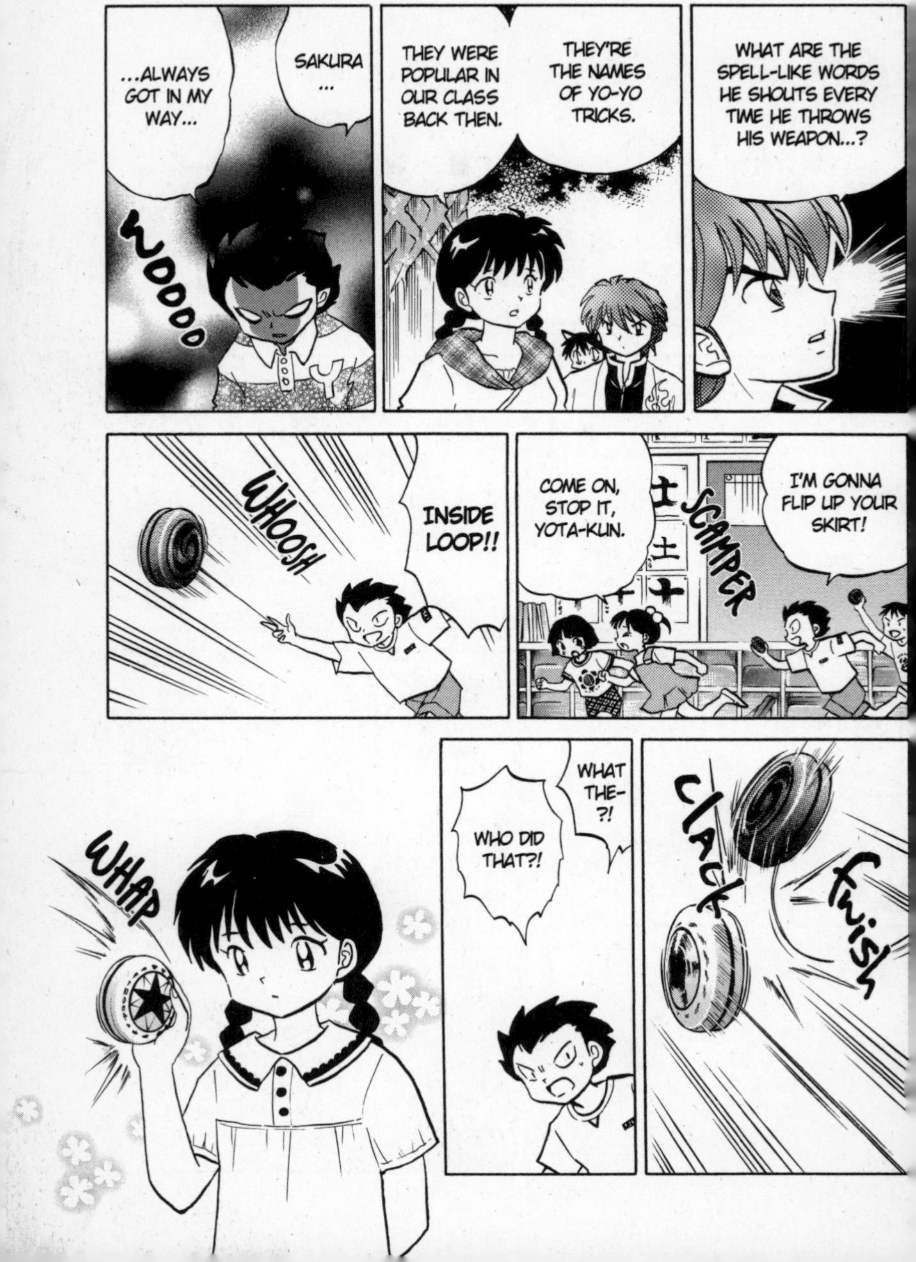
WHAT ARE THE SPELL-LIKE WORDS HE SHOUTS EVERY TIME HE THROWS HIS WEAPON...?
THEY'RE THE NAMES OF YO-YO TRICKS.
THEY WERE POPULAR IN OUR CLASS BACK THEN.
SAKURA ...
...ALWAYS GOT IN MY WAY...
WOOOOO
I'M GONNA FLIP UP YOUR SKIRT!
SCAMPER
COME ON, STOP IT, YOTA-KUN.
WHOOSH
INSIDE LOOP!!
CLACK
fwish
WHAT THE-?!
WHO DID THAT?!
WHAP

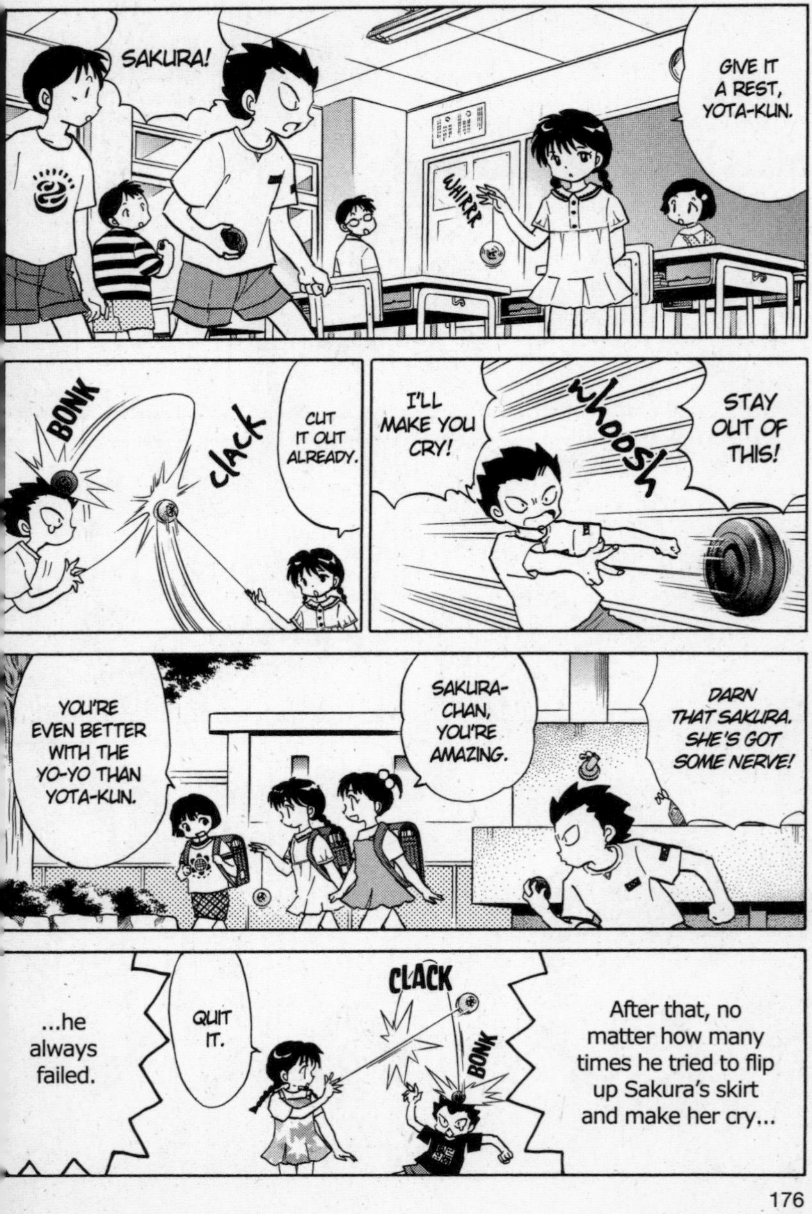
GIVE IT A REST, YOTA-KUN.
WHIRRR
SAKURA!
STAY OUT OF THIS!
WHOOSH
I'LL MAKE YOU CRY!
CUT IT OUT ALREADY.
CLACK
BONK
DARN THAT SAKURA. SHE'S GOT SOME NERVE!
SAKURA-CHAN, YOU'RE AMAZING.
YOU'RE EVEN BETTER WITH THE YO-YO THAN YOTA-KUN.
After that, no matter how many times he tried to flip up Sakura's skirt and make her cry...
CLACK
BONK
QUIT IT.
...he always failed.

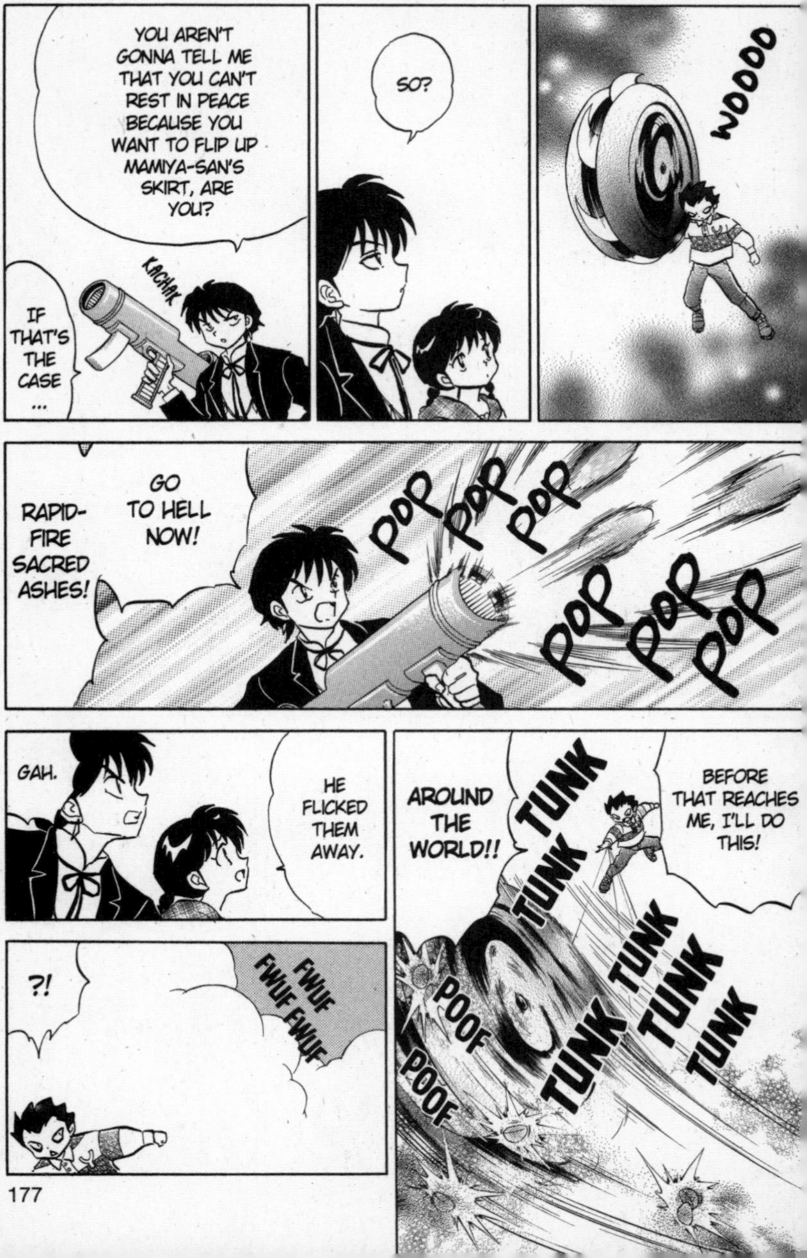
WOOOO
SO?
YOU AREN'T GONNA TELL ME THAT YOU CAN'T REST IN PEACE BECAUSE YOU WANT TO FLIP UP MAMIYA-SAN'S SKIRT, ARE YOU?
KACHAK
IF THAT'S THE CASE ...
GO TO HELL NOW!
RAPID-FIRE SACRED ASHES!
POP POP POP
POP POP POP
BEFORE THAT REACHES ME, I'LL DO THIS!
AROUND THE WORLD!!
TUNK TUNK
TUNK TUNK TUNK TUNK
POOF POOF
HE FLICKED THEM AWAY.
GAH.
FWUF FWUF FWUF
?!

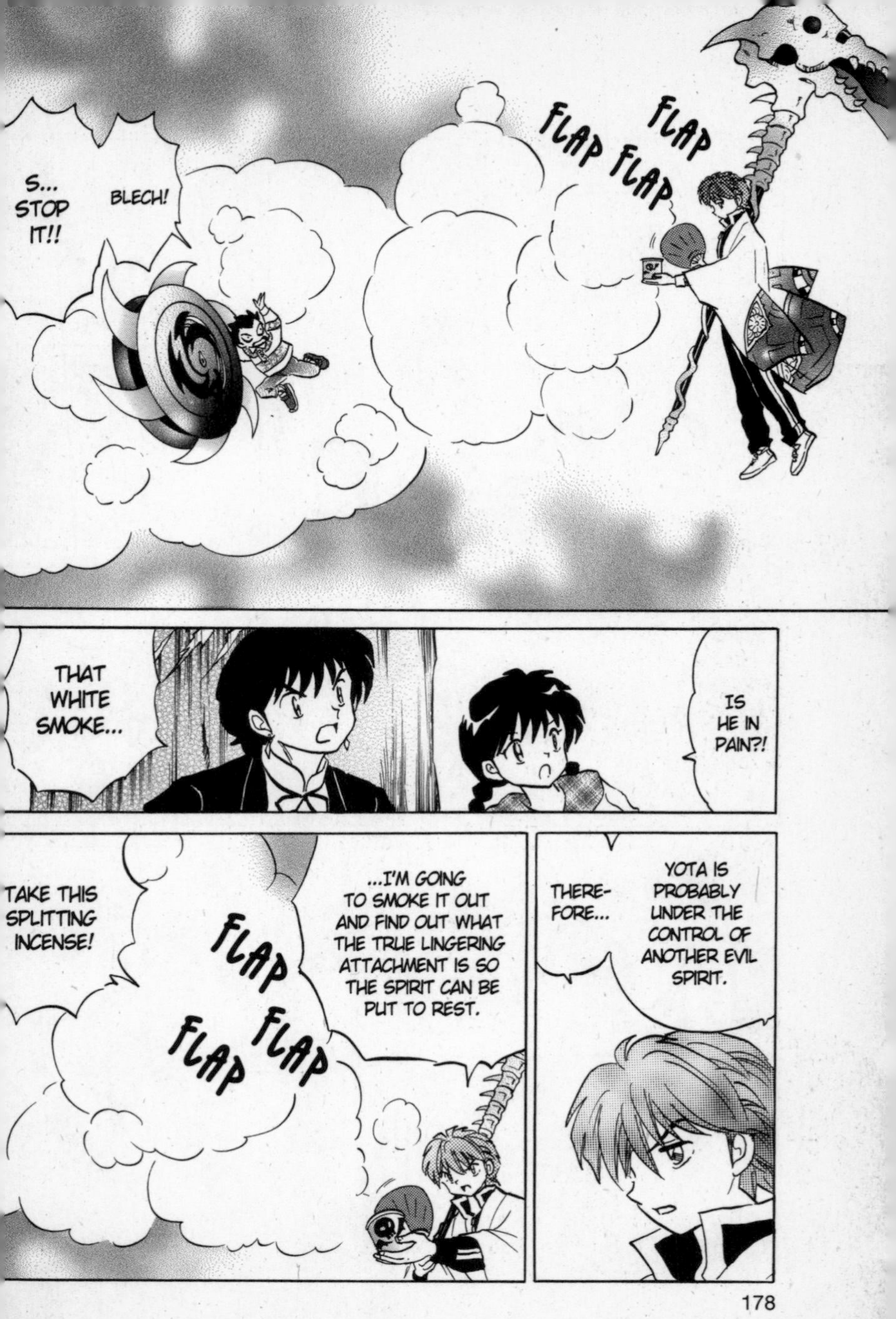
FLAP FLAP FLAP
BLECH!
S... STOP IT!!
IS HE IN PAIN?!
THAT WHITE SMOKE...
YOTA IS PROBABLY UNDER THE CONTROL OF ANOTHER EVIL SPIRIT.
THERE-FORE...
...I'M GOING TO SMOKE IT OUT AND FIND OUT WHAT THE TRUE LINGERING ATTACHMENT IS SO THE SPIRIT CAN BE PUT TO REST.
FLAP FLAP FLAP
TAKE THIS SPLITTING INCENSE!

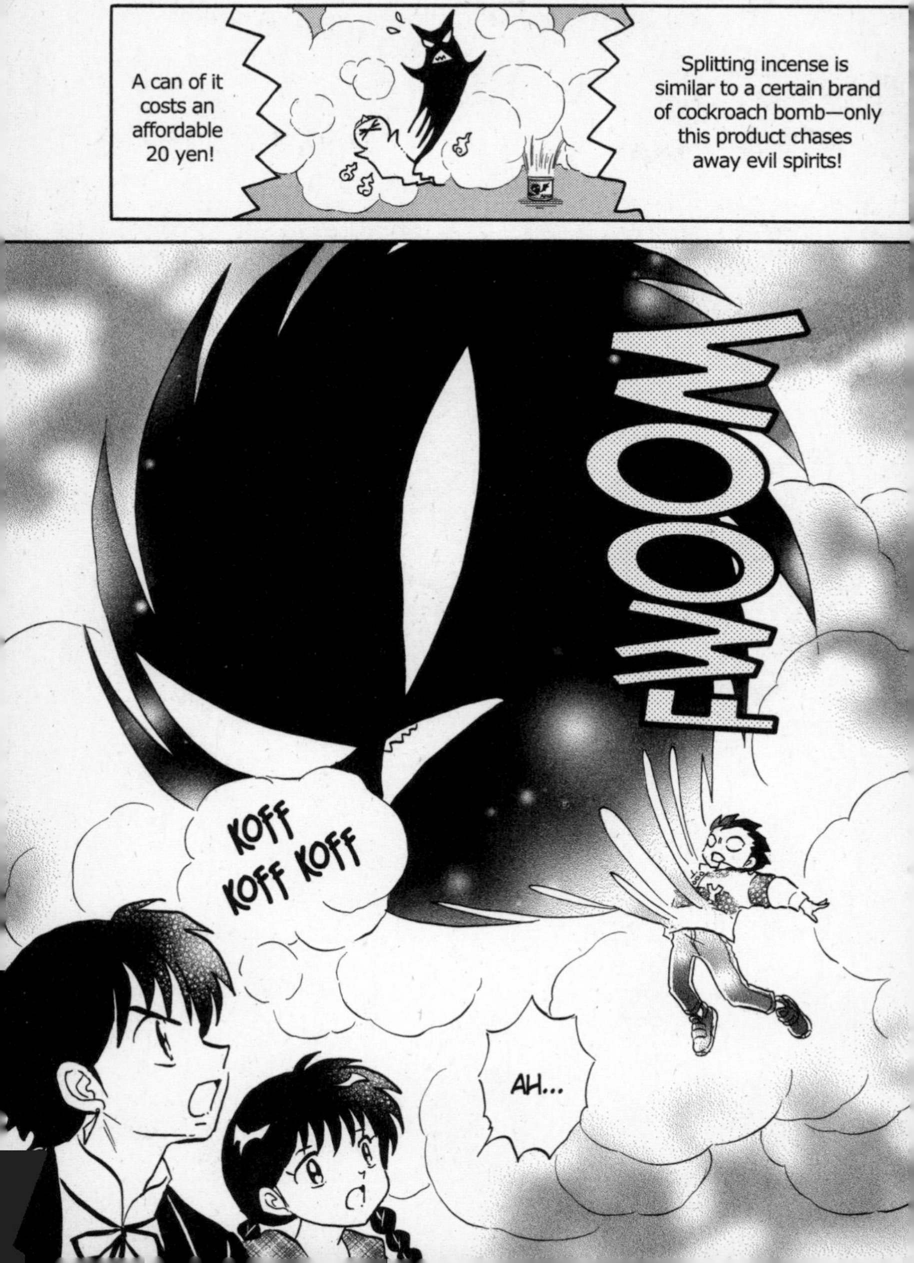
Splitting incense is similar to a certain brand of cockroach bomb—only this product chases away evil spirits!
A can of it costs an affordable 20 yen!
FWOOM
KOFF KOFF KOFF
AH...

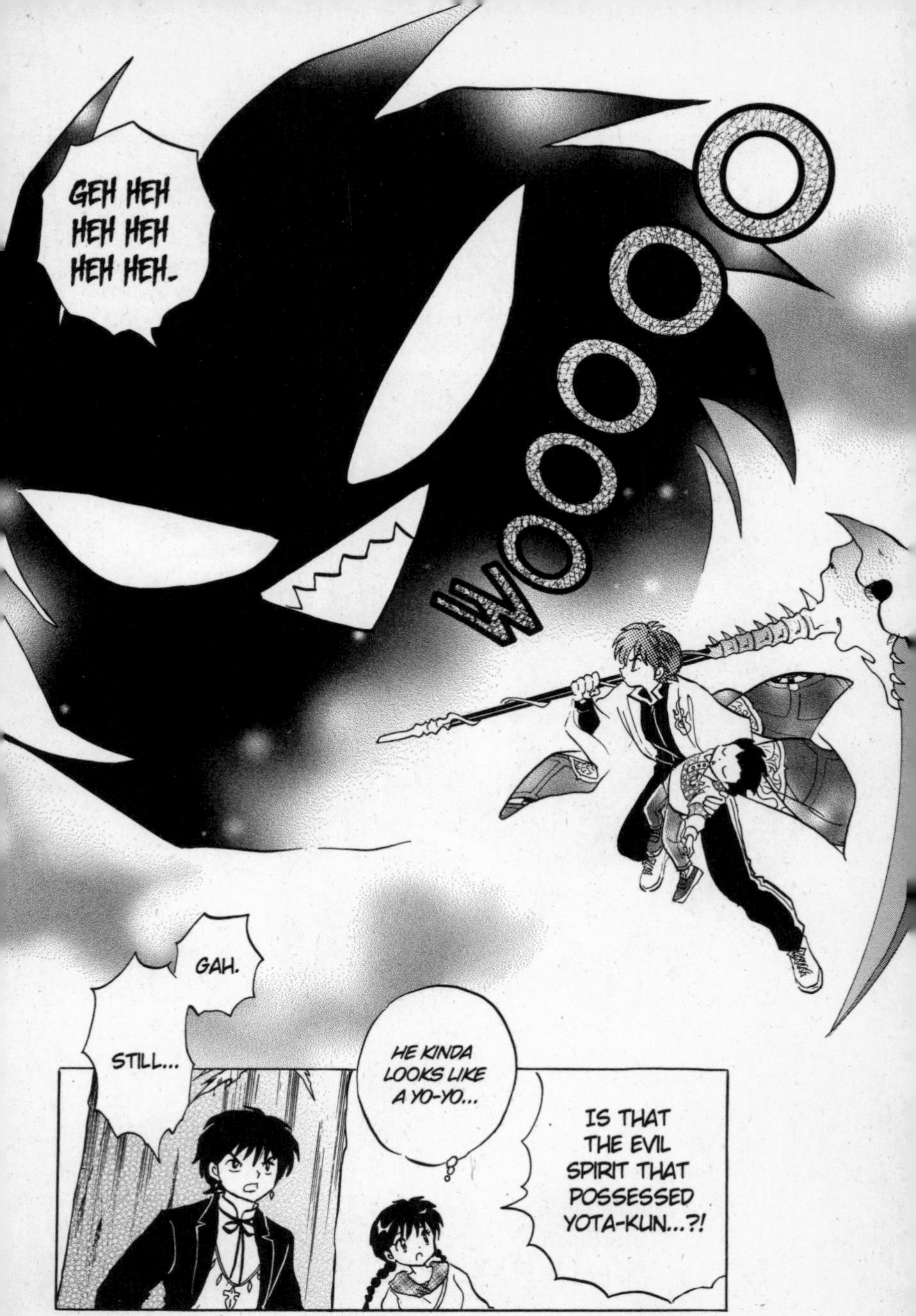
GEH HEH HEH HEH HEH HEH.
WOOOOO
IS THAT THE EVIL SPIRIT THAT POSSESSED YOTA-KUN...?!
HE KINDA LOOKS LIKE A YO-YO...
GAH.
STILL...

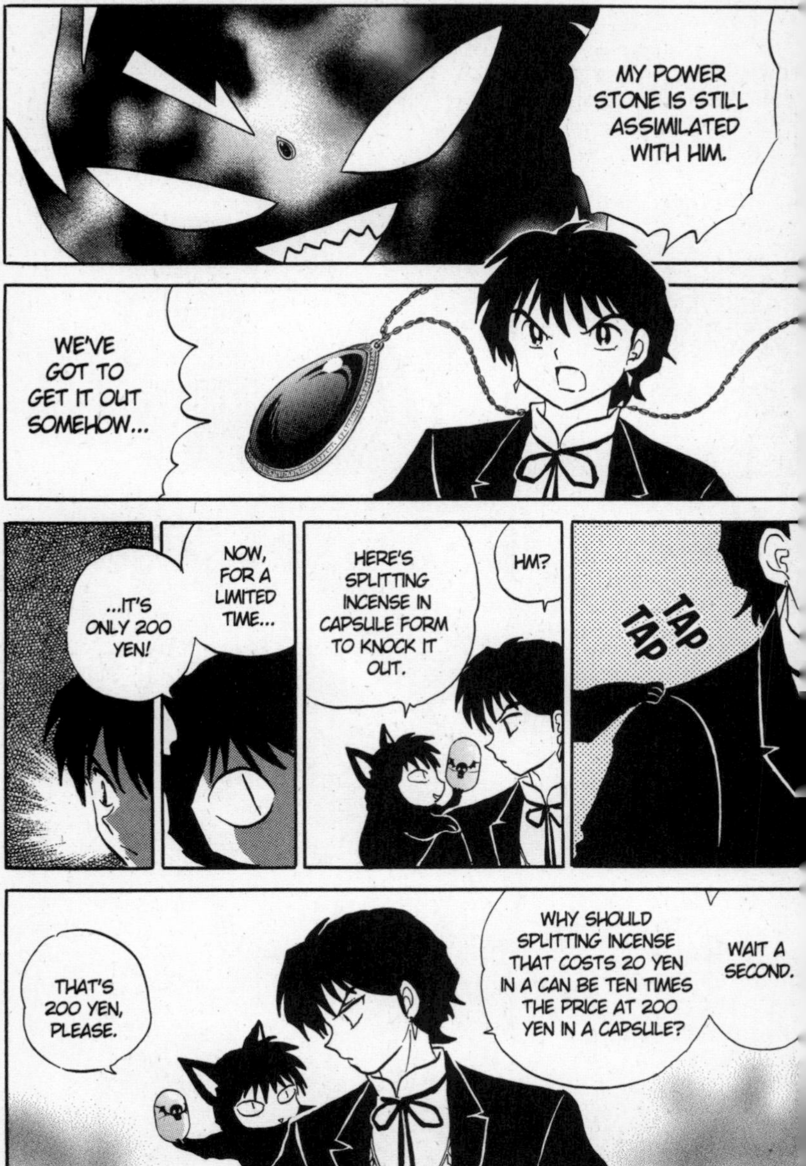
MY POWER STONE IS STILL ASSIMILATED WITH HIM.
WE'VE GOT TO GET IT OUT SOMEHOW...
TAP TAP
HM?
HERE'S SPLITTING INCENSE IN CAPSULE FORM TO KNOCK IT OUT.
NOW, FOR A LIMITED TIME...
...IT'S ONLY 200 YEN!
WAIT A SECOND.
WHY SHOULD SPLITTING INCENSE THAT COSTS 20 YEN IN A CAN BE TEN TIMES THE PRICE AT 200 YEN IN A CAPSULE?
THAT'S 200 YEN, PLEASE.

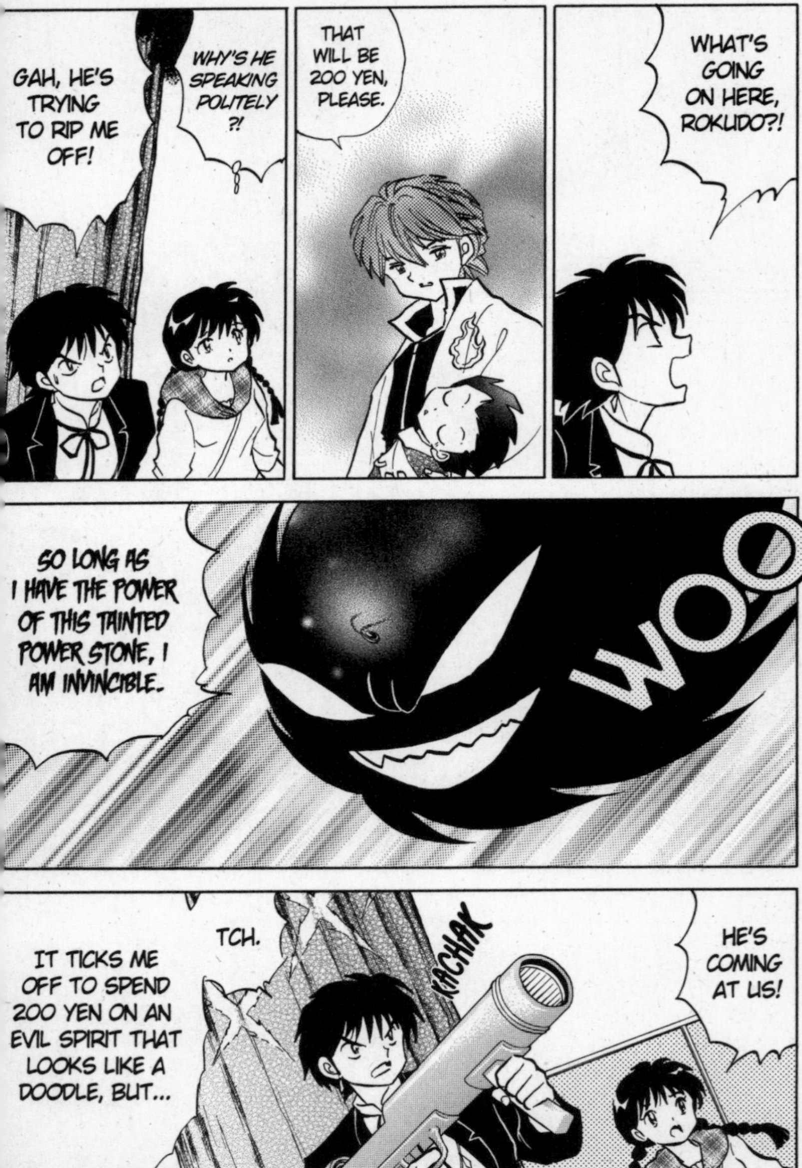
WHAT'S GOING ON HERE, ROKUDO?!
THAT WILL BE 200 YEN, PLEASE.
WHY'S HE SPEAKING POLITELY ?!
GAH, HE'S TRYING TO RIP ME OFF!
WOO
SO LONG AS I HAVE THE POWER OF THIS TAINTED POWER STONE, I AM INVINCIBLE.
HE'S COMING AT US!
KACHAK
TCH.
IT TICKS ME OFF TO SPEND 200 YEN ON AN EVIL SPIRIT THAT LOOKS LIKE A DOODLE, BUT...

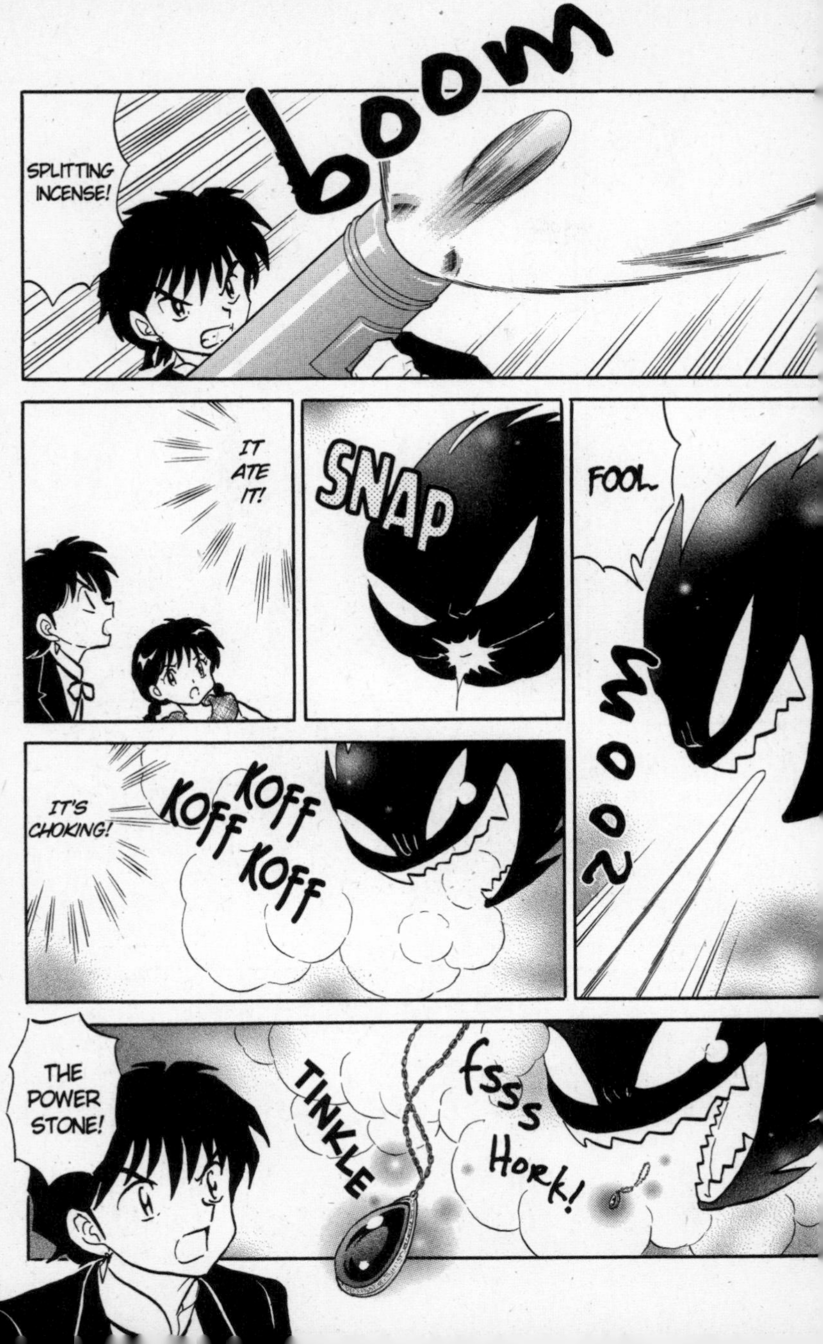
boom
SPLITTING INCENSE!
FOOL
zoom
SNAP
IT ATE IT!
KOFF KOFF KOFF KOFF
IT'S CHOKING!
fsss
Hork!
TINKLE
THE POWER STONE!

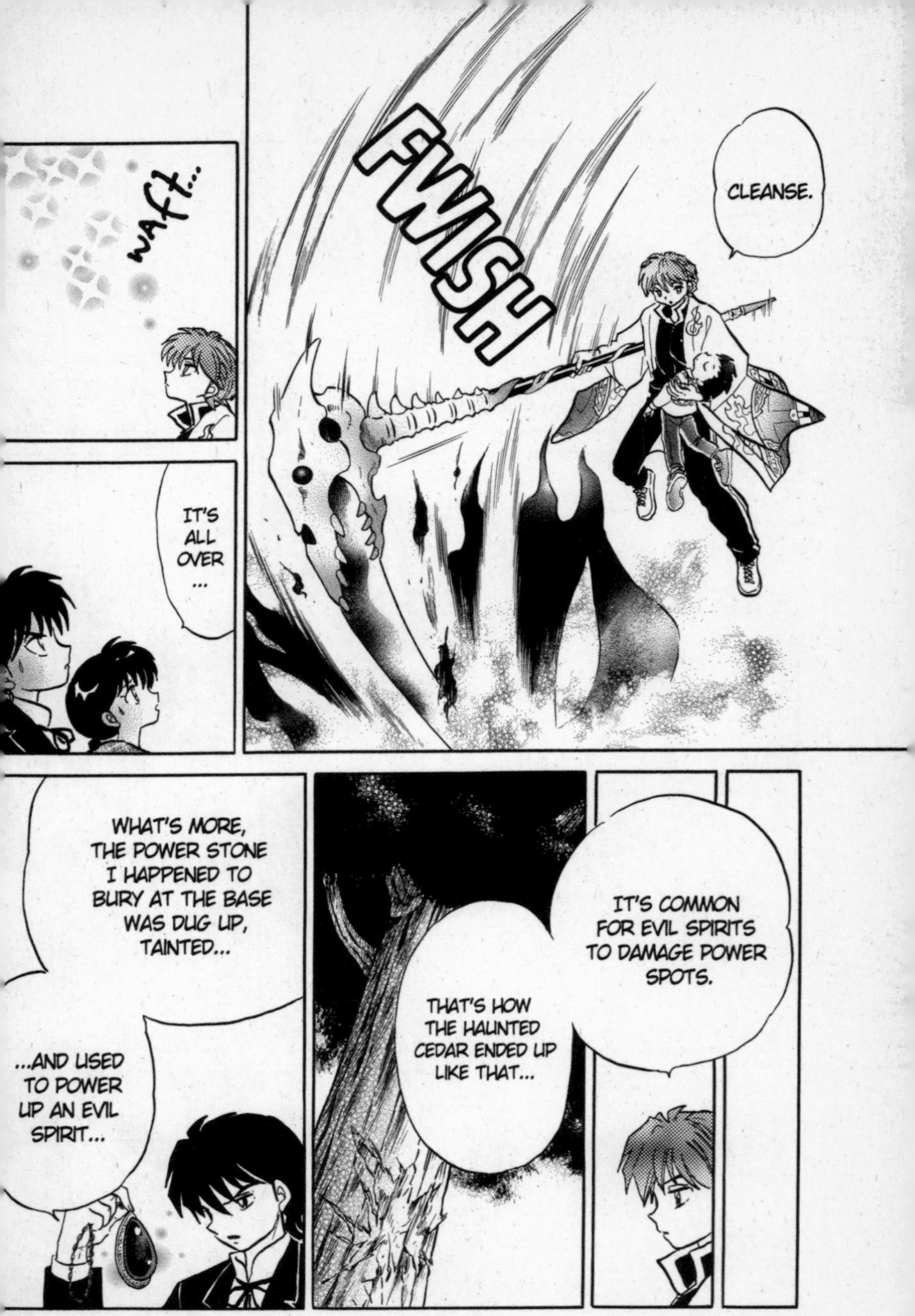
CLEANSE.
FWISH
waft...
IT'S ALL OVER...
IT'S COMMON FOR EVIL SPIRITS TO DAMAGE POWER SPOTS.
THAT'S HOW THE HAUNTED CEDAR ENDED UP LIKE THAT...
WHAT'S MORE, THE POWER STONE I HAPPENED TO BURY AT THE BASE WAS DUG UP, TAINTED...
...AND USED TO POWER UP AN EVIL SPIRIT...

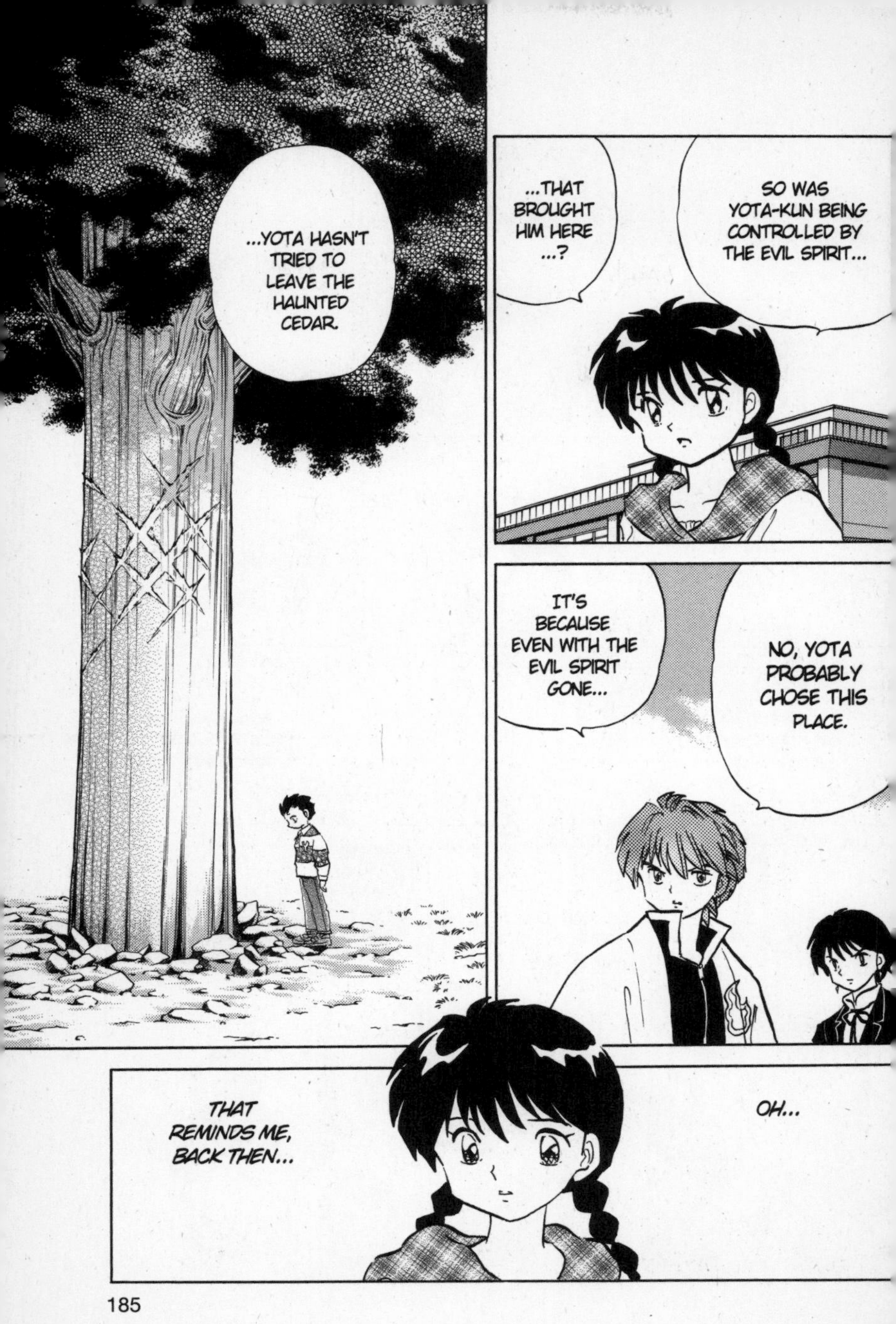
SO WAS YOTA-KUN BEING CONTROLLED BY THE EVIL SPIRIT...
...THAT BROUGHT HIM HERE ...?
NO, YOTA PROBABLY CHOSE THIS PLACE.
IT'S BECAUSE EVEN WITH THE EVIL SPIRIT GONE...
...YOTA HASN'T TRIED TO LEAVE THE HAUNTED CEDAR.
OH...
THAT REMINDS ME, BACK THEN...

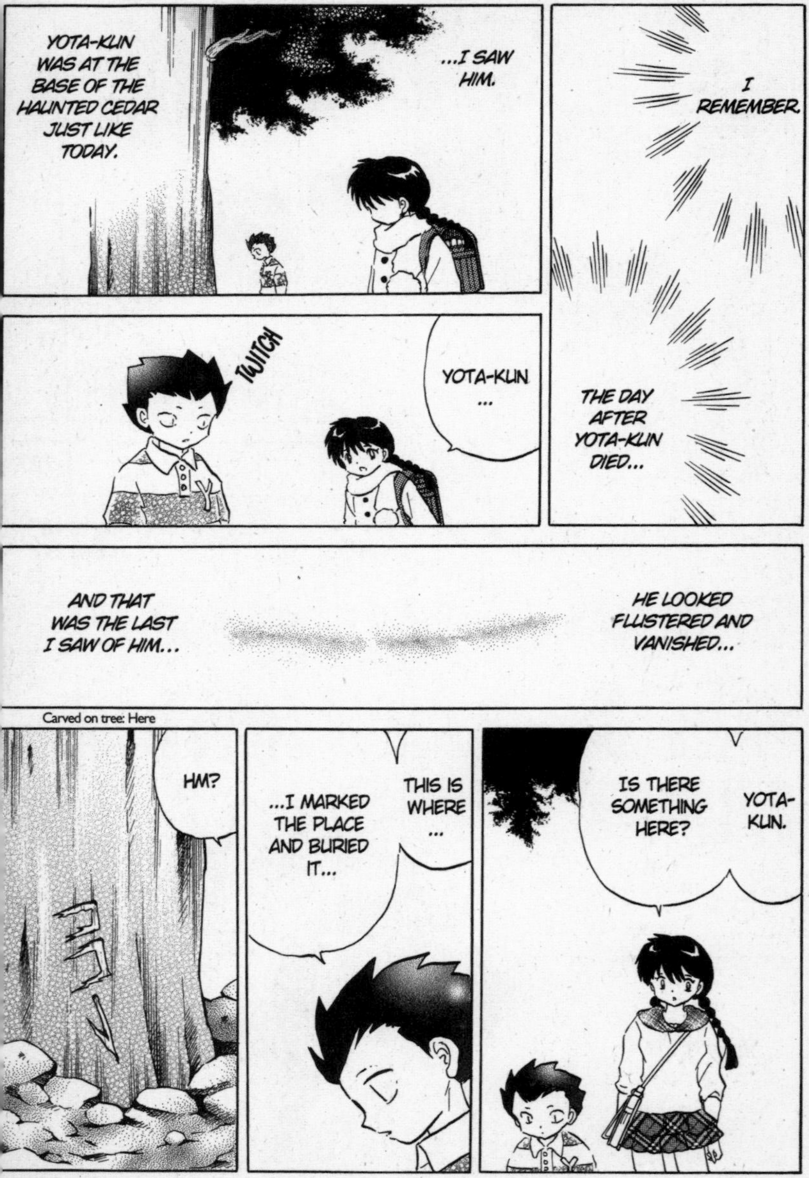
I REMEMBER.
THE DAY AFTER YOTA-KUN DIED...
...I SAW HIM.
YOTA-KUN WAS AT THE BASE OF THE HAUNTED CEDAR JUST LIKE TODAY.
YOTA-KUN ...
TWITCH
HE LOOKED FLUSTERED AND VANISHED...
AND THAT WAS THE LAST I SAW OF HIM...
YOTA-KUN.
IS THERE SOMETHING HERE?
THIS IS WHERE ...
...I MARKED THE PLACE AND BURIED IT...
HM?
Carved on tree: Here

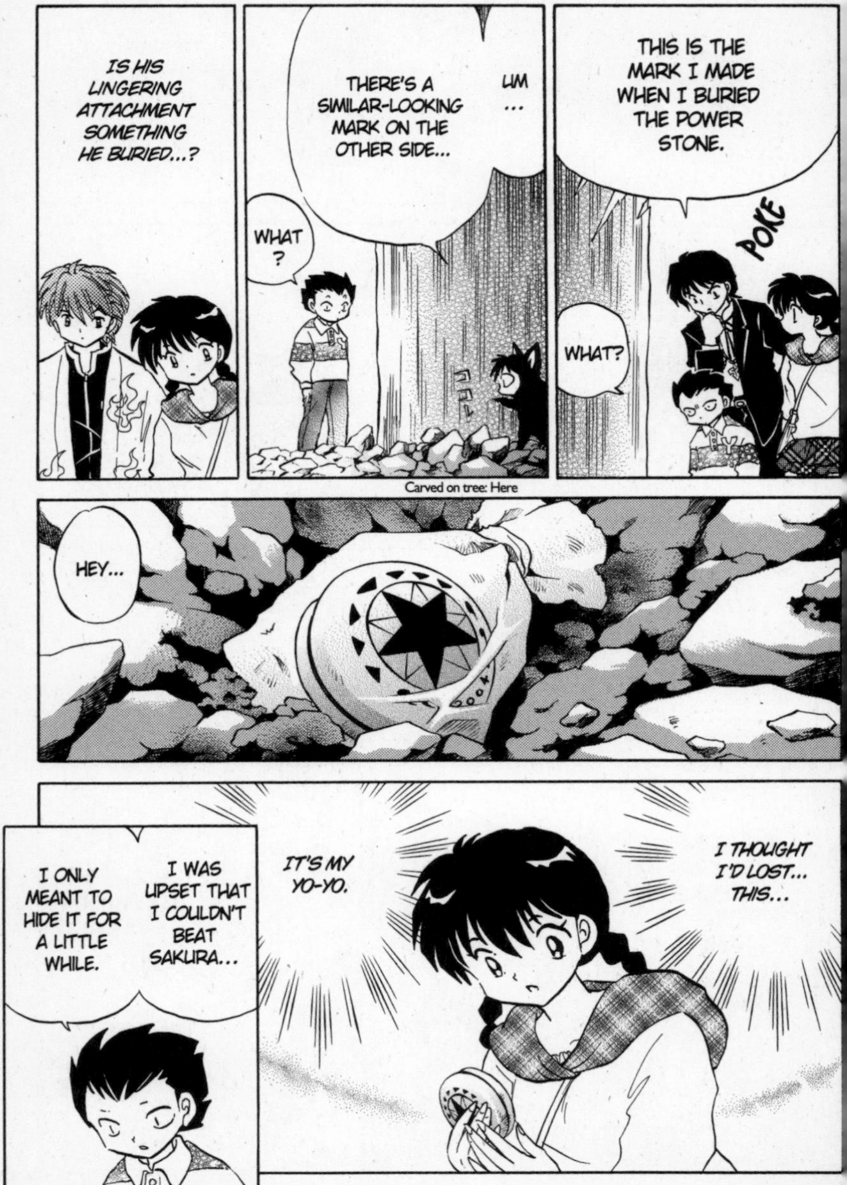
THIS IS THE MARK I MADE WHEN I BURIED THE POWER STONE.
POKE
WHAT?
UM ...
THERE'S A SIMILAR-LOOKING MARK ON THE OTHER SIDE...
WHAT ?
Carved on tree: Here
IS HIS LINGERING ATTACHMENT SOMETHING HE BURIED...?
HEY...
I THOUGHT I'D LOST... THIS...
IT'S MY YO-YO.
I WAS UPSET THAT I COULDN'T BEAT SAKURA...
I ONLY MEANT TO HIDE IT FOR A LITTLE WHILE.

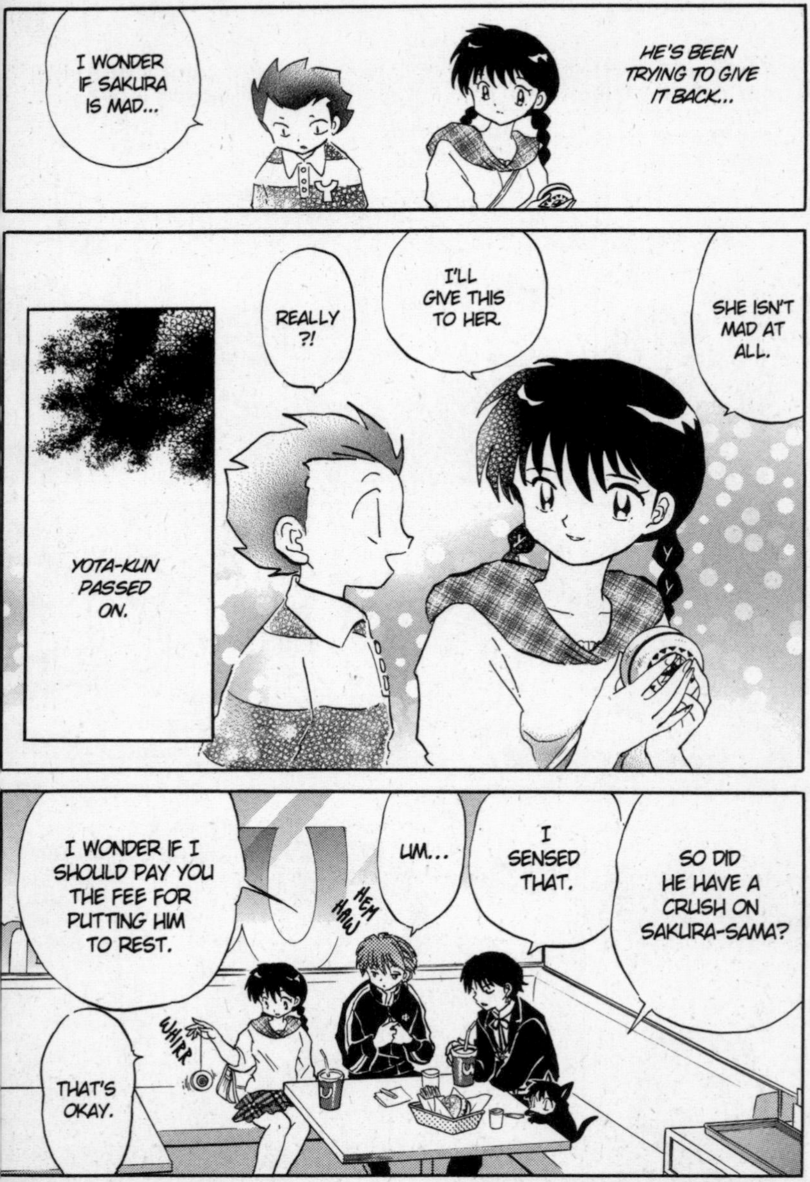
HE'S BEEN TRYING TO GIVE IT BACK...
I WONDER IF SAKURA IS MAD...
SHE ISN'T MAD AT ALL.
I'LL GIVE THIS TO HER.
REALLY ?!
YOTA-KUN PASSED ON.
SO DID HE HAVE A CRUSH ON SAKURA-SAMA?
I SENSED THAT.
UM...
HEM HAW
I WONDER IF I SHOULD PAY YOU THE FEE FOR PUTTING HIM TO REST.
WHIRR
THAT'S OKAY.

RIN-NE VOLUME 5 - END -

At Your Indentured Service

Hayate's parents are bad with money, so they sell his organs to pay their debts. Hayate doesn't like this plan, so he comes up with a new one—kidnap and ransom a girl from a wealthy family. Solid plan... so how did he end up as her butler?

Find out in *Hayate the Combat Butler*—
buy the manga at store.viz.com!

© 2005 Kenjiro HATA/Shogakukan Inc.

www.viz.com
store.viz.com

STUDENTS BY DAY, DEMON-FIGHTERS BY NIGHT!

KEKKAISHI
【けっかいし】

Teenagers Yoshimori and Tokine are "kekkaishi"—demon-fighters that battle bad beings side-by-side almost every night. They also quarrel with each other, but their biggest fight is the one between their families. Can Yoshimori and Tokine fight together long enough to end their families' ancient rivalry and save the world?

Join this modern-day Romeo and Juliet adventure—graphic novels now available at *store.viz.com*!

ONLY $9.99!

KEKKAISHI
Story and Art by
YELLOW TANABE

VIZ MEDIA

www.viz.com
store.viz.com

© 2004 Yellow Tanabe/Shogakukan, Inc.

Half Human, Half Demon—
ALL ACTION!

Relive the feudal fairy tale with the
new **VIZBIG Editions** featuring:

- Three volumes in one
  for $17.99 US / $24.00 CAN
- Larger trim size with premium paper
- Now unflipped! Pages read
  Right-to-Left as the creator intended

**Change Your
Perspective—Get BIG**

Story and Art by Rumiko Takahashi

On sale at

TheRumicWorld.com

...e at your local
...d comic store

STARTS ON SUNDAY
SHONENSUNDAY.COM

GLASGOW LIFE GLASGOW LIBRARIES	
C005570877	
SM	PETERS
22-Mar-2012	£6.99
TF	

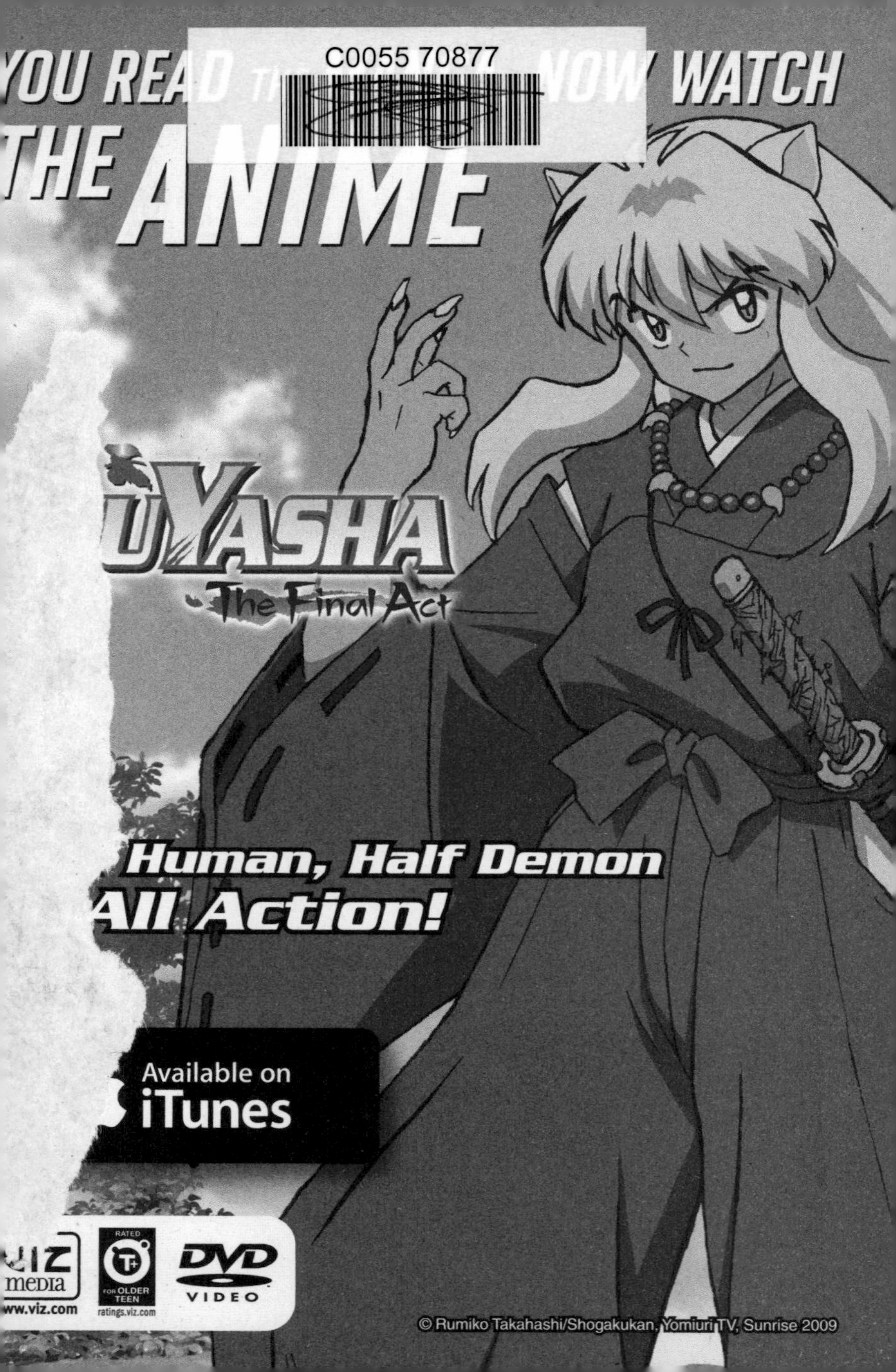
YOU READ
NOW WATCH
THE ANIME
UYASHA
The Final Act
Human, Half Demon
All Action!
Available on
iTunes
media
www.viz.com
RATED
T+
FOR OLDER TEEN
ratings.viz.com
DVD
VIDEO
© Rumiko Takahashi/Shogakukan, Yomiuri TV, Sunrise 2009